A GEOGRAPHY OF
WORLD ECONOMY

The Van Nostrand Series in
GEOGRAPHY

SAMUEL VAN VALKENBURG, *General Editor*

HANS BOESCH—*A Geography of World Economy*

Additional titles will be listed and announced as published

A GEOGRAPHY OF

HANS BOESCH
Professor of Geography, University of Zürich

WORLD ECONOMY

D. VAN NOSTRAND COMPANY, INC.

PRINCETON, NEW JERSEY | NEW YORK | TORONTO | LONDON

D. VAN NOSTRAND COMPANY, INC.
120 Alexander St., Princeton, New Jersey (*Principal office*)
24 West 40 Street, New York 18, New York

D. VAN NOSTRAND COMPANY, LTD.
358, Kensington High Street, London, W.14, England

D. VAN NOSTRAND COMPANY (Canada), LTD.
25 Hollinger Road, Toronto 16, Canada

EDITOR'S PREFACE

The present text represents the convictions of its author, one of today's ablest geographers, about what a course in world economic geography should contain.

First, such a course ought not to drown the reader in a flood of tables and statistics, with which our world is already drenched from scores of commercial and governmental sources. It should show the student how meaningful statistics are derived, selected, and used to maximum advantage. The author's charts and maps picture facts that are needful and enlightening, and they exemplify methods of clear presentation that are explained by the text.

A term course must also present a logical framework, within which basic and current ideas, principles, and methods can be discussed. A special chapter (Chapter 6) poses the open questions of modern geographic research—its nomothetic and idiographic aims, and the interplay of functional and "formal" structures. The framework is that of primary, secondary, and tertiary occupations in their world scope—i.e., production, processing, and service and administrative occupations. The point of view is a part of liberal education—human history embodied in the sequential stages of land use and in the ever more complex network of economic relations spreading over the landscape.

In the course of introducing fresh ideas that illustrate the work of the modern geographer, the author does present in some detail many central areas of fact: population and food consumption, land use in its historical dimensions as they affect the present in major countries, and the importance of the new frontiers of arctic waste and jungle. The major products are given their setting in world commerce.

The treatment of secondary occupations progresses from the sources and measurement of energy to an impressive list of major industries, which are described in selective detail. The keys to tertiary structures are urbanization and economic regionalism as a basis of world trade. Here the student finds a guide through statistical material and many examples of how charts are made and what they mean. A special chapter is devoted to the world aspects of recreation and tourism.

The up-to-date bibliography puts the reader in touch with the ideas and methods that move the modern geographer. Everywhere the treatment of facts and statistics, even when presented in detail, offers lessons in thought even more than exercises in memory.

Dr. Boesch does not stand alone in his view of the needs of today's student of economic geography. His presentation will supply a model for researchers and teachers who demand a serious and reflective approach to economic geography. It is gratifying to me to present his textbook to the English-speaking world of geographers.

SAMUEL VAN VALKENBURG

ACKNOWLEDGMENTS

As this book is going to the press, it gives me great pleasure to thank all those who helped to make it possible. H. Häfner, G. Ammann, T. Strüby, H. U. Wohlgemuth, A. Städeli, and Misses I. Kutschke, I. Niemann and H. Kishimoto, my assistants, have all contributed their efforts and are responsible for the drawing of the illustrations. Miss H. Kishimoto has read the manuscript critically and offered valuable professional comments; above all, she improved my English and assisted during proofreading and indexing. H. Carol, now at York University, Toronto, will recognize that our methodological discussions of many years ago have left their marks; his methodological publications, most of them in German, laid the basis and were most stimulating. In a way, this is our book, because we all shared the labor of preparing the manuscript; equally, we are all looking forward to the day when it will come off the press. Editor and publisher are assured of our thanks and sympathy for their uncomplicated and understanding cooperation.

HANS BOESCH

Zürich, January 1964

CONTENTS

ix

LIST OF ILLUSTRATIONS

INTRODUCTION

Economic geography has primarily to do with the mutual relationship of man and earth, which finds manifold expression in the variety of landscapes that the earth offers. As a science, economic geography knows certain techniques of its own, with the help of which its object, the landscape, is investigated and described; as a science, economic geography also employs a distinctive terminology and a group of specific concepts with which we conceive and describe our findings. In the introduction, we shall limit ourselves to a few of these; more will appear later as discussion demands.*

Economic geography is, above all, geography. As such, its object is the earth's surface, in contrast to neighboring sciences for which human society, say, or its economy constitutes the object of study. Such a definition of geography is in fact very old. Bernhardus Varenius, whose *Geographia Generalis* appeared in 1650 and was for centuries the leading geography text, had already defined the object, and implicitly geography as a science as follows: "The object of geography

. . . is the earth, in particular its surface and parts of it." Modern concepts accept the same definition in principle, though the terminology may have changed. The terms "landscape" and "earth's surface" have already occurred above to designate that object. Both of these terms are quite descriptive, but open to discussion and subject to misunderstanding, since they are popularly used to signify a number of different things. If we want to be quite clear, we had better use a term which avoids these difficulties. Such a term is "geosphere." Geosphere is the complex whole at, above, and below the immediate surface of our planet and is composed of the following spheres: lithosphere + hydrosphere + pedosphere + biosphere + anthroposphere + atmosphere. This complex whole is studied in its components as well as in its structure. The aim of geography, as was stated by a French geographer (Cholley, 1942), is a rational description of the earth's surface. In all these respects economic geography is no different from geography in general.

What then, is the distinctive feature of economic geography? It is primarily the standpoint from which we observe the geosphere. This gives economic geography its unique status. Man, *Homo œconomicus*, as an active agent, is the focal point to which we relate all the observable facts. This focal point enables us to sift the relevant from the irrelevant and to avoid the danger of permitting our investigation to become limit-

* When a book is written, there is always a basic idea at the outset as to what one wants to communicate and how it should be done. It is therefore appropriate to start a text on economic geography with some remarks on this basic idea. These may seem rather abstract at first but will become far clearer in the light of illustrative examples found here and there in the main body of the work. Accordingly, the student is strongly advised to come back to Chapter 1 after he has worked his way through the chapters which follow.

less or purely encyclopedic. There exist other systems or frameworks in geographic research with which we are not concerned here. Yet economic geography differs from general geography not in its object, but rather in the platform or standpoint from which we investigate and judge.

From this point of view, the earth's surface may be divided into two parts: the natural landscapes, which are not influenced or have not yet been influenced by man's activities, and the cultural or, better, humanized landscapes. Each has its place in economic geography. This is apparent as to the humanized landscape, but the natural landscape is also important as potential reserves for further human expansion. For practical purposes, the two terms are contrasted in the way that *ecumene,* the inhabited earth, is contrasted with *anecumene,* the uninhabited earth.

The central theme in economic geography, a theme of great fascination, is the change on our earth, unbroken since the earliest times, in the ratio and spatial distribution of these two main divisions as well as in the structure of the humanized landscape itself. No other scientists are concerned with history in just the way that the economic geographer is—namely, with the cultural and economic evolution of mankind as mirrored in thousands of different landscapes over the earth. The student of economic geography ought to grasp this fact in its full meaning. Studies in economic geography are not, in the first instance, collections of factual data made to be put to use later on. They should be great lessons in our ways of life, their limitations and possibilities.

Although most of economic geography is concerned with existing situations, studies in the history of humanized landscapes are profitable and even necessary, because only they can provide us with clues to many things we observe in the contemporary scene. While the historical geographer is also interested in the reconstruction of past landscapes, our interest in the past derives mainly from an analysis of the present-day landscape into elements that bear the traces of various past ages. The pattern of land distribution, communications, and settlements in the former public-land states of the United States is not an expression of conditions as they exist today, but of those of over a hundred years ago when settlement took place. Similarly, certain landscape elements in other countries date back to former times and conditions. Field patterns in central Honshu, Japan, are archaic elements from about the seventh to the eleventh century, while in the Mediterranean region they may go as far back as to Roman times. The observable landscape characteristics of the present may extend their roots deep into older and indeed ancient times and may have originated under conditions quite different from those prevailing now. We can speak of old and young humanized landscapes and learn once more the lesson that everything is subject to continuing and complex changes. Another great lesson of historical geography is that we can project the significance of our findings forward in time. Furthermore, the speed with which changes occur is totally different from place to place. There are dynamic and static landscapes, and it is sometimes hard to tell whether man or the earth is primarily responsible for such differences.

With these introductory remarks, we have already touched upon the fundamental questions of scientific methodology in economic geography. We have defined the object of study, in a general way the direction of approach, and the importance of the time factor. These principles will be recurrent throughout the book.

In the arrangement of chapters in this volume, we start with man as a producer of primary goods, i.e., with agriculture and similar pursuits; but the motive for this choice of a beginning is not merely an inclination to follow the system adopted by nearly all texts in economic geography. For thousands of years man has been actively influencing the earth's surface and expanding the ecumene by taking up land and cultivating it. During most of that time, far the greater part of his products came from such pursuits. Man's productivity was expressed roughly by the number of inhabitants multiplied by a factor which took into account his economical and technical status. Gradually, a primitive form of manufacturing in the root sense of the word—handicraft—grew up to supplement the economy with a productivity that was directly proportional to the number of people engaged in it, and service industries came into being. If we think historically—and we have stressed the importance of this above—there are good reasons to start our discussion with the primary occupations. These occupations have certainly undergone much change in modern times. They are highly mechanized and productivity has been increased a great deal. But, as will be seen later, methods of agricultural production have their limitations in this respect. The widening gap between agriculture and other pursuits in productivity is one of the greater economic problems of our days, especially when we think of the countless millions of agriculturists who still have no share in even modest improvements of modern production techniques.

Some two hundred years ago, man succeeded in inventing new methods of multiplying his productivity in one sector of his activities. In the course of the so-called Industrial Revolution, he not only mechanized manufacturing but also added the productive power of inanimate nature to the animate sources of energy utilized up to then. This was accompanied by the use of new raw materials—iron, and later steel, being the most important. The iron and steel industry can truly be called the basic industry of the nineteenth century. But the creative mind of man went further, and new results were brought forth one after another. The twentieth century has witnessed the advent of new production processes called chemical synthesis, whereby entirely new materials were produced which have no counterparts in nature. Invasion by these new materials into the fields of traditional materials, as well as into the fields hitherto reserved strictly for agriculture, is often alarming.

Parallel with this development, service industries have been growing. The organization of our economic life has become more complex, and the people who are responsible for its functioning have come to constitute a larger part of the actively engaged population than ever before.

In principle, these are the reasons for the breakdown of the present volume into three main parts dealing with original production, processing, and services or—to use the terms employed by most economists—primary, secondary, and tertiary occupations, respectively. Such a division has all the weaknesses of any analytic approach. Facts cannot be dealt with in separate chapters exclusively; what is discussed in sequence is in reality concurrent and in countless ways interrelated. Yet an analytical approach has advantages. It leads to greater clarity, a consideration of first importance in a textbook. The greatest advantage of the analytical approach proposed here perhaps lies in the fact that agriculture, manufacturing industries, and services respond to the controlling factors in entirely different manners, thus necessitating different methods of investigation and interpretation.

Agriculture, even in its most modernized forms, is still earth-bound, controlled by natural factors such as soils, climate, and the rest. In a primitive civilization where man does not yet command many techniques, he is at the mercy of the vagaries of nature. For long ages his mind was wholly occupied with unknown and uncontrollable forces; but gradually he began to master more techniques and learned to organize his activities within the framework given by nature. Sometimes he may even think in a prosperous year that he has conquered nature, only to learn the following year that she still has the upper hand. Thus agriculture is the best example to demonstrate man's struggle with nature. In this sphere of human activities environmentalistic points of view find more application than elsewhere—all the more so if the agricultural civilization is in a less advanced stage.

Industrial manufacturing brought an increasing freedom from the limitations imposed by natural factors. More and more manufacturing is taking place in fully air-conditioned factories where man has complete control of the natural environment. But in order to manufacture goods, energy and raw materials have to be assembled and products to be distributed. Therefore, locational factors become important. Industrial localization has little to do with the specific conditions of a given site, but rather with its relationships with places from which raw materials come and places to which finished or semi-finished products are shipped. Locational relations may or may not be subject to natural factors, but often human factors exert a powerful influence. Thus one observes a marked shift in the treatment of the problems involved.

Finally, services, even more than industries, are subject to human factors in location as well as in development. Other differences will be discussed at the appropriate points in the following chapters.

Let us return to the broad picture of the earth's surface as modified by man. Before our eyes appear wide expanses of lands agriculturally used, here and there are seen isolated towns, cities, and industrial agglomerations. Were we to judge from a map which only portrays land use of different types, both agricultural and non-agricultural, we could never evaluate properly the relative importance of various regions and areas. Yet land-use maps are of great value. They show us where the objects of our studies are located and how they are distributed. They represent an important component or element of the anthroposphere. But in order to analyze and interpret them, we must view them together with maps covering other elements of the geospheric whole. Taken together, they will help us to understand why diverse landscape elements, at a given place, did arrange themselves into a particular and distinct pattern, under the influence of natural and human factors.

As a rule, an economic-geographical investigation starts from a given site. The elements or attributes and their structural correlation at that particular place are first investigated and explained by judging the relative influence of natural and human factors upon them. No two places on the earth would yield identical results for our observations; at least one of the elements would undergo modifications as we departed from the place of our first observation. Therefore, the whole structure must also change. In the long run, our investigations will result in a large collection of studies at selected sites, each one differing in some respect or other from the rest. To bring order to such a huge mass of examples is a general problem in all kinds of scientific research. It is solved by replacing the individual with the type, through elimination of certain characteristics, and by limiting our description to a few features which are considered typical.

The countless particular cases are reduced to a limited number of types that can be grouped systematically or taxonomically. In geographical research such a procedure will automatically lead to the possibility of delimiting areas of uniform character, the size of which depends solely on the selection of the type characteristics, the degree of map generalization, and the grain of the landscape in question. Practically all economic geographers follow this procedure in order to establish economic regions or areas; yet there is no generally accepted system of landscape types comparable, for example, to systematic botany or zoology.

Once a typological order of landscapes has been accepted by an author, he may proceed from site studies towards the delimitation of uniform areas or economic regions. This is a process called induction, a method that proceeds from the particular to the general, as opposed to the deductive method or deduction, where we draw an inference from the general to the specific. There were times when the relative merits of inductive and deductive methods were hotly debated in the field of economic geography. In actual research, however, the two methods are often used side by side and by the same investigators. It seems logical to employ the inductive method in the early stages of investigation, since it starts from the reality of the object studied and is therefore less subject to wrong conclusions.

The absence of a generally accepted taxonomy of economic landscapes has resulted in many systems of economic regionalization, each representing the judgment of a particular author. An author may have good reasons for his own system, and a careful study of its legend or of the accompanying publication will do much to clarify the author's ideas, as well as the identity of the region. System-minded people may regret this state of affairs, but others may hold in esteem the individualistic approach so typical of today's geography.

The approach to the study of the geosphere that starts at a given site and proceeds toward regionalization, as described above, does not cover the entire range of geographic reality. The relationships radiating from a given site and having to do with the economic organization of an area by man are still neglected. The spatial organization of economy is expressed through countless functional relationships between places—as it were, multiple cobwebs superimposed over the landscape. These relations and the resulting functional structures are also geographic reality, though generally invisible and intangible. Consequently, our approach has to be different, and so do the methods and techniques to be employed. We come to the conclusion, then, that in order to grasp the full reality of the geosphere, the economic geographer must use two quite different approaches. The one is for obvious reasons called the functional approach; the other—for lack of a better term and an antithesis—the formal approach. In dealing with agriculture the formal approach will be relatively more important, but the center of gravity will gradually shift toward the functional approach as we proceed to industry and services. More will be mentioned in the course of our discussion to illustrate all this.

It is harder to write a small book on economic geography than to compile a massive compendium. There are enough figures and examples available to fill volume after volume. Difficulty begins when selections have to be made. The principle observed here is the following. As has already become apparent from this introduction, the main reason why this text has been written is not to present a small or a large number of factual data, but to set forth certain ideas. These ideas have been formulated in a preliminary way in this introduction and will be followed up in greater detail through the chapters to come. Factual data serve chiefly to illustrate and to substantiate the ideas. At the same time, a student will learn from the discussions how an economic geographer pursues his work scientifically so that he will be able to cope with similar problems in the future. This seems more important than mere factual knowledge.

For these reasons, the text, the tables, and the illustrations may, to a certain degree, be regarded as relatively independent of one another; they serve different purposes, though they are generally arranged in such a way that, with respect to their factual content, they fall within the same context. The function of the text is to develop a given theme and to discuss the problems. Few statistical data will appear in the text; if they do, it is rather to show the order of magnitude than for anything else. Tables, on the other hand, simply contain the facts which are treated separately from the text and additionally to it. They are self-explanatory. Since general statistics are so easily accessible nowadays, careful consideration was given to making a limited selection of statistical data for the present volume.

Finally, the illustrations serve as examples. They should be studied with reference to the text, as well as for themselves. Each together with its legend and explanatory note, makes a small object of study in itself, and each is meant to bring a kind of order to its topic. For instance, the last map (Fig. 100, p. 242) is simple in both visual and systematic aspects, since it must be legible at the reduced scale of reproduction. Beyond such practical necessities, simplicity is a great merit in itself as long as it is the outcome of careful study of complex phenomena. Many phenomena appear at first bewildering, complicated, and difficult to grasp. Gradually or suddenly, one comes to recognize the major points and lines. An ability to describe things in simple terms is the final achievement gained through long painstaking work. As someone once put it, speaking of the academic profession, "It's much easier to express something simple in a complicated manner than vice versa." The author may not always achieve this clear simplicity; but nowhere has he attempted to make something more complicated than it already was.

These, then, are some of the principles of economic geography, and hence of this text. They may sound dry and academic, but scientific research is often like that. Research can be cumbersome and exasperating. There are days with nothing but figures and calculations. But for students of economic geography there are also rewards, and the greatest of them is a better understanding of the ways in which man has changed and organized the earth's surface. He who wants to be a good economic geographer should be equally fond of the earth and of mankind; he should be proud of the privilege that, thanks to his geographical training, he is able to read the contents of the landscape like a script.

AGRICULTURE, FORESTRY, AND FISHERIES
PRIMARY OCCUPATIONS

ABOVE LEFT: Scarp of the Cotswolds, Gloucestershire, England. Two types of field patterns are separated by the scarp. The selions or Anglo-Saxon strips are clearly visible
within the enclosed pasture land in the upper part of the picture, indicating now
abandoned cropland. (Courtesy, Geographisches Institut, Zürich)

ABOVE MIDDLE: Rectangular field pattern of Jo-ri system near Nara, Japan. (Courtesy,
Geographisches Institut Zürich)

ABOVE RIGHT: Block fields and dispersed settlements in the Jura Mountains near St. Imier,
Switzerland. (Courtesy, Eidgenössische Landestopographie, Bern)

BELOW: Two contrasting types of land utilization in Malaya in the State of Negri
Sembilan: paddy and Malay villages in the river bottom lands and rubber plantations
in different stages of development on the hilly higher lands. (Courtesy, Survey General,
Federation of Malaya)

2 | PRIMARY OCCUPATIONS

AN HAS steadily expanded his *ecumene,* as we shall call the region organized for his habitation, by following his economic pursuits, and has thus altered the face of the earth and organized the different parts of the ecumene gradually into a complex structure of world-wide economic relationships. In doing so, man is guided by his own will as well as by the possibilities bestowed by nature. Geographers call the one group of influences the human factors and the other the natural factors.

It has been the traditional practice in treatises of economic geography to put primary emphasis on the natural factors and to follow this principle in arranging the material into the main chapters. Economic geography has therefore frequently been defined as the study of nature's influence upon man's activities, and the word ''environmentalism'' was coined to describe the basic philosophy of that school of thought.

Of course, environmentalistic considerations have their place; their applications will be rather frequent in the pages that follow. But the impact of nature declines in importance as we proceed from primitive to more advanced civilizations. Nature not only dominates but permeates every aspect of the life and thought of a primitive people; the rain god, the sun and the moon, the rivers, and the sea—all these are mighty powers that regulate and control life. But in a modern civilization, man's will and determination assume the priority (though the validity of

this philosophy may be debated). The natural environment can be considered the frame within which man operates. On this view the material ought to be presented according to human activities rather than according to natural regions.

MAIN GROUPS OF ECONOMIC OCCUPATIONS

In the present volume the three major groups of occupations—primary, secondary, and tertiary—have been recognized as the basis for dividing the text into the three parts. Part One deals

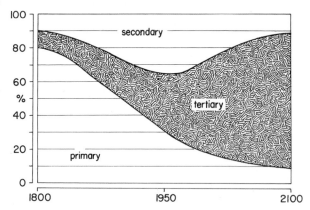

1 · DEVELOPMENT OF PRIMARY, secondary, and tertiary occupations. The chart, constructed by Fourastie for France, indicates the growing importance of secondary and tertiary occupations in the past and the prospective growth of the tertiary.

8

with the primary occupations, i.e., agriculture, forestry, and fishery (mining activities are relegated to Part Two together with the respective industries). Such a division of human activities is convenient since it is employed in most statistics and a further breakdown would frequently not be possible.

In a primitive society primary occupations are prevalent. The importance of the primary occupations as compared with the other two types decreases conspicuously with the passage of time and advance in civilization. National statistics and international surveys show this clearly. Recent surveys by FAO (Food and Agricultural Organization of the United Nations) give the ratios of agricultural population to total population, as well as to actively engaged population, as follows: in countries like India and Congo the ratio is as high as 70 and 80 percent,

respectively; in Japan and Italy it is 40 to 50 percent, but it drops below 20 percent in all the highly industrialized countries, the lowest being 5 percent in the United Kingdom. Such a decline, relative and often absolute, can also be observed in particular countries in the course of their development. In the United States the farm (working) population has dropped steadily from over 90 percent prior to 1820 to 12 percent today.

Perhaps the most significant implication of these figures is that despite this decline the farm population has been able to produce all the food needed. The primary occupations have been able to keep pace with the accelerated increase of mankind first by expansion of the producing area and second by rising efficiency in production. During the past three to four hundred years vast areas in the Americas, Soviet Asia,

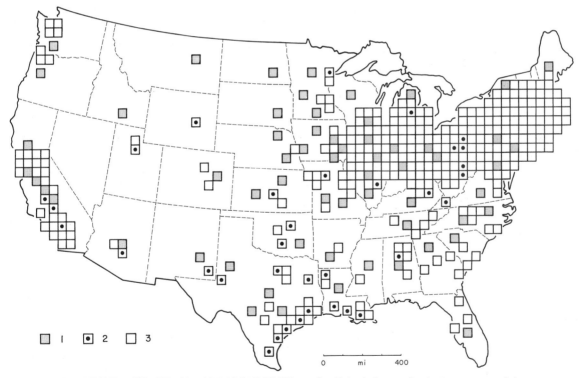

2 · PRIMARY AND SECONDARY PRODUCTION in the United States. Production measured in units of $500 million. Legend: (1) Agriculture, based on the value of the farm products sold in 1959. (2) Mineral production in 1959. (3) Manufacturing, based on the value added by manufacture in 1958. Unfortunately there were no statistical data available on tertiary production.

Australia, etc., have been settled and added to the ecumene; today the problem has shifted toward how to increase production per unit area with a minimum input of human labor.

THE OBJECT OF PRIMARY PRODUCTION

Mining excluded, those engaged in primary occupations provide mankind above all with food, clothing, and shelter. Even here only the production of the raw materials falls within the primary occupations: the preparation of food, making of textiles, sawing of timber, and building come under the secondary occupations—processing.

Furthermore, supplying shelter and clothing has become increasingly an object of nonagricultural activities. The second part of this book includes a discussion of the invention of artificial fibers and the inroads that new products have made into established markets. In construction, concrete and steel are replacing wood. Thus the production of food and feed becomes relatively more important and dominates primary activities increasingly.

With the exception of a number of textile fibers, rubber, forest products, and other minor products, primary activities have become more and more concentrated upon producing enough food for mankind and feed for animals. In these pages agriculture will be treated mainly in terms of food production, though its other functions will also be taken up at appropriate places. In food production competition from nonagricultural products is not so severe as, for example, in the production of rubber or textile fibers. There is a widely held view that naturally grown products are healthier than their man-made counterparts, and sometimes special laws protect the population from artificial food or food ingredients. Such an attitude is partly substantiated by medical science, but more often based on strong popular belief or misbelief. There are also certain sectors of human nutrition where our technical knowledge is not yet capable of producing artificial foodstuffs. These points have a bearing upon the importance of agricultural food production and tend to justify our concentrating here on the food-producing function of agriculture.

Man harvests both land and water, but for the world as a whole as well as for most countries the production from the land is paramount; fishing at its most productive supplies substantially less of our necessities than agriculture. For very few countries does the consumption of fish surpass that of meat in terms of weight. In Portugal annual per capita consumption of fish is 19 kilograms, of meat 16 kilograms. In Ceylon the figures are 6 and 3, in Japan 23 and 6, and in the Philippines 15 and 10. Here is another justification for stressing the importance of agriculture; fishery will be touched upon from time to time, but no special chapter will be allotted to it.

CHARACTERISTICS OF AGRICULTURAL PRODUCTION

The Interference of Man

In the natural landscape any change in the influencing factors takes place very slowly. Only over a long period of time may a change in the climate lead to a change in vegetation. It will also take a long time for the landscape to become adapted to the changed natural factors; eventually it attains a state in which the different landscape elements—soils, hydrology, biotic sphere, land forms, and so forth—can be described as being in balance, corresponding to the *climax* in vegetation. Natural landscapes are almost invariably more static than dynamic; only upon rare sudden changes of the influencing factors is the equilibrium upset.

Wherever man starts to occupy land, a new set of influencing factors are introduced. Abruptly some elements are eliminated, e.g., by extermination of wild life or by clearing of the forests, and new elements are implanted. As a rule this starts an immediate chain reaction throughout the structure of a given landscape; soils, ground water, surface streams, and even some climatic conditions quickly react. Not all of these changes are harmful to land use, though in newly settled areas and especially under conditions only imperfectly understood, grave consequences may result from human interference, such as destruc-

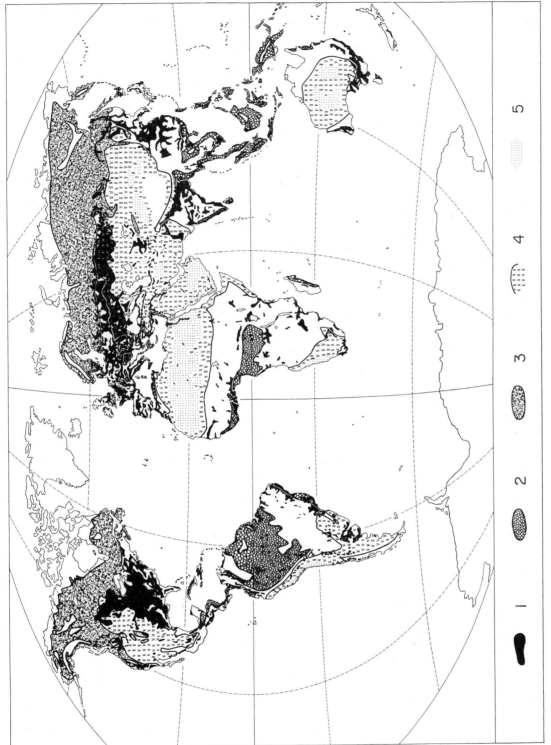

3 · NATURAL VEGETATION AND AGRICULTURE. Legend: (1) Cultivated area as defined in Fig. 20. (2) Tropical rain forest. (3) Northern coniferous forests. (4) Steppes—grasses and shrubs. (5) Deserts. The map shows, among other things, the extent of cultivated land as it extends from the mixed forest-zone in middle latitudes into the steppe lands (grain and livestock farming) and encroaches upon the subarctic belt of coniferous forests.

1   2   3   4   5

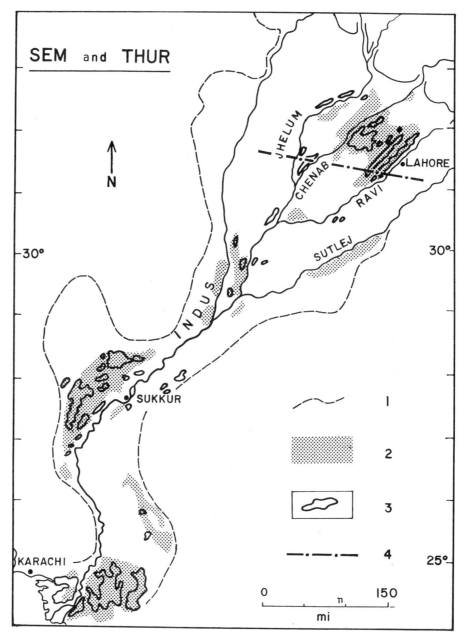

Boesch, 1962, after K. S. Ahmad et al.

4 · SEM AND THUR; problems of irrigation in West Pakistan. *Legend:* (1) Boundary of Indus Plain. (2) *Sem,* areas affected by severe waterlogging. (3) *Thur,* areas with highly increased salinity. (4) So-called Delhi-Shapur Ridge—a buried mountain chain which may possibly affect the ground-water situation. Waterlogging and salinity have increased in parallel with the extension of irrigation, but a causal relationship between them is not yet firmly established. West Pakistan currently loses about 100,000 acres of cultivated land through *sem* and *thur* annually; land recovered by way of reclamation is only a quarter of what is lost. This is a good example of the interference by man with the geospheric structure and the effects upon it.

tive soil erosion and lowering of the ground-water table. From an economic point of view, however, there are also enough examples to indicate that interference by man may improve overall conditions: in Europe, for example, agricultural know-how makes it possible today to bring ever-increasing returns from the soil, which is at the same time enriched and conserved.

A student of economic geography is therefore likely to examine the natural landscape to find first its component parts as well as the influencing factors. Then he may make an evaluation of the possible interferences by man. Conditions differ from one site to another in accordance with variations in the natural landscape. Hence site studies are of outstanding importance. Though nature's influence at a given site diminishes as we move from primary to secondary and then to tertiary occupations—i.e., the impact of nature is most pronounced in a primitive society and decreases with the march of time and civilization—yet no matter how far technical development in agriculture has progressed, site factors always weigh very heavily in our evaluations.

The Imprint of Farming Activities

No other human activity changes the face of the earth as much as agriculture does. This will become clearer if we think of a view from an airplane or take a look at a land-utilization map. Though large industrial and commercial agglomerations appear here and there, what generally dominates the view is wide expanses of crop fields and pastures. Yet this impression does not represent the relative importance of the various human activities. Judging a landscape by its physiognomy is apt to obscure what is most important. In many geography textbooks emphasis is put on the visible and tangible—the physiognomy of the landscape. To gain the full reality and meaning of the landscape we need both the modes of approach mentioned in the Introduction—the functional and the formal. The formal approach will play a particularly important role in dealing with agriculture, just as for industries and services the functional approach will take first place.

The changes brought about by man's interference at a given site are primarily changes in the formal structure of the landscape. In addition they often produce a characteristic pattern or texture of the landscape. A typical case is found in the settlement that took place in the former public-land states in the Interior Plains of the United States. Until about 1800 the landscape pattern was chiefly determined by the watercourses and to a lesser degree by topographical accidents. Through settlement the landmarks were almost completely wiped out and replaced by rectangular boundary lines and streets and a checkerboard arrangement of fields. Everywhere the three-dimensional structure of the landscape was altered through human activity; viewed on the two-dimensional earth's surface, an entirely different texture or pattern emerged. (Structure refers to the three-dimensional landscape complex at a given site; texture describes the two-dimensional arrangement on the surface which is characteristic for a certain area.)

Changes in formal structure are anchored in tangible things and thus remain visible for a long time. It is therefore important to ascertain when and under what circumstances the initial occupation of the land took place. In the case just cited, the pattern was established during the nineteenth century following the rules laid down in laws regarding surveys and distribution of public lands. Here we are confronted not only with a very young humanized landscape but also with one where the pattern originally laid out by man has undergone only minor alterations since its inception. In many parts of southern Europe similar rectangular patterns were established in the course of the Roman colonization. Today only traces of them remain among the lines of newer patterns that have since been superimposed.

Such patterns constitute extremely interesting objects for special studies. They lead us back through history to the beginnings of the humanized landscape; in most cases they were conceived in accordance with the economic conditions prevalent when they were installed. One important task for improving the productivity of agriculture consists in adapting the pattern

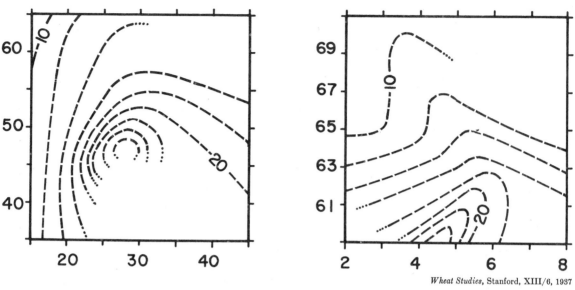

5 · RELATIONSHIPS between wheat yields per acre and the two major climatic factors temperature and precipitation. The left-hand diagram illustrates wheat yields relative to the average annual temperature (40°, 50°, 60°F) and precipitation (20, 30, 40 inches). The optimum is around 47°F and 29 inches. The diagram on the right shows wheat yields per acre plotted against the temperature and precipitation during the two months preceding the harvest.

of yesterday to the needs of today or tomorrow. Patterns also lend themselves very well to systematic studies, e.g., by distinguishing between long-lot farms, square-lot farms, etc.

The Controllability of Site Factors

Natural or physical site factors that play such an important part in primary occupations are scarcely or not at all controllable by man. For instance, hydrologic conditions are subject to improvement only by good management, and climatic conditions have virtually defied human control up to this day. Agricultural production is a highly hazardous affair and harvests fluctuate both in quantity and quality. This is in striking contrast to industrial production, which can be controlled down to the most minute details and adjusted to the demands of the market. The market for agricultural products is more static and less open to the influence of advertising. It is well exemplified by food products; variations in quantities consumed over a short period of time are relatively small, and definite

ceilings on consumption are observable, as will be shown in the section below on nutrition. In the complex structure of production, marketing, and consumption viewed as a whole, the major problems lie on the side of production. If the entire process is regarded as a sort of equation, most of the variables will be found in production.

A number of consequences result, affecting, for example, price behavior of agricultural commodities. At this stage it suffices to point out that in arranging the material and discussing the problems involved the order will be reversed as we proceed from agriculture to industry. Agriculture is considered in the order of production-marketing-consumption; in industry, market and consumption characteristics are taken first.

A Few Socioeconomic Facts about Agricultural Areas

The prevalent view that, economically speaking, agriculture in general and agricultural areas or countries in particular belong to the less developed parts of the world has almost axiomatic

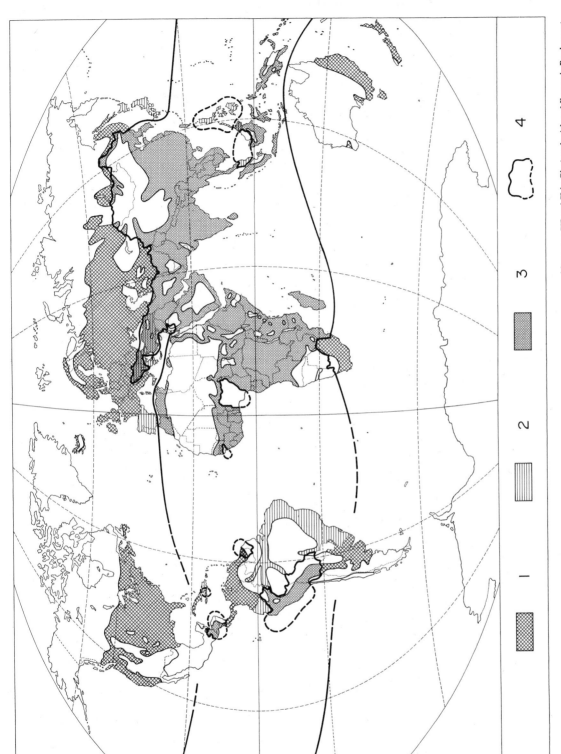

6 · GROSS NATIONAL PRODUCT and agricultural population. (1) and (2), Areas where the per capita GNP exceeds $307 and $200 respectively. (3) Countries where those engaged in agricultural occupations constitute more than 59 percent of the active population (the world average). (4), Boundary limiting the main agricultural belt of the world as well as the islands within it where the agricultural population is either higher or lower than the world average. The map shows that there are only very limited areas where a high gross national product and a high agricultural population coincide.

After maps III and X in Ginsburg's *Atlas of Economic Development!*

1   2   3   4

value. In reality, however, agricultural activities range widely from the primitive to the most advanced type. There is no doubt but that all agricultural operations are handicapped if compared with manufacturing industries and services. Not only is agricultural production hazardous and to a large degree uncontrollable by man, but also the means of increasing man's productivity through the utilization of inanimate energy, modern techniques, and the like, find only limited application in it. Agricultural production even in its most modern form has a touch of anachronism if placed side by side with the most advanced sector of the industrial world. As long as agricultural pursuits were part of a tribal or common village economy in which money did not yet play a role as a regulator of human relationships, it did not matter so much. Today products are sold on a market to distant consumers, farm hands are paid in dollars and cents, and farmers have to buy their necessities with cash. There are only a few places left on the earth where the situation remains as it was in bygone days.

In secondary and tertiary occupations man succeeded in multiplying his productivity by adding more and more value to a product with less and less man-hours of work of any kind, physical or mental. This heightening of productivity has also been tried in agriculture, but its technical development has never kept pace with that of the other occupational groups, for reasons beyond human control. This becomes apparent if a comparison is made between (A) the ratio of agricultural population to total population and (B) agriculture's share of the gross domestic national product. A few examples reveal the following discrepancies.

COUNTRY	A	B
Western Germany	15	7
Italy	44	19
United Kingdom	6	4
India	70	50
Japan	41	17
United States	13	4

The significance of these figures is simple: the agricultural population is at a disadvantage and

material remuneration in agriculture is inadequate relative to the amount of labor spent.

In the United States these inherent disadvantages have been successfully counteracted by raising the efficiency of agricultural production. In a more or less stable farming area, agri-

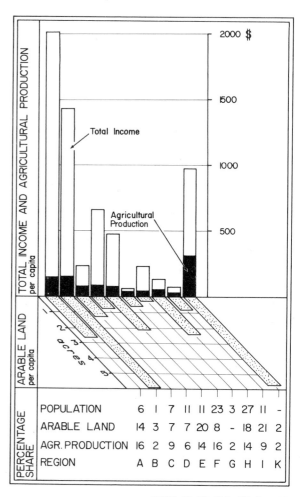

USDA, *The World Food Budget*, 1961

7 · COMPARATIVE DATA on world economy by major regions. The regions here distinguished are (A) USA, (B) Canada, (C) Latin America, (D) Western Europe, (E) Eastern Europe including the Soviet Union, (F), Communist Asia, (G) Japan, (H) Far East, excluding Japan, (I) Africa and West Asia, and (K) Australia and New Zealand. The diagram brings out the unevenness in the per capita resource distribution and the small share of agriculture in the total income.

cultural production has gradually increased to 150 percent (in constant value) of what it was thirty years ago with fewer farmers and a lower expenditure of man-hours. This is not the place to discuss the means by which the increase was achieved; they range from genetics to economics. But what was possible in one part of the world may not be a solution for another. In the United States it was possible to reduce the farm population owing to the high absorptive capacity of rapidly expanding industries and services. In other parts of the world no such alternatives exist. Growing cities in Asia, for example, have turned into unmanageable slums, nests of hunger, destitution, and political unrest. In places like this, agriculture at least gives people work and abode even if in a very inefficient form. In the United States the square lot system of land pattern, conceived more than a century and a half ago, is extremely well adapted to modern mechanical operation. In Europe a major task for raising agricultural efficiency consists in rearranging inadequate field patterns, property lines, and settlements which no longer serve current purposes. In the United States an economic structure of commodity exchange on a continental scale came into existence at the same pace as the frontier moved westward; in many parts of the world, however, trade areas have remained small and the creation of larger markets is hindered by economic and political difficulties. The economic history of the United States offers striking examples to illustrate the significance of land ownership and working contracts, which range from slavery, share cropping, and tenancy to individual owner operation, as well as the problems resulting. In other parts of the world also, agricultural improvement has been retarded by similar causes. In the United States the question of slavery led to the Civil War; the problem of land ownership and working contracts has often been and still is the cause of similar battles, wars, and revolutions in many other countries as well.

Such differences in the possibilities have led to an increasing gap between the better and the less developed countries in the world. The following excerpt from the 1961 annual report of FAO on the *State of Food and Agriculture* needs no further comment.

There is still an abundance, often a surplus, of agricultural products in the economically more developed half of the world, side by side with continuing malnutrition and even hunger in many of the less developed countries. . . . The greatest improvements in food supplies, however, have been in those parts of the world that are already better fed, so that the worse-fed areas are tending to lag still further behind.

The Farmer

Among the human factors to be considered, man himself is by no means the least. Perusing the geographical literature, we will come across excellent studies on variations in human behavior and thinking and their significance in economic geography. For the most part such studies are concerned with variations among different races or different parts of the world. However, significant differences are also observed among the occupational groups. On the one hand the farmers of the world differ a great deal among themselves; on the other hand they share certain traits which distinguish them from urban people and industrial workers.

Farmers throughout the world are harassed by similar problems, and their position in life and their view of the world around them come to bear many common characteristics. The life of a farmer is closely bound to the life cycle of plants and animals. In agriculture everything repeats itself with certain rhythm year after year. Accumulated experience weighs heavily when anything new comes along. Farmers are generally traditional; their activities are persistently seasoned with beliefs and tabus. They stay under the influence of the natural factors to a much greater extent than men in any other occupational group; even the most advanced among them still look out for the fair weather while the more primitive recognize the divine forces of nature everywhere.

There are many points to be observed in economic geography, but man himself is perhaps the most important of all.

3 | FOOD FOR MANKIND

MAN

The World's Population

Approximately three billion people are living today on this earth. National census returns and estimates during the intercensus period are regularly published in the *Demographic Yearbook* of the United Nations. In order to get more detailed knowledge of the population distribution, we must turn to national statistics and special publications.

The most noticeable characteristic of the world population is its rapid and accelerated increase in every continent, though the pace varies. The current rate of increase of the world population at large is 1.7 percent per annum. It is sufficient to bring the world total up to about 6 billion at the end of this century. This figure may be compared with 1.6 billion in 1900, 0.9 billion in 1800, and 0.5 billion in 1650. The annual rate of increase by continents around 1960 was as follows (in percent): Europe 0.8, Americas 2.1 (Middle America 2.7), Asia 1.8 (Southeast Asia 2.1), and Oceania (Australia) 2.4. These figures are self-explanatory.

This chapter does not deal with the fundamental causes of this staggering phenomenon; they will be discussed at various places throughout the text. The more immediate causes are sought in profound changes in the birth and death rates and gains and losses through migration in particular areas. The birth and death rates are usually expressed in number per thousand people and not in percent; they are indicative of the natural increase or decrease of a population.

Major population problems arise since the death rate is subject to a certain degree of human control. Improved medical care, the advance of medical science, better social conditions, and the like lead to a lowering of the death rate, especially among the younger people, in all countries in the world. In the United States the death rate dropped from 14.7 in 1910 to 9.4 in 1956, in India from 32.0 in 1911 to 12.7 in 1955, and so forth. The birth rate, on the other side, is largely regulated by considerations which defy outside interference and by causes that are sometimes difficult to comprehend. In contrast to the death rate, changes in the birth rate have been slower in most countries, though mostly in the same sense. In the United States it fell from 26 in 1913 to 24 in the early fifties; corresponding figures for Germany are 27 and 17, for France 19 and 20, and for England 24 and 17.

In view of the explosive nature of the natural increase of population, birth control (or as it is commonly called today, family planning, i.e., a restriction of conception or a reduction of births), has become a subject universally discussed. The only country which took effective legal and technical measures in this respect and where sufficient statistical data are available is Japan. There the propaganda for contraceptive

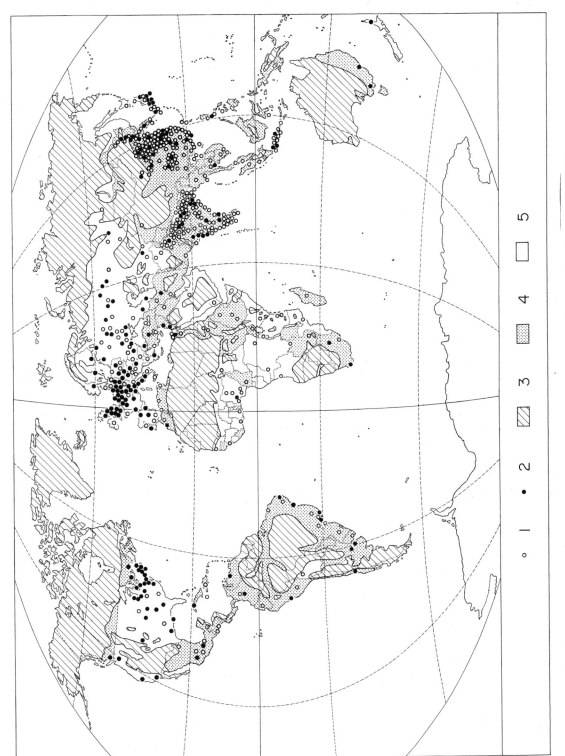

8 · POPULATION. *Legend:* (1) 6 million people, rural; (2) 6 million people, urban; (3) areas with less than 1 inhabitant per square kilometer or approximately 2.5 per square mile, which are generally considered uninhabited in the present volume; (4) countries in which the projected population increase for the period 1958–1962 is above the world average of 7.4 percent; (5) the same, projection below the world average.

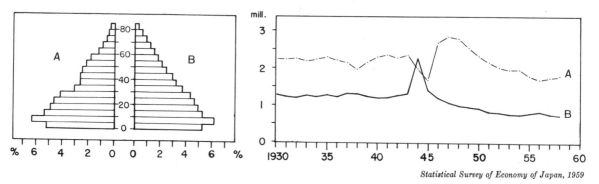

Statistical Survey of Economy of Japan, 1959

9 · DEMOGRAPHIC STRUCTURE: an example from Japan. *Left:* Age composition according to the 1955 census; (A) for males and (B) for females. Significant are the postwar baby boom and the effect of family planning in the following period. *Right:* Live births (A) and deaths (B) in Japan, 1930–1958.

measures that was spread in the wake of the Second World War was in no way successful. Only legalized abortion on a large scale was able to bring down the birth rate. Today about half of the babies conceived in Japan are eliminated before they are born. To adopt similar measures seems utterly impossible in other countries because public opinion would be strictly against them. In Japan, however, it has thus been possible to level down the steeply ascending population curve.

The reduction of the death rate was mainly achieved by saving the lives of babies and children. A number of consequences result. One of them is the prolongation of life expectancy; in the United States, for example, it increased from 50 to 68 years in half a century between 1900 and 1950, and in Western Europe, where records date back farther, it was 25 years around 1730 as against 72 for men and 74 for women at the present time. Of course this process will not go on indefinitely at the same rate. In Western Europe life expectancy is expected to reach 77 to 78 years in the year 2000. In earlier days about half of the children born died before they entered active life—an extremely wasteful investment from a purely economic point of view. Today an increasing number of them are reach-

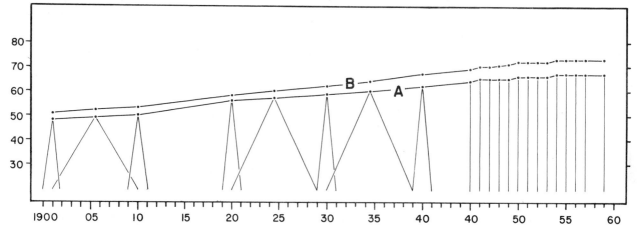

10 · LIFE EXPECTANCY of a newborn white child in the United States, 1900–1960. Life expectancy is expressed in the number of years. Between 1900 and 1960 it rose from about 50 years to 68 years for male babies (A) and to 74 years for female babies (B).

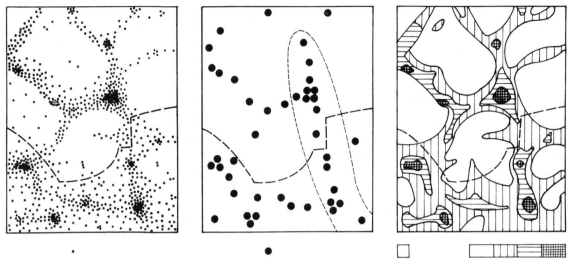

11 · CARTOGRAPHIC REPRESENTATION of population distribution. A hypothetical case of an unevenly distributed population. *Left:* the exact location of each unit is shown. One dot represents one unit. *Center:* an appreciable amount of generalization has been added by giving each dot a value of twenty units. *Right:* this cartogram was constructed on the basis of the dot map and shows the following population densities per square unit (from left to right of the legend: 0–2, 2–10, 10–25, > 25. The heavy broken line stands for a boundary of the statistical units. The light broken line (center) delimits an area chosen at random for which it is possible to determine the population number by counting the dots and hence to estimate the population density. Further explanations are given in the text.

ing the age group of the working population. This means that they reach marriageable age, too, and will start families. It also means that there is a constant increase in the number of those who live in retirement and again become an economic burden. In Japan the basic problems are not solved simply by adjusting the birth rate; as the children born before the birth control began to take effect grow up, a wave of population increase passes through all the age groups which is creating problems in schools and will soon affect employment and ultimately social securities and pension plans. In a different direction the reactions caused by famine and pest, war years, etc., all disturb the harmonious structure of a country's population. Such changes also lead to a shift in the relative importance of human diseases. Children's diseases are reduced, while diseases of old age, like heart failure and arteriosclerosis, become more prevalent.

Population Distribution

The distribution of population is first shown in statistical tables according to administrative and political units. For the student of economic geography this mode of presenting population data is often unsatisfactory because the exact location within the statistical unit is not specified.

A much better picture of the geographical distribution of population is presented by so-called dot maps. The unit value of a dot is suited to considerations of what can best be presented by graphical means, and the exact placing of a dot depends on careful analysis of data and, if necessary, checking in the field. In the present volume, dot maps of different kinds are used as examples; for technical details of mapping the reader is referred to special publications.

Dot maps of the first type have simply a

demonstrative value. Usually the dots are so numerous that their edges merge together in the areas of highest density. Nobody would think of counting dots on such a map. Maps of the second type are meant to transfer statistical data from statistical to geographical areas and allow dots contained within a given spatial unit to be counted. If the dots are correctly placed, this is the best method to break down or group together the original enumeration units into new ones of any kind. Dot maps of the third type are closely associated with maps of the second type and are intended for the calculation of population density. A widely employed method is first to calculate the densities of smaller areas, which together form a regular or irregular meshwork, and then to draw lines each of which represents a certain density value—*isopleths*—much as contours are drawn on a topographical map. The major difference between an isopleth map of population density and a contour map lies in the nature of the object to be shown; topography is a continuum while population is not. Another method which serves to establish areas of a given density or above is to select the size and the unit value of the dots in such a way that they merge together above the scale value selected; this makes it possible, for example, to define urbanized areas quickly by graphic procedures.

Directly or indirectly, dot maps form the basis of the centrographic method by which the center of gravity of a population within a certain area is calculated. A well-known case is the center of gravity of population distribution in the United States, which continuously moved westward from near Baltimore, Maryland, in 1790 to Columbus, Indiana, in 1900 and to Centralia, Illinois, in 1960.

Population density is the quotient of *population/area*. Generally people are enumerated at their place of residence; area means in most cases the political administrative unit which serves as the statistical counting unit. Sometimes this relationship makes sense, but in other cases it does not, for no true "relationship" exists between the two values in fact. Hence geographers have been particularly diligent in working out more meaningful relationships and have ar-

rived at different concepts of population density. The quotient *population/area* is commonly called the arithmetic density. In dealing with nonagricultural population it is better to correlate it with residential area, namely, the residential density. Similarly the agricultural density is the quotient of agricultural population and agricultural area, and physiological density the ratio of total population to the ecumene. There will be more such relationships, each serving a specific purpose in regional studies. No general standard or terminology exists, however, and the field is wide open to elaborate various ways of expressing man-land relationships or to select a way which helps to provide a realistic picture of the actual situation of a given area.

Closely related to the problem of population density is the problem of overpopulation. Though the term is frequently used, *overpopulation* in most cases is only loosely defined or not defined at all, and erroneous conclusions are apt to be drawn. Strictly speaking, overpopulation might mean a population density higher than can be supported from the agricultural use of the land concerned. But if overpopulation is conceived in relation to all the resources available, natural and other, it becomes noticeable when the material standard of living begins to decline and when a local shortage of food, if it occurs, can no longer be met fully by imports which are paid for by exports of another kind, including services.

Related to overpopulation are the concepts of the optimum and the maximum population. For the world as a whole, only the relationship of total population to total food production enters our calculations. The carrying capacity and hence the total population of the earth have been studied by a number of geographers; total figures varying between 7 and 15 billion people have been calculated, provided conditions of agricultural production remain the same. But a number of variables enter our calculations—the reproductive capacity of mankind, the amount and kind of food consumed, and the efficiency with which land and sea are utilized for the production of food and feed. Reproductive capacity has been referred to above, and the other

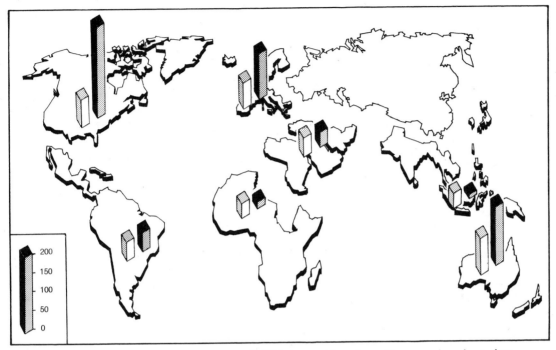

12 · ESTIMATED PER CAPITA FOOD SUPPLIES by world regions. The map, based on data supplied by FAO, shows price-weighted indices of livestock products (dark column) and crop products (light column) used for human consumption. It comprises all kinds of food. The period 1948 to 1952 is used as the base period (100). Eastern Europe, USSR, and mainland China are excluded for lack of data. The map is intended to facilitate rapid comparisons rather than for accurate measurement of individual columns; for this purpose a numerical tabulation would be decidedly superior.

two variables will be taken up below, since they represent the basic problems for the future of the human race.

Food Consumption

The amount of food consumption varies within relatively narrow limits and the market for food products is therefore relatively rigid, closely bound to the size of population. Yet, within these limits there are significant regional and social differences in both the quantity and the quality of food consumed.

It is customary to measure food consumption in calories. Calorie requirements vary from area to area, and of course individually too. The standard mean value of food requirements is frequently given as 2,700 calories a day. A recent

FAO publication further differentiates food requirements as follows: (A) the current levels of calorie supplies, (B) the daily calorie requirements per capita at the retail level, and (C) the ratio of A:B, by regions.

REGION	A	B	C
Far East	2,050	2,300	89
Near East	2,450	2,400	102
Africa	2,350	2,400	98
Latin America	2,450	2,400	102
Europe	3,000	2,600	115
North America	3,100	2,600	119
Oceania	3,250	2,600	125
World	2,400	2,400	100

The true meaning of these figures is somewhat obscured by the fact that in a greater number of

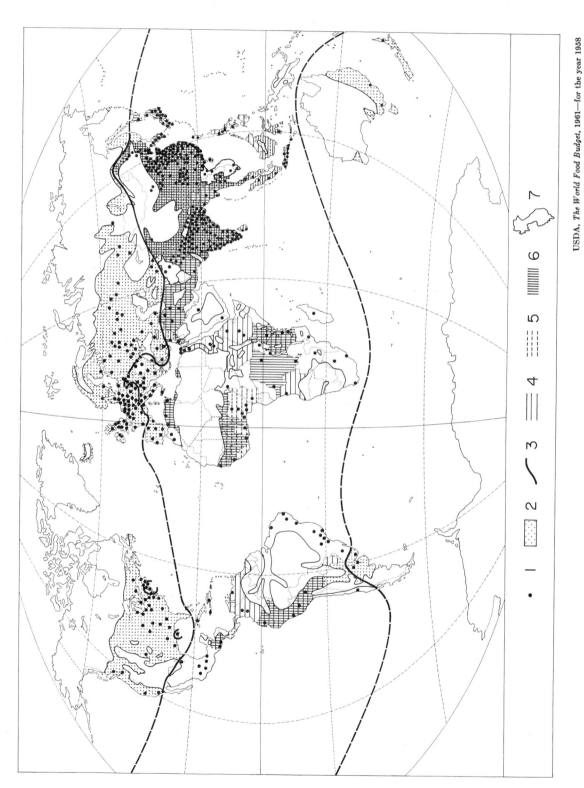

13 · THE GEOGRAPHY OF HUNGER. *Legend:* (1) population, identical with Fig. 8 but undifferentiated; (2) countries where daily per capita consumption of food is higher than 2,700 calories; (3) boundaries of the so-called hunger belt within which food consumption is lower than 2,700 calories and all sorts of deficiency diseases are found; (4) calorie deficiency in the average daily diet; (5) protein deficiency; (6) fat deficiency; (7) countries for which no data were available.

USDA, *The World Food Budget*, 1961—for the year 1958

regions supplies of food exceed the amounts required. However, the huge concentration of population in the Far East implies that the problem of malnutrition and hunger is much graver than appears from the table at first sight. Case studies made in the problem areas reveal that at least one-fourth to one-third of the Far Eastern population is underfed and that about one-fifth suffers from actual hunger. Since approximately half of the world's population falls within the deficit areas, it may be assumed "that between 300 million and 500 million people go hungry part of their lives even in normal times" (FAO).

The figure for the entire world suggests that preventing hunger is, at least for the time being, a matter not of production or consumption but simply of better distribution.

Another aspect of the problem of food consumption is the kind and quality of food con-

sumed. Regional differences are much greater for this than for quantity. As we move away from the highly industrialized countries toward the less developed ones, the diet shifts from animal to vegetable foodstuffs and consumption increases of cereals and starchy root vegetables and tubers. This shift is brought to light in the accompanying table which gives (A) percentage of calories derived from cereals, starchy roots, and

REGION	A	B	C
Far East	80	56	8
Near East	72	76	14
Africa	74	61	11
Latin America	64	67	25
Europe	63	88	36
North America	40	93	66
Oceania	48	94	62
World	70	68	20

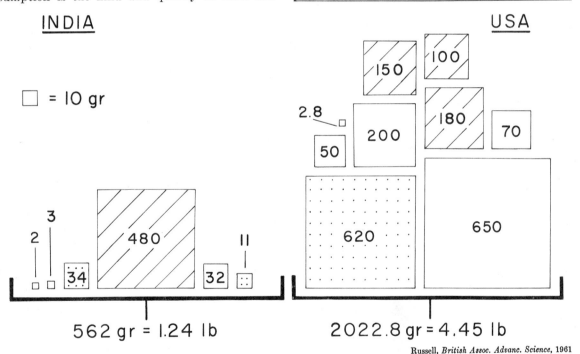

14 · THE DAILY BREAD. The typical diet of the working population of India is compared with that of the urban population in the United States. The figures represent the quantities of the component parts of the average daily diet per person in grams. *India:* 480 rice, 34 vegetables, 32 pulses, 11 fruit, 3 fats and oils, 2 meat. Other cereals, fish, eggs, milk, and sugar are negligible. *USA:* 650 milk and milk products, 620 vegetables and fruits, 200 meat, 180 cereals, 150 potatoes, 100 sugar, 70 fats and oils, 50 eggs, 2.8 pulses.

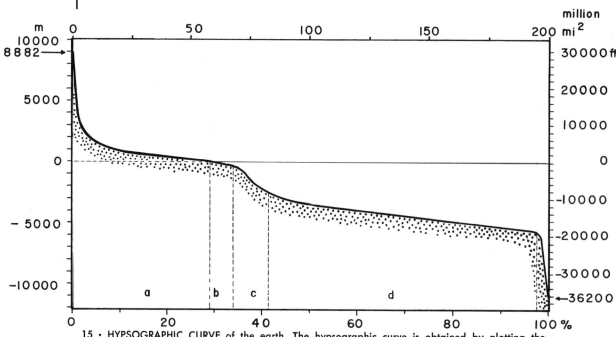

15 · HYPSOGRAPHIC CURVE of the earth. The hypsographic curve is obtained by plotting the extent of the various altitudinal zones (in square miles as well as in percent of the earth's surface) between the highest (8,882 meters in altitude, left) and the lowest point (36,200 feet below sea level, right) of the earth's surface. The major structural and morphological units can easily be recognized thereby, namely: (a) that part of the continental masses which is above sea level; (b) the continuation of a below sea level, the so-called continental shelf; (c) the slope of the continents toward the ocean floor; and (d) the ocean basins and deep-sea troughs.

sugar, (B) level of total protein in grams per day, and (C) level of animal proteins in grams per day.

The problem of undernourishment is thus coupled with that of malnutrition. Clinical cases are one aspect of malnutrition, while lessened physical resistance and working efficiency constitute another. Growing urban centers in the underdeveloped countries are the worst places in this respect; certain agricultural areas are almost as bad. Many diseases which have practically disappeared or are at least rapidly diminishing in the better-fed areas here take a heavy toll of lives, mostly from the youngest generation. A widespread disease of this kind is kwashiorkor, caused by protein malnutrition. Tuberculosis belongs ecologically to this group, and there are many more. On the one hand, as living conditions are improved, certain diseases disappear. On the other hand, an improvement in dietary habits gives rise to the problem of eat-

ing too much; medical science suspects that it also brings about the weakening of human resistance to some virus infections.

Usually unsatisfactory conditions of hygiene go hand in hand with malnutrition. A typical example is Egypt, where the greater part of the population suffers from bilharzia, a water-borne disease affecting the vitality, from dysentery, from tuberculosis, from trachoma which causes blindness, and from many more ailments. Life expectancy at birth there is only fifteen to twenty years, but once a child is five years old it leaps up to fifty years. Chronic and multiple diseases besetting an individual greatly reduce his working power and efficiency in the struggle for life.

The Food and Agricultural Organization, recognizing the grave importance of this problem, started a Freedom from Hunger Campaign a number of years ago. There must be found a solution to the problem for a number of reasons, but above all because we are all human beings and neighbors.

LAND AND SEA

The Configuration of the Earth

The primary division of the earth pertinent to the study of economic geography divides it into land and water; water covers 71 percent of the earth's total surface of 197 million square miles. The next division is based upon depths and altitudes. The summarized results can be plotted in a hypsographic (or bathygraphic) curve which reveals the major structural elements of the earth.

The coastline separates land and water. However, the hypsographic curve indicates that the continental block continues for some distance into the sea as a relatively shallow and gently sloping submarine platform until a rather sudden break in slope is reached and the platform starts to drop off. This break in slope generally occurs at a depth of 600 to 700 feet. The inundated edge of the continental mass may be hundreds of miles wide, but in some areas it is extremely narrow. This zone is called the *continental shelf*. It has gained in importance in many respects: for example, it contains important fishing grounds; offshore drilling for oil is becoming possible at greater and greater depths; territorial rights are extended into the ocean and, in certain cases, their limits coincide with the edge of the shelf.

Another thing to be observed is the cartographic representation of the earth's surface. Wherever a comparison between different parts of the earth has to be made, the only maps that ought to be used are those of equal-area projections. On the well-known Mercator projection, a given land area appears 2.5 times larger in southern Europe than it actually is in comparison with the same area near the equator, and 11 times larger in central USSR. The use of such maps in the classroom year after year impresses a greatly distorted view of areal relations upon the student's mind. The Mercator projection is not suitable for economic geography, where com-parative evaluations are of paramount importance.

Climate, Vegetation, and Soils

On an assumption that students of economic geography are already versed in physical geography, this section is made short and very general. In a course in climatology one deals with the causes of climatic differentiation and the problems of classification of climates. Here an entirely different point of view is assumed. In the economic geography of agriculture every climatic element is considered in terms of plant growth, e.g., how much warmth a certain plant requires, what extremes of temperature become harmful to its growth, how long the vegetative period must last, and so forth. This leads to the more specific problem of determining (*a*) the optimum conditions and (*b*) the limits of tolerable conditions. Some plants occur in highly restricted areas of possible growth, while others are almost ubiquitous.

The tropical zone comprises about two-fifths of the globe and one-third of the land surface, a fact which is often obscured by map projections which unduly enlarge the middle-latitude zones. The tropical climates are so different from all the others that it is difficult for the people living in other zones to understand them without abandoning certain terms or ideas which we take for granted. In tropical regions there are no middle-latitude cyclonic disturbances with well-defined fronts, rapidly changing cloud formations, and warm and cold air masses, no general circulation from west to east, etc.; the daily weather is different and so is the climate.

In the tropics the temperature requirements at a given place are met uniformly throughout the year without seasonal variations. There is generally a slight drop in temperature during the rainy season due to an increased cloud cover, but only such sensitive plants as rice show any noticeable reaction to that. Most important is altitude, since temperature decreases as altitude increases. At sea level the average temperature is about 77° F. It drops at the rate of about 1 F° for every 300 feet of rise (100 m, 0.5 C°); this is called the vertical temperature gradient. Con-

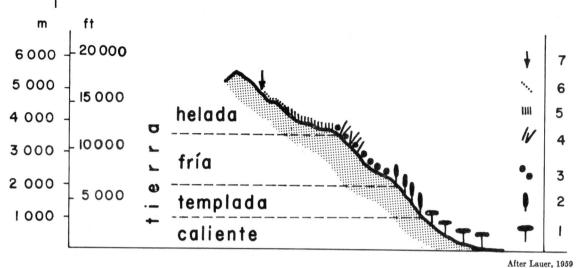

After Lauer, 1959

16 · ALTITUDINAL ZONES OF VEGETATION in the tropics (Central America). The four major zones are called *tierra caliente, t. templada, t. fría,* and *t. helada.* The legend indicates the characteristic types of vegetation: (1) tropical rain forests, (2) tropical mountain forests, (3) higher parts of tropical mountain forests—in northern Central America with boreal species, (4) bamboo, (5) paramo, scrubs, and grasses, (6) high-altitude rock deserts, (7) snow line.

sequently natural vegetation and cultured plants occur in levels or *stockwerks*. In Latin America the levels are commonly called *tierra caliente, tierra templada, tierra fría,* and *tierra helada* in ascending order. These different altitudinal zones have constant daily mean temperatures all through the year; as far as temperature is concerned there is no dormant season for living things nor any seasonal change. The same applies to the snow line in the tropics, which stays at about the same altitude all the year round with only a slight descent during the rainy season. It is therefore misleading to say that at higher altitudes in the tropics one finds a temperate climate comparable to a climate in middle latitudes, or to lump these two together in a climatic classification system as was done by W. Köppen.

Precipitation in the tropics is in the main of two types: convectional and orographic. Orographic precipitation occurs primarily in areas where the trade winds and the monsoons prevail. The maximum of convectional precipitation occurs during the high-sun period. Wet and dry seasons constitute the significant divisions of the year, just as summer and winter determine them in higher latitudes. It is confusing to speak of summer and winter in the tropics and should be avoided. The rainy season is the unpleasant season of the year. Everything becomes damp and moldy; the sky is overcast. Though temperature is slightly lower, humidity is high. It is the season that the Spaniards called *invierno* or winter in Central America even though it fell between June and September; likewise they called the time from about December to February the *verano* or summer.

With the exception of a narrow belt of "constantly wet" zone near the equator, the tropical lands show a division of the year into the wet and dry seasons, chiefly caused by convectional precipitation that occurs following the changing position of the sun. It can be either offset or reinforced by the trades and monsoons from which moisture is precipitated as they are forced to ascend. Rainfall distribution thus shows a marked difference between the windward side and the leeward side. The seasonal distribution of convectional precipitation in Central America has just been described. There during the (convectionally) dry season continuing precipitation occurs on the Caribbean side through the influence of the easterly trade winds, but drought is intensified by the foehn effect on the Pacific side.

Since temperature at any given place in the

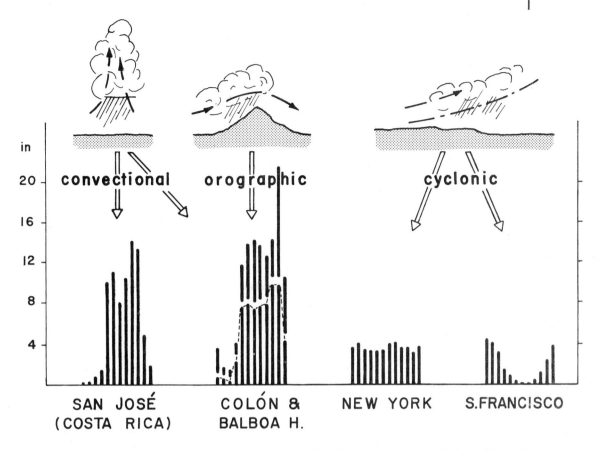

in

20

16

12

8

4

SAN JOSÉ
(COSTA RICA)

COLÓN &
BALBOA H.

NEW YORK

S.FRANCISCO

17 · TYPES OF PRECIPITATION. The types distinguished here are identical with those discussed in the text. Convectional precipitation (*left*) is most characteristic of the tropics. As a rule, two maxima are reached there, coincident with the high-sun periods, resulting in a typical rainfall curve like a camel's back. Orographic precipitation (*center*) plays an important role wherever there is forced ascent of moving air masses over a mountain barrier. The example shown here is taken from the zone of the trade winds; the two stations represent the conditions on the windward and leeward slopes of a mountain range. Cyclonic or frontal precipitation (*right*) is best developed in the belt of the middle-latitude westerlies. There the convergence of polar and tropical air masses produces cyclonic disturbances in which air is forced to ascend and yield precipitation without topographic obstacles. San Francisco occupies a more southerly position in this belt where such disturbances occur only in winter, while New York has a more even distribution over the whole year.

tropics does not vary with the seasons, limitations upon plant growth derive from the relation of wet and dry seasons as well as from the total amount of precipitation available after losses through evaporation and run-off have been taken into account.

In middle latitudes the situation is more complex because changes of temperature become effective in defining the seasons. Furthermore the effectiveness of precipitation depends to a large degree upon the temperature season, since much more evaporation takes place in summer than in winter. The duration of the vegetative period there is determined by a combination of temperature and rainfall effective for plant growth.

Perhaps the most noticeable change occurs in the direction of prevailing winds and the character of air movements. Middle latitudes are the major battlefields between polar-arctic and trop-

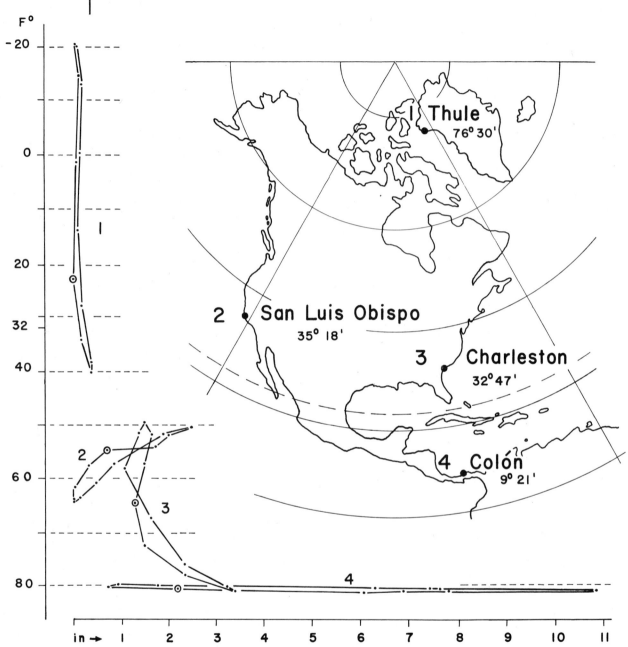

18 · CLIMATIC CHARACTERISTICS of various latitudinal zones. The four stations represent the climatic types characteristic of various latitudinal zones. The data are presented in the form of climographs. For each month of the year, temperature (°F) and precipitation (inches) are plotted on a system of coordinates and then joined together by a line. April is always indicated by a small circle. (1) Representative of the high arctic, characterized by meager precipitation and a large annual range in temperature. (2) and (3) Intermediate types of the middle latitudes, i.e., the east-coast type with a maximum precipitation in summer, and the west-coast Mediterranean type with a pronounced winter maximum and the dry summer. (4) Typical tropical climate in which seasonality is determined by precipitation.

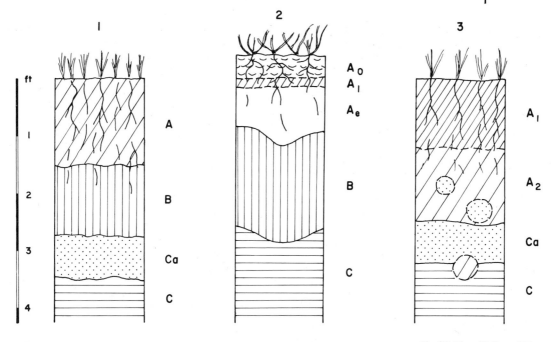

Simplified from Kubiena, 1953

19 · SOIL PROFILES of the temperate zone. The three types are (1) brown soil from Central Europe, (2) podzol, and (3) chernozem.

Type 1 is developed in humid lands of the middle latitudes under a natural vegetation of deciduous forest. The soil horizons indicated are: (A) eluviation, i.e., leaching of soluble material downward, and maximum biological activity; (B) illuviation, i.e., accumulation of material carried from above in suspension or in solution; (Ca) accumulation of calcium carbonate; and (C) parent material.

Type 2 is generally found in higher latitudes under a vegetation cover mainly of coniferous trees. (A_0) is partially decomposed raw humus, and (A_1) a dark-colored horizon with a very high content of humus. It is immediately underlain by a horizon of maximum eluviation (A_e—a gray layer characteristic of all podzols, (B) a horizon of illuviation, and (C) parent material.

Type 3 occurs in the more humid portions of the middle-latitude grasslands and is known for its fertility and ability to stand cropping year after year without fertilization. (A_1) is high in organic matter, decomposed and mixed with mineral matter; (A_2) is a faintly developed horizon of eluviation; (C_a) is an accumulation of calcium carbonate; and (C) is the parent material.

ical air masses which are drawn into a system of so-called cyclonic disturbances moving from west to east around the earth. Relevant to our discussion are the two primary effects. First, the cyclonic disturbances produce constant weather changes in every respect—cloudiness, precipitation, temperature, etc. Precipitation is to a large degree caused by a forced ascent of the air within each disturbance; mountain barriers are not essential to providing a trigger effect. Consequently rainfall is distributed more evenly than, say, in a monsoon country where a sharp contrast in rainfall is observable between the windward and leeward sides. The second effect is a distinct difference in climate between the eastern and western peripheries of the continents. Maritime air masses approach a continent from the west, and continental air reaches the east coast from the interior. The terms *maritime* and *continental* refer to temperature characteristics commonly found in maritime and continental locations; but even port cities in the east coast may have a continental climate despite their oceanic location.

A summer day becomes increasingly longer as we move poleward until the zone of at least twenty-four hours of daylight—which increases towards the pole to six months—is reached north of the Polar Circle. During the peak of the summer season, mean temperatures remain more or less the same for weeks and the total amount of solar energy received is astounding.

Climatic conditions are the principal control in determining the distribution of fauna and flora and for its differentiation. Economic geographers are mainly interested in the plant life and the great divisions of the natural landscape into forests, grasslands, and tundra, as well as deserts of all grades and kinds. Plant geography is the science which specializes in this particular field, while geographers regard the plant life as one of the elements constituting the geospheric whole. Thus soils, for example, are an expression of the versatile physical and human influence within that complex structure, and any change within it automatically brings about an alteration in the soil-forming processes.

Soil formation is the function of a given set of factors—parent material, vegetation, water conditions, etc. Soils generally develop to a depth which is shallow (a few feet) in temperate latitudes, but very deep (tens of feet) in warm tropical regions. The weathered derivatives of the parent material and the organic matter derived from plant and animal substances are altered through chemical and biological processes.

The significance of the soil in economic geography is that of the sphere where the plants extend their roots in order to obtain water and nutrients. Fertility of the soil may depend upon physical and chemical properties, the amount of nutritive elements available, porosity and permeability, and many other characteristics. Some soils are loose and are easily washed away once the natural vegetation cover has been removed and replaced by an inadequate cultural substitute; other soils are hard and can withstand even long periods of exposure to erosional agents. A soil is called mature if the soil-forming processes have led to the climax stage. On the other hand, soils may be constantly rejuvenated in alluvial floodplains, in volcanic areas, or on steep moun-

tainsides. In such settings there is frequently no time available for the soil to develop fully. Finally, we need to distinguish between natural soils and those which have been influenced and largely altered by human activities; soil conservation and improvement form a good indicator of high agricultural development. Examples of different soils will be given later from time to time, but no systematic description of the subject is attempted in this volume.

Habitable and Inhabited Areas

Strictly speaking, there is no place on the earth where man cannot survive, provided that he is properly supplied and protected. But the word *habitable* has generally been understood as referring to the parts of the earth where man can secure food and other necessities from nearby sources, be it sea, forest, or land. Sea and forest (fish and game) give rise to highly dispersed settlements or extremely low population densities; therefore they have often been excluded from consideration in connection with the term *habitable,* and the habitable area has become virtually synonymous with the potential agricultural area.

Habitability should always be considered in relation to conditions of time as well as of space. Agricultural techniques have been constantly improved and new varieties of cultured plants produced; such developments have helped to open up vast areas of virgin land for cultivation.

It is difficult to assess the amount of land that can be called habitable under present-day conditions. A classical example is an estimate given by an English economist in 1890; it classified about two-thirds of the habitable areas of the earth as "still unused." Since then the statistical situation has greatly changed. According to the figures given by FAO in 1960, 9 percent of the land surface is currently used as arable land and under tree crops, and 17 percent as permanent meadows and pastures, while 27 percent is covered with forests, used or not used. With the forests included, there remains 74 percent of the land surface to be considered. It is not surprising that the estimates vary a great deal as to how much of this land may be classified as "un-

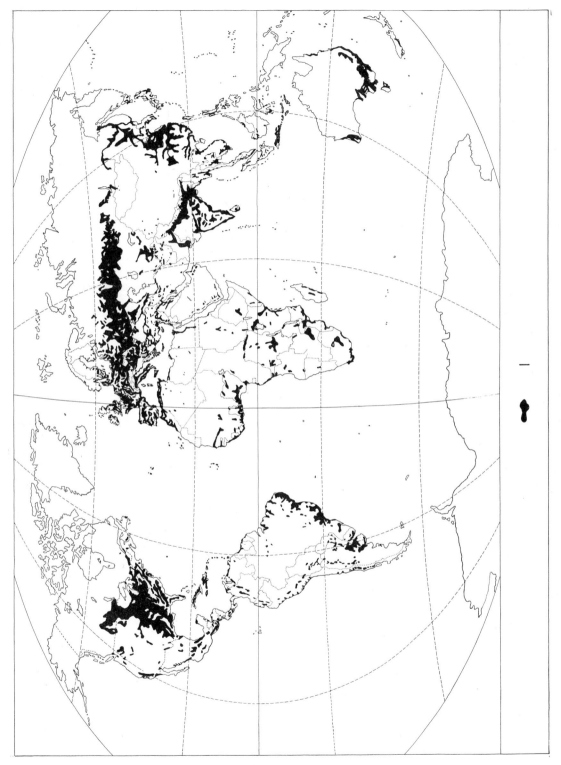

20 • CULTIVATED LAND. This map, compiled from a large number of sources, shows (1) the distribution of cultivated land which is equivalent to what FAO defines as "arable land and land under tree crops." Within certain limits it is in close agreement with the FAO statistics on land use.

used but potentially productive.'' FAO statistics for individual countries are far from complete and homogeneous. Estimates of FAO and of different authors vary within a range of 3 to 10 percent of the total land area (excluding the antarctic regions), which means that the area in use could only be increased by 10 to 40 percent in the future; the lower figure represents the more conservative estimate of FAO, and the higher more optimistic unofficial views.

During the past two hundred years the inhabited area has expanded more rapidly than the habitable area, owing to large-scale settlement that has come about throughout the world, especially in middle-latitude parts of North and South America and Soviet Russia, as well as in South Africa, Australia, and New Zealand. The origin of the settlers and the agricultural techniques developed and used by them were highly responsible for this fast expansion of the ecumene and for the concentration of it in the middle latitudes. The big question today is whether a similar development will be possible in the future in the parts of the tropics which have hitherto remained largely unoccupied. Essentially they may be considered ultimately habitable, but as will be seen later, their characteristics are not yet known well enough to warrant the most efficient utilization.

If the FAO estimates are to be accepted, it appears that utilizable land reserves have largely been exhausted. Unless new technical developments place some of the land areas that are at present unoccupied within our reach, the world's food situation can be improved only by raising the output per acre, a problem which will be dealt with in Chapter 4.

The expanding ecumene is bordered by a zone called the pioneer fringe; pioneers occupy a significant place in the history of the United States. Not infrequently economic and other human factors induce a reversed development, i.e., a contraction of the inhabited area. Today economic considerations lead us to recognize marginal and submarginal farm lands and to persuade the farmers there to move elsewhere. In other continents and under other conditions, pests and wars depopulated large areas, some of which have been permanently abandoned or reforested.

The area actually inhabited can be clearly delineated and its changes recorded by mapping and descriptions; but to give a fair estimate of the habitable areas of the earth is a problem which finds no clear solution.

Much of the earth's surface is not suited for efficient agriculture owing to its topography and soils. In former days mountainous areas in Europe were intensively cultivated by terracing; but small terraced fields are an obstacle to modern production methods, and the lower efficiency of the mountain farming in comparison with the agriculture in the plains gradually led to abandonment of mountain farms and emigration from them. One envisions with apprehension what might happen in some tropical areas where agriculture is at present based on terracing and unmechanized labor if a similar development were to set in there. Mountain areas are problem areas, and people living in them have to be compensated in some way or other for the disadvantages they have to put up with.

These problems are generally taken care of within each country according to the local possibilities. Yet some frontiers of the ecumene have become a matter of international concern.

The polar frontier in the Western Hemisphere is the special concern of Canada and the United States, and that in the Eastern Hemisphere of the USSR. Major agricultural problems involved in pushing the ecumene into the polar frontier zone include, for instance, the breeding of new hybrids adapted to a short vegetative period and constant daylight, and the management of the frozen soil, which thaws to a depth of no more than a few inches in summer for a period of only a few months.

Two other frontiers have invited international cooperation on a much larger scale to explore possibilities for future human occupation under the guidance of the United Nations and its subsidiary organizations. UNESCO has undertaken the Major Project of the Arid Zones, and a corresponding project for the humid tropics. These deal with the two great existing barriers to expansion of the ecumene. Research institutions in many countries are taking part in these programs; UNESCO stimulates their activities and organizes meetings on the international level to facilitate an exchange of basic information.

The Role of the Sea

The world catch of fish has been greatly increased since the Second World War; in fact, it has all but doubled to reach between 30 and 40 million tons per year. Fish (as was pointed out in Chapter 2) is in general of small importance in the world's food supply, except for a few countries; if compared with more than 250 million tons of wheat or rice or an equal amount of milk produced each year, the fish that the ocean supplies constitute a minor portion of the earth's food requirements.

The most important areas for salt-water fisheries are the continental shelfs and equally shallow banks in the cooler waters of middle and higher latitudes. While tropical waters contain a rich variety of fish species, cooler waters where the number of species is smaller are commercially more important because they have larger numbers of fish.

The annual climatic cycle in higher latitudes is reflected in a cyclic behavior of some fish that migrate in large schools to certain areas for spawning, etc. Such migrations make it particularly easy to catch them at a given time of the year. Fishing, therefore, is frequently combined in alteration with agriculture as a strictly seasonal occupation, at least as it is carried out near the coast. In the second half of the nineteenth century, steamers replaced sailing boats; fishing extended beyond the shallow coastal waters and the length of the journeys increased. In Europe the fishing grounds of Icelandic waters and the Barents Sea overshadowed those of the North Sea. Fishermen from New England sailed out to the banks off Newfoundland and the Labrador coast instead of to the much closer Georges Bank and South Channel. Fishing grew into a full-time occupation and a full-fledged sector of the modern economy.

Seasonality in fishing produces a number of problems. Slight changes in the salinity and the temperature of sea water induce the fish to shift unexpectedly from one area to another in an unforeseeable manner which is not yet fully understood. For example, sardines, the major catch of coastal Portuguese fisheries, suddenly disappeared after the last war. The result was financial distress in the whole country. On the other hand there was noted a simultaneous increase in sardine catches in Morocco.

The cod has been one of the most important commercial fish in Europe for many centuries. Cod are caught near the Lofoten Islands of Norway between January and April, and farther north in Finmarken in May and June. Depending upon the season, fishing settlements are either bustling with life or virtually deserted. Only a small part of the catch is sold for immediate consumption; the remainder is tinned, salted, dried, or frozen for preservation. Salted and dried cod, which appears just as stiff and long as the famous bread of France, had long been a commodity of trade between northern and southern Europe; it is still called *Stockfisch* in German, *stochefisso* in Italian, and *bacalao* in Portuguese, all of which mean exactly the same; *tierra de bacalao* was the Portuguese name for Newfoundland and Labrador, regions to which they had sailed for generations to catch the fish so much needed in their diet. In many Mediterranean countries salted and dried fish are still consumed as a delicacy; in Portugal they form the mainstay of daily diet.

Generally speaking, the Mediterranean is poor in fish. The major population centers in northern Italy or in Catalonia are supplied with fish either from northern Germany or from the Bay of Biscay by land transportation. Preserved fish of Scandinavian, North American, or recently also Japanese origin are sold everywhere.

In tropical areas abundant fish are found only in relatively cool waters—along the west coasts in the subtropics where there are upwellings of cold water from depths, or in cold ocean currents like the Humboldt Current off the coasts of Chile and Peru. In general tropical fisheries have remained in a primitive stage though they may be of highest importance locally, and the catch is consumed on the spot.

In response to the seasonality in catches, definite peaks are observed in fish landings. Since fish have to be shipped fresh as quickly as possible, fish markets assume a certain character which resembles that of the vegetable and flower

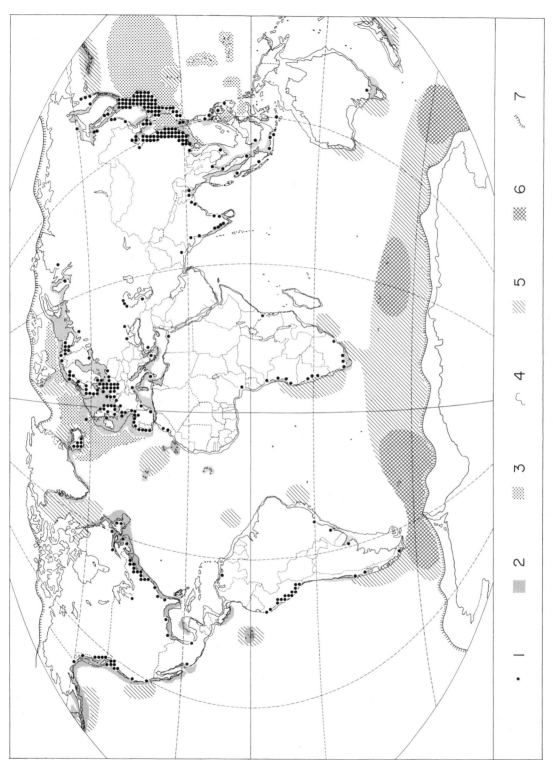

21 · FISHERIES. *Legend:* (1) Fish catches for 1958 in units of 100,000 metric tons. (2) Fishing grounds on continental shelves and banks. (3) Deep-water fishing grounds. (4) Isobath of 200 meters or 656 feet—the conventional margin of the continental shelf. (5) Whaling grounds of world importance. (6) Whaling grounds of lesser importance. (7) Limit of pack ice.

markets in many respects. The sale on the spot by way of bidding and immediate removal of the goods sold impart a unique color to the market. Fish are then delivered to inland markets by special fish trains and express trucks service and reach the ultimate consumer through special dealers and sometimes restaurants. Commercial fishing and fish trade therefore consists of a continuous chain of activities which are quite independent of other activities.

Whaling is not included in the statistics of fish catches since the whale is zoologically a mammal; in the technique of exploitation, however, whales may be considered together with fish. They have been a major source of oils and fats for industrial as well as for human consumption, accounting for about 10 percent of the world trade in these products.

The Atlantic Ocean used to be the scene of great whaling activities, and their contributions to capital formation in early America is well known. Gradually the center of whaling shifted to other seas, especially to the Antarctic. Already in 1909 more than half of whale oil production was coming from that source region. In the 1930's the proportion exceeded 90 percent. International control and regulatory measures for the conservation of whales have since reduced the contribution of Antarctic waters to 60 percent, which consists of fin whales for the most part.

Whaling is carried out in two forms: the catcher—the ship that actually captures the whale—operates either from a shore station or from a floating factory at which the carcass is immediately processed. Japan is the top-ranking whaling nation both in total annual catch and in number of catchers, closely followed by Norway and the United Kingdom. Japan has also shown the most rapid development since 1948. In the season 1958-1959, there were 54 shore stations, 23 floating factories, and 416 catchers in operation in the whole world, and the number of whales caught by them was 64,169. The share of Japan was 19, 8, 110, and 12,359, respectively. A number of nations possess no floating factories at all and operate exclusively from shore stations—for example, some Latin American countries (Argentina, Brazil, Chile, and Peru) and European countries (France, Spain, Iceland). The United States, where whaling is also performed only from shore stations, shares barely 1 percent of the world catch.

4 | THE USE OF THE LAND

FORMS OF LAND UTILIZATION

Many fine examples are drawn from the United States to illustrate the point that nature provides only the frame and does not act as the determinant in the molding of a certain form of land utilization. It is well exemplified by a historical succession of land uses of different types at a given place—hunting by Indians, invasion of white traders, pioneer subsistence farming, growing of some commercial crops that withstand long-distance transport, and then specialized commercial farming—or by the fluctuation of the boundary between the cattle-raising and wheat-farming regions of the Great Plains, which is chiefly caused by the price behavior of the respective produce. It takes a careful regional analysis to find out why a particular form of land use came to be chosen, for the decision hinges upon a large number of variables.

At present we are only concerned with the following question: How does man use the land? The answer is found partly in the statistics on agricultural production. Figures for the world were quoted earlier after FAO publications. These figures always refer to such statistical units as countries and provinces; consequently they indicate no details of the land use within each unit. For this reason geographers have undertaken a detailed mapping of land utilization. The earliest of these projects on the national scale was the Land Utilisation Survey of Britain started in 1930 under the leadership of L. D. Stamp. It was followed by others, and this kind of work has gained great momentum in recent years.

Land utilization maps present only one aspect of the agricultural landscape, particularly of its formal structure, and they should be supplemented by other maps and explanatory descriptions. A world-wide project of land-use mapping at the scale of 1 to 1,000,000 was initiated by the International Geographical Union in 1949; an integral part of the project is the memoirs to complement the maps.

According to the original key for the world land-use maps the following categories of land use were distinguished:

1. Settlements and associated nonagricultural lands
2. Horticulture
3. Trees and other perennial crops
4. Cropland:
   a. Continual and rotation cropping
   b. Land rotation
5. Improved permanent pasture
6. Unimproved grazing land:
   a. Used
   b. Not used
7. Woodlands:
   a. Dense
   b. Open
   c. Scrub

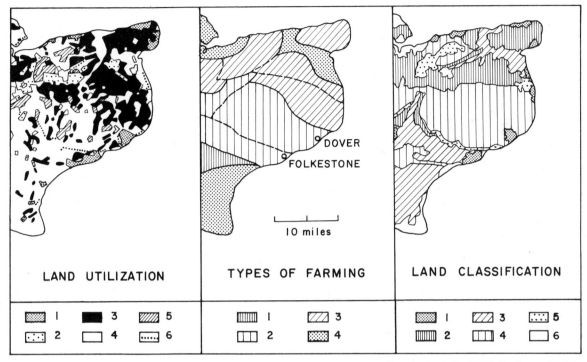

LAND UTILIZATION

TYPES OF FARMING

LAND CLASSIFICATION

After maps by the Land Utilisation Survey of Britain

22 · LAND USE MAPPING. The three maps of the same area in southeastern England show (left) the objective recording of land-use phenomena, (center) the evaluation of these data in terms of farming types, and (right) the classification of lands.

Legend: Left: (1) urban areas, (2) orchards and nursery gardens, (3) arable land, (4) meadowland and permanent grass, (5) forest and woodland, (6) heathland, moorland, rough pasture. *Center:* (1) pasture types, (2) intermediate types, (3) arable types, (4) various types, e.g., marshes. *Right:* (1) urban areas, (2) first-class, mainly arable, (3) first-class, mainly grass, (4) medium-quality land, (5) poor-quality land, (6) poorest land.

d. Swamp forests
e. Cut-over or burnt-over forest areas
f. Forest with subsidiary cultivation
8. Swamps and marshes
9. Unproductive land

This list is open to discussion and improvement; but once a system of classification has been established, land-use mapping becomes an objective recording of facts. Interpretation of these facts and the planning of the better use of lands for agriculture which follow the mapping involve on the other hand a great deal of subjective judgment. This underscores the great merit of land utilization maps in economic geography.

THE BEST USE OF LAND

What is meant by the best use of land? What are our criteria to be? In some instances the existing land use is evidently bad or wrong, but in others it is rather difficult to give an objective appraisal.

Land Use in General

When we approach the broad problem of how to use the land the first question is obviously whether it should be used at all. In many parts of the world the expansion of the humanized landscape has almost obliterated any traces of untouched natural landscapes. People who live in Western Europe, for example, scarcely know any longer what a virgin forest looks like; rivers have been regulated, and wildlife in its most primitive form has been virtually exterminated. Landscaping may have made the countryside more attractive in the eyes of many people, but in the meantime something was lost forever. The preservation of a few remnants of the virgin natural landscape has become the current major concern of a number of organizations for reasons which have little or nothing to do with economic or material considerations. In this case the best use of the land seems to be determined by immaterial values.

Similar, though not identical, is the use of lands as national parks, recreational areas, and the like. They carry a very specific value which is nevertheless difficult to express in dollars and cents. Recently, however, the preservation of natural conditions has been promoted from purely economic considerations, as in the tremendous wildlife parks of East Africa. It was pointed out that the potentialities of feed production and metabolism under natural conditions were superior to the cattle-raising of the Masai people. Since the latter keep their cattle only as symbols of prestige and wealth and do not derive material benefits from them, the ultimate value of animal products is not relevant to the comparison. Consequently, the natural state seems to be the ''better use of the land'' when the alternative is native cattle-raising.

As might be surmised from the mention of recreational areas, a broad meaning is attached to the words *land utilization*. In the original Land Utilisation Survey of Britain all the land which was not used agriculturally was grouped together and called wasteland! The point of view was obviously one-sided and strictly agricultural; there is in fact a great variety of nonagricultural types of land use. One of the basic problems in regional planning is to give each user the amount of space he needs and to make a selection in such a way that due consideration is given to every available factor of site and location. The purpose of zoning is therefore to reserve the land best suited, e.g., for agriculture. Site factors, such as soils, topography, ground water, microclima-tology, and similar physical features, should be favorable, but equally important are the locational factors—consolidation of holdings, relation to markets, etc.

Agricultural Land Use: Economic Evaluation

Apparently we must distinguish between the best use of land on the whole and the best use for the agricultural purposes. As far as the first is concerned, the question of best use can be answered only in very general terms. It is primarily a matter of assigning priorities on the basis of demands and availabilities. In many parts of the world where land is scarce and demand is much diversified—e.g., in highly industrialized and densely populated Western Europe—the problem of priorities is the major concern of all planning agencies. On the other hand, answers to the question of the best use of land for agricultural purposes are easier to formulate in more concrete terms.

One means of estimate is commonly used by economists as well as by individual farmers under the system of free enterprise: This is the measure of the best use of land in terms of monetary values. Obviously this approach would lead us nowhere in countries where money is not the prime regulator of economic relationships and considerations. Agricultural operations are called successful if the value of the production, whether for sale or for consumption by the farmer himself, is higher than the production costs involved, which include labor, fertilizer, interest charges for all kinds of capital investment such as buildings, grounds, equipment, etc.; in other words, if there is an excess of output over input. If this balance increases, we can speak of an improvement. This gives a satisfactory yardstick for measuring the best use of the land. A number of important economic rules or laws derive from it, some of them being of large importance for economic geography, too.

The relationships between input and output can be plotted (see Fig. 23) on a system of coordinates in two different ways. The first (a) simply represents the value of input x against that of output y. If there is no input, the output will likewise be nil. With an increase in input

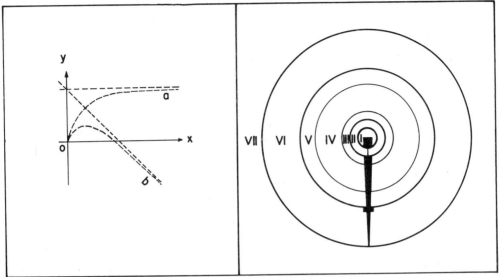

After Otremba, 1953

23 · ECONOMIC EVALUATION of agricultural land use. The diagram on the left illustrates the relationships between input (x) and output (y) as discussed in the text; likewise, (a) and (b) refer to the two relationships mentioned there. The diagram on the right illustrates the principle of economic regionalization by Von Thünen in a simplified form. Around a market town in the center the concentric zones of land utilization may be found in the following order: (I) intensive market gardening and truck farming; (II) intensive forestry or timber cropping; (III) crop rotation; (IV) associated crop and livestock farming; (V) three-field rotation including fallow; (VI) animal husbandry; (VII) unused but potentially usable land. The relative intensity of land utilization in the various zones is indicated by the thickness of the arrow.

the curve rises steeply at first, but after a while a further increase in x value will bring about only a slight increase in y value. There is a definite ceiling; in other words, the curve is asymptotic. The second (b) is to plot the input x against the net returns y. The curve starts again at zero but soon reaches the summit, after which it drops back to zero and finally assumes negative y values. In either case there exists an optimum point which may represent "the best use of the land." It does not pay to invest more money and effort beyond this point, since no proportional increase in output is observed and the net returns diminish thereafter.

The two curves may serve as a model which brings out a number of important considerations in agricultural operations. One of them is the intensity of land use. Intensity is directly proportional to the value of input; more intensified activity implies an increased input, be it in

terms of more man-hours, harder work, more fertilizer, or more farm machines. The model demonstrates that within a given production line intensification is not such a self-evident way to obtain a better use of land as is commonly believed. It all depends on what point on the curve one starts with. The output could be increased anywhere along the curve, but if the optimum has already been passed, the increment is perhaps very little. Still more important, any further increase in input may even result in diminished returns. Hence, increased intensity does not always lead to a betterment of the agricultural situation. On the contrary, more profitable operations may frequently be attained through changing over to more extensive land use—and in many instances this is exactly what a farmer does, at least under a system of free enterprise. He will always try to adjust his operations in such a way as to obtain the maximum returns.

A classical example of the spatial arrangement of different types of land use is found in the concentric zonal theory of Von Thünen, a German economist, formulated as early as 1826. It was assumed that, all the site and locational factors being equal, the costs of transportation for shipping farm produce to consumers should be considered the sole parameter in our model. According to this theory, the land-use zones may be found around each market town in the following order as concentric rings: horticulture—crop rotation—crop fields and animal husbandry—three-field system of crops with fallow—pasturing. Case studies have substantiated the theory of Von Thünen in certain instances, but in others have pointed to quite different relationships. This is understandable, because the assumptions of Von Thünen were based on his contemporary situation and are not valid for all times and places.

Areas producing the same agricultural product are often compared simply in terms of yields instead of using the whole of our complex model. Yields should be expressed as production relative to input, but this is generally simplified by replacing input by that part of the total expenditure which weighs most heavily. In the United States and Western Europe, it is usually the man-hours and the agricultural land, respectively. Yields are therefore measured either as production per man-hour or per acre. Both ways are possible and justified. It is not surprising that some authors in Western Europe regard agriculture in the United States as less efficient than their own because yields per acre are lower, while Americans may reach just the opposite conclusion. From a strictly economical point of view higher yields are not always a better solution; actually it may not pay at all for a farmer to raise the yields of his crop, since the rise might be achieved only by an increased input and he may have already gone beyond the optimum in this regard. Yields are rather an ambiguous yardstick to measure the best use of the land.

Agricultural Land Use: Nutritional Evaluation

Another way to evaluate land use is by the nutritional value of the agricultural production.

Understandably this is not a point of view that would serve as the guiding principle for individual farmers; but it most certainly will be a major consideration in overall governmental planning. Thus farmers might frequently be forced to adopt a mode of production which is, from the money point of view, not the best for them; in most cases, however, they will be compensated in other ways.

In judging agricultural production by nutritional value, two major groups should be distinguished. The first group comprises vegetables, and the second animal products. In the strict sense of the word, only the first is called the primary production. For animal products, feed is processed into milk, meat, eggs, etc., with a relatively low efficiency measured in calories, but perhaps with a high net return in money. From the standpoint of energy balance animal husbandry is the most wasteful use of the primary products of agriculture and is economically feasible only where the food situation is satisfactory. Animal products, especially proteins, are on the other hand an essential part of a well-balanced diet and should be produced regardless of economic considerations. Today many countries have a special board to study the nutritional situation and make recommendations to the ministry of agriculture, which in turn sets up a system of price support, etc., for inducing the farmers to produce the desired and needed products.

In the highly industrialized countries of Western Europe, state support and national planning have influenced agriculture in many ways. Yields have been raised beyond the economic optimum and are among the highest in the world; production has been diversified within national boundaries as a safeguard against emergencies even if natural and economic conditions do not particularly favor certain production lines. This has all been achieved with complicated systems of national price controls, production aids, tariffs, and so forth. The Common Market scheme for agricultural products, comprising all of Western Europe, is therefore very difficult to carry out. In the New World, where the above-mentioned considerations had not affected the development of agricultural production at least until the

1930's, an entirely different agricultural structure emerged.

In the United States about two acres of agriculturally used land is required to feed one person. Yields per acre are relatively low and the share of animal produce is large. In Western Europe, by way of contrast, one acre is sufficient to support one person, though there are relatively large regional variations; if the share of potatoes or grains increases, less than one acre is required, but more if animal products occupy a higher percentage. Interestingly, nearly the same relationship between agricultural land and population to be fed, i.e., one acre per head, is observed in India, where yields are much lower. This is explained by an almost complete lack of animal food in the Indian diet and much lower food consumption. In Japan a most intensive form of agriculture and extremely high yields per acre —but not per man-hour—have reduced the amount of land necessary to feed one person to about 0.2 acre.

These two methods of evaluation—economic and nutritional—are the most important for judging whether or not the land in question has been well used. Frequently the evaluations produce contradictory results, and the question of how the land may best be used can be answered in more than one way. Even if one solution is accepted as the best, we should always keep in mind the many obstacles which might be encountered on the way to attaining its realization. They may be of almost any kind—political, sociological, economical, to name but a few in the group of human factors. The sections that follow present a number of examples of land use.

ANIMAL HUSBANDRY

Cultural history and historical anthropology provide us with a clue to the beginnings and evolution of civilization. Early man was a hunter and collector; tilling of the soil entered the scene much later. Several theories have been put forward in an attempt to establish a genetic order of the various forms of cultural development. Early in the present century Krzymowski developed a theory of the three-stage evolution— hunting and fishing, nomadism, and agriculture

(restricted to "tilling the soil"). Later it was found that nomadism actually came after agriculture; the domestication of animals which forms the basis of nomadic life took place under settled conditions. A better and more advanced theory, developed by Hahn (1856–1928), depicts the evolution of the various primary occupations as follows:

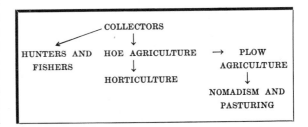

From our point of view, a classification of nongenetic order is of more significance. We shall make a primary distinction between a subsistence economy and a market economy; in many instances—but not in all—these terms are coincident with natural and money economy or with primitive and advanced economy. The first examples are drawn from animal husbandry to illustrate its very wide range. They also introduce the reader to a number of technical terms frequent in economic geography.

Examples of Animal Husbandry

The buffalo-hunting Indians of the North American plains and the caribou-hunting Eskimos of northern Canada are outstanding examples of hunting economy which never developed beyond a primitive and subsistence stage. The caribou hunters migrate with the animals from their winter pasture in southerly forests to the summer feeding ground in the tundra. The animals are instinctively directed by the seasonal changes in nature; they are truly wildlife and the Eskimos who follow their migration somewhat resemble packs of wolves. The term "animal husbandry" cannot yet be applied at this stage. Gradually man gains control over wild animals, and with that there occurs a change in their nomenclature, e.g., from caribou to reindeer. This stage is best represented by the traditional way of life of the Lapps in northern Scandinavia, though the past decades have witnessed certain changes in it. It exemplifies the transition from the prehusbandry to the husbandry stage. Even if reindeer cannot in the true sense of the word be called domesticated, they now supply milk in addition to meat, hides, etc.

Outside the tropical areas wild animals have to migrate seasonally from summer to winter pastures over long distances. So do all domesticated animals which graze the whole year round on natural pastures. Their owners are compelled to follow these wanderings; hence the term "migratory animal husbandry."

The best-known form of migratory animal husbandry is nomadism or nomadic migratory husbandry. It is found primarily in those parts of the middle latitudes where a broad zone separates the desert from the originally forested humid area, the semiarid steppe or grasslands; occasionally true nomadism is also found as a migration between high- and low-altitude pastures in well-watered regions. Nomadism is characteristic of the Old World extending from the Atlantic through northern Africa and the Middle East into Central Asia.

Frequently nomadism is called a primitive form of human economy, with some truth. Among

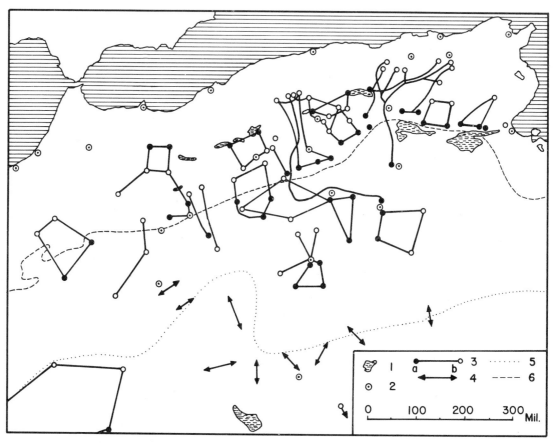

Niemeyer, 1955

24 · NOMADISM IN NORTH AFRICA. *Legend:* (1) *shotts;* (2) larger permanent settlements; (3) migratory pasturing between (b) fixed summer pastures and (a) winter pastures; (4) other types of migratory pasturing; (5) isohyet of 20 mm (0.79 inches); (6) isohyet of 100 mm (3.94 inches). (3) and (4) represent the type of nomadism described in the text.

nomadic herdsmen the material standard of living is quite low, medical care is practically non-existent, and social organization remains on the tribal level. The products of their economic activities are exclusively of animal origin and must be supplemented by wheat, rice, dates, and the like, for which their animal products are traded in markets of the neighboring settled zone. The nomads are basically opposed to the organized state and its officials. In place of written laws, tradition regulates their lives; instead of a state territory with a fixed boundary, they recognize pasturing districts with fluctuating boundaries. In most countries administration over the nomads is by way of their own tribal authorities, in contrast with the settled farmers and townspeople.

Yet in other respects nomadism is far from being primitive. Not only does it represent the most perfect form of adaptation of life to the specific natural conditions in the steppe lands; it is actually the only possible way of life there. Furthermore, the contribution of the nomads to the gross national product is by no means negligible. In the bordering zones of sedentary agriculture based on irrigation and dry-farming, production is almost entirely vegetable; thus the exchange of products between the two zones is quite important in quantity, value, and nutritional quality.

An organized state has, of course, a great interest in gaining control over the nomadic tribes within its territory and bringing them within the framework of its administrative hierarchy. To settle the nomads and to bring them under the same legal code as the other citizens is one of the major objectives of many development plans. However, to realize this objective means turning vast productive areas into wasteland and causing an undesirable imbalance in the national production.

Except for the above-mentioned relationship between nomads and bordering sedentary agriculturists, nomadism presents an economic unit complete in itself. Some of the big tribal leaders may own landed property and houses with adjoining gardens and fields, but as a rule there is no settled habitation and the whole population migrates with the herds, carrying with them tents and other transportable possessions. During the dry season a few large camps of nomadic herdsmen and their families may spring up around a few scattered wells, but during the humid season when forage and water are available everywhere, the families are widely dispersed. Animals must be adapted to the particular conditions and to the distance of migration; in the Middle East a characteristic difference exists between the Bedouin tribes who possess in the main small animals, such as sheep and goats, and others who keep camels and dromedaries and migrate greater distances.

In the Mediterranean countries a very special form of migrating animal husbandry known as *transhumance* is practiced. Sheep are the predominant species involved. They are driven from high-altitude summer pastures to low-lying winter pastures over long distances—e.g., from the Pyrenees to southern Spain, from the French Alps to the Rhone delta, from the Apennines to Apulia. The distinctive feature of transhumance is not so much the migration of herds as the fact that this type of economy occurs side by side with sedentary agriculture. The latter in all Mediterranean countries fills only a fraction of the land available, while large tracts remain untilled as rough pasture or secondary scrub, known in different languages as *macchia, monte bajo, maquis,* etc., which can be used only as rough grazing land for sheep or goats. It does not belong within the economic unit of a village because its seasonal counterpart may be hundreds of miles away. As a result two entirely separate forms of agricultural economy are found juxtaposed.

The word "transhumance" is of relatively recent origin and signifies the type of economy which is to be found "beyond (*trans*) the good earth or the tilled fields, vineyards, and olive groves (*humus*)." (No wholly satisfactory explanation is offered by etymologists, but this is the most satisfactory.) The migrating flocks and herds may be the property of village folk, but unlike nomads, these do not accompany their animals personally; they hire herdsmen instead. Proprietors are frequently nonagricultural people or institutions, for whom livestock owned in this manner is a capital investment. It has its particular advantages in troubled times in com-

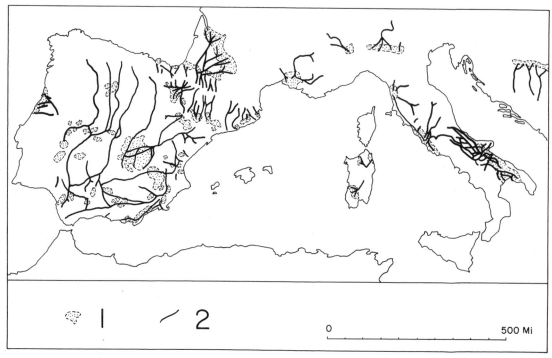

Müller, 1938

25 · TRANSHUMANCE in the western Mediterranean region. *Legend:* (1) Winter pastures for migrating herds. (2) Major routes of transhumants.

parison with landed property. During the Reconquista and thereafter, a transhumance economy was greatly favored in Spain in every way and organized in the powerful Mesta endowed with special privileges by the Spanish kings. We may also note that the word "pecuniary" derives from the Latin word for sheep (*pecus*) and points up the economic importance of this form of livestock management in Mediterranean countries. In the present century transhumance has suffered and lost its importance because more and more attention has been given to settled agriculture; today sheep are seldom driven in the traditional way but are transported by truck or railroad.

Away from its original Mediterranean setting the word "transhumance" has been applied in other parts of the world where similar practices are found. Even in this extended meaning, transhumance differs from nomadism insofar as only the herdsmen accompany the herds, and from

other types of animal husbandry, which have not yet been discussed, in the complete absence of any sort of coupling with sedentary agriculture.

Migratory animal husbandry occurs in various other cases in conjunction with settled conditions. A well-known example is the combination of pasturing in the early stages of livestock raising with feeding on the farm in its later stages just before slaughtering. In the United States, for example, wide expanses of otherwise unusable land in drier parts of the prairies or summer pastures in the Rockies are utilized for pasturing, which at the same time serves to build up the health of the livestock. Later fattening on the farm puts the cattle exactly in that physical condition which suits the demand of meat consumers. Another example is the alpine economy in Central Europe or the *säter* economy in Scandinavia. Essentially it is a combination of the valley farm which provides winter forage for the time of stabulation and the summer pastures at high altitudes. The pasturing season in the Alps, at least at the higher levels, lasts about three months, and for a few additional months the animals are able to graze on lower improved grasslands which also furnish hay for the winter. They are kept in the stables up to six months and fed with hay, and sometimes also with silage. The operational center of the individual farming unit is the valley farm. Frequently, at the peak of the pasturing season, hundreds of cattle which belong to a large number of different owners are pooled, and herdsmen are employed to look after them. This form of cooperative enterprise is regulated by centuries-old corporations which own alpine pastures, forests, etc.; in order to send cattle up to the high pastures one has to be a member of such a corporation or to own so-

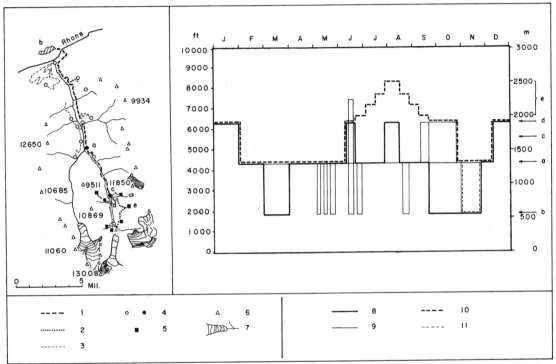

Gyr, 1942

26 · VAL D'ANNIVIERS, SWITZERLAND: a classic example of alpine economy. Illustrating the various forms of displacement that take place in the course of one year among the inhabitants of the village of Mission. The letters stand for the places where they live for a longer or shorter period each year: (a) the village of Mission; (b) the town of Sierre where Mission people own vineyards; (c) the hamlet of Zinal, which serves as a center for the early and late summer pastures in the surrounding (d), or so-called *mayens*; (e) alpine pastures. The location of these places is indicated on the map, and their altitude on the diagram.

Legend: (1) main valley road used by all the family units; (2) paths giving access to the alpine pastures; (3) other valley roads, not involved in the wanderings of the people of Mission; (4) villages (those mentioned above are shown in black); (5) chalets, centers of pasturing; (6) mountain peaks on both sides of the valley; (7) glaciers and rivers; (8) displacement which involves the whole family; (9) displacement for individual members only; (10) displacement for the entire cattle population; (11) displacement for groups of cattle only. Cattle are kept in stables in the localities *a* and *b*. In *d* and *e* protection against bad weather is provided; otherwise the animals are always kept on open pastures.

called cow rights, which are somewhat similar to shares of the stock in a modern industrial or commercial enterprise. Even though the animals migrate in both the cases cited above, it would be quite wrong to call them either transhumance or nomadism; yet some authors have done so, and popularly the words "nomad" and "nomadism" have been applied to alpine migrations.

The final steps along this line take us to various forms of animal husbandry in which livestock no longer migrate but remain on the farm all through the year. In middle latitudes this necessitates stabulation during the winter season and consequently the preparation of winter fodder, hay, or silage as well as feed cakes. In the tropics similar precautions may be taken in areas where the dry and wet season alternate, though it is a more common practice either to move cattle or to sell them before the dry season starts.

Until the eighteenth century the animal density in all the farming regions of Western Europe was extremely low; crop land was reserved for the production of grains, and during the warm season animals had to seek their food in nearby forests and on fallow crop land. An important step in modern scientific farming in Western Europe was taken when fodder production was incorporated into the crop rotation system and thereby the cattle not only were increased in numbers but were stabled so that the manure could be collected and later applied to the crop fields. The combination of crop and livestock farming has proved to be the right solution and, with the exception of a few highly specialized forms of agricultural production, is the most common type found in Western Europe. In the United States this combination is less widespread, since specialization is more prevalent.

Finally, mention should also be made of some special cases which are not in accord with the systematic classification here employed. We have already referred to the Masai people in East Africa, for whom animals form the basis of life though less for economic reasons than as symbols of wealth and an expression of social standing. India has the largest cattle population in the world, more than 150 million head or about 18 percent of the world total; it can scarcely be said, however, that they form an incorporated part of the farming system. They find their food almost anywhere, and the dung is used as fuel. Yet they consume a staggering amount of food, while their economic value is small; except for the milk and as beasts of burden they are hardly used at all.

TILLING THE SOIL

A number of cases discussed in the next few pages will be summarized later in Chapter 6, "The Economic Geography of Agriculture." The characteristics selected in each case are intended to bring out one specific point; the present chapter should not be regarded as a collection of case studies in regional economic geography.

The New World: The United States

FOUNDATIONS

Except for the areas of early British, Spanish, and French colonization, the larger part of the United States has been settled within the past one hundred and fifty years. A few Indian trails and later military roads are the only recognizable human elements from earlier days in the present landscape of this truly New World. All the rest is of more recent origin and therefore much less complicated than in the areas of older settlement. The landscape analysis is further facilitated by the existence of a wealth of historical documentation; in other parts of the world such documents are either scanty or entirely lacking, so as to preclude a clean picture of the beginnings of landscape development. Not only is this an outstanding characteristic of the American landscape as such, but it also gives American landscape studies a unique place in systematic geography through the specific methods that must be employed.

The second characteristic is the fact that, in contrast to the earlier colonial period, later settlement was guided by definite social and economic principles. The farm as a one-family operational unit (the "homestead") was the element of settlement. In accordance with a rectangular survey system and the principles expounded in the ordinances of 1785 and 1787, land was allotted to the settlers in the whole of the public domain.

The area thus involved in the original survey and allotment covered most of the United States west of the Appalachians; the public domain comprised originally about 75 percent of the aggregate territory. The system was applied throughout regardless of the nature of the land.

Among the most conspicuous results were the checkerboard pattern of fields and lines of communications, defined by the section lines running in the cardinal directions, and the dispersed type of settlement. Unlike its Spanish counterpart, American settlement proceeded on the basis of farming families; the founding of urban communities was not its prime objective. At first only the part of the land granted to each family as homestead was cleared of the forest to be put into agricultural use; as time went by, the land gradually filled up with an expansion of agriculture, but the typical pattern of settlements and fields persisted.

Agglomerated settlements functioning as administrative and trading centers for the surrounding farm areas appeared wherever they became a necessity. In early times the nonagricultural population was small; only a few buildings existed, housing such typical functional centers as postoffice and general store. They formed the nucleus of many small and medium-sized towns that emerged as secondary and tertiary occupations became more important.

The third most important characteristic is the fact that all or most of these farms, after a short initial stage of settlement, found themselves served by a growing system of transportation lines. This connected them with large centers of distribution and rapidly expanding markets and brought all within a single economic unit, finally encompassing the entire United States from the Pacific to the Atlantic. Generally each farm in its pioneer stage had to concentrate on subsistence crops. There followed products which could withstand long transportation; this explains the preference for wheat and other grains or their liquid form, whiskey. The wheat-producing belt moved westward behind the frontier. The arrival of the railroad considerably shortened the time of transportation and permitted the development of regional specialization in production in accordance with natural endowment and economic opportunity. In the Interior Plains the total of these factors varied only slightly over some distance, and consequently all farmers within a relatively extensive area found their optimum of production along similar lines. Only over very large distances did such physical factors as temperature or precipitation vary sufficiently to induce a change in the direction of production. Distance from markets became less important as means improved for shipping perishable products, such as milk and meat. Furthermore, the freight-rate structure could be rigged in such a way that long hauls cost the farmer no more than short ones.

The three factors mentioned above have given rise to a number of characteristics in American agriculture which are not found elsewhere. A high degree of specialization in one or a group of marketable products has made it possible to classify American farms primarily according to production specialty. Subsistence farming is negligible and confined to very remote districts. Even general or mixed farming makes up less than 10 percent of all the commercial farms. All the rest are specialized, i.e., more than half of the total value of production is derived from products of a particular kind, such as grains, poultry, fruits and nuts, cotton. This feature makes it possible to distinguish between different "types of farming areas" on the basis of crop and livestock specialization.

Site and locational factors being nearly equal over a large area, only the individuality of the farmer himself seems to be able to produce some degree of differentiation within any type of farming area. Since many of the American farmers or their immediate forefathers were foreign-born, traces of their diverse background—cultural, technical, racial, etc.—are still recognizable; but on the whole it is amazing how thoroughly such differences have been wiped out in rural areas and especially in the frontier zone. The most traditional groups have been religious ones, like the Pennsylvania Dutch, whose farms are recognizable wherever they settled. Generally it is very difficult to discern individual racial and cultural heritages in the settlement pattern or house forms. On the other hand, specialization in production based on the farmer's background

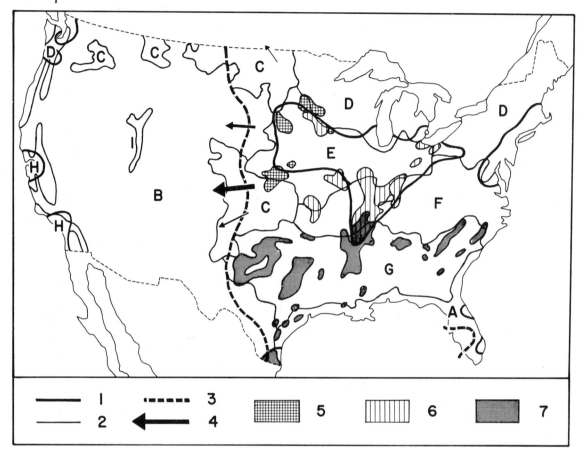

USDA, Weaver 1954, and Prunty 1951

27 · AGRICULTURAL REGIONS of the United States. *Legend:* (1) Area where the average value of land and buildings is very high. (2) Boundaries of agricultural regions, i.e., A, Gulf Coast and Florida—fruits, vegetables, special crops, as well as general farming; B, permanent and seasonal pasturing; C, wheat farming; D, predominantly grass and hay—dairy belt; E, corn belt; F, general farming and tobacco; G, cotton belt; H, Pacific area—intensive agriculture and specialized farming; I, dry farming and irrigation in Utah. (3) Boundary between East and West based on the average size of the farm unit of approximately 1,000 acres. (4) Direction of the postwar expansion of wheat farming. (5) Areas where a considerable increase in corn production occurred during the decade 1939–1949. (6) The same, for soya production. (7) Major centers of cotton production within the cotton belt with more than 8.5 percent of the cropland planted in cotton.

is more frequently found, like the cheese industry of the Swiss in Wisconsin or the vineyards operated by Italians in California.

All this has resulted in a broad zonation of agriculture controlled primarily by physical factors such as climate and topography and secondarily by human factors—for example, the relation to urban agglomerations.

EVOLUTION

American agriculture is one of the most rapidly changing. Earlier remarks about the farmer and his traditional inclinations are only partially true in the United States, for there are no well-established traditions rooted in a long history, and accumulated experience weighs less than elsewhere. In many instances the farmer never reached the stage beyond that of feeling his ground and gaining experience. A classical example is the advance of agriculture into the grasslands of the Plains. The American pioneer's experience of agricultural colonization had been gained through the clearing of forests in the humid East. Before the vast expanses of the Prairies with their unknown qualities the frontier halted, and the land that lay ahead of the settlers was first used as open range and later for cattle ranching. Agriculture extended into the Plains hesitatingly and not before the late 1870's; in the outer fringes it became possible only after the new technique of dry-farming came in. In dry-farming the crop fields lie fallow for one year to allow restoration of the moisture in the soil and subsoil. Agriculture was also probing possibilities at the northern frontier, often with unsuccessful outcomes based on economic reasons. The agriculturally used area has therefore changed a great deal in the past; not only has there been a general process of expansion during settlement, but also one of adjustment to physical and economic conditions often accompanied by contraction.

One of the best-known changes in physical conditions is soil erosion ensuing upon the removal of the natural vegetation cover. Running water destroyed the topsoil, especially where corn or cotton left relatively large surface areas uncovered; grass or grain crops offer a better protection. Gully and sheet erosion by water, and wind erosion in the drier parts of the Plains, have put much agricultural land out of production.

Among the economic factors, the most influential is the price behavior of agricultural products. For example, whenever the price of wheat rose, grain farming in the Plains expanded while ranching retracted. This was the situation during the First World War and for some time thereafter, and the same thing happened again during the Second World War. In both periods the expansion went past the boundary beyond which wheat farming was no longer physically reliable; when the humid years were followed by the dry ones, grain farming broke down. In the early 1930's, when this happened for the first time,

American agriculture was still relatively unprotected, and drought brought financial disaster. Today the protective measures by the government are such that the impact of natural and economic factors of an adverse nature are minimized.

Interesting as they are in themselves, these examples should be viewed in the present context as an expression of a continuing process of adjusting agriculture to the framework within which it operates. This is the usual process in a country where settlement started only a few generations ago. In addition to these adaptations there are, however, certain trends of a more constant nature to be observed.

American agriculture even in its infant stages was put at a disadvantage by the high cost of labor, though this was offset by the cheapness of land. We have already spoken of how yields and efficiency are related to man-hours, why agriculture had to be mechanized, etc. A few astounding results of that situation are the following: while the past half-century has witnessed a very slight increase in the amount of farm land, the number of farms, which remained

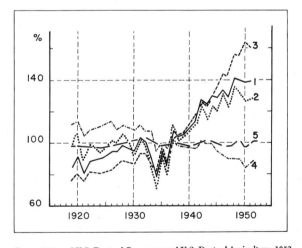

Raper 1952, and U.S. Dept. of Commerce and U.S. Dept. of Agriculture, 1952

28 · DEVELOPMENT OF FARM PRODUCTION in the United States. The following characteristics are compared in terms of index numbers (index: 1935–1939 = 100): (1) Farm production in volume available for ultimate human consumption. (2) Per acre production of all crops. (3) Output per man-hour. (4) Labor required on the farm in man-hours. (5) Total crop land.

practically stationary until 1940, has since declined rather abruptly. The implication is that the size of the individual operating unit has grown; actually the medium-sized farms decreased in number, whereas both the very small (under 3 acres, mostly part-time farming) and the large (over 260 acres) farms increased. There has been a decided shift of emphasis from crop to livestock farming since about 1930, measured in cash returns. On the whole the value of agricultural products has greatly increased, but so have the expenditures, both capital and operational. In other words, American agriculture has become much more intensive than before, with more universal application of fertilizer and the results of scientific research (genetics and insecticides, to name but two) as well as increased capital investments. The result has been much larger yields per acre as well as per man-hour, though no consistent trend is observable in net profits, which fluctuate from year to year.

American agriculture has been so much in-

tensified and so successfully operated that a major problem today is surplus production. Changed eating habits have added to this problem; since 1910 the consumption of potatoes has steadily declined to about 50 percent, and grain products to 70, while fruits, vegetables, eggs, and milk products rose to 125 and 150. The consumption of meat has shown minor fluctuations with economic conditions but remains fairly stable. In order to help the farmer, surplus products are bought up by the government (Commodity Credit Corporation). Technical improvements and price policies have contributed to increasing stores of all major products. In the case of wheat the increase was fivefold in the fifties and the stored grain represented about one annual harvest at the end of the period!

THE SOUTH: A DIFFERENT STORY

Little of what has been stated so far applies to the South; its story is altogether different. The South is the single major region where economic

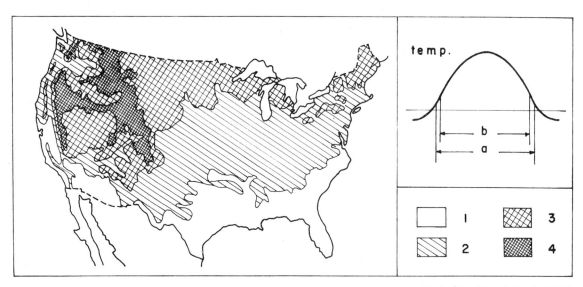

Handbuch der Klimatologie and official data

29 · MAJOR CLIMATIC CHARACTERISTICS in middle latitudes. The diagram on the right illustrates the characteristic annual temperature curve together with (a) the frost-free season and (b) the vegetation period. No absolute values of temperature are given since the periods a and b may be defined in different ways. The vegetation period is frequently defined as the period during which the temperature curve lies above 40° F. The map depicts the average number of frost-free days in the United States: (1) more than 220 days; (2) 140-220 days; (3) 90-140 days; (4) less than 90 days.

regionalization proceeded in another direction.

The early colonies in the South enjoyed not only the benefits of an unglaciated topography, better soils, and a milder climate as compared with New England, but also the possibility of bilateral exchange of commodities with England following the prevailing economic principles of the colonial period, i.e., raw materials and agricultural products traded for manufactured goods. From the beginning, agriculture was the dominant occupation in the South and the possession of the means of agricultural production stood for prestige and wealth. Tobacco was the first major crop and has since remained characteristic of the area occupied at the time, i.e., Maryland, Virginia, parts of the Carolinas, and Kentucky. Land was plentiful, but agricultural workers were scarce; the most important source was the indentured servants brought over from the Old Country. Operational units were generally quite large, agricultural management was much more in accordance with the feudal concepts of contemporary Europe than with the group settlements in New England or the later family farming in the public domain across the Appalachians.

The first big change came about when cotton began to replace tobacco as the major crop. It was directly caused by the invention of the cotton gin in the year 1793 and the concurrent development of a market for raw cotton in the English textile industry, later followed by other countries in Europe as well as by the United States. Production of cotton led to a rapid westward expansion of the agriculturally used area and the center of cotton production, first to the Piedmont of the Appalachians, then to the Black Belt of Alabama and the Mississippi Delta, and finally to Texas, Arkansas, and beyond. Land, the prime ingredient of agriculture, was easily and cheaply acquired; it did not pay to invest heavily in land, and consequently land was wasted. Behind the advancing cotton frontier and after a flourishing period of lucrative cotton farming one saw impoverished soils, decaying farm buildings, and people without means or hope for the future. The major portion of capital invested in cotton growing was represented by the labor force. For the cotton growers, slavery

proved to be the most economic form of working contract; the worker, under this contract, was bound to his master for good and could be moved together with other equipment again and again westward to areas of new and untouched soils. The high cost of slaves, the maintenance of them as well as of their families, the expenditures which today would be summarized as social securities and insurance, etc.—all this and more was compensated by the impossibility of securing an adequate labor force in any other way. Within eighty years following 1790 the number of Negro slaves increased from 700,000 to about 4,000,000. The size of operating units grew, and the large plantation came to be the typical form of settlement throughout the South.

The economic historical geography of the Southern States would be an interesting topic for a student of modern colonialism and of underdeveloped countries. In a way the South became almost a colonial area situated within the mother country. In the first place the function of the South was to supply the industrialized areas with the much needed raw material, cotton. The profits gained by these Southern States came exclusively from growing and handling cotton up to the point where it was ready to be shipped off by water; the profits made thereafter through shipping, manufacturing, and marketing were none of their concern. What emerged was the concentration of wealth in a handful of people and a generally underdeveloped status of the region as a whole.

The period of Reconstruction after the Civil War gave rise to an entirely different agricultural structure. Cotton remained the major crop. The role of the South as a supplier of raw materials did not change, nor was the land taken away from its owners. But the workers, who had been their most important asset, were liberated. Having no land of their own, these ex-slaves had to enter into a new working contract with the landowners, most of them as sharecroppers and some as tenants. The plantation remained as a unit of property, but operationally it was split up into many small units. The former servants' quarters were replaced by numerous dispersed and poor huts. Centrally directed efficient farm operations of former days were supplanted by

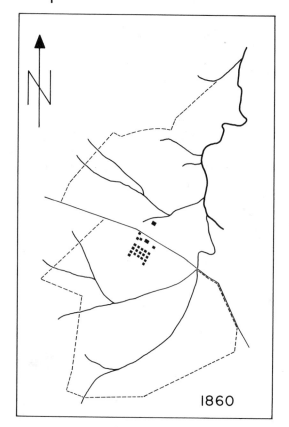
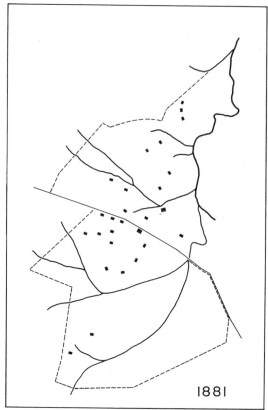

M. Prunty, *Geogr. Rev.*, 1955

30 · PATTERN OF SETTLEMENTS in the southern United States in the ante- and post-bellum periods. The change in the pattern of settlements is exemplified by the 2,000-acre Barrow Plantation in Oglethorpe County, Georgia, in 1860 and 1881. See the text for further explanation.

inefficient "one mule" units. Seed deterioration became a major problem. Most important, however, was the prevailing economic aim to satisfy urgent short-term needs resulting from borrowing money on exorbitant terms rather than acting on a long-term basis as before.

While the South continued to be a cotton-farming area, the formal as well as the functional structure of the landscape altered considerably, mainly for the worse, because the problems related to the post-bellum reconstruction, and especially to agrarian reform, were only imperfectly understood. The general state of underdevelopment was the first major problem of the South; the second was agrarian re-

form. In the case of the South there was ample time available for the reform to take effect through evolution. Over the decades following the Civil War agricultural production became gradually diversified. Livestock and fodder crops were introduced into the former monoculture. The previously closed Cotton Belt broke up into individual areas and the reign of King Cotton came to an end. Industrialization appeared in earnest around 1910; it proceeded slowly at first, but at an accelerated pace after 1930. The South may be regarded as an underdeveloped area of the world which had time to change through evolution; today, in other parts of the world, the time factor has become so pressing that the technique of agrarian reform has had to be elaborated to prevent drastic turnovers through revolution.

The Old World

WESTERN EUROPE

The story of Old World land use presents a sharp contrast with the story in the New World. The differences are those between a newly settled area and an area that has been under settlement for a much longer time.

The cultural landscape in Europe dates back to prehistoric origins. Many present patterns of settlements and main arteries of communication, for example, are traceable to a past of which no written records exist. Even historical periods are very often devoid of documentary evidence. Consequently there is close cooperation between geographers and archeologists in Europe and the working methods are on the whole quite different from those in the United States. Perhaps more important is the prevalence of the historical approach among geographers. Contemporary geographical conditions can only be fully understood and explained by tracing back the components of landscape through time to their origins.

The European cultural landscape is not only complex but also very heterogeneous. Western Europe embraces a wide variety of climates, and hence of natural vegetation and soils, which range from the Mediterranean through the middle-latitudes west coast to the Arctic type. Thus far there is basically no difference from the United States. However, upon this diversified natural groundwork a multitude of different cultural units grew up side by side; most of them attained in time some sort of political cohesion, each solving the problems of agriculture under its own political and economic system. Only during the height of the Roman Empire did there exist a unified administration and civilization for the greater part of Europe; traces of that period are still recognizable in the rectangular field pattern of the Roman centuriation and also in the street pattern of the most ancient part of many European towns. It is therefore exceed-

ingly difficult to make generalized statements on the cultural landscapes of Europe, because the foundations as well as the later processes of evolution vary a great deal from region to region and from country to country.

European agriculture did not grow up under a single unified economic system of a continental extent. With a few exceptions, there had always been a very close relationship between the producers and the nearby consumers until recently. In earlier days transportation costs for agricultural products were prohibitive. In consequence nonagricultural people had to see to it that all their necessities, grains being the most important, were produced within a small radius; this applies to the cities, monasteries and convents, nobility, etc., who were in possession of land and people and directed agricultural production in order to guarantee self-sufficiency. Later, the modern state followed more or less the same principle within its own national boundaries.

The initial stages of land occupancy and subsequent intensification of agriculture date back to very early times in European development. In the Middle Ages the forests of Europe were already greatly reduced. Primitive forms of grass-cropfield rotation were replaced by a two- or three-field system with intermittent fallow even earlier. The three-field system was found in the more northern and centrals parts, while the two-field system characterized the South of France and the Mediterranean lands, in response to the different natural conditions. The next step toward intensification consisted in eliminating the fallow and thus increasing the harvested area by at least by one-third. This was achieved in the course of the seventeenth and eighteenth centuries, and first in England; this country was at that time the most advanced in the science of agriculture, as later in industry. A scientific system of crop rotation established in England not only eliminated the fallow but also provided the necessary feeds for animals; this made it possible to abandon the old system of pasturing in forests and on fallow fields, to take better care of the animals, and to collect and to utilize the natural manure. These were the beginnings of modern scientific agriculture. They have per-

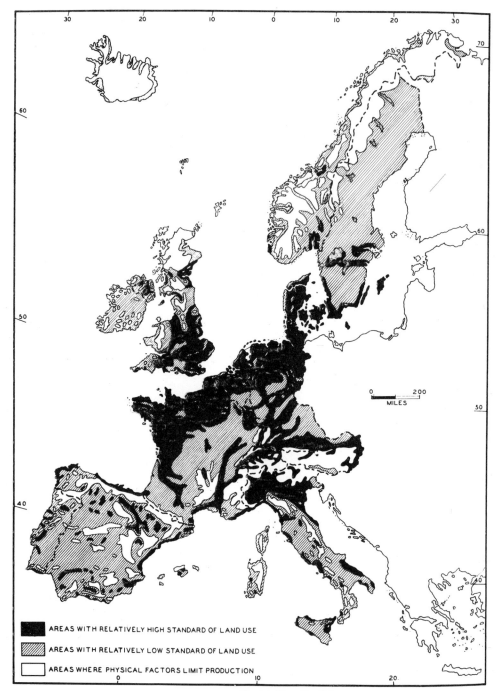

AREAS WITH RELATIVELY HIGH STANDARD OF LAND USE

AREAS WITH RELATIVELY LOW STANDARD OF LAND USE

AREAS WHERE PHYSICAL FACTORS LIMIT PRODUCTION

Reprinted from Van Valkenburg, 1960, *Economic Geography*, Vol. 36, p. 284

31 · STANDARDS OF LAND USE IN WESTERN EUROPE

sisted ever since, and continued improvements have given rise to a very intensified form of agriculture which boasts some of the highest yields per acre in the world.

Another evolutionary aspect of European agriculture is the constant adjustment of its formal structure to current needs. Individual farms and settlements and their distributional pattern may have been in harmony with the way of life in the remote past. However, agricultural production concentrated more and more on animal husbandry, to take one example, instead of on grains as it once had. Consequently certain farm buildings became obsolete and had to be remodeled. Similarly, fields had to be rearranged to permit mechanized work and to fit into the new forms of operations. This has been a major problem in every European country, and most of them have taken the necessary steps toward redistributing farm land and reorganizing farming settlements.

In England a significant change of that kind occurred as early as the sixteenth and seventeenth centuries, when the original village type of settlements with open fields was gradually replaced by compact private holdings and their enclosures. Through such changes, agriculture was able to achieve greater yields per acre, which was a major motive in carrying out the so-called enclosure movement.

Relatively early change in the agrarian structure was also observed in the countries of northern Europe. The oustanding example is perhaps Denmark, where the old village type of settlements gave way to dispersed farmsteads, and compound farms were created by rearrangement of landed properties during the seventeenth and eighteenth centuries. In Sweden such a change-over was accomplished in two steps, (*a*) the revision of property rights (*storskifte*) in the eighteenth century and (*b*) changes in the settlement pattern as in Denmark in 1830-1880 (*lagaskifte*). In most other countries, however, similar projects were not undertaken until the end of the eighteenth century. In the middle of the twentieth century agrarian reforms of that kind were going on in all European countries. Some countries like Ireland and Denmark have practically carried it through; others have hardly begun. To the latter group belong all the Mediterranean countries (Spain, Italy, and Greece) where an agregate of 50 million acres of farm land are badly in need of reconstruction along the lines mentioned above.

Redistribution of farm land thus far discussed does not involve redistribution of wealth. Upon the completion of the project, each farmer will be the owner of land the total value and size of which are about the same as before but which consists of plots more conveniently grouped in view of modern production systems. Quite different from this is the problem of landownership and, implicitly, the size of operational units which we encounter in many European countries.

As in the United States, most parts of Europe have a farming population who operate family-sized farms with additional hired hands and an increasing degree of mechanization. In most countries there is also a tendency toward an increased size of the farm in view of the new possibilities offered by modern production methods. The development has not yet gone quite as far and productivity in relation to farming population or man-hours is not yet as high as in the United States. Various reasons account for this; one is the belief that the existence of a large farm population and hence an intensively cultivated land consisting of medium-sized operational units has demographic and political advantages. Other causes are to be sought in the more traditional inclinations of farmers. Even a tenant farmer enjoys great independence in making his decisions, and his life is on the whole not very different from that of an owner-operator.

In southern Europe, however, another problem appears, namely, large landholdings with absentee landlords on the one hand and landless farm workers on the other. Coupled with overpopulation and lack of industrialization, this type of landownership has largely been the cause of general backwardness and an extremely low level of material life such as occur in southern Italy—the so-called *mezzogiorno*—and in southern Spain. Large properties are seldom operated as unified production units; the prevalent forms are, as in the post-bellum period in the South of the United States, share cropping and tenancy,

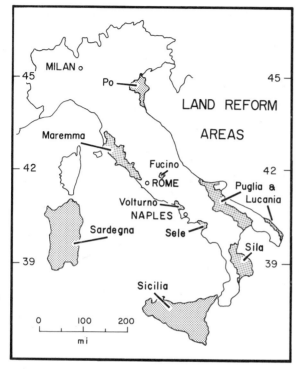

After Dickinson, 1954

32 · LAND REFORM AREAS IN ITALY

frequently on a fifty-fifty basis (called *mezzadria* in Italy). Farming is extensive; yields are low in relation to land and labor. Farmers are not capable of obtaining the necessary capital for bettering their operations and landlords are only in exceptional cases interested in overall improvement. In these areas state intervention became a social and political necessity and we find that the most progressive plans for land redistribution were formulated. The foremost of them is in Italy. There much land has been expropriated and sold to farmers, who in this way become owner-operators, paying off their interest in cash as the years go by.

A very important change, which was to a large degree revolutionary in nature, occurred in the wake of the French Revolution. In most countries of continental Europe the farmer had been a servile subject of a mundane or an ecclesiastical landlord. He had been told what to produce and paid his rent in kind. Farming op-erations had been generally regulated down to the minutest details within a village community. Following the ideals of equality, liberty, fraternity, his position underwent a radical change. His obligations toward the landowner were capitalized in terms of money and his rent was thereafter paid in cash; he was free to choose the mode of production which he considered the most profitable. The agricultural landscape was modified little by little, finally to appear very different from what it had been. Uniform grain fields in former times, where individual property lines had been concealed through common field operations of compulsory nature, assumed a new look. Individual farmers followed their own crop-rotation schemes, and soon a bewildering mosaic of crop fields came to emphasize individual property rights and the new order. Lanes had to be built through fields to reach each plot at any time, and property units needed to be rearranged in such a way that efficient field work was possible. This naturally involved a heavy capital investment, but it was compensated by a greater freedom of action and the possibility of saving and accumulating money. In times of decreasing value of currency—and devaluation has been almost continuous in all countries concerned, to a certain degree—the farmer who can pay his rent in cash is of course much better off than the one who has to pay it in kind.

Even if this last development may be called revolutionary, it applies only to the legal situation. Changes in the landscape came slowly. There are still certain areas in central Europe where farmers have found it more profitable to put up with some of the age-old restrictions than to change the formal structure of the agrarian landscape, change which would involve too heavy expenditures.

The most distinctive change during the last century was the replacement of small self-sufficient regional groups by larger national units and a growing dependence on extra-European supplies of food. Regional specialization in agriculture came about within the national economic areas and to a limited degree on a continental scale. For example, the Netherlands became famous as a supplier of potatoes and vegetables and Denmark of eggs, bacon, and dairy products.

The Mediterranean countries ship early vegetables and citrus fruits as well as wine to the north. Switzerland is known for her cheese exports. Still, each country is trying to produce a maximum of basic foodstuffs within its own domain for emergencies. European countries are high-cost producers and must protect their agriculture by tariffs, government subsidies, etc. Enormous differences exist in this respect from one country to another, and the project of a common market for agricultural products for the whole of Western Europe is therefore difficult to achieve.

Despite the intensity and the resulting high yields, Europe is the single largest deficit area as regards foodstuffs and consequently the greatest buyer of practically every agricultural product. Western Europe takes 40 percent of all wheat imports of the world and 75 percent of the butter imports, to name just two examples. This is but another aspect of the basic difference between the Old and the New World.

EASTERN EUROPE AND USSR

Some regions in Eastern Europe have long been settled; problems there were similar, in principle, to those discussed in the foregoing section. Other regions have been settled recently and are therefore more comparable in certain respects to North America. Such settlement was already actively going on in tsarist days; it has been even more vigorously pursued under the Soviet regime, moving in every direction—northward into the forests, eastward into eastern Siberia and the Far East, and southward into the steppe and desert country. The importance of the guiding principles (free enterprise and private captial, farm and family, etc.) has been stressed in the discussion of the United States. In the USSR the political factor plays an even greater role. It applies not only to newly settled areas but even more to the parts settled before the Revolution. There problems of the kind which have been dealt with in the preceding section found their solution not through evolutionary procedures, but by the Revolution with which the Soviet regime came into being and through the revolutionary changes that have ever since been made.

In this development the question of land ownership occupied a central position. Prior to the Revolution slightly less than one-half of the total farm land was in the hands of large landowners. The Revolution put an end to every type of private ownership of land, and as the first step, the expropriated land was handed over to the farm workers (or actual farmers) with the right to use it. The average size of an operating unit was then about 11 acres. Collectivization of these small units into larger ones began in 1928, when the First Five Year Plan took effect, and was completed before the Second World War. A new form of large farms came into being; they were not large holdings in the pre-Revolutionary sense, since all the land belonged to the people, but rather, large operational units which permitted more efficient methods of production and assured a larger surplus of products to supply the growing proletarian population, i.e., the industrial and urban centers.

Two types of such operational units should be distinguished: the collectivized farms (*kolkhozy*) with an average size of 1200 acres, and the state-operated farms (*sovkhozy*) larger than 6500 acres. The collectivizing process from small to large units has thus gone further in the USSR than anywhere else. The advantages of this system become apparent especially where mechanized farming is feasible and profitable as, for example, in the production of grains and cotton. Collectivization did away with many aspects of the previous formal structure of the agrarian landscape; it also destroyed the traditional type of farmers, replacing them with agricultural workers with fixed wages.

The success of this development can be measured either against the preexistent situation in tsarist Russia or the situation in another area of similar magnitude and with comparable natural conditions. If a comparison is made between the USSR and the United States, the index numbers (US = 100) of total population, arable land and land under tree crops, as well as permanent meadows and pastures, are somewhat higher for the USSR, i.e., 118, 118, and 144, respectively. In both countries the combined area in grains (wheat, rye, barley, oats, corn, millets, and rice) occupies the largest portion of the arable land,

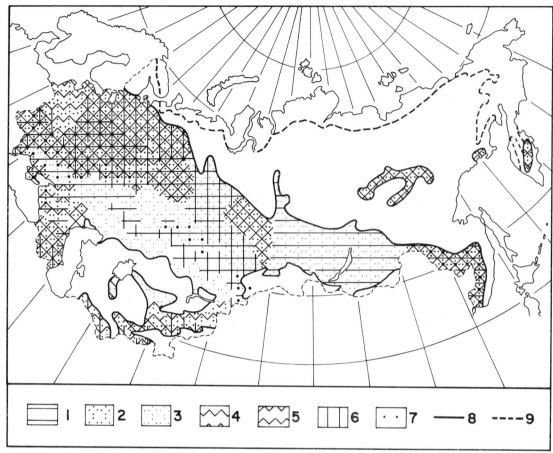

33 · ZONES OF AGRICULTURAL LAND UTILIZATION in the USSR. The map was compiled from the information contained in an article by V. P. Sotnikov ("Farming Problems in the Zones of the USSR and the Tasks of Soviet Geographers," *Soviet Geography*, 1960). *Legend:* (1) grains; (2) intensive livestock farming; (3) livestock and animal husbandry in general; (4) truck farming; (5) root crops and others, mainly potatoes; (6) fiber plants—cotton, flax, etc.; (7) oil plants—soya, sunflower, etc.; (8) limit of agricultural belt, which gives way to forests, deserts, and mountains; (9) northern limit of forested area. Agriculturally unused lands (forests, tundra, deserts, and mountains) are shown in white.

namely, 42 percent in the United States and 52 percent in the USSR. So far one sees no significant differences between the two. However, per acre yields for all the grains mentioned are without exception higher in the United States, with the largest difference in the case of corn, for which the average yields are about 2.5 times that of the USSR. Output per agricultural worker is also very much higher in the United States. The agricultural population of the United States

is only one-third that of the USSR, or 16 percent of the total population, as against 46 percent for the USSR. (These figures are quoted from the *FAO Statistical Yearbook* for the year 1959.)

Such a comparison may be misleading, as it leaves out two important factors to be taken into account. One is the significance of historical development; in contrast to the pre-Revolutionary days, agriculture in USSR has since made enormous strides, both in its areal extent and intensity. The other is a set of natural factors that can be altered by man hardly at all or only slowly.

The alignment of the major natural regions (forests, prairies or steppe, deserts, mountains, and plains) is quite different in the USSR than in the United States even if the two countries show certain similarities. The main grain-farming zone occupies the borderland between grasslands and forests, stretching eastward from Ukraine through southern Russia into Siberia. Especially in the more humid western section the combination of grains with sugar beets on dark grassland soils represents one of the most favorable forms of agriculture. Decidedly less advantageous are the natural conditions for the growing of corn; nothing comparable to the combination of high humidity and a dependable supply of moisture, high temperatures, and good soils that is found in the North American Corn Belt is available, and the production of corn has become one of the weakest sectors of the Soviet agriculture in recent years. The above-mentioned grain-farming zone approximates also the distribution of sunflowers, an oilseed plant of primary importance in the USSR. In the originally forested northern parts, hardier grains are grown and, among other important products, flax and linseed. Cotton is a product of irrigation culture in the Asian part of the USSR and in Transcaucasia.

The recent trend in various sectors of agricultural production can be summarized as follows: (a) a greater emphasis placed upon all crops other than grains, especially industrial crops, and (b) a growing concern in every form of animal husbandry. This reflects the increasing importance of manufacturing and improved nutritional conditions.

An interesting case is presented by the agrarian changes that occurred in the countries of Eastern Europe. They had before the Communist regime essentially the same agrogeographical characteristics as Western Europe. In most cases the example set by the USSR has been followed by the new regime, i.e., first, the disposal of large landholdings and creation of small farming units, and secondly, the collectivization of these

into large units operating within the framework of planned economy.

Difficulties seem to be considerable, and understandably so. The formal structure of the agrarian landscape is too firmly established to be done away with by changing the political and social order. In a way history repeats itself, if we remember what has been said in the preceding section about the changes following the French Revolution. In addition the social order and especially the position of the farmer therein were quite different in the Eastern European countries than in Russia: he was, like his neighbors on the other side of the Iron Curtain, an independent operator or at least one with a large stake in profitable operations. It is therefore not surprising that the agrarian reforms in these countries are on the whole proceeding rather slowly and can only be achieved against strong opposing forces.

The East: Japan, China, India

If the New World, the Old World, and the East are viewed from the standpoint of agricultural geography, just about the entire spectrum of possibilities is encompassed. At the one end we find the United States with an extremely fortunate man-land ratio, a favorable set of natural factors, and a young agrarian landscape. Western Europe holds an intermediate position, while the East is at the other end, less favored

	A	B	C	D	E
United States	465	24.4	178	12.4	2.6
West-Central Europe	80	37.5	121	19.0	0.7
USSR	546	9.9	210	46.2	2.6
Japan	15	16.4	93	38.7	0.2
China (mainland)	270	11.2	670 / 476*	83.0	0.4 / 0.6*
India	395	48.5	403	62.0	1.0

A = arable land and tree crops in million acres
B = (A) in percent of the total land area
C = population in million
D = agricultural population in percent of total population
E = acres of land (A) per man (C).

in every respect. The table brings it out clearly (1959; items marked with an asterisk are 1937).

Other significant differences are also revealed by these figures. The ratio of agricultural land to agricultural population provides an average of 21.1 acres per head in the United States, 5.6 and 3.5 in the USSR and Western Europe respectively, but only 0.4, 0.5, and 1.6 in Japan, China, and India. Agriculture is consequently labor-intensive in the East, which in little-industrialized countries means a generally low standard of living and underdeveloped state. Since most of the tillable land is fully used and not enough jobs in the secondary and tertiary occupations are available, living conditions deteriorate rapidly as the population increase goes on unchecked. In India the land available per person was curtailed to 50 percent during the first half of this century. There are at least twice as many people living on and off the land in the East as are justified from the point of view of agricultural operations; however, they have no other alternative of place or work to live by.

The history of the agricultural landscape is still older in the East than in Western Europe, with the exception of Japan and some peripheral areas of younger colonization. As a result an even more pronounced state of stagnancy is observed. Everything is so entangled in a vicious circle that it seems almost impossible to break it up. In Europe the Industrial Revolution opened the way to drain the overpopulated and inefficient agriculture and at the same time to revive and reconstruct it with new impetus. An agrarian reform meets with far greater difficulties in the East, for it is neither just a political nor a technical and social problem, but embraces the totality of life. Agriculture plays a basic role in this part of the world and it is badly in need of a change; agrarian reform is therefore the problem with the highest priority in all these countries, even though more publicity is today given to industrialization.

Not only is agriculture beset by such human factors as have been mentioned above, but nature is less kind there than elsewhere. These countries are situated within the so-called monsoon realm where certain climatic hazards to agriculture are always present. Kinds of crops are in the first instance determined by the mean values of temperature and humidity. The climatic hazards are then defined by the frequency and the degree of deviation from such mean values. During a given season there is a constant monsoon airflow from a certain direction, though its intensity may fluctuate from time to time; prevailing air masses are from the same source region, and consequently extremes of temperature seldom occur. The only significant exceptions are northern India and northern Japan, where the outer limits of the monsoon realm are reached and non-monsoonal invasions of cold air masses occur, in summer frequently damaging the rice crop in Japan. Precipitation, on the other hand, depends upon the intensity of the monsoon air flow, and deviations from its annual mean values are large. At the same time the dry and wet seasons are so well defined that a delay of only a week or so in the break of the monsoon should be considered a major climatic hazard. Precipitation is therefore the crucial point in agriculture; it is either too dry or too wet, the crop may be destroyed by droughts or flooded. Crop yields fluctuate much more than in Europe with its temperate humid regime of cyclonic character.

Long use and an exceedingly small amount of crop land per head almost exclude animal husbandry and invite extreme exhaustion of the soils. Statistics on the dietary conditions (see Chapter 3) indicate that a very large part of diet consists of cereals, while it is very poor in animal protein; statistics of agriculture likewise point to the predominance of grain crops. Little manure is available, and hence yields per acre are extremely low. In the following table yields indices of two major crops, wheat and rice, for five countries and one region are given (the average of all six = 100):

	YIELDS PER ACRE	
	WHEAT	RICE
United States	101	99
Europe	134	163
USSR	76	56
Japan	168	154
China	63	84
India	60	43

The obvious way out would be sought in artificial fertilizer. Its application is made possible only when the farmer has the means to purchase it or when the state undertakes the initial investment required. Europe and Japan through an extreme intensification of their agriculture have attained the highest yields per acre. In the United States and the USSR high yields per acre are less essential than high yields per man-hour. India and China, where more intensified agriculture would be so essential, seem to have all the odds against them, natural as well as human factors. Japan, China, and India were selected here not only because they are the most populous but also because they represent three different stages of agricultural development. Japan has made a remarkable achievement in intensifying and rehabilitating her agriculture by well planned and directed evolution; in China the gigantic task has been undertaken by the Communist regime to break up and reconstruct by revolutionary measures an agrarian structure thousands of years old; and finally India, with an equally long tradition, has sought the same goal through evolution, showing due respect for acquired rights and individual freedom.

JAPAN

Japan is an extremely mountainous country where only 15 percent of the land surface is considered agriculturally usable for the time being. Practically all of it consists of coastal and fluvial plains, and more than half is used for the production of the staple food, rice. The average per capita consumption of cereals is somewhat less than a pound per day, and the cereals make up almost 70 percent of the total calories consumed.

For some two centuries after about 1700 the population in Japan increased only very slowly, reaching 35 million in 1868, a year which marked the end of the feudal period. Land reserves had long been exhausted by then. With the opening of the country in that year a spectacular progress set in. In 1912 population was 50 million; by 1960, 40 million more had been added. More land for agriculture was made available only in very limited amounts—for example, by land reclamation along the coast; this was quickly offset by losses resulting from the expansion of cities, industrial plants, railroads, etc., which also claimed level land, in the main in competition with agriculture. The total area under crops has only slightly changed since 1868 and so has the absolute number of farm families, though the working population in agriculture fluctuates seasonally and also with the general economic situation of the country a great deal. In short it may be said that 5 to 6 million farm families together with 5 to 6 million extra farmhands (about 20 to 25 million people all told) cultivated all the time slightly over 12 million acres. The farming population has decreased from 75 percent to 40 percent of the total working population since 1880.

Characteristic of Japanese farming has always been the small family unit. So-called ''large farms'' with more than 5 acres made up only a few percent of the total number of farms; two-thirds had less than 2 acres. This, however, refers to the size of the operating units and not to the property rights, for most of them were tenant farmers who paid their rent in kind, i.e., in rice, which often went up as high as 40 to 50 percent of the harvest per annum. Farmers were not free in their decisions; to have some savings of their own was simply out of question. In 1945, 7.5 percent of all the landowners owned more than half of the agricultural land. Such a situation was not necessarily unique for Japan; in fact it was very similar to the situation in Western Europe at the end of the eighteenth century.

The agrarian landscape is likewise in need of readjustment, since it was conceived to meet the economic conditions prevailing generations ago. The typical rectangular pattern was laid out before the eleventh century; it is the *jo-ri* system of *han-den* (i.e., land distribution) for the old villages, in sharp contrast to the shoestring villages and long fields of *shin-den* (i.e., new villages) of the late Tokugawa period. The effects of feudalism, which lasted for a long period, and pronounced traditionalism hindered a thorough agricultural reformation.

The first measures taken after 1868, the year of the Meiji Revolution, mainly comprised technical improvements, primarily in raising yields per acre by heavy application of fertilizers,

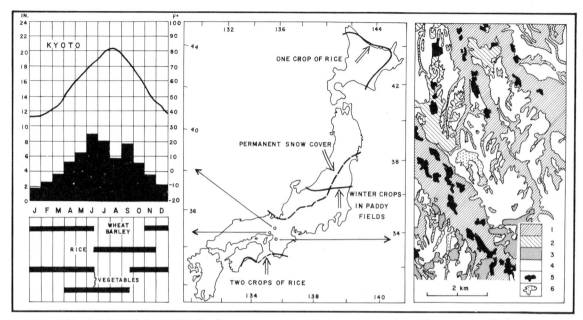

34 · LAND USE IN JAPAN. Students are encouraged to compare and correlate geographic facts using these climatic chart and crop calendar (left), general map (center), and detailed land use map (right). The three localities, as indicated by circles and arrows, are not identical, but sufficiently close to one another to justify such a comparison.

Legend for land use map: (1) rice; (2) dry fields; (3) orchards; (4) woodlands; (5) settlements; (6) ponds.

breeding of new strains of rice, etc. Nevertheless large-scale imports of rice became necessary; before the Second World War Japan was one of the major importers of rice.

Following the Second World War an agrarian reform was carried out by the Japanese government as demanded by the Allied occupational forces. The aim was definitely political, namely, to remove certain causes of the militant expansion policy of the thirties. The Japanese agrarian reform consisted of the following steps. (1) Absentee landowners were expropriated and small owner-operated farms became the universal form. Within a few years one-third of the agricultural land was bought up by the government to be sold to 2.7 million farmers. (2) Rent in kind was replaced by rent in cash. Farmers benefited a good deal in terms of rice (about 1 million tons per annum at the start in the aggregate) and even more through the devaluation of the national currency in the following years, despite several adjustments that were made. Today they pay something equivalent to a few percent of their rice crop in the way of interest (only 1 percent in 1950!) instead of the 30 percent or more of former days. Not only did the farmer become an independent operator but he also could have savings, make investments, and ask for credit. Consequently Japanese farming has been undergoing continuous intensification since the agrarian reform. Thanks to a number of consecutive bumper crops, imports of rice have been reduced to a negligible amount.

CHINA

Chao Kuo-chün, summarizing the agrarian situation in China prior to the Communist Revolution started in 1949, states in the American journal *Focus*: "The basic features of rural life in pre-revolutionary China could be summarized in two words: poverty and hopelessness. In a typical village a few landlords owned almost all the arable land, and the great majority of the farmers rented tiny plots. Rents were exorbitant, up to 40 percent of the value of the year's harvest. . . ."

China was essentially an agrarian nation when the Communists took over in 1949 and still is so despite considerable efforts and achievements made in the field of industrialization. Agrarian reform is therefore a pressing issue of paramount importance. In this matter China has gone her own way, though certain similarities are recognized between her case and the Russian example. In the beginning only the so-called "large landowners" were eliminated. The really significant development then was on the operational side, i.e., in the formation of producer's cooperatives. Land still remained private property, but the cooperative was operated as a unit. Thus 110 million family-sized farm units, on which about 500 million people were working, had been merged into approximately 700,000 cooperatives by 1957.

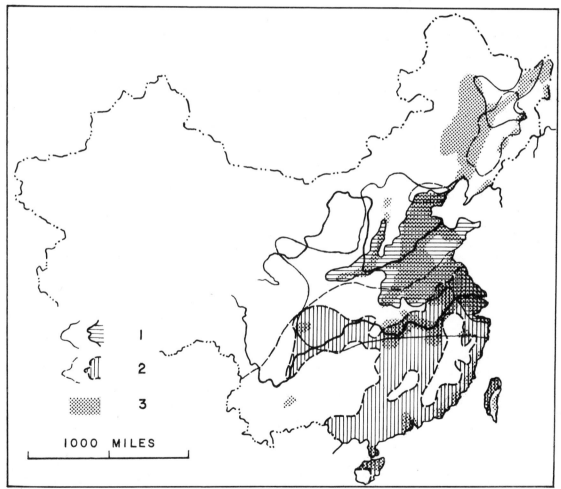

After Cressey, *Land of the 500 Million,* 1955

35 · AGRICULTURE IN CHINA. *Legend:* (1) principal area and limit of wheat cultivation; (2) principal area and limit of rice cultivation; (3) areas where physical conditions are favorable for agriculture.

The next step consisted in the formation of agricultural communes which comprised more than one operational unit and had a regional character. These communes are directly responsible for the overall direction, the technical training of the farmers, and technical improvements on a large scale. Communes number about 25,000, with an average population of 20,000. The 500 million farmers became agricultural workers who earned wages and were insured by a social security; with the exception of personal belongings they own no property. Under the so-called capitalistic system the inherent differential between the agricultural and industrial sectors has always been considered to be canceled out by the fact that the farmer has remained to a large degree his own master. In China no difference any longer exists between the agricultural worker and an industrial worker in this respect; it remains to be seen how the parity is to be maintained between them in the future as industry goes on expanding.

Land reform in China extends beyond collectivization, though this is the most discussed, and perhaps the most debatable, aspect of it. Diversification of agriculture in the direction of noncereals, primarily animal husbandry and industrial raw materials (cotton), is equally significant as is also the promulgation of pest control, plant breeding, artificial fertilizers, and so forth. Large-scale water control appears to be the only way to counteract to a certain degree such natural hazards as floods and droughts; however, it has been clearly demonstrated in recent years that droughts will continue to be a major hazard in the northern part for all non-irrigated crops like wheat and the millets.

Chinese are convinced that the execution of any project related to the reconstruction of agriculture is possible only on the new structural basis of collectivized operations. More than ten years of experience since 1949 have, in fact, given promising results with increased acreage and yields in general. Rice and wheat production has doubled, while cotton, the third major crop, has tripled.

It cannot yet be ascertained to what extent the formal and the functional structure of the agrarian landscape has gone through a basic change; as in most other cases this will take much longer to accomplish. Functionally the outstanding characteristic of former times was the lack of an adequate transportation system. If one region suffered from a crop failure, people there had only two alternatives, either to move to another more fortunate region or to stay and starve (and they died literally by the millions) for it was impossible to ship foodstuffs to the affected region. Similarly, coastal areas imported foodstuffs from overseas and not from the hinterland. Economic regionalization and industrialization under the Communist regime will be described later, in Chapter 9; its effect upon agriculture will undoubtedly be the widening of a functional unit, giving rise to problems of interregional marketing and crop specialization.

The problems of pre-Communist China were not much different from those in other countries of the East. However, the way she chose to overcome the stagnation is unique and will certainly be studied carefully in other parts of the world.

INDIA

The major problems of India are nearly identical with those of China—an age-old stagnated agricultural system, natural calamities, accelerated growth of population, and impoverished soils giving extremely low yields. In one respect India fared better than China: a well-coordinated transportation system built during the colonial period facilitated the shipment of foodstuffs to famished areas, whether from other areas of the country or from overseas through ports. Big famines, once a regular occurrence in India, could thereby be eliminated. Nevertheless, the situation did not improve basically.

On the contrary, population has been increasing by leaps and bounds from 235 million in 1901 to 438 million in 1961; the productive land available per capita was reduced to almost one-half during the same period. It implies that all the farming units have become too small and overequipped with manpower. As Indian economists have correctly pointed out, as much as one half of the actual agricultural population would have to be removed from the land even to attain that man-land ratio which existed at the beginning of this century. It means that there are

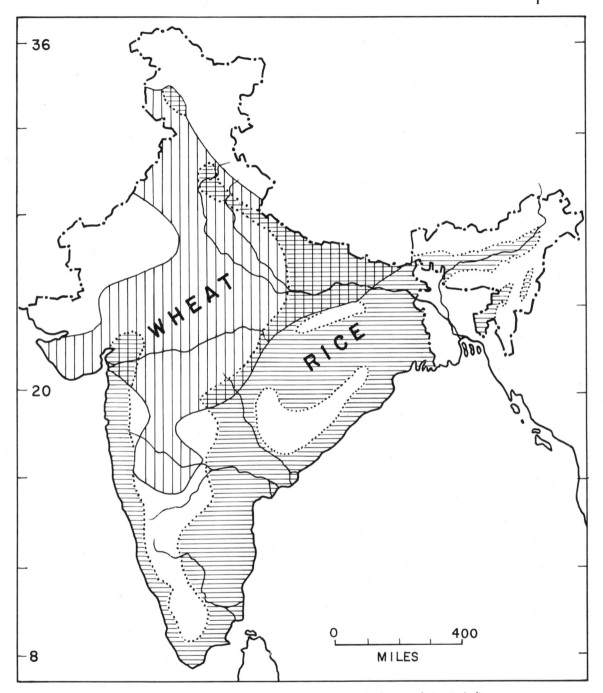

36 · AGRICULTURE IN INDIA. Major crop areas of wheat and rice in India.

no alternative means of making a living for more than 150 million people; industrialization on a large scale could only take care of a fraction of this huge surplus population, particularly since strong emphasis is placed upon the relatively labor-extensive iron and steel industries in the Indian development plans. It is indeed difficult to point to a way out of this basic dilemma.

Manpower is practically the only capital asset other than the poor land upon which Indian agriculture rests. Sample surveys in agrarian regions of India have demonstrated that the net annual income per farm family averages roughly $50. Two-thirds of it are spent for securing additional foodstuffs, one-tenth for clothing, and the rest for all the other necessities. No savings are possible under these circumstances, and cash may be obtained only at exorbitant interest rates.

Animal husbandry is practically nonexistent even though India has one of the largest cattle populations in the world. Consumption of their meat is prohibited for religious reasons. Cow dung is collected, mixed with leftovers from threshing, and used as fuel. Forests are in a derelict state and will remain so as long as they serve as unprotected pasturing ground for goats. Without the application of animal or artificial fertilizer, soil exhaustion ensued, and yields are among the lowest in the whole world.

One of the most inspiring lessons in the field of agrarian geography is presented by the development plans of the Indian government, particularly in the face of the almost hopeless situation outlined above. Agricultural production has been accorded a high priority in the Indian five-year plans and an unusually large share of capital investment has gone into that sector.

An expansion of the agricultural lands can be achieved only through extended irrigation. The treaty concluded between India and Pakistan in 1960 regarding the utilization of water resources in the Punjab is of major significance. However, even if these plans are carried out in full, the increase in arable land will scarcely match the corresponding increase in population during the period of construction.

Relatively successful were the attempts to raise crop yields per unit of area, especially for basic food crops such as grains and pulses. Far more

difficult to achieve are structural changes. Mechanization is hindered not only by the fragmentized and extremely small property units, but also because it would bring about an enormous increase in both landless and jobless population. Many evolutionary measures have been taken in order to improve the general situation without uprooting the basic social structure: they include, for example, the elimination of large landholdings, revision of the rent system, revival of ancient village communities based on cooperative farming and private property rights, increased availability of credit and marketing facilities, and so forth.

The Middle Latitudes of the Southern Hemisphere

The countries situated in the middle latitudes of the Southern Hemisphere (Chile, Argentina, Uruguay, South Africa, Australia, and New Zealand) occupy an aggregate land area of approximately 3 billion acres, of which about 6 percent are now used as crop land and for tree cultivation. They are discussed in the following with respect to two distinct characteristics. (1) They represent a part of the globe where the expanding ecumene met conditions not very different from those in the Old and the New World. (2) Because of a physical similarity, they were able to play a unique role in providing the industrialized countries in the Northern Hemisphere with foodstuffs and industrial raw materials.

The continents of the Southern Hemisphere taper off southward, and their poleward ends are reached at much lower latitudes than in the Northern Hemisphere. The southernmost part of South America corresponds to Prince Rupert in British Columbia or central Labrador in North America; the southern tip of South Africa corresponds to Morocco in northern Africa; the Australia–New Zealand realm occupies a position midway between the two. They are all separated by vast bodies of water, about 70 degrees in longitudinal extent between South America and South Africa, and 90 degrees between South Africa and Australia. Few airlines and ocean routes connect them directly because there is nothing to draw them together; in every respect their orientation points elsewhere, mostly toward countries in the Northern Hemisphere.

The pattern of climatic distribution corresponds to that of the northern continents. The arrangement of climatic types of the western side of a continent follows the same sequence as in the Northern Hemisphere, i.e., the subtropical desert and steppe, the Mediterranean (dry summer), and, if the land mass extends far enough poleward, the humid temperate climates. The east coasts lack the dry regions of the west separating the middle latitudes from the tropics. In the Southern Hemisphere, where land areas are relatively narrow, continentality in climate is much less pronounced, particularly with respect to the winter minima; summers are sufficiently hot and humid to permit the production of corn, but less so than in the east-central United States.

THE AGRARIAN LANDSCAPE

In general, in all the countries concerned the humanized landscape is relatively young. Few traces of pre-colonial days remain. Any generalization beyond this is hardly appropriate, since conditions governing later development differed widely from area to area.

The importance of pursuing a definite policy of land settlement was recognized early in the United States, though it was conspicuously absent in colonial North America, at least in the British sector. Spanish colonization followed a specific line, though quite different from the North American example discussed earlier. In the Spanish colonial realm the keynote was the city rather than agriculture and family and farm. Spanish culture at home was essentially an urban culture; rural areas were characterized by absentee landowners, large holdings, and landless agricultural workers. Principally it was this socioeconomic structure that was transplanted into the Spanish colonies. Cities were laid out in a standardized pattern. They were supported by local, mostly indigenous agriculture, but otherwise agriculture hardly went beyond the subsistence stage. Exports from the colonies consisted almost exclusively of mineral products. The creation of large landholdings also dates back to the colonial

period; frequently large tracts of land containing a number of villages were given to officials of high rank as *encomiendas* or trusts, as we would say today, which in the course of time became private property. All the details of colonial development were carefully laid down in the form of royal laws and decrees, and though many changes have taken place through the postcolonial development of a century and a half, the typical landscape and social structure have remained to this day.

Areas in South America which were settled later than the colonial period, such as the southern part of Chile, present a quite different aspect, and so of course, do, the areas which were formerly Portuguese territories. Similarly the absence of a colonial land policy in South Africa and in Australia, comparable to the North American or the Spanish example, resulted in the lack of a typical settlement and field pattern. On the other hand such characteristics as may be attributed either to the origins of the settlers (e.g., the Dutch influence in South Africa) or to natural factors of site have become more conspicuous here. The rural landscape of New Zealand as well as urban life strikes the foreigner as more English in many respects than that of the Old Country; in other respects it contains something different. Perhaps it is precisely this duality that may be called typical of New Zealand.

POSITION IN THE WORLD ECONOMY

When the natural conditions in a colony were similar to those in the home country, it had in the long run two advantages. First, it was easily colonized and cultivated by the people whose agricultural know-how had been acquired in the northern middle latitudes. Spanish America offers an interesting example. The Spaniards took to the dry country everywhere they went; in the Amazon Basin and in southern Chile the beginning of the forest zone marked the outer margin of Iberian settlement. Forested areas became the main sites of settlement later for those who came from northern Europe, chiefly Germany. In short, people from Europe were well qualified and well equipped to occupy and to develop the land. Secondly, products from the

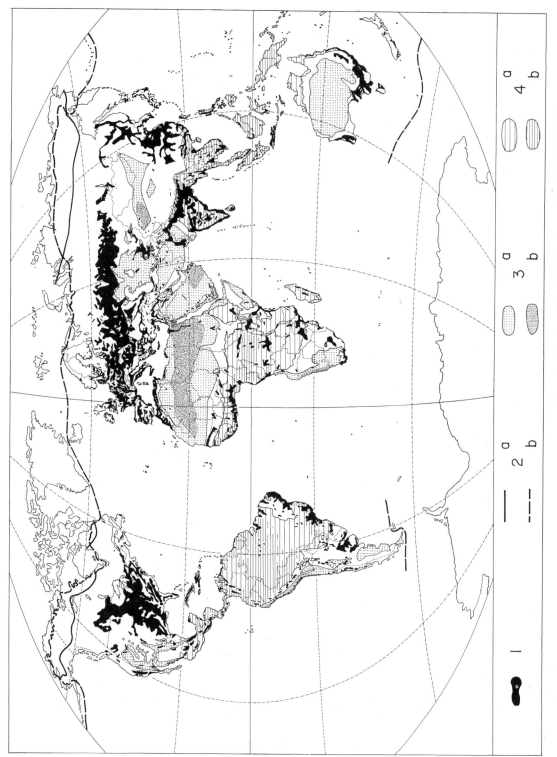

37 · FRONTIERS OF AGRICULTURE. *Legend:* (1) Extent of cultivated land (see Fig. 20). (2) Cold frontier—(*a*) southern limit of permanently frozen soils and (*b*) poleward limits of forest. (3) Arid frontier—(*a*) arid lands and (*b*) Extremely arid lands. (4) Humid tropical frontier—(*a*) more or less periodically wet lands and (*b*) more or less permanently wet lands.

Sources: 2a—Kimble and Good, 1955; 2b—Hermes, 1955; 3—Meigs-UNESCO, 1952; 4—Küchler, 1961 land were those for which there was rising demand in the industrialized countries of Western Europe. Grains, meat, fats, and wool became major export products for Europe as transportation improved and demand increased.

In all the countries considered in the present section, modern developments brought about a certain degree of industrialization and urbanization, and with it a large nonagricultural population came into existence. Still, agricultural products rank very high in export trade. In Argentina meat, wheat, and wool make up almost 100 percent of the exports; equally important are dairy products, meat, and wool in New Zealand (94 percent) and wheat and wool in Australia (83 percent). In South Africa agricultural products (fruits and wool) account for only 40 percent of the total exports, while in Chile they are negligible (3 percent). All these commodities are primarily destined for Western Europe.

This particular relationship creates certain common problems among them with regard to their economic policies. All these exporters of agricultural products are exposed first to the fluctuations of world market prices and secondly to the effects of the protective agrarian policy of their customers in Western Europe as mentioned earlier. They protest that world trade in agricultural products should be made free or liberalized on the same principle as advocated by the industrialized countries with respect to manufactured goods exported by them. Despite the fact that they are separated from one another by large water bodies, they can be logically grouped together for these and other reasons.

The New Frontiers

The idea of the frontier and the role of the pioneers have been discussed earlier. Though there are many different kinds of frontiers—in sociology, in science, in other fields—it is the geographical frontier that we are here concerned with, i.e., the peripheral zone of the ecumene where settlers are faced with a set of unfamiliar and often hostile natural conditions and the best or a possible way to use the land has to be worked out carefully at first. Frontiers of this kind are found primarily in three directions.

THE POLEWARD FRONTIER

There is a poleward limit of growth to every cultured plant. The limit is not firmly fixed, but is liable to shift with technical advance in agricultural management.

One of the chief problems is the conditions of soils which are characteristic of the polar areas. During the long cold winter the soil and the bedrock are both so deeply frozen that the melt water in summer cannot permeate them; it saturates only the uppermost layer or runs off. As soon as the temperature drops below the freezing point, water in liquid form ceases to be available. The zone where these conditions prevail is called the *zone of permafrost*.

Soils in the zone of permafrost show little chemical weathering or decomposition and are poor in humus and soil bacteria. These characteristics make it necessary for agriculturalists to find special techniques of improving the soils by raising their temperature and modifying other physical, chemical, and biological properties.

A second problem is concerned with features of the climate in the polar areas. Most of the poleward frontiers today lie beyond the polar circle, in regions where polar days and nights occur. People living in other parts of the world hardly realize the importance of long summer days for the total amount of solar energy received. When the sun does not set, the diurnal range of temperature becomes very slight. A daily mean temperature of about 40° F is considered to mark the lower limit of the growing period. In the middle latitudes this temperature is reached in the early spring, but for a long time as the year advances temperatures above 40° F occur for only a small number of hours during the day. In the polar regions, on the other hand, though the growing period is much shorter, temperatures remain constant for some weeks.

An obvious way to solve the problems of temperature is to breed new hybrids of cultured plants which can take advantage of certain characteristics of the polar climate, i.e., can grow continuously and complete a life cycle within a short period. According to the scientific reports available at the present time, it seems that much research has been done along these lines in the USSR and that the northern limit of grains in

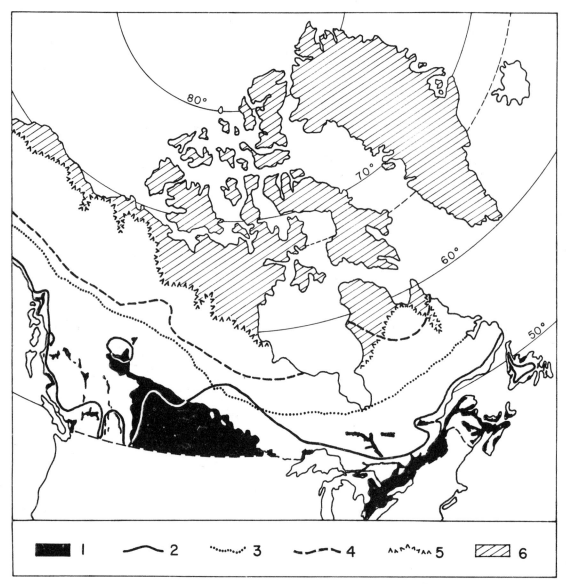

Bennett, 1959; Kimble and Good, 1955

38 · POLEWARD LIMITS of agriculture on the North American continent. *Legend:* (1) land in farms, 1951; (2) northern limit of area with more than 90 frost-free days; (3) southern limit of permafrost; (4) southern limit of perpetual permafrost; (5) northern tree limit; (6) tundra and ice. The United States is left blank, since only the conditions in Canada, Alaska, and Greenland are shown.

Siberia has been pushed toward the pole. The problem is less pressing in North America because of the abundance of better land further south.

Under subarctic conditions agriculture may alter the interrelation of the various landscape elements in a manner quite unknown to and different from the middle latitudes. What, for example, would be the result if the permafrost should disappear through clearing or plowing? It would certainly affect the hydrological conditions within the soil, which might be rendered dry, especially if precipitation is negligible. At present, however, little is known about all these processes.

It is quite another matter to create artificial conditions in the lands of permafrost for growing special vegetables and fruits, as in the greenhouse or in artificial soil. Bananas are successfully grown in Iceland, and fresh vegetables are available at many outposts in the subarctic regions.

Plainly in such an unknown environment as the polar frontiers people confront problems which cannot be solved in the light of their previous experience. The solutions await a new kind of systematic basic research.

THE ARID REGIONS

Lack of water constitutes a major obstacle to the expansion of agriculture and hence of the ecumene. Yet a precise definition of aridity is not so simple as it first appears.

Rainfall figures are frequently employed in determining the boundaries between the humid and the dry lands, or in measuring the degree of aridity. But they permit only a first-order approximation. More important than how much water falls on the land is how large a part soaks into the ground and is afterward available to plants through their root systems. Another part of the rainfall is removed by run-off, and the rest is evaporated. The exact portions of the respective parts are difficult to determine and are known in only a few experimental cases. Since the amount of evaporation increases with tem-

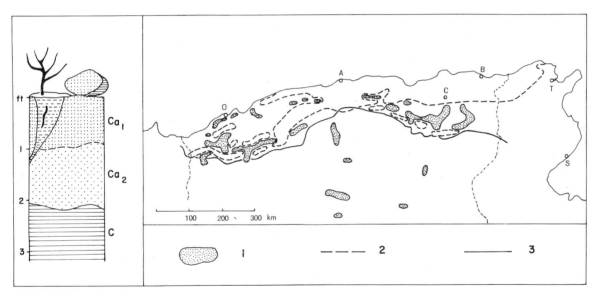

Jaeger, 1936

39 · A CHARACTERISTIC SOIL TYPE of arid regions in North Africa: its profile and distribution. *Left:* The profile is indicative of the soil type which is developed in the border zone between subhumid and semiarid wet-and-dry climates. Its characteristic is the accumulation of calcium carbonate formed as a result of evaporation. Ca_1 represents the hard crust cracked and filled with blown-in material, Ca_2 the weathered rock material loosely cemented together by calcium carbonate, and C the bedrock. *Right:* The distribution of soils of this type in North Africa (Algeria) is shown by (1); (2) is the humid-arid boundary according to A. Penck; and (3) is the limit of rain-fed agriculture. The localities indicated are (O) Oran, (A) Algiers, (C) Constantine, (B) Bone, (T) Tunis, (S) Sfax.

perature, among other factors, it may be stated in a somewhat simplified way that aridity is directly proportional to precipitation and inversely proportional to temperature. The so-called aridity index i has been defined in principle as

$$i = \text{precipitation}/\text{temperature}$$

with various modifications and refinements by different authors. It was used in the classification of world climates by W. Köppen, who also took into consideration the seasonal distribution of the rainfall. W. Thornthwaite further elaborated upon these principles, introducing the concept of precipitation and temperature effectiveness.

While the underground circulation of water in humid regions is mainly downward, it moves upward in arid lands through the different layers of the soil, finally evaporating at the surface. This was recognized more than half a century ago by the German geographer A. Penck as one of the characteristic differences between humid and arid climates. The upward movement of water leads to the precipitation of certain substances at or near to the soils surface; of these calcium carbonate is the most common. Thus soils of special types are found in the boundary zone between humid and arid climates; they are made up of loose material cemented together by these precipitated substances into a concretelike mass, sometimes several feet in thickness. These soils make it impossible for the plants to extend their roots into the moister lower strata; consequently bunch grass and shrubs and many annual plants that grow during the wet season when the surface layer is wetted constitute the vegetation. Plowing merely serves to scratch the top soil, and annuals, mostly grains, grow during the wet season. In order to plant vines or trees, the hard crust must be blasted so that the roots are able to reach below.

In many respects there is no clear-cut boundary between humid and arid regions; rather, we may speak of a zone of transition, use such terms as "subhumid" or "semiarid," or apply a sliding scale of aridity. In moving from less dry to very dry climates, one observes that each plant has a dry limit different from the others. In any type of dry-wet climates, such as the Mediterranean, the most important distinction is recognized between the annuals and the perennials. Annuals conclude their life cycle within the wet season and therefore only the climatic conditions prevailing during that period are relevant; perennials, on the other hand, must withstand the drought. Forests and tree culture disappear long before the first dry limit for grains is reached. Barley extends into still drier parts than wheat because it matures more quickly. From an economic point of view the grassland bordering the forest constitutes a unique zone because the grassland meets the physical requirements for pasturing as well as sedentary agriculture, though mostly in a monocultural form.

Up to this degree of aridity, agriculture is still basically dependent on the rainfall, though irrigated plots are also in use for the production of special crops during the dry season. In the Mediterranean countries the classical trinity of grain-grape-olive has been increasingly supplemented by irrigated crops of subtropical and tropical origin, such as rice, citrus fruit, and cotton, which are grown during the hot and sunny summer months. Similar combinations of crops are found in the other areas with an identical climate, like California, central Chile, and the southernmost part of Africa.

With a further decrease in precipitation the variability from year to year increases. In the drier parts of the grasslands one enters a zone where the bad years and good years hold the balance, but finally the hazards become so great that one reaches the limit of grain-farming based upon rainfall. Special techniques have made it possible to push grain-farming still farther. Such techniques, designed to restore and preserve moisture in the soil and subsoil, had already been highly developed in Roman times in the Old World though some of them were rediscovered in the dry West of North America by white settlers. One common feature of these techniques, collectively called dry-farming, is the alternation of fallow and crop on the same land. Another is that during the fallow the land is usually carefully plowed to minimize moisture losses.

The outer boundary of rain-fed agriculture is subject to fluctuation for many reasons: changes in climate, technical advances, competition from

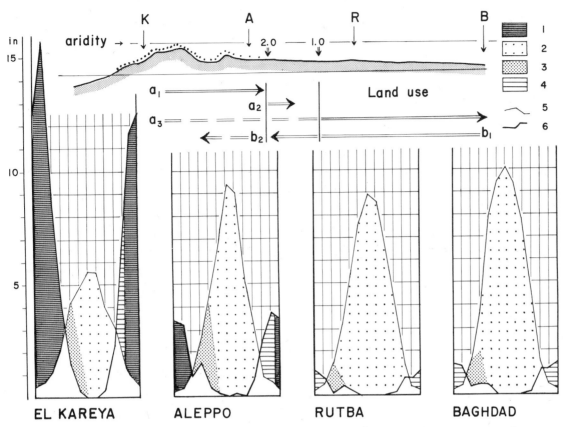

40 · TRANSITION FROM HUMID TO ARID LANDS. The cross section is a schematic representation of the climatic transition in the Middle East. *K, A, R,* and *B* indicate the relative position of the stations shown by the climatic diagrams. The numbers 2.0 and 1.0 are aridity indices by Köppen, denoting the boundaries between the tree climate (*Csa*), the steppe climate (*BS*), and the desert climate (*BW*). Characteristic types of land use are: (a_1) Mediterranean agriculture; (a_2) sub-Mediterranean zone, predominantly wheat; (a_3) irrigation culture, either exclusively or in combination with rain-fed agriculture of a_1 and a_2; (b_1) nomadic economy, prevalent in all areas outside of irrigated lands; (b_2) infiltration of nomadic people into settled agricultural communities during summer.

The legend for the climatic diagrams denotes (1) excess of water, (2) deficit of water, (3) deficit covered by water available in the ground, (4) use of excess water to replenish empty underground reservoirs, (5) potential evapotranspiration, (6) precipitation. The months run from January to December in the order of a calendar year and not of an agricultural year.

livestock grazing upon the price basis, etc. A very important cause for such fluctuations in the sub-Mediterranean zone used to be the varying strength of the political powers. Whenever the power of the states in control was weakened, nomads invaded the settled agricultural communities, destroying settlements and plantations.

In modern times an important change was introduced by tractorization of plowing. Once the rain starts to come in autumn, the land should be prepared as quickly as possible. With old-fashioned implements only a small portion of the land could be cultivated at a time, but the use of tractors has considerably enlarged the possibilities. As a consequence, large areas are being added to the crop land, as in Syria after the Second World War.

Finally one encounters the absolute limit of agriculture based upon precipitation. From there onward agriculture is only possible with artificial irrigation. Every region which depends solely upon irrigation has its special problems, but these may be summarized as follows: (1) A balance should be established between the needs and the availabilities of water. The unit of measurement frequently employed is the acre-foot, i.e., the volume of water needed to flood an acre of level ground to a depth of one foot. This should take into consideration the seasonal distribution of water availabilities and needs and the short-term fluctuations from year to year.

(2) Measures must be taken to equalize any discrepancies which may appear in this supply-and-demand relationship. In most cases it means the storage of water in artificial lakes so that the supply curve is smoothed. In areas of continuous irrigation (flow irrigation) it is obviously the minimum supply of water that determines the amount of land to be irrigated; excess water can even be harmful and should be taken out of the irrigation system, as has to be done for the great Mesopotamian rivers, Euphrates and Tigris. In the traditional irrigation practice of Egypt the big flood arriving at the beginning of the cool season—contrast with Mesopotamia, where it occurs in early summer—was allowed to inundate the land completely (basin irrigation) which was later planted with winter crops. Where rivers

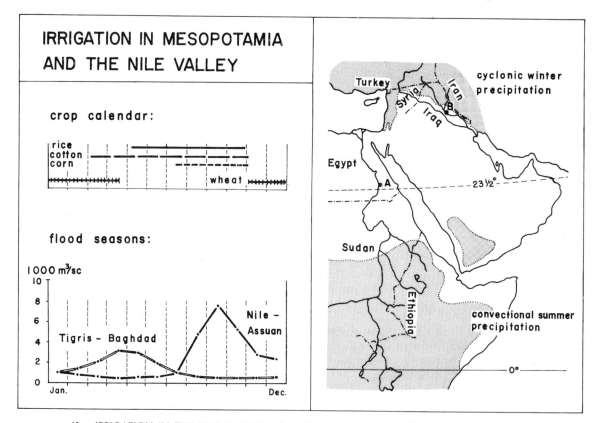

41 · IRRIGATION IN THE NILE VALLEY and in Mesopotamia (Iraq). This shows in contrast the size of the river basin and the rainfall regime (right), the occurrence of floods and the volume of water (left, top), and the crop calendar for the characteristic winter and summer crops grown in both areas (left, bottom).

flow at a level lower than the land to be irrigated or where groundwater is used, another type of irrigation is found—lift irrigation. If groundwater is utilized for irrigation, the amount drawn should never exceed what is replenished. This simple rule has been often overlooked, with the result that the groundwater table is lowered and finally the reservoir emptied. It sometimes happens that groundwater reservoirs are old and were filled under more humid conditions than those existing today. For example, in North African deserts extensive aquifers came into existence some 20,000 to 30,000 years ago during the last ice age. Water has remained stored in them up to this day, but no more replenishment takes place under the present climatic conditions. This, of course, makes it impossible to project any long-term development plan based on these reservoirs. (3) The actual amount of water required for irrigation has to be determined by experience, and the necessary precautions be taken for proper drainage of the irrigated land. Application of too much water would cause a rise of the groundwater table and thence a widespread waterlogging, especially when drainage is inadequate. Another consequence resulting from too much or too little water is the precipitation of salt crystals in the upper layers of the soil. Most plants do not tolerate salts and consequently they deteriorate and disappear altogether. No universal rules can be established for the precise amount of irrigation water required in each case. Experimental stations in all arid lands are engaged in working out the correct formula for certain specific local conditions and cultures. Numerous examples of wrong management may be cited; in many cases the causes are to be sought not in too little, but in too much water, as in parts of Egypt, Iraq, and Pakistan. This kind of mismanagement usually accompanies new projects; in the age-old irrigation areas the farmers have an accurate knowledge of water requirements and soil management.

Though irrigation is but one phase of the exploitation of arid land, it is among the most frequently discussed and highly publicized topics at the present time. There are many reasons for this, but only two are considered in the following. First, irrigation necessitates large-scale planning and heavy capital investment in dams, canals, and the like. It is usually a governmental enterprise, constituting an essential part of the national development program and thus receiving widespread publicity. Second, irrigation guarantees more constant harvests; crop failures due to droughts or floods do not occur. A high intensity of production in every respect is therefore economically justified by secure returns and high yields per acre.

The problems of the development of the arid zone are multifarious and complex. Arid-zone research is being undertaken in various parts of the world, covering different fields of science and engineering. Under the program of the Major Project of the Arid Zone UNESCO has organized an international platform for the exchange of information and subsidizes research institutions and research projects.

THE TROPICS

The third and the most extensive frontier of the present is represented by tropical lands. Though there are different ways of delimiting the tropics, they agree that the tropics comprise about one-third of the land surface of the globe. A large variety of natural landscapes and economies are found within the tropics. Logical subdivision of the tropics is made in two ways: (1) into the equatorial zone of the evergreen rain forest and the adjacent savanna lands, and (2) into the altitudinal zones that ascend to the zone of perpetual snow and ice. It is therefore difficult to give any generalization about the tropics as a whole unless they are viewed from a specific point of view.

Tropical climates and other natural elements have been outlined earlier (Chapter 3) and more facts will be added at appropriate places. It is not intended here to present a short regional geography of the tropics, but rather to substantiate the thesis that they represent a zone of frontier similar to the poleward and the arid frontiers discussed above. On first thought such a statement may not sound convincing since the tropics have been settled since as far back as historical and archeological records can take us. The origins of many cultivated plants, if not of human culture as such, are sought in tropical lands. Why, then, should they still be regarded as a frontier?

In every estimate of the future population growth of the earth, the tropics are rated highest as to potential agricultural production and carrying capacity; in other words, one finds here the largest agricultural resources that have so far been little used for the production of foodstuffs and industrial raw materials. At present this zone stands out because of its low population densities—though some restricted areas are highly productive and densely settled—and also because of its small share in world commerce. There arises a question: Are these estimates wrong? Are we actually confronting one of the largest and potentially richest zones of the globe? The tropics are for the time being not known well enough to permit an answer either way, nor are the agricultural techniques known that might bring in modern methods of production. Not only the Industrial Revolution but also what may be called the Agricultural Revolution of the last two hundred years took place outside the tropics. With a few exceptions, tropical agriculture, compared with that of the middle latitudes, has remained static and the basic research into its possibilities has been limited. To quote L. D. Stamp, "There is much to be learned, before we can teach" (*Land for Tomorrow*, 1952).

Thus our lack of knowledge, a large number of popular misconceptions, and a need for intensified basic research constitute one theme of our discussion. Another is the results of colonialism which affected the larger part of the tropics for several centuries until recently. Together these themes underline the frontier characteristics of the tropics and at the same time throw light on the possibilities of future development.

For these reasons UNESCO initiated a project of global scope, similar to the one on the arid zone; it is called the Major Project of the Humid Tropics.

Probably more misconceptions are found in schoolbooks and in the minds of people about the tropics than about any other part of the world. The natural and the human habitat in the tropics strikes anyone from the middle latitudes as totally unfamiliar so that he often finds himself without the correct concepts to describe a situation. It is senseless to speak of winter or summer

there. Equally wrong is such a generalization as "the tropical climate is hot and humid"; undoubtedly, there are such climates, but there are also climates of many other types.

A very common misconception is the proverbial fertility of the tropical lands. As a matter of fact, tropical soils are for the most part very infertile, especially if they are not properly managed. Soil forming processes mainly consist of chemical alterations under the influence of constantly high temperatures and constantly or seasonally high humidity, at least in the tropical lowlands. Biological activity is also highly accelerated; organic material decomposes quickly, and the humus content of soil is only a fraction of what is common in good soils of the middle latitudes, even though leaf shedding takes place all the year round. In wet-dry climates concretional soils of the lateritic type are formed which, as the name implies, are as hard as brick. With the exception of alluvial lowlands and young volcanic areas, mature residual soils in the tropics turn out to be decidedly infertile once the natural vegetation cover has been removed.

Moreover, after the forest is cleared, the deeply weathered soil is easily washed away, and there results a rapid decrease in fertility. It forced the native agriculturist to adopt a special form of land use called shifting cultivation, which is today found in the more mountainous parts of the tropics. It involves clearing the ground for cultivation that will last for only a few years. When the soil is exhausted, it is abandoned and new land is cleared; the old fields thereupon revert to forest. It takes up to twenty or thirty years until the same land may be used again for cropping. Over wide areas, therefore, what is commonly observed as primeval forest is actually secondary forest; virgin stands are rare even in such a vast realm of tropical rain forest as the Congo or the Amazon basin.

A priori, it is to be expected that soils which are chemically and physically so different from those in the middle latitudes require a different management. Throughout the tropical world indigenous agriculturists use the hoe and in some areas the light plow. When modern plows and heavy agricultural machinery were introduced into the tropical agriculture, these implements, admirably suited to agriculture in higher lati-

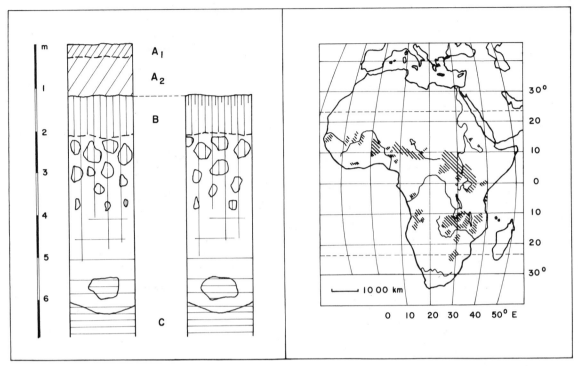

Profiles after Duchaufour, 1960, and map after Prescott and Pendleton, 1952

42 · TROPICAL SOILS. The profiles illustrate the development of typical lateritic soils. On the left is the normal profile with an A_1 horizon (accumulation of organic matter) and an A_2 horizon (zone of eluviation); such a profile may be found under a forest cover. On the right is a so-called degraded soil profile where the A horizon was washed away and the lateritic B horizon (zone of illuviation) with a characteristic hard crust forms the surface. C represents the parent material, which in this case is reached at a depth of 6 meters (19.7 feet). The map shows the distribution of laterite in Africa.

tudes, proved to be a complete failure because they brought about a heavy destruction of soil qualities. It follows then that our present inadequate knowledge of soil management, application of fertilizer, production techniques, etc., in the tropics should be completed first before the indigenous systems of agriculture, often termed "primitive," are thrown overboard.

Viewing the agricultural situation in the rice-growing regions of Southeast Asia, for example, one becomes aware of many parallel instances that existed in Western Europe in the eighteenth century. There is the problem of breaking up the vicious circle of continuous monoculture by introducing a crop rotation which includes a fodder crop. This would enhance the possibility of raising more and healthier livestock and in turn of manuring and obtaining higher yields per acre. There are all the problems associated with plant breeding and pest control. Last but not least, similar problems are met in the socio-economic sphere: tenancy, cash rent instead of sharecropping, and many others. Though the problems are similar, the solutions will have to be different; at the moment many of the questions remain unanswered.

These are but a few of the characteristics of the natural as well as immediately related human conditions. Many other human characteristics must have appeared equally strange to colonizers who came from western or southern Europe. Much of the land before them looked as if it were not inhabited at all, while other parts seemed to have a very low population density. What the colonizers failed to take notice of was the fact that different types of economy might have totally different requirements for land and that the association of high density with large expanses of crop fields and closely spaced villages is applicable only to certain types of economy. In the collecting and hunting economy, for example, a vast area is required to support even a few persons; the aggregate amount of land used by a shifting cultivator over a long period of years is many times larger than the acreage that a rice farmer in a kampong cultivates year after year—his continuously cropped rice fields or sawah. Another fact which the first colonizers were not fully aware of was that by taking up the land seemingly unused, they were actually breaking an essential link of an existing economy without which its proper functioning was no longer possible.

The coming of colonizers also led to the breakup of the existing social structure. Usually this consisted of the tribal organization in which each member had certain obligations to fulfill for the common good. Not only were people of the younger generation, when recruited to work on plantations, isolated from their traditional background, but the rest of the group was also left incomplete. These and many other things, such as tribal taboos and their importance for the functioning of the daily routine, became gradually known through the work of ethnologists and sociologists. But in most parts of the tropics the precolonial social structure has already been destroyed beyond repair, and nothing equivalent has yet been offered as a substitute.

The aims of economic activity were likewise different for colonizers and for indigenous people. Over large areas the indigenous economy was based on subsistence agriculture which provided no surplus production for sale or barter. Barter trade was the first step for obtaining certain commodities from the colonies. A short-term philosophy and limited desires of the natives resulted in small quantities of products offered for bartering and later for sale. Forced labor, head taxes, and so on were thus regarded as legitimate means to wring out an exportable surplus and to induce the natives to work toward that end more than they were used to working up to that time. What method was applied depended upon the

colonial policy in individual cases. Well known is the Dutch policy in the former Netherlands East Indies. Under this policy, which was introduced in 1830 but abandoned later because of its detrimental effects on food production, each village was obliged to produce a specified amount of surplus products for export.

More and more, therefore, the colonizers established their own producing units. Principally they were of two types: white settlers and farmers on the one hand, and large plantation with native labor on the other. The first type is only to be found where the white settlers are able to live and work and maintain good health. Outstanding examples are in parts of the Antilles, the Central American highlands, Andean South America, the highlands of Brazil, and parts of East Africa. In some of these areas white settlers have completely uprooted the indigenous economy, while in others they are concurrent with native farms.

A plantation is a large operating unit with a large indigenous labor force working for wages under a centralized direction. In contrast with the indigenous economy, it is characterized by a high capital intensity and a long-range outlook. The following example will illustrate the difference between the short- and long-range econo-

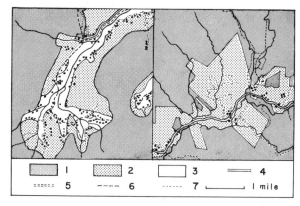

Ooi Jin-Bee, *Journal of Tropical Geography,* 1961

43 · RUBBER CULTURE IN MALAYA. *Legend:* (1) jungle; (2) rubber; (3) paddy; (4) road; (5) jeep track; (6) bridle path; (7) foot path. Houses are indicated by dark dots. Rubber trees are grown in conjunction with paddy on native smallholdings, occupying the lower hillsides hitherto unused (left). Rubber cultivation on estates is a monocultural form of production (right).

mies. An indigenous cultivator whose main interest is to obtain a certain amount of cash from the sale of his products will have to increase production if market prices drop. Under similar circumstances, however, the estate or plantation-owner will begin to restrict production if over-production happens to be the cause of the lower prices. The latter's action, based on the long-range prospect, will therefore correct the causes and eventually reestablish a balance between supply and demand, while the native producers will continue to act as a disturbing factor. In many countries special marketing organizations have been established for the specific purpose of maintaining stable prices; these organizations are usually created by the responsible governments.

Plantation agriculture appeared also wherever agricultural products had to be processed immediately after harvesting, like sugar cane, or where a large volume of a product had to be delivered on very short notice, like bananas. Not infrequently plantation production is augmented by indigenous production.

These examples suffice to stress the point that a thorough investigation of natural as well as human factors is a prerequisite of any promising development project. The problem has become grave because we no longer find a static situation to start from, but are instead thrown in the middle of extremely dynamic states. Centuries of colonial development carried out in accordance with ever-changing policies and frequently by trial and error have brought some changes into the framework of nature, but above all they have revolutionized human society, and nobody will be able or willing to turn the wheel back.

Colonialism established certain economic characteristics of the countries concerned, and its marks cannot be obliterated simply by changing them in political status from colonial territories to independent states. The role they play in world commerce is still as producers of raw materials, agricultural or mining, and as markets for manufactured products. Not only is their share in the world export and import trade small, but they are now put in a more disadvantageous position than in former days because the prices of manufactured goods have tended to rise while those of primary products have been falling since

about the end of the last war. For the most part, however, the colonial period has also served to prepare them for nationhood, providing them with fairly well functioning administrative machinery, the fact not to be overlooked at the time when the last traces of colonialism are being uprooted by the young nations emerging all round the world.

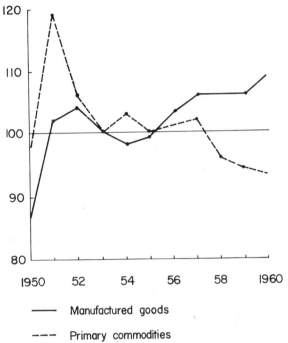

44 · PRICE INDICES of international trade for manufactured goods and primary commodities, 1950–1960 (1953 = 100).

Prior to the Second World War, about one-fourth of the earth's land surface consisted of the colonial territories, of which four-fifths were situated in the tropics. It follows that problems of tropical development are not only technical but also include the intricate matters that fall under social and political geography and are the outcomes of a long period of colonial development. Comparatively speaking, these countries are underdeveloped, but the nature of their underdevelopment is such that what they need is more than just technical assistance and basic research; tact and understanding of their peculiar situation are equally indispensable.

5 | WORLD MARKET PRODUCTS

INTERNATIONAL TRADE IN AGRICULTURAL PRODUCTS

Until recently nearly all agricultural products have been consumed near the place of production. Notable exceptions were found, e.g., in the European spice trade with the Southeast Asian and Indian realm, or in the grain trade of the ancient Greeks. One of the first mass products of modern international trade was cane sugar, which was exported from the colonies in the New World to Europe from about the sixteenth century. Large-scale international trade in agricultural products began only in the course of the nineteenth century. Though it was greatly facilitated by the development of modern mass transport means, the prime causes that necessitated an international exchange of agricultural products were elsewhere.

One of them is the ratio of agricultural production to population, which has undergone drastic changes in recent times for a number of reasons. Western Europe or Japan may illustrate one aspect of this. Despite highly intensive agricultural production, these regions turned into deficit areas as a result of demographic changes. They are overpopulated from the point of view of autarky in food supply; furthermore, the secondary and tertiary occupations are so highly developed that they are able to cover the deficit in primary products through imports as long as it is possible to counterbalance it with exports of manufactured goods or with services. On the other hand, the United States, whose demographic pattern followed similar trends, still produces enough (and of some products considerable surpluses) of the basic foodstuffs, thanks to her more fortunate natural endowments and an extremely efficient agriculture. This area has a considerable surplus to offer and imports only certain products that cannot be grown there. Similarly the newly settled lands in the middle latitudes of the Southern Hemisphere produce exportable surpluses to be sold to deficit areas. Growing industrialization in these countries, however, will bring a corresponding decrease in the exportable surpluses of primary products.

Demographic and the economic changes in all these regions have moved faster and faster for the last century or two, giving rise to surplus and deficit areas in agricultural production of both foodstuffs and industrial raw materials. The more recent spreading of manufacturing industries, especially of textile manufacturing, has somewhat smoothed out regional differences in the sector of industrial raw materials. In principle, surplus and deficit areas balance each other in a free economy, since price acts as a regulator between supply and demand. Several times in the past, however, this regulator has not functioned properly, and the failures prompted planned

82

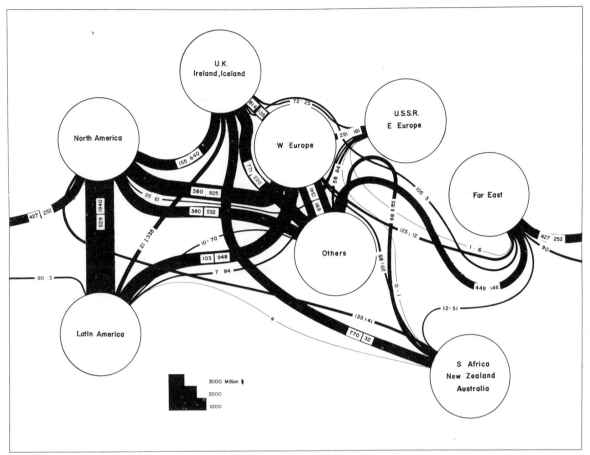

45 · INTERNATIONAL TRADE in agricultural products, 1958. The commodities composing this international trade are those in the SITC Sections 0 and 1, i.e., food, beverages and tobacco; other agricultural products, such as fibers, are excluded. This is a type of schematic presentation which is about halfway between a flow map and an abstract diagram. The figures stand for export totals in millions of U.S. dollars, e.g., 925 million dollars of exports from North America to Western Europe and 380 million dollars in the reverse direction.

production and marketing. Well known are the international regulations in wheat, sugar, coffee, etc.

Another and the most disturbing case is presented by countries which turned into deficit areas only through population increase. Most of the former colonial territories also belong to this group. Their economy shows a marked imbalance as a result of the mercantilistic economic policy which has imposed upon them the role of raw-material producers. India is the largest and most populous of this group, though there are many other countries in which the situation is qualitatively even worse. None of them, in general, has adequate export-based capacity to import.

It should never be lost from sight that certain products are grown only under specific climatic conditions. Since the major deficit areas are situated in the middle latitudes, their import needs must be satisfied primarily by middle latitude products. Yet, as has been proved by a number of cases, these may be replaced by tropical products, or a market may be created for products of tropical origin by altering dietary habits.

The most important of the middle-latitude products are the cereals. It is very significant for marketing and especially for price behavior that the growing seasons in the Northern and the Southern Hemisphere alternate. The supply of fruits and vegetables is much more stabilized now than before for the same reason, as Southern Hemisphere products reach Northern Hemisphere markets. Among the tropical products which may be substituted for middle-latitude products are cane sugar, oils and fats, and certain industrial raw materials. Bananas belong to the third group for which the market had to be created first with the help of much advertising. Similarly rice has found an expanding market in some European countries.

Agricultural Products in World Trade

The annual foreign trade of the world—measured by the total of all exports—was valued at about 100 billion dollars in the late fifties. According to the Standard International Trade Classification (SITC) employed by the United Nations, food, beverages, and tobacco are classified together. They account for about one-fifth of the total value of international trade, or if nonfood products are included, for one-fourth of the total, while chemicals, machinery, and other manufactures have an aggregate share of more than 50 percent. The role of agricultural products in international trade is therefore decidedly secondary.

The following tabulation brings out in a very simple manner the position of the major trade regions of the world. The three columns refer to the percentage share of each region (A) in world exports, (B) world imports, and (C) the difference between the two, for the SITC commodity group of food, beverages, and tobacco.

A large part of the trade in agricultural products is still carried on within the political unit. This will be indicated later by the ratio of exports to total production for particular products. As a rule this ratio is low even for major products which enter world trade, though in a few cases it reaches high values. A good many agricultural products do cross international boundaries, but trade remains within a single one of the major regions mentioned in the above table. This is particularly true in Europe, which is divided up into a large number of countries. Intra-European trade in itself constitutes more then one-tenth of the total world trade in agricultural products. In the other areas intraregional trade is smaller; nevertheless, its aggregate accounts for one-fourth of the world trade. Notable cases are trade between Mexico or Canada and the United States, Argentina and Brazil, China and Hong Kong.

In the discussion that follows only a limited number of products which play a significant role in the foreign trade of the world will be taken up. Products which do not enter into international trade in important quantities are omitted even if they may be regionally of great significance, as potatoes are in Europe, sunflower seeds in Russia, and millets in Africa.

THE MAJOR PRODUCTS

Agricultural products, food and nonfood together, make up about one-fourth of the total world trade. The following table shows the vari-

	A	B	C
North America	20	21	+1
Latin America	19	5	−14
Western Europe, incl. UK	28	51	+23
Eastern Europe and USSR	2	2	—
South Africa, Australia, New Zealand	7	2	−5
Far East, incl. China	7	5	−2
Others	17	14	−3
	100	100	

1. Cereals [wheat, rice, maize]	17%
2. Oils and fats	11
3. Meat, meat products [beef]	10
4. Milk, milk products, eggs [butter]	6
5. Tea, cacao, coffee	13
6. Sugar	6
7. Fruits, wine, tobacco	12
8. Fibers [cotton, wool]	18
9. Natural rubber	7
Total	100%

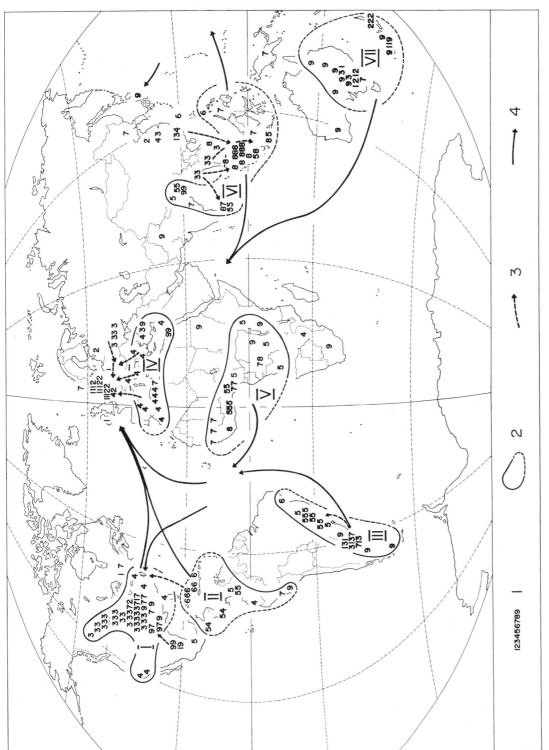

46 · AGRICULTURAL EXPORTS. (1) The numbers 1 to 9 denote groups of agricultural commodities: 1, meat and meat products; 2, milk, milk products, and eggs; 3, cereals; 4, fruits, wine, and tobacco; 5, tea, cacao, and coffee; 6, sugar; 7, oils and fats; 8, natural rubber; 9, fibers. Each number represents a total of $100 million. (2) The distribution of these numbers brings out the principal exporting areas of agricultural commodities: I, United States and Canada; II, Caribbean America and northern South America; III, Argentina–Uruguay–Brazil; IV, the Mediterranean region; V, West and Equatorial Africa; VI, South and Southeast Asia; VII, Australia–New Zealand. (3) Major intracontinental trade relations. (4) Major intercontinental trade relations. The map is based on average figures for the late fifties.

ous subgroups and their relative importance; products in brackets individually account for more than 500 million dollars worth of trade.

These groups will form the subheadings of the following discussion. Emphasis will be placed upon production and trade; the processing of agricultural products will be discussed in Chapter 9.

Cereals

The cereals are the single most important group among foods, constituting 17 percent of world trade in agricultural products. Together with starchy root crops and tubers, cereals are the filler of the stomach for the hungry population, and the proportion of cereals consumed in the daily diet may well serve as an indicator of the material standard of living. Tubers and starchy roots, though their role is of considerable importance in various diets, are negligible in international trade because their specific value is low and they deteriorate during long transportation. They are generally consumed near the place of production—potatoes in Europe, cassava and yams in tropical and subtropical countries. Grains on the other hand have a higher specific value and withstand long-distance transportation without deteriorating.

The following table shows for each of the major cereals: (A) approximate annual production in million tons during the late fifties; (B) average export price in dollars per ton, which is as a rule 10 to 20 percent higher than the local price, for 1959; (C) volume of exports as percentage of (A).

PRODUCT	A	B	C
Wheat	250	$ 62	11%
Rice	250	121	3
Rye	60	44	3
Maize	200	51	5
Barley	83	52	8
Oats	37	47	3

WHEAT

Wheat is the traditional bread grain in the Middle East, the Mediterranean, and most parts of Europe, especially in the South. Changes in food habits among many peoples have been decidedly in favor of wheat, and this cereal has found a much expanding market area. It is replacing other cereals in all parts of the world, particularly among the urban population, for example, rye in Europe, maize in Latin America, and rice in Asia. On the other hand its consumption has been declining in Europe and in the New World, especially in the United States, as a result of the gradual shift toward higher-quality foodstuffs.

Wheat is found practically all over the world, though high humidity and temperature render its production unprofitable, and owing to the long growing period required, the latitudinal and altitudinal limits of its cultivation are reached earlier than for other grains. The two main wheat-growing zones are the humid temperate middle latitudes, where it is found in combination with other crops in a rotation system, and dry-wet climates, where it is the leading crop and frequently the only one grown (monoculture). The latter zone, originally grassland and steppe, has become the major source of surplus wheat which supplies the deficit areas.

The first and for a long time the only deficit area of importance was Europe. Around 1850 the steppe lands in southeastern Russia became the chief supplier of wheat, successively followed by the North American prairies and the irrigation lands in Pakistan (then British India) after 1870, the middle-latitude countries of the Southern Hemisphere after 1880, and Canada and Siberia (the latter for the USSR and Eastern Europe) in more recent times. Secondary markets developed later in Latin America (Brazil), Pakistan, and India, the urban agglomerations in Southeast Asia and the Far East, especially Japan and coastal cities of southern China.

Some of the surplus areas disappeared in the course of time, like Pakistan and India, or declined in importance in intercontinental trade, like Argentina, South Africa, Australia, and the USSR. North America became the largest exporter as a result of a number of factors mentioned in the foregoing pages.

Since the time prior to the First World War, the world's wheat acreage has more than doubled, while yield per acre has increased by one-third.

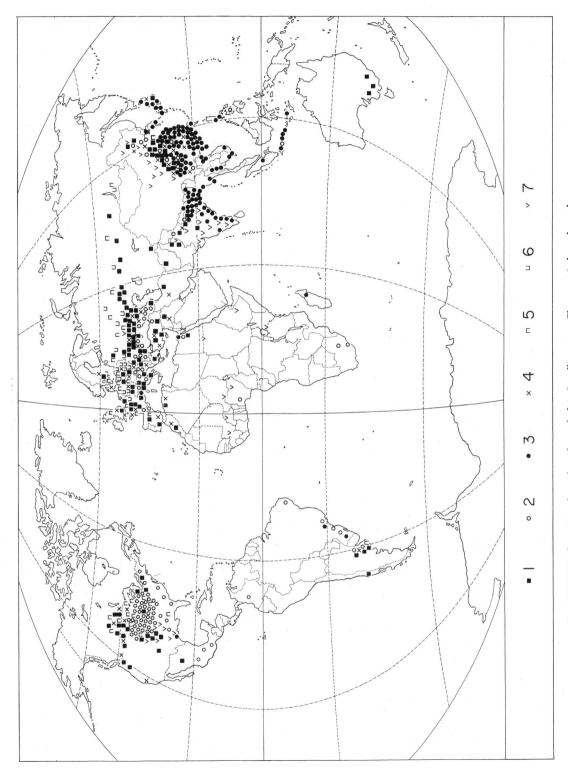

47 · GRAINS. The unit value of each symbol is 2 million tons. The map is based on the average production figures for 1957/8–1959/60. Legend: (1) wheat; (2) corn; (3) rice, expressed as paddy; (4) barley; (5) oats; (6) rye; (7) millets and sorghum.

■ 1   ○ 2   ● 3   × 4   ⊓ 5   ⊔ 6   ˅ 7

Large increases of the acreage in Canada, the Mediterranean countries and the Middle East as well as in Pakistan, India, and China were chiefly responsible for this. In Europe the area devoted to wheat has remained about the same, but yields have increased considerably. Thus increases of acreage occurred chiefly in the monocultural zone of grassland or in irrigation areas; in the zone where wheat is grown in rotation with other crops, such possibilities are limited, but yields may be increased by more intensive cultivation.

In a more detailed study of wheat, attention should be given to its different types, especially with respect to various baking qualities. Marketing of wheat is also an interesting study, for wheat exchanges are the oldest major produce exchanges where the prices are established in accordance with supply and demand, and a large part of the crops is sold in a speculative way long before it is harvested.

RICE

Rice is the staple food in the East. While wheat is processed by milling and baking and distributed to the ultimate consumer through an extended system of wholesalers and retailers, rice is only husked and polished; it is prepared daily in individual homes. Rice is also, in comparison with other cereals, a high-quality food and expensive, as is evident from the above table; even in the rice countries of the East it is sometimes beyond the reach of the poor and is more and more being replaced by bread grains and by millets.

Rice makes exacting demands with respect to temperature, sunshine, and water. Dry cultivation is rare; most rice is grown either as wet or as irrigated rice. Wet cultivation is characteristic of the monsoon countries, where the necessary water is supplied by the heavy rainfall during the monsoon season. Fields resemble those in irrigated areas; they are level and have small dikes all around to hold the water. Irrigated fields are supplied with water through canals.

Usually in wet-dry areas a single rice crop is harvested yearly. With adequate facilities of irrigation it is possible to carry out double-cropping, provided that the temperatures are high enough. Further north, as in Japan, rice fields

are sometimes replanted to a second crop in winter, for example, wheat. In many parts of Asia rice is sown broadcast and little or no fertilizer is applied; consequently yields are low. Transplanting is a step toward intensification; the seedlings, when they are four to five weeks old, are removed from the seedbeds to the fields. Usually four or five months must pass before the harvest is reaped. Heavy application of fertilizers is another way of intensifying rice production. For example, in Japan where both transplanting and heavy fertilizing are practiced, yields are about four times higher than in Burma or Thailand, the main rice-exporting countries. In all these countries much labor is involved and yet yields are low, expressed per man-hour. In some European countries, and above all in the United States, many operations have been mechanized. Instead of small terraced fields, extensive fields and few settlements are found there. As a result of heavy investment in every sector of rice production, yields per unit of area are as high as or even higher than in Japan.

Two-thirds of the world's rice acreage is still in Asia despite the fact that rice cultivation has spread all around the world. Rates of increase in acreage have been greater in non-Asian territories, especially in South America, but the highest absolute increase has occurred in Asia. There the pressing needs resulting from the continuous growth of population induced every government to give special attention to expanding the crop-bearing areas and raising yields from lands already in use. The following figures bring this to light:

	1925/29	1948/53	1959/60
World production (annual average) in million tons	75	164	258
Yields in lb/acre	1392	1427	1963

Rice trade is in the main intracontinental. The surplus areas are Burma, Thailand, some parts of mainland China (with local surplus in spots, but not China as a whole), and in normal times the countries constituting the former Indochina. The deficit areas comprise Southeast Asian countries which have devoted much of their lands to exportable products during and since the colonial period (Ceylon, Malaya, Indonesia), urban centers (Hong Kong and Singapore), as well as Japan and India-Pakistan—the latter with import necessities that vary much from one year to the next. European producers (Italy and Spain) supply the European market, which absorbs only small quantities in addition. The United States has been recently exporting increasing quantities of her surplus rice, mainly to Asian markets.

Consequently, rice trade in Southeast Asia represents one of the most important movements of agricultural commodities outside the trade orbit dominated by the Western World. It is mainly in the hands of Chinese rice merchants, and a high degree of governmental control has been exercised over it in recent years in the countries concerned.

RYE

Rye is another important bread grain. It is grown in cool temperate climates, since it is hardier and less particular about soils than wheat. It has been the traditional bread grain in northern Europe, and is traded within Europe, additional supplies coming from North and South America.

Rye bread is coarser than wheat bread and therefore less preferred by the consumer. Still, rye was the dominant bread grain in Germany as late as the 1930's. The following table shows the present situation in rye production and trade

	Western Germany	Eastern Germany	Poland	United States
Wheat:				
production	4,008	1,331	2,041	32,119
+ imports	2,547	1,235	1,258	237
− exports	28	7	—	10,029
Balance	6,527	2,559	3,299	22,327
Rye:				
production	3,804	2,244	2,056	685
+ imports	80	252	261	87
− exports	83	1	480	160
Balance	3,801	2,495	1,837	612

as compared with wheat (the annual averages for the years 1957-1959, expressed in thousands of tons).

The shift from rye to wheat as the preferred bread grain increased the dependence of the countries concerned upon imports from overseas sources. As a consequence, their governments made all sorts of attempts to check this tendency; for example, rye bread was much advertised as being healthier, or an order was imposed to mix rye flour with the wheat flour for normal daily bread.

MAIZE

Maize was the mainstay of the diet among the inhabitants of the New World at the time when the first settlers arrived there; hence the name "Indian corn." In contrast to rye, climate and soil requirements for maize are much less flexible and more exacting. Not many parts of the world possess what W. Köppen called the typical maize climate (Cfa in his systematic classification), i.e., a humid temperate climate with high summer temperatures (more than 72° F). Maize is actually grown outside of this climatic type, but the product is then either of inferior quality or used mainly for silage.

Among Indians, maize was above all for human consumption in the form of porridge (mush), as a sort of bread (tortillas), or as an alcoholic beverage. In Southern Europe maize has been particularly well known in Rumania and northern Italy, where it is eaten as *polenta*. However, by far the largest part of maize production is today used as feed for cattle, hogs, and chickens. In the United States, where nearly half of the world's maize is produced, practically all of it is consumed by livestock. Only a very small part is industrially processed into a number of products of various uses. For these reasons maize plays a relatively insignificant role in international trade.

An interesting development in recent years, also in the United States, is an amazing rise in productivity for maize. Despite a drastic reduction of the planted area, which is at present not more than it was at the turn of the century, maize production has since gone up by one-half. This is mainly the result of the successful breeding of new hybrids. No comparable development has been observed with any other grain.

BARLEY

This is one of the oldest grains used by man; it was already widespread in the Old World in neolithic times. Owing to its higher tolerance of adverse physical conditions, barley is cultivated along the peripheries of the grain culture today. It is found at the highest altitudes of the crop area and in parts of the wet-dry climate where the wet period is shortest. In the following table different grains are compared in terms of (A) the length of the growing period in days and (B) the necessary amount of heat, expressed as the cumulative of average daily temperatures during the frost-free period.

GRAIN	A	B
Spring wheat	120-140	1900-2300
Spring sown barley	80-160	1200-1800
Buckwheat (middle latitudes)	70-90	1000-1200
Subtropical millets	90-120	2000-2800

Barley is now used almost exclusively as a fodder and a raw material for the brewing industry.

OATS

In Western Europe oats had been traditionally used for making bread as well as in preparing thick porridges. Today oats serve mainly as feed. Like barley and rye, the oat plant is hardier than wheat and is found at more than 5000 feet of altitude in the Alps and 6000 feet in Asia; in northern Europe it is cultivated as far north as 66° latitude.

International trade in oats is small. It originates in North America, Argentina, and Australia and is exclusively directed to Europe.

Oils and Fats

For a number of reasons, oils and fats are interesting subjects in economic geography. Next to the grains, the supply of these basic products is most likely to create major bottlenecks in the industrialized countries of Western Europe,

necessitating large imports from other areas. The geographical structure of this commodity group, however, does not represent a simple and straightforward relationship of production–marketing–consumption.

Oils and fats are used not only as human food and animal feed, but also for technical and industrial purposes. They are obtained from both vegetable and animal sources. Most of the animal fats are produced in temperate-zone countries, while vegetable oils are more characteristic of tropical and subtropical regions; minor quantities of both sources come from the other zone, too. Oils and fats of diverse origins and hence of diverse characteristics can be processed in such a way that they become interchangeable for many purposes. Nevertheless, there are strong regional and national preferences in oils and fats for cooking. For instance, in the United States one finds a large market for vegetable shortening and coconut oil. In Europe, especially in central Europe, peanut oil (in French, *huile d'arachides*) is preferred; the particular odor of certain olive oils is associated with Mediterranean cookery, as ghee or sheep fat with the Middle East, and soybean oil with the Far East.

Final products represent many different raw materials. Processing may be done in the form of home industry, but generally it is carried on in large manufacturing establishments. International trade involves both the raw materials and the processed products, e.g., soybeans as well as soybean oil. By-products obtained in the course of processing are valuable as feed or for technical uses. Before the Second World War the United States was chiefly importing the processed products while European countries preferred to have the raw material so that the refined oil and the feed cakes could both be obtained.

Within Europe a clear distinction should be made between countries in which an intensive form of crop farming has been developed in combination with the production of livestock and other countries; for the latter import mainly oils while the former prefer the raw materials.

Besides the oil-bearing materials and the oils, the by-products of the milling process also enter international trade. These by-products, e.g., oil-

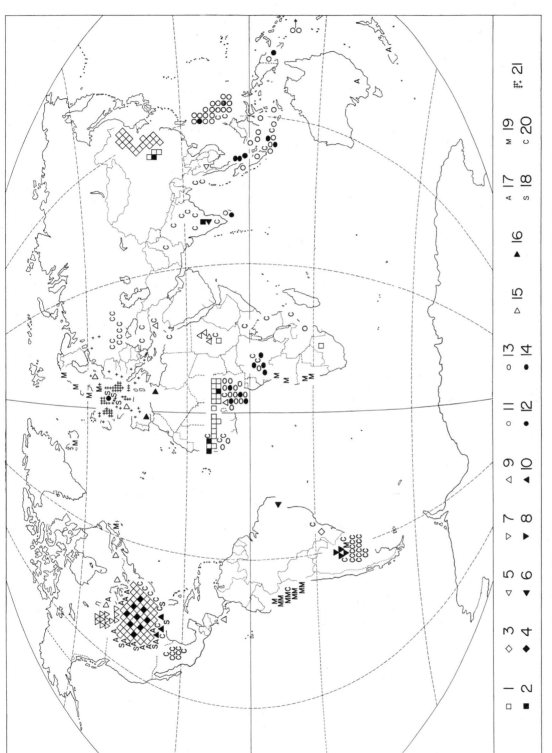

48 · OILS AND FATS. Each symbol represents 50,000 tons of exports (1957–1959 average): (1) groundnuts; (2) groundnut oil; (3) soybeans; (4) soybean oil; (5) castor beans; (6) castor oil; (7) linseed; (8) linseed oil; (9) cottonseed; (10) cottonseed oil; (11) copra; (12) coconut oil; (13) palm kernels; (14) palm oil; (15) rapeseed, mustard seed, and sesame seed; (16) olive oil; (17) animal fats; (18) lard and shortening; (19) meat and fish meal; (20) oilseed cakes and meal; (21) imports of oils and fats, expressed in oil equivalents.

seed cakes, often come from less developed countries in which oil plants are grown chiefly for human consumption of the oil obtained from them; livestock industry is either lacking or in a poor state. But the oilseed cakes which could improve such a situation are exported to better-developed countries, together with raw materials and oils.

Oils and fats are not basically different. Oils are liquid at normal temperatures while fats are solid. Through chemical processes, however, oils may be solidified or fats liquefied. They can accordingly be referred to together as the fat group, though a particular product is still called an oil or a fat.

It is hard to find a common denominator for the statistical treatment of such a diversified group of products. In accordance with the FAO statistics the volume of production or trade, expressed in tons, is here employed as the basis of comparison. The second solution would be the respective value, and the third, the oil-value or oil-weight obtained by multiplying the two other measures by a certain coefficient which varies from product to product.

Oilseed cakes and meal	4
Meat meal and fish meal	1
Lard and shortening	0.5
Groundnuts	1-1.5
Copra	1.5
Palm kernels	0.7
Soybeans	3
Linseed	0.7
Cottonseed	0.4
Castor beans	0.1
Rapeseed and mustard seed	0.2
Sesame	0.1
Animal fats	0.9
Linseed oil	0.3
Soybean oil	0.4
Cottonseed oil	0.2
Groundnut oil	0.3
Olive oil	0.1
Palm oil	0.6
Coconut oil	0.3
Palm kernel oil	0.1
Rapeseed oil	negligible
Sunflower oil	negligible
Castor oil	negligible

The accompanying map shows world production of the more important vegetable oils; the similar map for animal products is found on page 94. Whaling accounts for another small part of the total production. The contributions of these three groups to the world fat supply are approximately as follows: vegetable 74 percent, animal 18 percent, and whale oil 8 percent.

The table below lists raw materials and oil products and their approximate volume of foreign trade in million tons; it also suggests how large a variety of products make up this group.

In contrast to this bewildering array, the structure of international trade in oils and fats seems simple. Before the Second World War the two largest deficit areas were Europe and North America. About one-fourth of the total world net imports were directed to North America alone. Immediately after the war, however, its share dropped to 5 percent, subsequently disappearing completely during the fifties. European countries—and the USSR with a very small amount—remained the only importers, absorbing an increasing quantity of oil seeds, oil nuts, and oils. So far as the vegetable group is concerned, Africa moved up to first place among net exporters with more than two-fifths of the world's net exports, surpassing Asia, whose net exports declined from 50 percent to one-fourth of the world total. Another significant change in the postwar period was the emergence of North America, a former net importer, as an exporter taking equal rank with Asia. These should be regarded as significant changes in the world economic geography of commodities; the precarious position of Europe has been intensified. It relies on Africa more heavily then on any other region of the world for supplies of fats and oils, while the United States has become independent of Southeast Asian sources.

Another change of significance, though a comparatively minor one as yet, is a gradual shift in world trade from oil seeds and nuts to oils. It reflects the general trend in the producing countries toward building up their own processing industries. Trade in oil seeds and nuts was about the same at the end of the fifties as prior to the Second World War, but trade in oils increased by more than 50 percent.

Finally, a momentous change in the relative positions of products has come about through the rapid increase of the soybeans and the soybean oil in international trade. Mainland China, particularly the northern part and Manchuria, used to be the major suppliers of soybeans to the Far Eastern markets and other minor outlets. Soybean production in the United States was started in the middle twenties and rose sharply after the outbreak of the Second World War; by the end of the fifties the United States production had surpassed that of mainland China, making up about one-half of world production. Parallel to this development is the increase in soybean exports of the United States; in 1959 they were 2½ times those of China. In the case of soybean oil the supremacy of the United States is even more pronounced, since practically no oil is exported from China.

Meat and Meat Products

For this commodity group the statistics cover the animal population on the one hand and international trade in animals and animal products on the other; comparable statistics on the products as such are not available. The distribution of the various animals is presented on the accompanying map. The relationship between the natural environment and the distributional pattern is in most cases so clear that little has to be said in this respect. The different types of animal husbandry have been discussed in Chapter 4.

The amount of meat and meat products is generally proportional to the result of multiplying the number of animals by two factors—(1) a factor for rejuvenation or reproduction and (2) a factor for the weight of the animals. The weight factor shows great regional differences. The average live weight of the cattle exported from Argentina or central European countries is about half a ton per head, while the average for cattle of southern European and tropical provenance is about one-fourth to one-third of a ton. Similarly, Danish hogs weigh on the average twice as much as hogs in most other European countries, and at least three times as much as hogs of the African and Asian exporters.

The output of meat is further influenced by a third factor which fluctuates over the time. In regions where the supply of fodder varies considerably through the year, the animal population is periodically reduced in order to adjust the number of animals to the fodder available. This brings about an increase in meat output, usually accompanied by a decline in its prices. It is a regular occurrence in the middle latitudes at the beginning of the winter season, and in wet-dry climates at the beginning of the dry season. Similar but irregular are the repercussions of a shortage of fodder from natural or economic causes. In Europe, where pigs are fed with potatoes instead of maize as in the United States, another regulating factor appears, because potatoes are also valuable as human food and therefore the farmer's decision whether to sell his potatoes for human consumption or to feed them to the pigs depends upon the price relation between the two products.

The supply of meat and meat products within a given area is thus dependent on a number of factors and must be studied separately for each case. The following discussion deals only with the foreign trade.

Cattle are the most important of the livestock that enter international trade; the number and the live weight involved are about 3 million head and 1.0-1.5 million tons. Trade in cattle takes place mainly among neighboring countries. Its greatest concentration is found in Europe, where Ireland, Denmark, Austria, and Yugoslavia are the chief exporters while West Germany, the United Kingdom, and Italy (northern) constitute the importing group. In North America cattle are exported from Canada and Mexico to the United States. In Asia there are local exports from Syria to Lebanon as well as from China (and Mongolia) to the nearby countries, foremost to Hong Kong.

In hogs the predominance of intra-European trade is even more pronounced. Denmark and Sweden in Western Europe and Bulgaria, Hungary, and Poland in Eastern Europe are exporting to the adjacent countries, West Germany and Austria. The United Kingdom, a large importer of cattle, does not import hogs. In the rest of the world similar situations prevail—

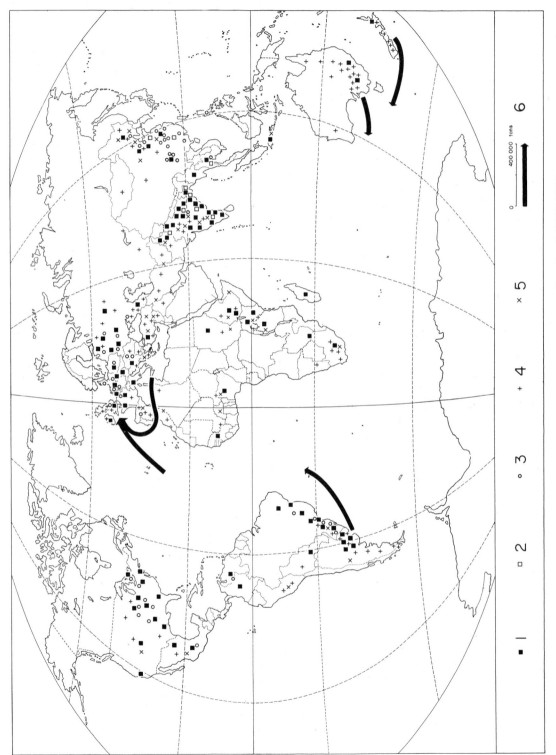

49 · LIVESTOCK. Each dot symbol from (1) to (5) represents 10 million head (1957–1959 average): (1) cattle; (2) buffaloes; (3) pigs; (4) sheep; (5) goats; (6) export trade in fresh meat, only by major exporters.

■ 1   □ 2   ○ 3   + 4   × 5   ⟶ 6

0   400 000 tons

e.g., exports from Honduras to Salvador, and from China to Hong Kong. The latter represents the most important trade relationship outside of Europe and accounts for about one-third of the world trade in hogs.

Technical advances in canning and freezing have made it possible to ship meat products over considerable distances and in consequence opened up new supply areas in distant parts of the world. Trade routes for frozen meat and meat products are longer than those for live animals.

Approximately 2 million tons of fresh meat, mostly frozen, annually finds its way into world trade. Beef and veal make up 45 percent. Practically all the imports are destined for European countries, and of these the United Kingdom is the single most important importer; the United States receives relatively small quantities. Roughly one-half of the total volume of exported beef and veal originates in Argentina and Uruguay and about one-third in Australia and New Zealand. Nearly all the mutton and lamb, which represent 20 percent of the total exports of fresh meat and meat products, comes from Australia and New Zealand, with a small addition from Argentina. They find the largest market in Europe, primarily in the United Kingdom, which absorbs practically all the mutton and lamb.

World trade in poultry, with 15 percent of the total, is mainly intracontinental, the only exception being a large flow from the United States to Europe, particularly to West Germany. Finally, pork, which ranks about equal to poultry in tonnage traded, is for the most part an intra-European trade commodity flowing from the eastern to western countries. Additional imports to Europe originate in Argentina. The only other flow of consequence is between Canada and the United States.

As in the case of oils and fats, Europe appears as the only significant deficit region which is supplied both from within, i.e., by European countries with a more agricultural structure, and from far distant sources. The trade between China and Hong Kong is statistically significant, but geographically speaking, it can be viewed as the trade between a large urban center and its agricultural *umland* and is international only by political accident.

Milk, Milk Products, and Eggs

Like sugar, dairy products constitute one of the smallest groups of agricultural commodities in world trade both in weight (2.5-3 million tons) and in value (6 percent of all the agricultural products involved). However, this does not apply to milk production itself. As with meat, production of milk may be estimated if the two factors, i.e., the number of milk-producing animals and the milk yields, are known. The milk yield varies even more than the meat yield. The average annual yield per milch cow is more than 4000 kilograms in the Netherlands and more than 2500 kilograms in most European countries; comparable yields are obtained in the United States (about 2900) while those in the USSR are somewhat lower (1800). The corresponding figures for Latin America, Asia, and Africa are 1000, 500, and less, while they again reach 1900 in Australia and 2700 in New Zealand. Israel boasts the highest yield with more than 4300 kilograms. The FAO calculated total milk production for 1959 to be 335 million tons, the bulk of which consisted of cow's milk. Note that this total exceeds that of wheat or rice.

Most of the milk is consumed on the spot or marketed within a small radius of its production. Practically no fluid milk enters international trade. In the present context we are concerned only with the processed forms of milk, i.e., condensed or powdered milk, butter, and cheese.

Probably butter presents the simplest relationships. The outstanding deficit region is Western Europe with a net import of more than 200,000 tons (this and the following figures refer to annual averages for 1956-1959). Most of this butter comes from Australia and New Zealand (combined net exports 245,000 tons). Other countries and regions represent only small fractions in the world trade of butter, either as exporters (North and Latin Americas) or importers (all the rest). The only exceptions are intraregional trade relations—e.g., between the USSR (combined exports 37,000 tons) and the countries of Eastern Europe, or Denmark and the Netherlands and other European countries. The world total of butter exports averages about 0.6 million tons per annum.

Cheese, with 0.4 million tons, ranks lower than

butter and its trade structure becomes more complex. Western Europe as a whole is a net importer. However, the difference is extremely small. Intra-European trade is lively and many-sided; France, Italy, and Switzerland join Denmark and the Netherlands with large volumes of special kinds of cheese. The United States together with Latin America and many other countries make up the rest of the net importers, while Australia and New Zealand remain the only net exporters in the world's cheese trade.

In terms of weight, condensed and powdered milk together form the most important item of the present group, with total exports of 1 million tons equally divided between the two. Large markets for these products are found in the tropical and subtropical countries of all the continents. Especially Venezuela, India, Burma, Malaya, Thailand, the Philippines, Japan, and Egypt are heavy importers. Europe is the prominent exporter of condensed milk, and North America of powdered milk. Australia and New Zealand contribute considerable quantities of both to the world export trade. By far the single most important exporter of condensed milk is the Netherlands.

Eggs are usually included in this group. International trade in eggs is considerable both in weight (about 0.5 million tons) and in value (about 300 million dollars). Unlike the other products in this group, the trade in eggs takes place mainly among neighboring countries or within a single regional unit. In Europe the flow is from Eastern Europe, the Netherlands, and Denmark into West Germany and Italy; little is directed to the United Kingdom. Small amounts are also exported from the United States, Canada, and Argentina to various countries of the Western Hemisphere and Europe. Last but not least, mainland China exports considerable quantities of fresh eggs to Hong Kong and powdered eggs to the world market in general, mostly to Europe.

Tea, Cacao, and Coffee

Sometimes these three products of tropical origin are collectively called the "colonial prod-ucts." This name characterizes them very well; for even though the crops differ in environmental requirements, the present pattern of their distribution over the world is attributable rather to colonial economic policies than to any other cause. Tea is a product of Asia, cacao mainly of Africa, and coffee almost exclusively of the Western Hemisphere. The current trend of production is to smooth out this regional division somewhat. Countries who export these products generally have a typical "colonial" structure in their export trade, i.e., their economy depends so much upon the price and marketing conditions for a single crop or limited group of crops that a sound development of the country is often hindered. These characteristics stand out more markedly in this group than in any others and therefore the products will be discussed here in particular.

Tea requires a tropical highland climate with sufficient humidity. Picking of leaves continues the whole year round and has to be done by hand. Tea production is therefore labor-intensive. The curing of tea, which may be done in different ways, takes place either in small or in large establishments. In China and Japan production of tea has traditionally been a small-scale operation. In the former colonial areas of South Asia the present structures of production have evolved according to different colonial policies—i.e., extensive commercial plantations in combination with indigenous producers in Indonesia, and mainly large estates in the former British colonies of Ceylon and India.

The table below shows an overall increase in production and the prominence of South Asia. The recent slight decline of South Asian supremacy is largely due to expanded production

	1909/13	1925/29	1948/52
Total production (1000 tons)	286	406	627
Percent in:			
Ceylon	30	25	22
India[a]	43	44	48
Indonesia	10	16	9

[a] Including all areas of former British India.

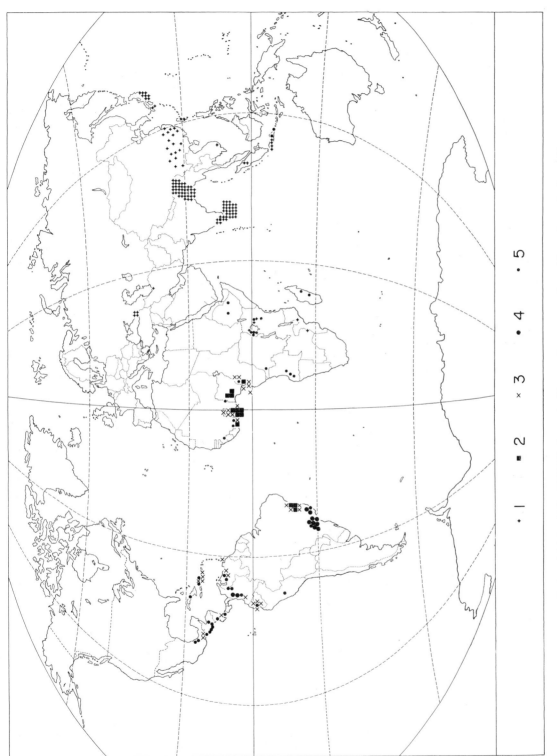

50 · TEA, CACAO, AND COFFEE. *Legend:* (1) tea, 1 percent of world total production; (2) cacao, 5 percent; (3) cacao, 1 percent; (4) coffee, 5 percent; (5) coffee, 1 percent. The world total of each product is the average of the annual totals for 1956–1959.

· 1   ■ 2   × 3   · 4   · 5

in other parts of the world; in Africa (especially Nyasaland and Kenya) and the USSR, where tea is the preferred beverage, production has increased at a rapid rate, supplementing in the USSR the traditional supply from China. China is altogether excluded from the present table because production figures for earlier years were unobtainable.

In Ceylon and India, tea still holds the first place among the export commodities. The share of tea in the national export trade was 64 percent for Ceylon and 21 percent for India (the average for 1956-59); the corresponding figure for Indonesia was but 2-3 percent. Tea is a product with an unusually large part—as much as three-quarters—of its production going into the export market. Both India and Ceylon export most of their tea production; their share among the producers and the exporters is practically the same and amounts to 70 percent.

Coffee occupies lower altitudes than tea and is found between 2,000 and 5,000 feet or even higher. In most producing countries there exists a seasonal rhythm of production which is conditioned either by the dry and wet seasons of the tropics or by influences of the extratropical winter season. Coffee may be produced on family-sized farms as in Colombia, in medium-sized to large units or so-called coffee *fincas* as in Central America, or in large plantations as in Brazil. The processing of coffee berries to render them transportable and marketable, i.e., removal of the pulp, drying, milling, and sorting, is conducted in different ways. When producing units are small, processing is generally done on a cooperative basis; such is the case in Colombia, where the Federación de Cafeteros holds a very strong place in the country's economy. The larger the size of the producing unit, the more complete will be the installations for processing to be found on the *finca* or coffee plantation. In most of the coffee-producing countries, however, the marketing of the crop for export is supervised and frequently even handled by a state organization. This is understandable: the national economy is highly dependent upon coffee exports as shown by the following list, based on averages for 1956-1959.

COUNTRY	RANK OF COFFEE AS AN EXPORT	SHARE OF COFFEE IN TOTAL EXPORT, %
Brazil	I	62
Colombia	I	76
Costa Rica	I	51
Nicaragua	I (or II)[a]	38
Honduras	II[b]	17
El Salvador	I	73
Guatemala	I	72

[a] Alternating with cotton. [b] After bananas.

These Latin American countries were together responsible for 74 percent of the world coffee supply in 1959.

One characteristic common to all the three products of this group is that they are tree crops.

	1909/13	1925/29	1948/52	1959
Total production (1000 tons)	1208	2106	2240	4605
Percent in:				
Western Hemisphere	87	90	84	82
Brazil	66	66	46	57
Colombia	4	9	16	10
Central America[a]	8	7	9	6

[a] Comprising Guatemala, El Salvador, Honduras, Nicaragua, Costa Rica, Panama.

Consequently shifts in production occur slowly. The age of a coffee tree is several decades; old trees are continually replaced and coffee areas consequently have a high degree of stability. The annual crop of coffee, on the other hand, is subject to violent fluctuations from year to year; especially in Brazil the trees are liable to damage in the early stage of the vegetation period, i.e., when they blossom, by the invasion of cold air from the south. The equilibrium between supply and demand is thus easily disturbed and large fluctuations in price result. In 1956 Brazil exported about 1 million tons of coffee valued at 1,030 million dollars; however, the 1 million tons exported in 1959 brought only 733 million dollars in return! The total economy of these countries is extremely sensitive to the behavior of coffee prices and it would be most difficult to change this economic structure within a matter of a few years.

The following table shows that coffee is primarily an American crop even though African producers (West Africa, Angola, Uganda, Ethiopia) are entering the world market with increasing quantities.

Of the three products, production of cacao has undergone the greatest areal shifts since the turn of the century. The tree was brought from the Western Hemisphere to the densely settled areas of West Africa, where the wet tropical climate at low altitudes proved to be well suited to the growing of cacao. It is now firmly established there as the following figures show:

	1909/13	1925/29	1948/52
Total production (1000 tons)	235	532	760
Percent in:			
Western Hemisphere	62	36	34
Brazil	13	13	16
Ecuador	16	4	4
Dominican Rep.	8	4	4
Africa	35	63	66
Ghana	15	43	33
Nigeria	4	8	14
S. Tomé e Principe	15	3	1

Growing cacao and processing the beans do not require large mechanical installations with corresponding capital investment; consequently, cacao culture is very well adapted to an indigenous mode of production which operates on a small scale and where the land, manpower, and trees represent the main operational capital. In West Africa the cacao-growing industry is par excellence a concern of small native growers. On the other hand, cacao trees are very susceptible to a number of destructive diseases which are difficult to control and combat in the structure of native production. Moreover, the significance of the cacao exports in the national economy (in Ghana as well as in Nigeria cacao takes first

rank among the export products, representing 56 and 20 percent, respectively, of the total value of exports average for 1956-1959) leads to repercussions from fluctuating exports which go far beyond the economic sphere.

The ratio of exports to production for cacao in quantity is over 90 percent, which gives it a unique place among the products discussed; cacao-producing countries themselves have very little use for this product and their dependence on distant market conditions is thereby increased.

Sugar

Sugar is today a very important single item in world commerce, representing 1.4 billion dollars' worth of trade (exports) or 6 percent of the total value of the agricultural exports in 1959. It occupies an important place in our diet though its consumption varies a great deal from one country to another. In the industrialized countries, per capita consumption of sugar runs from 70 to 100 pounds annually, but in the so-called underdeveloped countries it drops to 40 or 30 or even less. In the Middle Ages sugar was an item little known in Europe. Honey and other things were used instead to sweeten food and beverages. With the acquisition of colonies, first in Brazil and later in the Antilles, cane sugar began to flow into world trade in increasing quantities; it was the first product of tropical origin exported in bulk. Gradually its role changed from a luxury item to one of the daily necessities.

Sugar is the best example of an agricultural product which can be produced in the tropics as well as in the middle latitudes though based on entirely different raw materials and manufactured in very different manners.

Sugar cane—or rather sugar canes, for there are many varieties—is a product of the tropics and the subtropics. The plant requires a mean annual temperature above 70° F and an annual precipitation of 40 inches. The sugar content is considerably increased, from 9 to 15 percent, if the growth period is followed by a dry period. The latitudinal range of sugar cane culture is very wide, reaching as far north as 30° in Louisi-

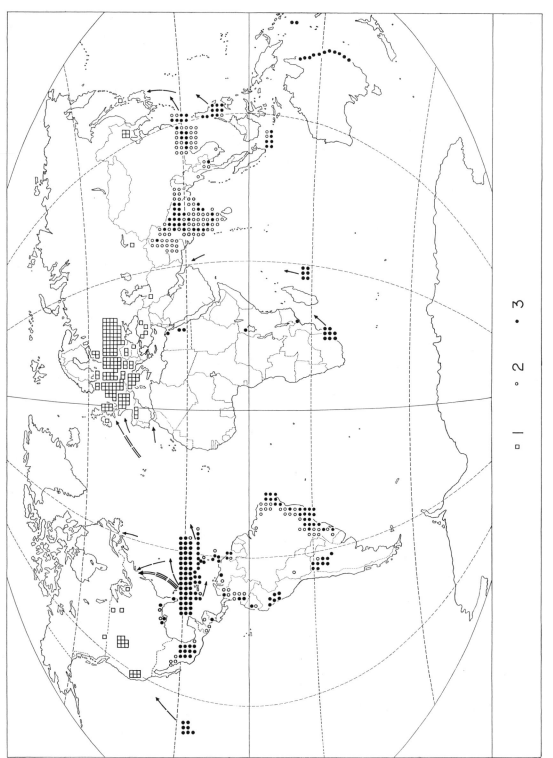

51 · SUGAR. World production of sugar cane and sugar beets as the average for 1958/9–1959/60. The unit value represented by the three symbols is varied in proportion to the sugar content of cane (12–15%) and of beets (20%). Legend: (1) production of sugar beets, each symbol representing 850,000 tons; (2) production of sugar cane used for the extraction of non-centrifugal sugar with about one-half of the efficiency of producing centrifugal sugar, each symbol representing 1,000,000 tons; (3) production of sugar cane used for the manufacture of centrifugal sugar, each symbol representing 1,000,000 tons. The arrows indicate major international trade relations, each bar representing half a million tons of sugar.

□ 1   ° 2   • 3

ana, 33° in Spain, 33° in Japan, and 30° in Natal. In the marginal zones, planting has to be done for every crop, but in lower latitudes several crops may be obtained from the same plant (ratoon crops).

The primitive way of extracting sugar is first to press the cane and then to boil down the sugary liquid until it crystallizes. This sugar is classified in the FAO statistics as noncentrifugal sugar and is known throughout the world under many different names—*panela, piloncillo,* and *chancaca* in Latin America, *gur* in India, etc. In all these countries most of the crop may be processed in this way to be locally consumed. As far as quantities are concerned, India and Pakistan are the most important producers of noncentrifugal sugar; their share of centrifugal sugar is correspondingly small. Sugar as an export commodity is centrifugal sugar, extracted and refined in large establishments where economic and technical considerations require a steady supply of cane in large quantities. Land around these sugar mills or *centrals* is therefore devoted exclusively to cane growing, whether the cane is produced by the sugar mill operators themselves or by independent growers who deliver the cane under a contract system. In some areas the cane land is intermittently used as pasture land for the draft animals, but in others it is strictly monocultural. Heavy fertilizing is therefore another characteristic.

It is well known in history how the war between England and France in the early nineteenth century cut off continental Europe from major sources of sugar and how Napoleon took the initiative in solving the problem of extracting sugar from beets. Today sugar beets constitute the second source of centrifugal sugar and are characteristic of the higher middle latitudes. Though the making of beet sugar was originally a typical European division of the world's sugar economy, it has since spread to all other middle-latitude countries, especially to the USSR, and also to the United States. Its initial objective, to make the countries in question independent of colonial sources of cane sugar, has become of less importance today. For a number of reasons the sugar beet is admirably suited to modern crop rotation and is therefore grown for other reasons

than just to secure the supply of sugar. The area from which a beet sugar mill draws its raw material has a considerable radius. Sugar beets stand long-distance transport and even prolonged storage much better than sugar cane, which deteriorates rapidly.

An important economic aspect of sugar production is that the industry yields valuable by-products—alcohol and molasses on the one hand and the refuse on the other. Sometimes the rum brings more profits than sugar. The refuse is equally important, especially in beet sugar, for the remains of the milling process are returned to the farmers to be utilized as very valuable feed.

Whether a country relies chiefly on cane sugar or on beet sugar is determined by a number of factors. Beet sugar is ruled out in all areas where sugar cane can be grown, because its cost is higher. In other areas such factors as economic policy (autarky, or national self-sufficiency) and considerations of protecting one's own colonial producers of cane sugar or of helping one's own farmers by creating a market for sugar beets and thereby improving the farming operations at the same time have played their parts to varying degrees in different countries and at different times.

The following statistical tabulation represents annual averages for the years 1957-1960.

The pattern of international trade in sugar is relatively simple. In the second half of the fifties the only large deficit areas in the world were North America, with 4.0 to 5.0 million tons of net imports, and Western Europe, with 3.5 million tons. The Middle Eastern countries also constitute a net importing area of a minor order, with 1 million tons. Europe relies for sugar supplies partly on Eastern Europe (1 million tons of beet sugar) and to a larger degree on her former colonial possessions in different parts of the world which are still within the trading orbits established by the British Commonwealth and the French Union. Additional supplies of cane sugar came from Latin America to be sold on free markets. North America, mainly the United States, depends in the first place upon Hawaii and Puerto Rico; imports from these islands are, however, not considered interna-

Total production:

Centrifugal sugar	48,060,000 tons
Beet sugar	19,770,000 tons
Cane sugar	28,290,000 tons
Noncentrifugal sugar	7,650,000 tons

Sugar cane and cane sugar (total production of sugar cane 369 million tons):

	Sugar cane	Cane sugar
North and Central America	30%	42%
Cuba	13	21
South America	22	21
Brazil	13	11
Asia	35	20
India	20	12
Pakistan	4	1
Africa	6	13
China mainland	3	1

Sugar beets and beet sugar (total production of sugar beets 147 million tons):

	Sugar beets	Beet sugar
Europe	53%	56%
Eastern Germany	4	4
Western Germany	8	7
France	7	7
Italy	6	5
Czechoslovakia	4	4
USSR	31	28
United States	10	10

tional trade by definition and are therefore excluded from the total mentioned above. Until recent years most of the sugar imported by the United States was of Cuban origin, and Cuban sugar enjoyed preferential import duties. Latin America was the major exporter, with 8.0 million tons: 5 million tons came from Cuba, 0.9 from Commonwealth territories, 0.2 from French territories, 0.6 from Brazil, 0.6 from the Dominican Republic, and 0.4 from Peru. Finally, Oceania also contributed a small share, 0.7 million tons, to world sugar exports. All the other world regions, i.e., the USSR, the Far East, and Africa, show insignificant quantities of net imports or exports and have little effect upon the international movements of sugar.

Most of the sugar moves within trading areas where some sort of preferential policy has established the relationships, and only minor quantities can be considered free-market sugar. The Cuban political problem of the 1960's had repercussions in the world economy as well as in the Cuban economy itself, in which sugar made up 72 percent of total exports by value and 65 percent of exports destined for the United States.

Fruits, Wine, and Tobacco

This is a very heterogeneous group of products and is put together here for convenience. Among the fruits that enter international trade, only bananas and citrus fruits are of outstanding importance. Together their world trade exceeds the half-billion-dollar mark, equaled by wine but surpassed by tobacco by another half billion dollars.

Citrus fruits have quite distinct locational characteristics and physical requirements. Originating on the subtropical east coast of monsoon Asia where no irrigation was required, they were introduced into the summer-dry Mediterranean regions to become irrigated crops. In the New World the corresponding locations are in Florida on the one side and California on the other. Secondary production centers in various parts of the world also belong to either one of these two major climatic types. The largest flows of citrus fruits occur mainly within two areas—from the producing regions in the United States into Canada, and from the Mediterranean region into central and northern Europe. The citrus belt of the Mediterranean regions extends from Morocco and Algeria through Spain and Italy as far east as Israel and Lebanon. Taken together, these countries constitute the major exporting area of the world. Exports in smaller quantities come from South Africa.

Bananas are grown in the tropical and subtropical lands all around the world, either with or without irrigation. They appear on local markets in many varieties, forming an important part of indigenous diets as vegetable or fruit. Bananas on world markets are of a special variety which can be harvested before it is ripe; ripening takes place during transport and storage. The variety which is marketed internationally also has to meet certain other requirements —pleasing taste, size, tough skin, etc. With the exception of the Canary Islands and West Africa (less than 10 percent of the world exports in value) exported bananas are a product of the Western Hemisphere. A few characteristic features of banana production relevant to economic geography require special mention. (1) Bananas provide an outstanding example of a tropical product for which every possibility of advertisement was exploited to create a market in the middle latitudes. (2) Commercial banana production is virtually monopolized by large, foreign-controlled companies outside of the countries of production. The local price for bananas is so low that it does not pay for independent producers to grow bananas for sale unless they are subsidized in some way or other, usually by the banana companies themselves, which in this manner provide for additional sources of production. Profits are made on the way to the consumer after bananas have left the country of production. (3) Bananas are generally grown by the large companies in monocultural form. In Central America they are so much affected by two virulent diseases (sigatoka and Panama disease) that a plantation must be abandoned after five to fifteen years. Therefore these companies are always in need of large land reserves which are for the moment unused. Another consequence is that banana production shifts rapidly from one area to another within a country, and also from one country to another. (4) Bananas are grown in hot lowlands not far from the ports of shipment. Before the banana-growing venture was started, these lowlands had been practically uninhabited because of their unhealthy conditions. The banana companies made an enormous investment in the way of building settlements, railroads, etc., as well as bringing in workers by the thousands. All these characteristics throw light on the reasons why banana companies are often bitterly attacked by nationalists and unions despite their enterprise and economic importance and why the stigma of colonialism is upon them, whether justifiably or not.

Grapes and wine are interesting for two reasons, i.e., the structure of their production and processing and the distribution of the industry.

Grapes are grown for immediate consumption, for the preparation of raisins, and for wine. World production is succinctly presented in the following table.

	GRAPES	GRAPES FOR WINE	WINE	RAISINS
Total world production (1000 tons)	41,050	31,000	22,300	650
Europe	64%	74%	72%	23
France	18	22	21	—
Italy	22	27	26	a
Spain and Portugal	10	13	12	—
Algeria	5	6	7	—
United States	6	4	4	—
Argentina	5	4	7	—

a Greece 21, Iran 10, Australia 13.

Even more noteworthy are the facts about the international wine trade. France, generally considered to be a wine-exporting country, actually accounts for only 5 percent of the total world exports while taking in 62 percent (!) of the total world imports. In absolute quantity, this means 20-40 million gallons of wine exported from France against 350-450 million gallons imported. The most important wine-exporting country is Algeria, with a share of 48 percent; 4 percent comes from Morocco and an equal amount from Tunisia. Italy contributes 6 percent, Portugal and Spain 7 percent each to the total wine exports. These are the only countries which yearly exported more than 22 million gallons of wine (1 million hectoliters) between 1957 and 1960. On the importing side, West Germany is a distant second after France, with 11 percent; Switzerland ranks next, with 4 percent. All other countries import less than 22 million gallons.

Only one-fifth of the total volume of tobacco production moves into the channels of international trade as unmanufactured tobacco. Europe is the only major importing area, followed by the USSR and Australia by a wide margin. The exporting countries can be grouped according to the kind of tobacco they produce. The most important group, which accounts for one-third of the world exports, consists of Turkey, Bulgaria, Greece, and Yugoslavia, exporting the Balkan type of tobacco much preferred by many European cigarette smokers. The other group is the United States (about one-fourth), which exports tobacco of the Virginia type also to Europe. Minor exporters are Cuba (until recently exporting to manufacturing plants in the United States, mostly in Florida), Brazil, and mainland China (exporting to neighboring countries, especially to the Soviet bloc). Finally Rhodesia-Nyasaland has been exporting significant amounts in recent years.

Rubber

Natural rubber is obtained from the tree *Hevea brasiliensis,* indigenous to the Amazon Forest. It was introduced into other parts of the world and has been improved by scientific breeding to yield a maximum amount of latex. Around 1880 the first seedlings were brought from Brazil via London to botanical gardens in Ceylon and Singapore. This was the beginning of the rubber plantation industry in Southeast Asia, where *Hevea* found excellent soil and climatic conditions. The rise of the automobile industry after the turn of the century created new needs for natural rubber and a rapidly expanding market.

The mode of rubber production is of three types: (1) wild rubber, which is collected from natural stands in the tropical forest; (2) native production by small holders; and (3) plantation industry. The first type played an important role in the last century and made a come-back during the Second World War under the emergency when the rest of the world was cut off from Asian supplies by the Japanese occupation of the supply area. But collecting wild rubber is an inefficient and uneconomic mode of production and the quality of rubber is inferior. Native production is possible in conjunction with subsistence farming; therefore it is frequently found as a cash crop in the rice-centered kampong economy of Malaya and in Indonesia. Rubber trees may be planted on hillsides, which are

otherwise unutilized. The latex can be processed by native farmers into rubber sheets with a minimum of technical experience and capital, and thus they obtain a marketable product. For plantation production, large capital investment is necessary; that is why most rubber estates are either European or Chinese concerns. The laborers on these plantations work for wages and purchase part of their food. The latex is collected from the rubber trees every morning. It is immediately treated and made into rubber sheets. Plantation rubber is of superior quality and fetches higher prices. Today more and more latex is shipped as it is, without being coagulated, and processed to special-quality rubber in the industrialized countries. The different reactions of the plantations and the native producers to rubber price fluctuations have been discussed above.

In one respect rubber production differs from other tree cultures, e.g., coffee. The output of latex can be regulated by increasing or reducing tapping within certain limits set by the number of producing trees. For production to be stepped up beyond this point, at least several years are required before newly planted trees become ready for tapping. If the imbalance between supply and demand is caused by an oversupply of rubber, it may be corrected by controlling production through a joint effort of the producing countries. Two-thirds of the world's natural rubber is produced in the Federation of Malaya and in Indonesia, or 90 percent in Southeast Asia. This whole region used to be a colonial realm before the Second World War, with the exception of Thailand, and agreement on a restrictive policy was not difficult among the interested parties. After 1922 restrictions of exports had to be imposed in the form of various regulating plans and schemes in order to assure a supportable minimum price and to safeguard the rubber industry as well as the economy of the colonial territories concerned.

During the Second World War supplies of natural rubber virtually ceased and most of the world had to resort to secondary or synthetic rubber. The synthetic rubber industry, which is based on oil, natural gas, or coal, will be discussed in Chapter 9. It was highly developed in

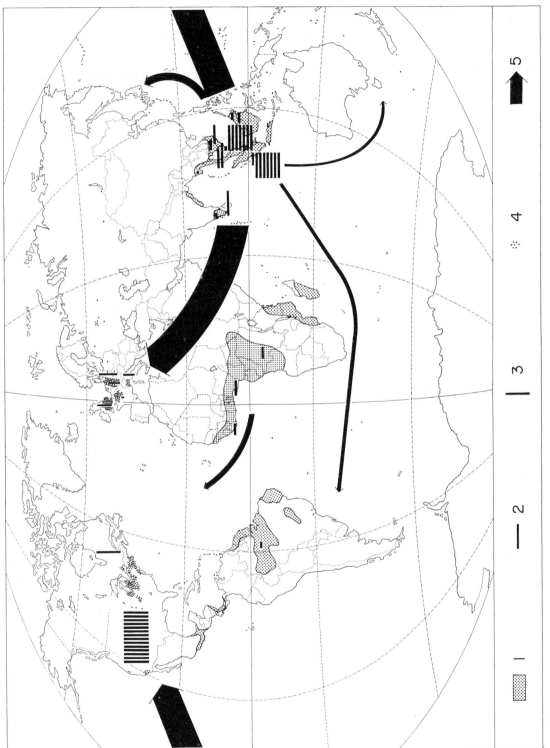

52 • RUBBER: production and trade. *Legend:* (1) areas of natural rubber production, after *Inst. Int. d'Agricult.* (FAO), 1944; (2) production of natural rubber in 1959 (one bar = 100,000 tons); (3) production of synthetic rubber in 1959 (one bar = 100,000 tons)—data incomplete, especially for the Soviet Bloc; (4) automobile production in 1959 (one dot = 50,000 motor vehicles); (5) world trade in rubber, relative importance indicated by the width of the arrows.

the United States. After the war synthetic rubber production was at first much curtailed, since the Asian producers of natural rubber were again able to supply the world market. This shift back to natural rubber was motivated by economic and political reasons. The countries in the rubber-producing area had meanwhile attained independence and their national economy was heavily dependent on the export of such commodities as natural rubber. In Malaya the share of rubber in the national export trade was 63 percent, in Indonesia 40 percent, and in Ceylon 17 percent (1956-1959). Furthermore, as most of the rubber was sold to the United States, the returns from this transaction constituted one of the major sources of dollar earnings for the Commonwealth. These rubber-producing countries preserve to a remarkable degree the colonial economic structure and suffer from price fluctuations in the same manner as the Latin American coffee countries.

While the unbalanced situation of supply and demand in the interwar years was mainly a result of the overproduction of natural rubber, the present cause of high instability lies just in the opposite direction: supply falls short of rising demands. Consequently rubber prices have increased considerably and so has the danger that synthetic rubber may invade the world market hitherto reserved for natural rubber. Production of natural rubber remained more or less stationary during the fifties at 2 million tons; new plantings do not become effective before several years have elapsed. In consequence, the share of synthetic rubber in total rubber marketed has risen rapidly, surpassing that of natural rubber in recent years. Synthetic rubber has certain technical advantages. It is also cheaper and prices are stable. In certain sectors of industry it has completely eliminated the natural product, for example, in the chewing gum industry.

A comparative tabulation of recent rubber prices sheds light upon the problems touched upon above; (A) represents the wholesale price of rubber smoked sheets No. 1 (RSS. No. 1) in New York, (B) the same for No. 3 blanket crepe, and (C) the price of standard quality synthetic rubber, f.o.b. (free on board) at plant in the United States.

PRICES OF RUBBER IN CENTS PER KILOGRAM			
YEAR	A	B	C
1950	90.6	82.1	41.9
1951	130.3	109.2	55.1
1952	85.1	67.7	51.8
1953	53.4	46.8	50.7
1954	52.0	50.0	50.7
1955	86.3	72.7	50.7
1956	75.4	63.3	52.5
1957	68.8	61.6	52.7
1958	62.0	51.9	52.7
1959	80.7	76.7	52.7

Fibers

In value of output, fibers constituted the largest group among all agricultural products, with a share of 18 percent. The output comprises a large variety of fibers which differ widely in export price and quantity as shown in the following table. The table contains, for each fiber, (A) the average export price per ton in U.S. dollars; (B) the percentage share in the value of world exports of the fibers listed, which amounted to 3,966 million dollars; and (C) the percentage share in the volume of world exports of the fibers listed or 6,609,000 tons; all the figures are for the year 1959.

As the table shows, cotton and wool are of outstanding importance. They are high-value products providing the bulk of textile raw ma-

53 · COTTON AND WOOL. Symbols with the same unit value are used on both maps so that they are strictly comparable. *Legend:* (1) production of raw material, one dot = 50,000 tons; (2) production of yarn, one square = 50,000 tons; (3) import or export of raw materials, one bar = 250,000 tons. *Note:* Raw cotton is calculated on the ginned basis and wool on the greasy basis. For wool exports, however, the wool clean basis had to be employed without changing the unit value.

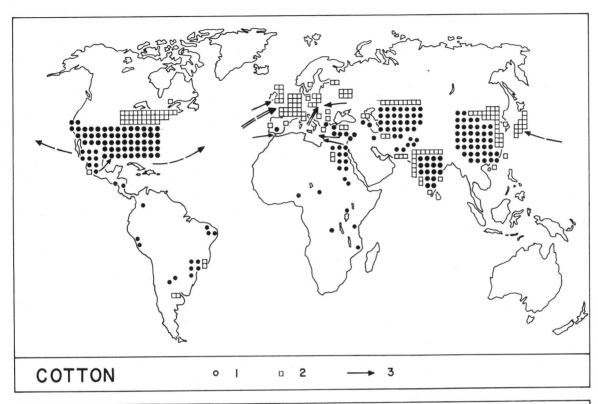

COTTON   ○ 1   □ 2   ⟶ 3

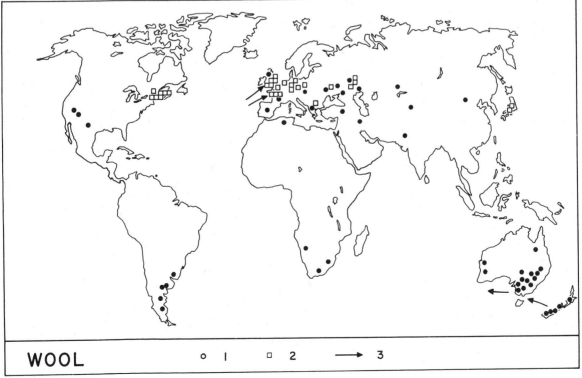

WOOL   ○ 1   □ 2   ⟶ 3

FIBER	A	B	C
Silk, raw	8363	2.1	0.1
Wool, greasy	1088	33.9	18.7
Wool, scoured	1457	7.7	3.2
Cotton	569	46.4	49.0
Jute	177	3.9	13.2
Flax (excluding straw)	290	1.6	3.4
Hemp	265	0.5	1.0
Sisal and other agave fibers	173	2.8	9.7
Abaca	375	1.1	1.7

terials. Their aggregate share in the total export value is seen to be considerably higher than in volume. In fact, silk ranks highest in value, but it has been practically eliminated from international trade as a result of competition from artificial fibers. The other fibers furnish raw materials for coarse textiles, ropes, etc.; not only are they of less importance in both value and quantity, but the relationship of (B) to (C) is the reverse of what it is for silk and wool; cotton holds an intermediate position.

The relationship of natural fibers to artificial or man-made fibers as well as the processing of these fibers will be taken up in Chapter 9. Consequently the present discussion is brief, especially since the regional distribution of production and major trade flows of cotton and wool are clearly indicated on the accompanying map.

Cotton is a product of tropical and subtropical agriculture. Commercial cotton growing is largely confined to regions in which the duration of the frost-free season is at least 220 days. Where there is a combination of high temperature and heavy precipitation, as in the South Atlantic states of North America, monsoon countries, wet-dry regions of the outer tropics, or equatorial regions, cotton requires no irrigation. In a summer-dry climate or where precipitation is not sufficient, compensating facilities for irrigation are necessary, as in California, the Southwest of the United States, the Middle East, and Pakistan. This difference cannot be overrated in a geographical appraisal of the cotton-growing industry because it involves significant differences in its regional organization and hence in its economic and social structure. Immediately after the cotton is picked, it is usually treated in a cotton gin, a machine which separates the seeds from the cotton fiber or lint. Production statistics of cotton refer to the production of cotton lint, which makes up approximately one-third of the picked cotton by weight but is sold for about three-fourths of the combined value. Cottonseed yields many products—cottonseed oil, feed cake, and others.

Cotton is classified into many types according to specific qualities. The most important basis is the length of the staple, for it influences the spinning process. Short staples make a thick yarn, and very short staples are not spinnable, but can be used only in manufacturing felts. Fineness of a yarn is measured by "counts," i.e., the number of hanks (840 yards for cotton yarn) per pound of weight; hence the higher the count, the finer the yarn. Typical examples are given in the table.

COUNTRY	VARIETY	STAPLE LENGTH IN INCHES	COUNTS
United States	Sea Island, S.C.	2	300
	Georgia and Florida	$1\frac{5}{8}$	200
	Upland middling	1	40
India	Average	$\frac{7}{8}$	30
China	Average	$\frac{3}{4}$	20
Egypt	Sakellaridis	$1\frac{1}{2}$	150

Together with other characteristics like luster and color, the staple length largely determines the price and the end-use of cotton lint.

A noteworthy development in recent decades has been the diffusion of cotton production and manufacture of cotton textiles from original centers of early industrialization toward less-developed countries in subtropical and tropical regions. In quantity, the outstanding example is India, and to some degree Pakistan; these countries used to be important exporters of cotton but are now beginning to draw on external sources of raw material for their textile industry. In other places the domestic production of cotton can still supply the fast-growing regional textile industry, but export possibilities are being greatly reduced, as in Latin America (except Mexico) or Egypt. This is revealed in the following table, which summarizes the content of the accompanying map, listing by continents the percentage shares in the world totals of cotton production, exports, imports and cotton goods manufacturing.

Wool is a traditional apparel fiber in cooler

REGION	PRODUC-TION	EX-PORTS	IM-PORTS	MANU-FACTURING
North America	29.2%	25.8%	3.2%	21.6%
Latin America	18.9	22.8	1.4	2.1
Western Europe	1.6	1.8	45.0	21.1
Eastern Europe and USSR	14.6	10.7	19.2	19.4
Asia excluding China	13.3	12.0	28.8	20.3
China mainland	22.2	2.5	1.3	14.0
Africa	8.2	24.4	.5	1.3
Oceania	0	0	.6	.2

climates. Its production and manufacture are conspicuously absent from low-latitude zones. Australia and New Zealand stand out among the exporters of raw wool; minor quantities come from South Africa and Argentina. On the importing side Europe, especially the United Kingdom, is prominent, followed by the United States, Japan, and the USSR.

Flax grown for fiber is almost exclusively a crop of Western and Eastern Europe, including the USSR, where more than half of world production originates. Hemp is grown for seed and for fiber; in fiber production we observe about the same distributional pattern as for flax, though hemp is found in a more southerly and warmer zone stretching from the Balkans to southern Russia. Jute is centered in East Pakistan and Bengal, and an important secondary center is found in southern China (Chekiang). Most of the abaca comes from the Philippines. Small quantities come from Central America, where abaca plantations were laid out during the war when supplies from South Asia were curtailed. Sisal is produced in a number of regions, all of them climatically or edaphically dry, but favored by high temperatures; centers are the Yucatan Peninsula, Tanganyika and Kenya, Angola, and the northeast of Brazil.

6 | METHOD IN GEOGRAPHY

O N T H E B A S I S of the foregoing topical and regional discussions the present chapter summarizes some methodological principles of economic geography, also applicable to the discussions in Part Two and Part Three, reviews some fundamental problems of economic geography, and defines our study in more precise terms than in the Introduction.

PRINCIPLES OF A GEOGRAPHIC INVESTIGATION

The Object

The concept of the *geosphere* and its components was expounded in Chapter 1, and our discussion has stressed the importance in a geographic investigation of considering interrelations among the various spheres. No study which singles out one sphere or one component part can rightly be considered geographical even if such work is carried out by geographers in the course of preliminary analysis, as often happens.

A geographer is trained and will use a method which consists essentially of analysis and synthesis. Analysis establishes the distribution and the properties of particular geospheric elements within the various spheres, their changes under the influence of geospheric controls, and their interrelationships. Synthesis, in contrast, implies viewing all the component parts together and understanding the complex as a whole.

The geosphere, then, is the object of geography. As such it is of global extent. There is as yet no generally accepted concept for parts of the geosphere. Such parts may be continents, countries, smaller areas, or even single locations. The tern *geomer* (from the Greek word *meros*, a part) was proposed and its use has been found helpful in methodological discussions.

Space and Time

The geosphere is a three-dimensional unity and consequently has a three-dimensional structure. Texture, on the other hand, refers to the arrangement of one element or a combination of elements on one plane, usually the horizontal one. However, the geosphere has also a fourth dimension, viz., time. It is undergoing unceasing changes under the influence of factors, some of natural origin and others attributed to man. A full understanding of the geospheric structure cannot be attained merely through the knowledge of the actual situation. We recognized, for example, the existence of young and old landscapes and distinguished between some that change rapidly and others that change at a slower rate. Extrapolation on the basis of past and present trends of landscape development renders possible a certain amount of prognosis or forecast—in other words, contributes to scientific regional planning.

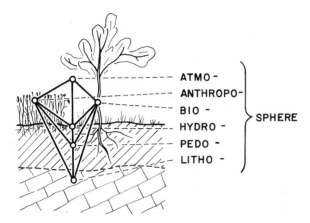

54 · GEOSPHERIC STRUCTURE. The various elemental spheres (indicated by the circles) and their interrelations (indicated by the heavy solid lines). Other instances where one or more spheres are missing could easily be imagined. For example, the absence of the anthroposphere would result in a so-called natural landscape, and the absence of all but hydrosphere and atmosphere would create a landscape that may be found at the North Pole.

Systems or Points of View

Geographical investigations fall under many systems which, while not differing from one another with respect to the object of study, examine it from different points of view. One such system is economic geography, within which agricultural geography forms a subsystem. The system or point of view determines which of the various geospheric parts primary attention is directed to and serves as a guiding principle for the selection of the relevant facts.

Scientific Order and Scientific Working Methods

It was stated in the Introduction that students of economic geography are acquainted with the use of certain common concepts and working methods. We must admit, however, that this is only partially true at present. There exist no generally accepted and standardized methods such as are known in other scientific disciplines. Almost every geographer develops his own individual method and a good deal of discussion is expended on defining concepts, methodological problems, and the like.

In a general way we can recognize two types of geographers. Those of the first type favor the *idiographic* approach and study the peculiarities of particular regions and places. On the whole this approach is characterized by the subjective evaluation of a situation and a free selection of working methods. The other approach may be called *nomothetic* (Greek, "establishing law"); its principal characteristic consists in standardized methods of research which guarantee the comparability of results obtained by different investigators and quantification of significant traits.

So far all attempts to set up generally acceptable working rules and a taxonomic order of geomers have failed. The reason for this may rest with the geographers themselves or with the peculiarities of the object of geographic research; no attempt is made here to give a conclusive opinion to this matter. However, the students of a younger generation will undoubtedly be thrown into these discussions in time to come and will have to find their own ground.

As to this apparent dichotomy in geography, the author is of the following opinion. There is no doubt but that a nomothetic approach would greatly enhance the scientific prestige of geography, especially among natural scientists, economists, and engineers; however, it goes far beyond expressing trivialities in the form of equations! One of the greatest advantages of the nomothetic approach seems to lie in the fact that the diverse results of different workers become directly and numerically comparable, thus enabling one result to be added to another. A scientific order which is sound and objective may be ultimately achieved in this way. Attempts in this direction have been made in various fields of geographical research with fruitful outcomes. They are usually restricted to studies in which a large number of individual cases are to be examined, or to relatively simple or elemental sectors of the analysis. However, regional studies deal, generally, with a small number of cases and a highly complex structure which virtually excludes generalization and defies numerical evaluation and the establishment of general laws that can survive the test of practice. The best regional studies are idiographic and the best geographers have used their subjective but sound judgment to the fullest extent. Neither of the two approaches should exclude the other; each should be used according to the circumstances. Geography is a complex science and cannot measure with one scale only.

There is one last remark to be made: whether one approaches a problem quantitatively or approaches it qualitatively has no influence upon the scientific nature and value of geographic research. Our findings are not more and not less scientific whether they are expressed numerically or not.

ANALYSIS

The meaning of geographic analysis can best be understood by considering first the difference between a sum and a whole. If two or more values are added together the total is called a sum; the value of a sum is not more than the total value of all the component parts. The whole, however, is something more than the sum total; it includes a certain new value that has been created through assembling the parts into a complete organization; this value is lost when the whole is dissociated into its components. Other terms which are equivalent to *sum* and *whole* are *totality* and *unity,* respectively.

The geosphere is most certainly a whole and not just the sum total of its elemental or component parts. In any geographic analysis not only the individual component parts but their interrelation and interdependence are also studied. Analysis of the latter brings to light the newly added value of a whole which is responsible for the specific character of the geosphere.

This consideration explains in a very simplified manner why geographic analysis consists of two steps, (a) analysis of component parts or elemental analysis and (b) analysis of their mutual relationships. Obviously, the first procedure frequently leads to the recognition of distributional patterns or textures, while the second provides a clearer understanding of the geospheric structure.

We have already been concerned repeatedly with the two basic aspects of regional economic geography. The one had to do with the way man organized his economic activities. Different localities and areas were evaluated with respect to their functions in a far-reaching organizational pattern—for example, as producing or consuming regions, as marketing and transshipment places, or as collecting or distributing centers. The other aspect was the geospheric structure at a given place—specifically, its typical characteristics and their areal extension, yielding a regionalization quite different from the first one. Two different approaches are used for the study of these two aspects; the first we called the functional approach and the second the formal approach. These two approaches constitute the primary divisions of our analytical study.

The Study of Functional Aspects (Functional Approach)

The functional aspects within a given area should be studied by methods that are specifically adapted to that approach. The economic organization of an area is usually not visible and hence cannot be inferred from maps or by mapping using the standard procedures in the field. Instead the information is obtained from interviews and from statistical and other documentary sources.

This limitation of sources may be illustrated by a simple example. A detailed mapping of a countryside depicts the correct locations of crop fields, forests, houses, etc., but it offers no clue to the actual organization of the area's agricultural economy. In order to record the ownership of crop fields, for example, it becomes necessary to interview informants. In a map the fields that belong to the same operator may be represented by a certain color to identify a particular functional aspect. However, such a map is basically different from a land-use map of the conventional type.

It is not difficult to cite many other examples illustrating the same characteristic approach. It would apply to delineating the milkshed of a metropolitan area or to differentiating the food surplus and deficit areas of the world. Functional relationships are of many different orders.

Some are only of local importance; others extend over the entire earth. If they are studied systematically, a certain order may be seen to emerge out of high complexity. All the functional relationships together form what is called the functional structure.

Historical development has drawn the center of gravity within the functional structure toward ever higher levels in modern times. In the less developed countries characteristically the lower orders of the functional structure prevail.

In most countries the lowest level of the agrarian functional structure is represented by the individual farms, but in parts of the world where the land is communally or collectively tilled, the lowest level may be the tribal domain or the village area, which is usually part of the second platform that extends above and over the farm level. In the feudal period of Europe the functional structure terminated at the level fixed by the relationship between agriculturists and landlord, at least for the bulk of agricultural production. Modern developments have added new and higher levels, regional, national, and international in character. Within the functional structure an individual operates simultaneously on different levels, for he is connected with and dependent on more than one point of the whole system.

Comparatively speaking, agriculture shows a functional structure in which the lower levels are preponderant, while the secondary and tertiary occupations are characterized by a functional association that is not only more complex but also rapidly establishing itself on higher levels. This is particularly true of areas where a simple subsistent agricultural economy prevails. The case of sugar production may be recalled in this connection. Wherever a larger portion of the harvested cane is used to produce noncentrifugal sugar, the center of gravity in the functional structure of the area it at the lower levels. On the other hand, in a country like Ceylon where agricultural production is highly export-oriented, the level stands very much higher as far as agriculture is concerned.

In agricultural geography most of the functional studies are concerned with the following problems:

- On the level of individual farms; the operational units.
- Local markets for agricultural products, city supply areas, etc.
- Functions of agricultural regions in the matrix of national economy.
- International trade in agricultural products.

The Study of Formal Aspects (Formal Approach)

The study of the formal aspects of an agrarian landscape follows two different lines. One is to study a given locality as a geospheric whole and to proceed from there to a differentiation of the earth's surface into regions of varying sizes. The other is to dissociate the geospheric whole into its various spheres and further into component parts of each sphere and to study their distribution. The two methods of investigation have been employed by geographers to about an equal degree.

In the first approach, the particular geospheric elements of a given site are uncovered and their mutual relationships established; taken together they form the geospheric structure of that particular place. Such geospheric elements comprise topography, soils, hydrological conditions, atmosphere, various biotic spheres, anthroposphere, etc. This complex structure, undergoing changes affected by the two sets of factors, the natural and the human, tends to attain a state which might be termed, to use a biological analogy, the climax of the geosphere at this site. The whole structure may be thought of as an experimental model in which different states are obtained by changing the operations of the factors.

By pursuing an investigation of as many localities as possible, we will come to possess a large collection of the results of topological studies. At this stage it will become necessary to bring scientifically sound order into the collected material by selecting meaningful criteria.

ITALY   JAPAN   U.S.A.

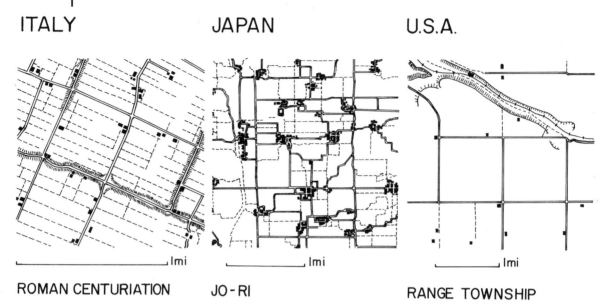

ROMAN CENTURIATION   JO-RI   RANGE TOWNSHIP

Topographical maps, and R. Hall, 1931/2

55 · SETTLEMENT PATTERNS in different parts of the world. The three plats show rectangular field patterns which are in many respects alike. Yet they represent wholly independent developments and may therefore be termed the "formal convergence." The example on the left is from Bagazzano (Bologna), Italy, a very pure relic of Roman centuriation. The center is a typical Jo-ri pattern in the Yamato basin south of Nara. The situation in Grant County, Washington, is shown on the right. One should observe the varying scale and the density of farming settlements. In Bagazzano each cluster is an individual farmstead consisting of a few buildings, while in the example of the Yamato basin such a cluster represents a village of fifteen to twenty family units.

For economic geography, here are a few criteria that permit generalization of a mass of individual cases. (1) Sites may be first sorted out into two groups distinguished by the presence or absence of the anthroposphere, i.e., into natural landscapes and humanized landscapes. (2) Further differentiation is made according to the intensity of the human influence in humanized landscapes and according to potential economic use in natural landscapes. Sorting our site studies in this way will eventually lead to systematic regionalization based on a standardized method and a meaningful principle according to which we replace the individual by the type.

Another procedure has proved helpful for practical work. It is well known in the United States under the designation *fractional-code system* and its ultimate goal is to recognize the so-called *unit areas*. First a set of geospheric elements are selected for observation and then a scale for measuring is assigned to each of them. According to the fractional-code system physical elements are expressed as the denominator, and human elements as the nominator. The association of phenomena at a given location is thus expressed by an abbreviated code-symbol. In order to avoid any misunderstandings we should realize that such a fractional notation does not possess any mathematical qualities. It serves only as a quick and efficient way to record the results of a field investigation. All the places with the same code figures are considered to represent an identical association of phenomena. By a process of gradual generalization we can proceed from the first code-types, obtained by field observation, to more general types and in this way establish a hierarchical order of landscape types. Similarly we can then delineate unit areas for the different stages of generalization.

However, we should observe that any regional

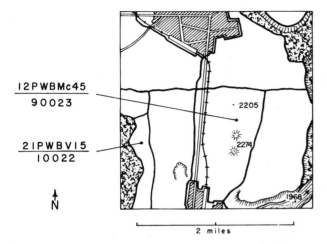

I2PWBMc45
90023

2IPWBVI5
I0022

↑
N

2 miles

After Kirchen, 1949

56 · AN EXAMPLE of the unit-area method, taken from Bonaduz in the Grisons, Switzerland. The land use is noted above the line and the physical conditions below the line. For example, the unit area on the left is characterized by the following features: *above the line* (2) mainly grass, (1) crop fields in addition, (PWBV) potatoes, wheat, barley, vegetables, (1) fruit trees, (5) yields good average; *below the line* (1) flat, (0) no surface water, (0) no unproductive land included, (2) stoniness medium, (2) soil depth 1-2 feet. The unit area on the right situated in the middle of a large alluvial plain about 250 feet above the main river differs from the first in the following respects: the ratio of crop land to grassland is reversed; maize and colza are added to the crops; fruit trees are only a few; small hills in the plain form a characteristic land-form feature; the soil depth is less than 1 foot.

method such as this depends on selecting criteria relevant to a purpose. No regional system is self-determined or innate in the geosphere; any system is a result of our intellectual work. We are in full agreement with R. Hartshorne when he declares (*The Nature of Geography*, 1939): "The regional entities which we construct on this basis are therefore in the full sense mental constructions; they are entities only in our thoughts, even though we find them to be constructions that provide some sort of intelligent basis for organizing our knowledge of reality." Regional entities are thus like time periods in historical or geological studies. The fact that they are mental constructions in no way disqualifies them for status on a par with the concrete subject matter of most systematic sciences.

With this second procedure the investigation goes further to analyze the geosphere along various planes or spheres. Studies relating to geomorphology, climatology, etc., using a procedure such as has been described above for integrated geospheric studies, are included here. Excellent examples of such works are the geomorphological division of the United States by Fenneman and the climatological systems by W. Köppen and W. Thornthwaite.

Another group of examples are found in the study of settlements, which has received much attention of geographers. Field patterns have already been mentioned. They have proved to be a particularly informative source for understanding certain areas. Equal in value are the settlements themselves, which may be studied with regard to the component parts (individual buildings) or as a totality, projected on a vertical plane or on a ground plan. Settlements and fields are outstanding examples for the process of typification; typical field patterns and forms of settlements have been distinguished in many parts of the world, though a world-wide comparative study is still lacking that would warrant a world classification into types.

SYNTHESIS

The analytical method provides an understanding of the functioning of the geosphere; yet the very essence of geographic work is synthetic. Geographic training urges the students at all steps to go beyond analysis. In this respect geography holds a position that differs a great deal from the general trend in scientific research in modern times. Human knowledge is now so vast that advances can come about only through intensifying specialization. The further we progress in scientific research, the more important the role of the specialist becomes.

Current geographic publications on methodological problems frequently support the opinion that the geographer should follow this general trend and become a specialist in a certain field in order to gain scientific recognition. Seldom do geographers succeed, however, in competing with real specialists, either because they may be lacking in the expert knowledge and training of

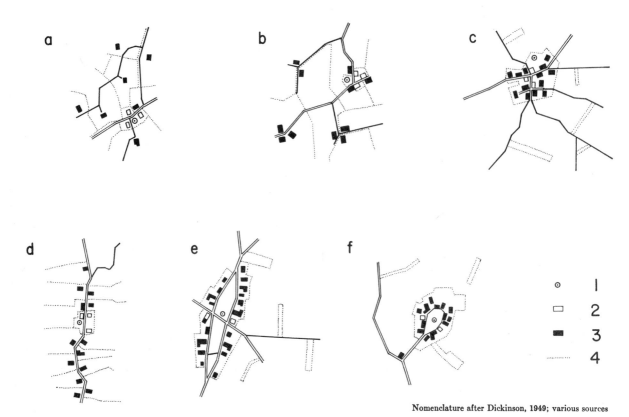

Nomenclature after Dickinson, 1949; various sources

57 · TYPES OF RURAL SETTLEMENTS in Central Europe: (1) church; (2) service building; (3) farmstead; (4) property line. (a) Isolated farmsteads, irregularly scattered. The village center consists only of service buildings and church. Property is consolidated. (b) A hamlet. (c) An irregular clustered village. The houses are surrounded by trees and gardens. Cropland is of the open-field type, and individual property (only one is shown here) is fragmented. (d) A street or linear village, of which there are many well-known subtypes. (e) A village with an elongated common in the center or so-called *Argerdörfer*. This type is frequently found in eastern parts of Germany. (f) A place village (*Rundling*). This is also found in eastern Germany and dates back to an earlier period of the Slavic settlement.

systematic scientists or because they invariably fall back upon what their own training has emphasized, namely, that their work consists in viewing the unity rather than dissecting it further and further. Moreover, if a geographer attained the status of an efficient specialist, it might be rightly questioned whether he could any longer be called a geographer.

It seems that those who advocate a trend toward specialization are overlooking the fact that viewing particular phenomena as a whole offers a certain distinctive perspective and results. Such an approach also represents specialization in its way. In other words, synthetic viewing is precisely the specialization in which the basic training of a geographer consists. In modern rational Western thinking, analytical procedures generally carry more weight; however, this bias should not deter geographers from doing what is expected of them and what is inherent in their field of study.

The presentation above of the formal and

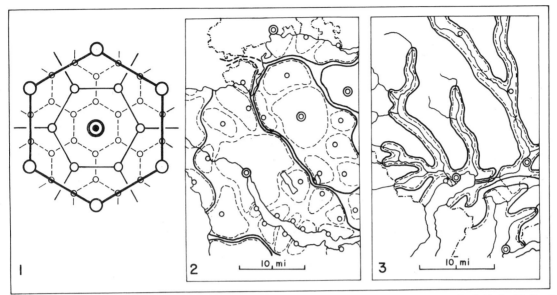

(2) After Carol; (3) after Wydler, 1952

58 · FUNCTIONAL STRUCTURE OF CENTRALITY. The figure shows in comparison: (1) the concept as developed by Christaller (1933), i.e., the hexagonal structure of trade areas with four classes of central places; (2) an actual case, though much simplified, in which only two classes are distinguished. The area shown is in the northeastern part of the Swiss Plateau, and the places with the highest degree of centrality are Zürich, Winterthur, Schaffhausen, and Frauenfeld; (3) another case illustrating how the functional pattern is influenced by the topography. The example was taken from Ticino in southern Switzerland, and the three major places are Bellinzona, Locarno, and Lugano.

functional approches should have clarified the process by which formal and functional structures are recognized through analysis and partial synthesis. Possibilities of the final synthesis of these two now remain to be considered.

Formal and functional structures have entirely different qualities. Only in a few very exceptional cases are they likely to coincide in terms of areal expansion. A model of the functional structure could be so constructed that the vertical or z axis represents the level of the respective functions, while on the horizontal plane (x and y axes) we are plotting the correlated functional areas. Such a model thus has three-dimensional qualities. As far as the formal structure is concerned the following differences should be observed. (1) In contrast to the virtual model of the functional structure, the formal structure has the qualities of being tangible and physiognomically perceptible; a model of the formal structure will also have the three dimensions of space, plus the fourth dimension of time. Formal and functional structures are, however, different with respect to their specific qualities. (2) The arrangement of formal unit areas, following the hierarchical order established by generalization, is in every respect different from that of the functional unit areas.

As a matter of fact there hardly exists any unit area or region which is homogeneous in both function and form, as every geographer knows quite well. The hinterland of a port does not coincide with any formal unit, nor does the umland of a city. An isolated village in a primeval forest or an outlying farmstead may be exceptional, since their functional structure possesses only one platform and the hierarchical order of their formal structure consists of but one representative.

Of the two approaches, partial synthesis allows

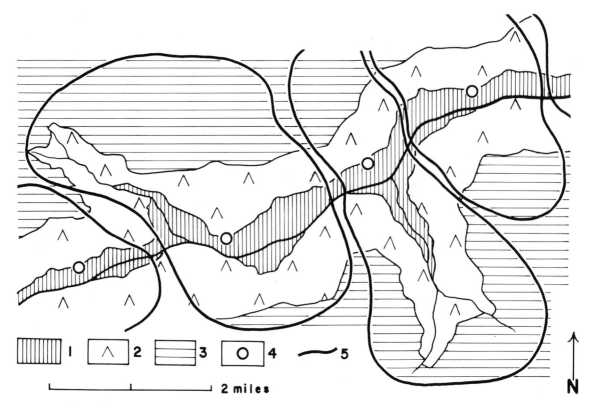

59 · COMPARISON OF FORMAL and functional structures. *Legend:* (1) grass and crop fields in the valley bottom; (2) forests; (3) pastures and unused lands at higher altitudes; (4) villages; (5) boundaries of the functional areas of villages. The map does not represent any actual case, but the kind of arrangement illustrated here is typical of many mountain valleys. Note that the formal and functional structures do not coincide. The formal structure consists more or less of an altitudinal arrangement of land use zones parallel to the longitudinal axis of the valley. The functional area of a village, on the other hand, stretches across the valley and its longitudinal axis is at right angles to the valley axis. The arrangement is therefore rather that of a cellular chain.

to a very large degree standardization of procedures and quantification of results, as has been demonstrated by the fractional-code system and the unit-area method; examples could likewise be discussed from the fields of functional research. Some of these methods have reached such a degree of perfection that we can actually devise a process for obtaining results electronically.

It seems to lie in the nature of the object of geography that final synthesis defies any such methods. In view of the basically different nature of the results of partial synthesis, namely, the formal and the functional structure, only two ways are open to reach the goal: either the reader is left with the results of the partial synthesis to work them out in his own mind and arrive at an understanding of the unity, or the author selects on the basis of his experience and subjective judgment what he considers the relevant facts to present a comprehensive view to the best of his ability.

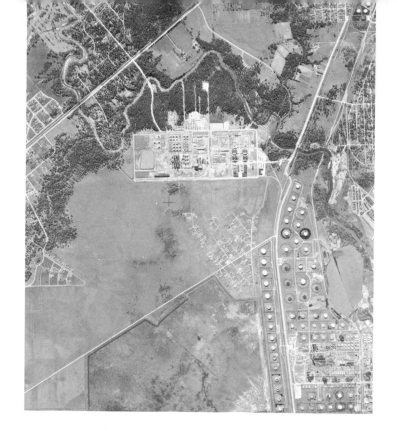

Part Two | INDUSTRIALIZATION SECONDARY OCCUPATIONS

ABOVE: This oil refinery in Texas (Harris Company) shows the spaciousness and the well-planned outlay of this modern type of industrialization: tank farm, refinery, and settlements.

BELOW RIGHT: Grand Coulee Dam in the State of Washington, showing the dam, the artificial lake and the power station. (Courtesy, U. S. Bureau of Reclamation)

BELOW LEFT: Gold-mining area in the city of Johannesburg, Republic of South Africa. (Courtesy, WILD)

7 | INDUSTRIALIZATION

WHAT IS THE MEANING OF INDUSTRIALIZATION?

Industrialization is a word widely used, but difficult to define. It is a process which defies precise and quantitative measurement, involving a large number of fundamental changes in the economic structure of an area or a country, and its manifold aspects are expressed in the economic geography of that particular region. The word derives from the Latin *industria* which simply means the steady application to business or labor. The English language still uses the word "industrious" in the sense of hard-working. In French, the meaning has slightly changed, the term *industrie* refers to all operations by which raw materials are processed and goods are produced. Finally, in German, *Industrie* is reserved for processing on a large scale with the use of machinery and modern methods of working. Similarly, the term "manufacturing" is used differently in different countries. In English usage, the word usually connotes fabrication from raw materials, while *manufacture* in French is a large mechanized establishment; in German, *Manufakturwaren* are the products of the textile industry. Any student reading foreign texts or making international comparisons should be aware of this rather confusing situation.

All this will become much clearer if we view the problem not linguistically, but historically and economically. Industrialization then means a development in economic history through which man's activities were directed along new paths and his productivity multiplied by leaps and bounds. This development, called by historians the Industrial Revolution, first took place in certain European countries during the latter part of the eighteenth century. England took the lead in this development, just as she was also the foremost in agricultural improvements during the same period. Primarily, the roots of the Industrial Revolution must be sought in a highly developed civilization and in an area where thought and research had prepared the ground.

EFFECTS OF INDUSTRIALIZATION

Economically, the most significant change caused by the Industrial Revolution seems to be the increased productivity of man. By supplementing the animate energy of men and beasts with different kinds of inanimate energies, and by utilizing machinery and new production techniques, the industrialized nations commanded a greater economic potential. However, more important may have been the increased output per man-hour. Industrialization thereby leads to a higher material standard of living. At the same time, increased productive capacity makes it possible to provide large funds for research, which demands a staggering amount of money in modern times.

Another equally important result of industrialization is a fundamental change in the demographic structure. Not only was it possible to absorb the agricultural surplus population into various industrial pursuits, and to ease in some measure the ever-pressing problem of population increase, but the Industrial Revolution brought about a new pattern of population distribution by creating industrial agglomerations. The process firmly established new centers of production and distribution and resulted in an increased flow of goods in national and international trade. This in turn led to a great expansion of all the services needed for the organization and management of the complex economy, but not directly involved in manufacturing. Industrialization expresses itself in the ratio of primary-secondary-tertiary occupations as clearly as in its physiognomy or what is popularly called an industrial landscape.

All this is said here in rather general terms, but it represents the considerations that move an increasing number of countries to seek industrialization as a way out of their underdeveloped status. Indeed, industrial projects play a much greater part in most development plans than agricultural projects, because industrial techniques are transplantable, for instance, to a tropical environment with much less difficulty than the agricultural know-how of middle latitudes.

In accordance with certain economic theories of the day, the spread of industrialization was at first viewed with disfavor by the industrial countries, and it cannot be denied that in many instances they have actually suffered economically from such a spread. Yet, developing industries of one's own is quite different from having them transplanted from other countries. We ought to differentiate more and more between countries which take over well-established industrial techniques from others in order to bring about a change in their economic structure and countries which constantly develop new techniques and new branches of industries. The textile industry is probably the best example. At the first stage of its development, Europe was able to export textiles to almost all the other continents, thanks to a tremendous increase in production. At the second stage, countries that had been buying from Europe began to establish their own textile mills, and this curtailed European exports disastrously. At the third stage, the creative mind of European industrialists, backed by innumerable research laboratories, succeeded in developing new processes and synthetics, and thus European textile industry was able to come back into the world market.

Industrialization cannot be measured solely by counting the numbers of manufacturing establishments or of workers. Perhaps statistical data on inventions or patents granted would make a good additional indicator.

If we speak of the industrialization of underdeveloped countries, the following point should also be born in mind. Both in Europe and in America, industrialization started with the consumer-goods industries and then proceeded to iron and steel and capital-goods industries. As is well known, the USSR reversed the sequence in her various five-year plans by first establishing heavy industry centers; similar are the plans in China at present. It is only natural for the countries undergoing the process of industrialization to look to the highly industrialized world. Japan, for instance, followed almost scrupulously the European and American example. Today, countries in Asia and Africa are more and more turning to the USSR and China for guidance in the belief that industrialization there took place under conditions more similar to their own than those in Western Europe prior to the Industrial Revolution.

The generalities outlined above point to one of the fundamental differences in the mode of production between agriculture and industry, one which has great influence upon economic geography and our working methods. An appraisal of natural and human factors involved in agriculture brought us to the conclusion that nature provides the frame, often a very rigid one, within which man can exercise his own will. The introductory remarks on industry, on the other hand, have stressed the fact that our primary consideration should be given to man and his creative abilities. We can even declare

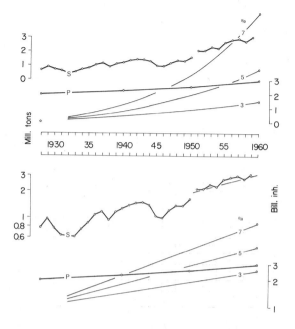

60 · RATE OF INCREASE: population and crude steel production, 1928–1960. The figure shows in contrast two different ways of plotting changes from one year to the other. In addition to the two curves portraying changes in population (world total, *P*) and crude steel production (world total, *S*), three curves were plotted to indicate different rates of increase—3, 5, and 7 percent, respectively. The chart at the top represents an arithmetic line chart, and the one at the bottom a semilogarithmic or ratio chart. Since an increase at a constant rate is shown by a straight line on the latter, it is more helpful in comparing *P* and *S* curves.

succinctly that industry differs from agriculture precisely at the point where man came into possession of means of production which were subject to his own will and increasingly freed himself from the vagaries of nature. An environmentalistic philosophy, as was explained earlier might be applicable to agricultural problems, yet for industry it necessarily distorts the relations and is liable to invite wrong conclusions.

Most economic geographers have probably placed undue emphasis upon the presence or absence of so-called natural resources. To be sure, they are important and valuable and must be carefully taken into account, but Switzerland and Japan clearly demonstrate that natural re-

sources are by no means factors of the primary order in industrial development. Whether a country is poor or rich, actually or potentially in terms of industrial productivity, is in the first place determined by the human factor in the broadest sense.

Economic Geography of Industries: Methods and Techniques

In the study of individual industries, we need to consider factors of three kinds—topical, locational, and structural. (1) Topical factors affect a specific site. They are of paramount importance in agricultural production, but play only a minor role in industry, which is mostly carried on in an artificial environment. The building grounds of a manufacturing plant remain as an important topical factor, from the physical point of view as well as from the economic. (2) Location differs from site, representing the external relations of an industry. Since industry involves the continuous assemblage, processing, and distribution of raw materials and semifinished to finished products, as well as the constant flow of goods, money, and ideas, locational factors become extremely significant. Most of them relate to the flow of goods. Consequently, possibilities and costs of transportation have to be given first consideration. Other locational factors are relevant to the exchange of ideas, banking and trading facilities, and the like, and still others have bearing upon sociological conditions. Locational factors constitute an important field of research in economic geography relating to industries. They are viewed, for example, in relation to raw materials, energy supplies, labor and capital, market, research facilities, etc. (3) Finally, structural factors affect the vertical structure and its ramifications for a given manufacturing process. They are indispensable in understanding the technology and economy of an industry before we attempt to analyze its problems in economic geography.

Studies of industrial economics differ from those of agricultural economics in another respect. In the latter it is logical to start with production and to proceed to consumption. Similar procedures have been followed in practically all texts of economic geography in dealing with industry as well. This can only be explained by the fact that there seems to be a tendency to stick to the beaten paths of tradition. In agriculture, demand is rather static, changes occur over longer periods of time and are likely to follow steady trends. Supply, on the other hand, is characterized by considerable fluctuations and is in large measure beyond the control of man, for reasons which are both natural and human. Industrial production, as contrasted with agricultural output, is highly controllable, changeable, and adaptable to the demands of the market. Here it is the market—the economic geography of consumption—that should be taken up first. In industry, production responds to market demands; if the demand justifies it, raw materials will be assembled, whatever the difficulties or costs may be. If logic is to be followed, we must do likewise in our presentation.

On moving from studies of specific industries to studies of the overall situation within a country we are confronted with such problems as measuring the degree to which a country is industrialized and making comparisons between countries in these terms. The question immediately arises: How are we going to measure industrialization?

The first obstacle is the incomparability of the various national statistics. International statistics are much less complete for industry than for agriculture. Difficulties start with the various definitions of the so-called statistical unit, an individual factory, and thence lead to varying definitions of an industrial worker. Such criteria as density of factory distribution, number of industrial workers, etc., may be used for regional studies and comparison within one country, but the same criteria cannot be employed for making international comparisons, since the quality and availability of statistical information also vary a great deal from one country to another. Nearly complete statistics are available in the United States; there we find practically all the items which are required for viewing the distinctive characteristics of different industrial groups, such as number of workers employed, raw material consumption, power consumption, value added by processing, output, and so forth. Most European statistics are in this respect incomplete, and many European scientists have been compelled to turn to the United States to study the economic geography of industry. Incomparability and incompleteness of statistics thus constitute the major drawback at present in making compartive studies on the international level. It is to be hoped that the United Nations Economic and Social Council meets with success in establishing international standards for basic industrial research.

The commonly adopted way of expressing the degree of industrialization in a country, namely, by number and ratio of people engaged in industry, can hardly be recommended. Such figures should be viewed with scepticism. If we group secondary and tertiary occupations together, as seems justified from a certain point of view, we can express the degree of industrialization as the reciprocal value of the ratio of people engaged in the primary occupations. This seems to be a much less debatable and more accurate indicator than the direct method. The respective figures are published regularly in the statistics of the FAO for most countries.

There are two other ways which enable us to approximate a measure of the industrialization in a country with some degree of accuracy. One is to evaluate "the industrial origin of the gross domestic product," and the other (to be discussed in detail later) is to measure energy consumption. The relevant figures for the former are published regularly in the *United Nations Yearbook*. Though not strictly comparable with one another, they are much better than the employment figures.

8 | ENERGY

ENERGY CONSUMPTION

Industrialization and economic development can be expressed in terms of energy consumption. Recently (1960) Guyol has demonstrated the close relationship between energy consumption and gross national product; he also agreed with Zagaroff (1955) that "in long term investigations of growth and in global comparisons of economic power, the energy approach is to be preferred to the money approach." One advantage of this indicator is the availability of numerous and full statistics, such as the United Nations *Statistical Papers on World Energy Supplies* (WES), an earlier study by the U.S. Department of State (1949), *Energy Resources of the World* (ERW), and the proceedings of various World Power Conferences.

Measuring Energy

A simple statistical appraisal of the quantities of coal, oil, etc., consumed as fuels is only a rough approximation of the true magnitude of energy consumption. The problem is more complex because the efficiency coefficient in transforming these raw materials into usable energy is highly variable, depending upon such factors as source material, technology, and so on. Actually, the transformation of coal, etc., into usable forms of energy is perhaps the most wasteful of all the processes in modern economy, even if people everywhere try hard to improve the ef-

ficiency. In underdeveloped countries, where energy is largely derived from fuelwood, the efficiency is well below 20 percent; in the United States it is about 40 percent today, but was only about 30 percent thirty years ago; and in Norway over 60 percent. Such differences not only reflect various degrees of development in energy utilization, but also its varied sources. Coal has in general an efficiency coefficient averaging 20 percent, but a much lower one in locomotives. For hydroelectricity, it is 100 percent; in thermal plants, however, only one-fifth to one-quarter of the energy in the coal burned is transformed into electric energy.

For the sake of comparison, each source of energy in WES is measured in terms of its coal equivalent. Comparisons between fuels are made on the basis of the heat energy which can be obtained from each under ideal conditions. By multiplying this quantity by the appropriate coefficient—e.g., 1.3 for crude petroleum, 0.3-0.6 for various lignites—all the fuels can be expressed in terms of coal. Metric tons are used throughout, which facilitates international comparisons a great deal.

ERW, on the other hand, converts every source of energy into an electric power equivalent, "assuming that 20 percent of the energy contained in fuels, and all the energy contained in electric power, is available for consumption." In this study, the kilowatt hour is the unit of measurement. For example, 1 metric ton of bituminous coal is equivalent to 1630 kw hr, 1000 cubic

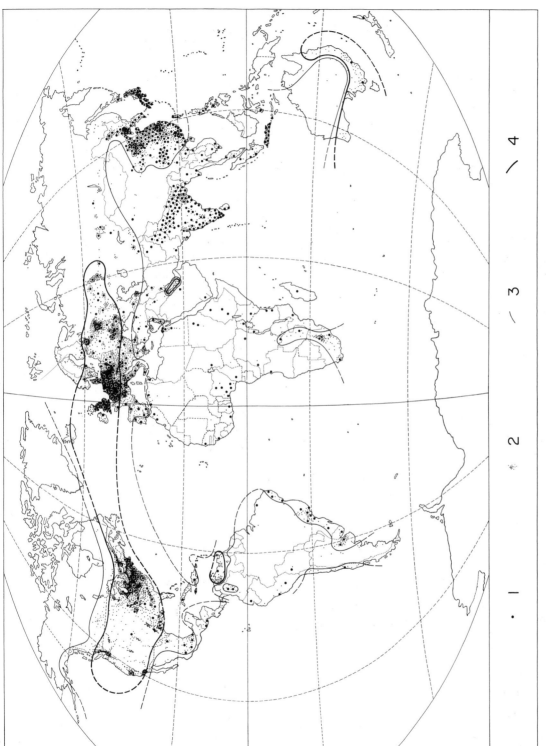

61 · ENERGY: animate vs. inanimate. A map comparing animate and inanimate energy expressed in kilowatt hours. A heavy dot (1) represents animate energy produced by 6 million people, and a light dot (2) an equal amount of inanimate energy. Three major areas are distinguished on the map and delienated by (3) and (4). The first is the huge belt of underdeveloped countries; the second and the third represent two stages of industrialization and consequently increasing consumption of inanimate energy.

meters of natural gas to 2240 kw hr, and so forth.

Such approaches to the energy problem enables us to convert all the different sources of inanimate energy into some standard unit of measurement. We may go further and include the animate energy in our comparison as well. If we assume—as in ERW—that a horse has a capacity of 800 working hours per year, approximately, we can also express this amount of work as 600 kw hr. A workman with $\frac{1}{12}$ hp attains only 150 kw hr per year, even if he works 2400 hours a year. He is no better than a donkey with $\frac{1}{4}$ hp, because the latter would take his time and limit his effort to 800 hours! In this way, we are able to compare animate energy consumption with inanimate, and the ratio between the two figures may be considered an excellent indicator of the uses man has made of the available materials to increase his productivity.

If an efficiency coefficient of about 20 percent for inanimate energy has already sounded quite fantastic, it is even more surprising to learn that a comparison between the food intake of human beings and animals and its equivalent in kilowatt hours will uncover an efficiency coefficient of only 5 percent! This is, of course, a materialistic and one-sided way to look at man's activities and purpose in life, but in this context it is justified.

Using ERW first for comparison, we reach some idea about the differences in magnitude among various sources of energy. The amount of animate energy is proportional to the number of human beings and draft animals; the world total shows that about two-thirds of all animate energy is of human origin; the remaining third is derived from draft animals. The absolute figures can be calculated from the conversion factors mentioned above. At present, the colossi in the use of human energy are China and India; the former is incidentally one of the countries with an extremely low consumption of animal energy.

Energy Sources and Usable Energy

In discussing energy problems one has at all times to differentiate clearly between the sources or "raw materials" of energy and the amount of energy which can be made use of. The latter, as we have seen, is usually considerably less, the ratio of the two depending as much on technical mastery as on the specific kind of energy which we need. The lowest ratio discussed so far characterizes the transformation of food into animate energy; a still lower one will be discussed later for the conversion of solar energy into heat energy. Locomotives represent a much lower efficiency of recovering the latent energy of coal, oil, etc., than stationary steam engines or turbines. The shift from coal to oil and natural gas permits a further increase of the efficiency ratio, as was shown in the case of the United States.

To measure the energy resources of a given area in terms of source materials, expressed, say, in bituminous coal units, represents therefore only a very rough approximation. These figures give only an accurate indication of the kind and the quantity of energy sources needed and consumed, but not more. If we want to know something about the energy balance of a country, we have to study how the source materials are employed for the production of usable energy, how much is lost as waste, and what kind and quantity of usable energy is finally produced.

Apparently both ways have advantages and disadvantages. WES and ERW have been selected above to illustrate the two approaches. Of course, a general efficiency coefficient of 20 percent as used in ERW, allows only a first approximation, and the study of individual cases poses quite difficult problems.

The various sources of inanimate energy will be discussed in the chapters that follow. The present section is concerned with the energy problem as such.

Animate and Inanimate Energy

Around 1800 inanimate energy began to play a certain role in the world energy balance, but even as late as the second half of the nineteenth century inanimate energy was less important than animate energy, at least in the overall picture. Only in a very few countries, first exclusively in Europe and later in the United States, did inanimate energy supplement animate to any appreciable extent. Before the end of the century

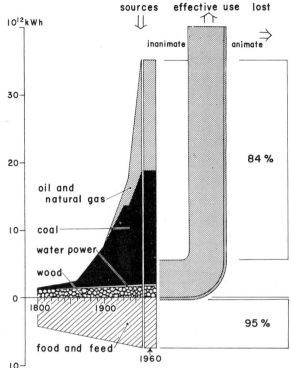

sources   effective use   lost

62 · WORLD ENERGY CONSUMPTION, 1800–1960. This diagram should be studied carefully because it provides a clear picture of what has taken place during the nineteenth and twentieth century in the use of energy derived from the various sources. The left-hand column shows the increasing amount of energy consumed and the changing composition of the energy sources. To its right is indicated the situation in 1960. The amount of potential energy wasted in the process of conversion (95 percent of the energy derived from food and feed and 84 percent from all the other sources) and the amount which is actually made available and used, most of it being of inanimate origin, are shown on the right.

the relationship had definitely changed. Even though the two sources of energy practically equaled each other in terms of coal equivalent as late as 1870, the higher efficiency of the technical machinery brought a higher energy return. From that time onward, a phenomenal increase in the importance of inanimate sources has been witnessed. Until 1900 the whole development was essentially carried on a single base—coal. Subsequently, oil and natural gas took over an increasing share, while water power remained almost

negligible in the world picture. Difficult to assess, but quite important even in the modern energy balance, is fuelwood. The best way to visualize the revolutionary changes in human economy within the last two centuries is to study a graph illustrating the various forms of energy.

Two hundred years ago, the energy balance of the world was dominated by animate energy. Man and his draft animals accomplished almost all the work, and only a meager amount was contributed by waterwheels, windmills, and above all, fuelwood. Today, we find the situation roughly as follows. (*a*) *Animate energy* is now equivalent to $3 \cdot 10^{12}$ men, according to ERW, or $0.45 \cdot 10^{15}$ kw hr; but since only about two-thirds may be considered actively engaged, it had better be assumed that only $0.3 \cdot 10^{15}$ kw hr are really effective. We shall further include in this approximation the draft animals by raising the figure to $0.5 \cdot 10^{15}$ kw hr. (*b*) *Inanimate energy* in total consumption is $4 \cdot 10^{12}$ tons coal equivalent; according to ERW with its 20 percent efficiency rate, it is converted to $6.8 \cdot 10^{15}$ kw hr, or about 14 times the total of animate energy. Figuratively speaking, this means that for every man who works on this earth, fourteen invisible slaves are serving to increase his productivity. Such average figures for the entire earth, however, mean less than figures for individual countries or areas. For all of America the ratio is 41, but for the United States alone it is more than 100. Corresponding figures for the other parts of the world are Europe 25, USSR 29, Middle East 2, Far East 2, India 1.5, Japan 9, China 3, and Africa 4. A student of economic geography should view these figures with the greatest interest because they disclose the unbalanced energy equipment of mankind. In many places on the earth man himself still does practically all the physical work and has no chance to compete with his brothers unless he too can benefit from technical advances in full measure.

The Users of Energy

General discussions on energy should include its differentiation into various forms of utilization. It is obvious that certain users demand certain kinds of energy. A waterfall is not of much help if the power is needed miles away, and a coal mine is of little use in running a car. Apart from these platitudes, we can think of important energy consumers, like metallurgical plants, which depend on energy in a specific form, electricity; or we can enumerate the advantages and disadvantages of steam and electric traction in railroads. Since an energy consumer demands energy in a specified form, a primary energy source often has to be transformed into a secondary one. A common secondary source is electricity, which will be treated separately in Chapter 9. But if the material remains much the same after processing, as when crude oil is converted to gasoline, wood to charcoal, or coal to coke, we do not consider the product a secondary source. The importance of the market demand has to be fully understood as it influences the way in which various energy sources are utilized. Coal-rich Germany and the USSR, for example, are both changing important sections of their railway systems from steam to electric traction for certain technical and economic considerations. For this, coal has first to be converted to electric energy in thermal plants. Electricity has many advantages, which will be discussed later; but it should always be regarded as proper for certain special uses and users, and also generally as "high-quality energy," obtainable at a higher price.

Other sources of high-quality energy are oil and natural gas. Liquid fuels and natural gas together constitute 72 percent of the total energy consumption in the United States, but only 13 in the Federal Republic of Germany, 18 in the United Kingdom, and 30 in the USSR. The world average for 1958 was 44.5 percent, and the general trend, as has already been seen definitely moves toward an increasing importance of liquid fuels and natural gas.

Such a remarkable increase in the consumption of energy immediately gives rise to three major questions. The first has to do with the future availability and replenishment of *sources* utilized at present. The second is the problem of improving the efficiency quotient of the *machinery*. The third is concerned with *new sources* and ways of utilizing energy.

From the point of view of power use, modern machinery is certainly far better than human beings and draft animals; still, a loss of 80 percent, which occurs in converting the source material into usable forms of energy, seems tremendous. Most of it is caused by the fact that our energy sources have first to be transformed into heat and then into mechanical energy. According to the laws of thermodynamics, unavoidable losses of energy are incurred through these transformations.

Our calculation has so far been based upon the figure 80 percent, in accordance with the literature cited. But we should be aware that the shift from solid to liquid fuels, natural gas, and electricity has also resulted in a higher efficiency coefficient. The United States had a coefficient of 37 percent in 1937, but 42 percent in 1955, both being well above the assumed world average. It is perhaps a fair approximation to assume that through this shift and through technical improvements, the efficiency of energy and power production has increased from about 12-15 percent in 1900 to 20 percent in 1937 (ERW) and to 25 percent at present.

Energy balances have been constructed for many countries, and ERW gives a summarizing picture for the whole world. The amount of loss is found to be the smallest in the case of electricity, once the conversion has been accomplished; only a small amount (increasing with increasing distance) is lost in transmission.

The three problems named above will appear repeatedly in our discussion of energy sources; they all have to do with the *energy materials* and *machinery*. As for new sources of energy, it is safe to assume that the future will witness a continuous increase at rates similar to rates in the immediate past, but that consumers' preference will probably shift toward high-quality and special types of energy.

SOURCES OF ENERGY

Coal

It is hard to realize today that coal appeared so late as a source material for the production of energy. As late as the thirteenth century, wood and peat were practically the only fuels used, and even in the sixteenth century in England, coal was still considered a fuel for the poor. The Industrial Revolution created an ever-increasing demand for coal as a source of energy as well as for the making of coke in iron metallurgy. Nevertheless, the production figures for 1850 were still very low: England 35 million tons, Germany 4, France 2, and the United States 6. By 1860 the world production had risen to 200 million tons and thereafter increased steadily up to 1200 million tons in 1910. During that whole period coal was almost entirely responsible for the rising curve of energy consumption. Following the First World War, however, other energy sources gradually made their appearance, e.g., oil and natural gas; and until the Second World War, coal production in the United States, Great Britain, and Germany, which had constituted 85 percent of the world total in 1910, remained stationary around 1000 million tons, finally dropping appreciably in the wake of the war. On the other hand, total world production was still increasing, though at a reduced and much fluctuating rate, because the newly industrialized countries, such as the USSR, India, South Africa, Australia, and China, based their development mainly on coal. It seems that the development in the USSR has in this respect all but reached "stage 1910" of older countries, for a definite shift away from coal toward oil and natural gas has been observed in recent years. We shall come back to this competitive situation of the coal industry later when discussing what is commonly called the coal problem.

THE MARKETS FOR COAL

The utilization of coal as a source of energy involves its transformation into heat first and then into mechanical energy, in most cases. An appraisal of the various grades of coal, therefore, takes into first account their calorific value: anthracite, semianthracite, and semibituminous coals have 8,000-8,900 calories, bituminous and subbituminous 5,500-8,800, and lignite 4,000-6,000 calories (all in kcal/kg).

Generally, processing of coal is possible only within narrow limits. Such operations as washing out inorganic admixtures, breaking, and screening into specified sizes are becoming more and more important. In Europe, lignite or brown coal is powdered and then pressed into handy briquettes for domestic use. A large-scale modern central-heating system uses powdered coal which is automatically injected into the furnace. Yet the possibilities of accommodating a wide range of consumer demands are strictly limited for coal.

Another large group of coal consumers is the metallurgical plants, where coal is used not as a source of energy alone but also as a raw material, essential in certain processes. The most important consumer, the iron and steel industry, will be discussed in detail in Chapter 9. This industry demands a special kind of coal—coking coal, the source of coke. The manufacture of coke takes place in the modern by-product coke ovens or cokeries. About 30% of the original weight is removed from coal in the form of various gases and tar to be recovered as valuable by-products. Earlier, coke was made in so-called beehive ovens from which all the volatile by-products escaped without being utilized. The coking process may be manipulated in many ways by regulating the temperature. Even so, not every type of coal is suited for making coke, at least the dense, hard metallurgical coke; some may give "gas coke" and others no coke at all.

The third group makes use of coal simply as a raw material. This is the branch of chemical industry which deals with hydrocarbons and their derivatives. It utilizes primarily the by-products of coke-making and need not be included here; it will be taken up later under Chemical Industries.

In the two major groups, i.e., the group using coal as a source of energy and the group demanding metallurgical coke, the basic difference lies in the fact that, while the former could switch to other sources, the latter has no technically feasible alternatives. Since iron and steel plants are the largest consumer group within the latter, demands for coke, and hence for coking coal, are influenced by iron and steel production.

The behavior of these various consumer groups in the immediate past, as indicated in statistics

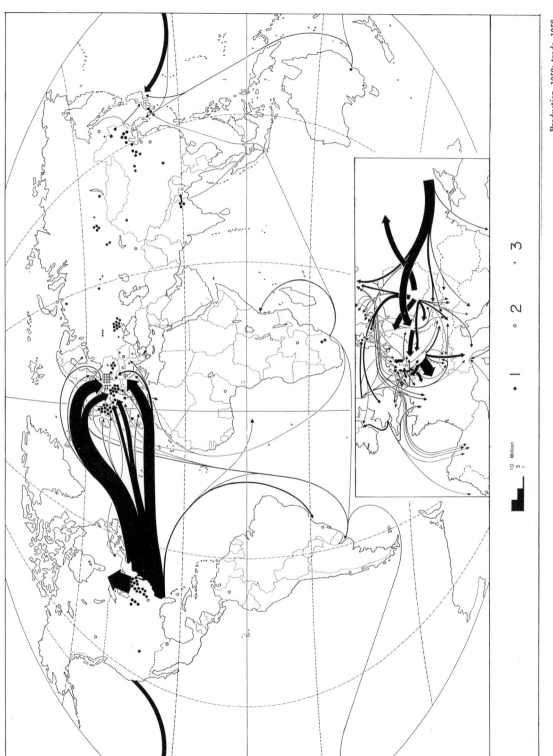

Production, 1959; trade, 1958

63 · COAL. (1) Each dot represents 1 percent of the world production of bituminous coal. (2) Coal-producing centers of lesser importance. (3) Lignite (brown coal) production. In terms of potential energy 3 tons of lignite is equivalent to 1 ton of bituminous coal. Each symbol represents an equal amount of energy contained in one dot worth of bituminous coal. International movements of coal are shown by the flow lines. The scale indicated in the legend also applies to the inset map showing intra-European movements of coal.

10 Million
5
1
· 1 ° 2 + 3

for the United States, is revealing. The years between the two world wars saw no drastic changes. The heaviest consumers of steam coal were the railroads and the electric power utilities; the former showed a decline from about 25 to 20 percent of the total coal consumption, while the latter increased their share from 5 to 10 percent. Big changes did not occur until after the Second World War, when the share of the railroads dropped to but a few percent. It was compensated, however, by a swift rise of electric power utilities to more than 30 percent. This shift also means a more efficient use of coal as a source of energy. With an efficiency ratio of 20 percent, 1 ton of coal equals approximately 1,600 kw hr; however modern thermal power plants are capable of realizing 2,000-2,200 kw hr. On the other hand, mechanical users may produce only as much as 1,000 kw hr or even less. Heavy industry, i.e., the coking industry, steadily in-

creased its consumption from about 15 percent in 1920 to more than 25 percent in the late fifties.

If electric power utilities had not risen to such an important position as a steam coal consumer, the problem of marketing coal would have become even more pronounced. Domestic users, as well as land and sea transportation, are gradually shifting to other energy sources. The premium placed upon coking coal is particularly felt where the same mining area produces both steam coal and coking coal, or in Europe, where some countries are well endowed with one but not with the other kind. In the Campine Basin of Belgium 40 percent of the coal reserves are of coking quality, in Northern France 23, in the Ruhr 68, in Upper Silesia 9, and in the Donetz Basin 16, but more than 80 in Northumberland-Durham in the United Kingdom. The coke problem presents quite a different aspect from the

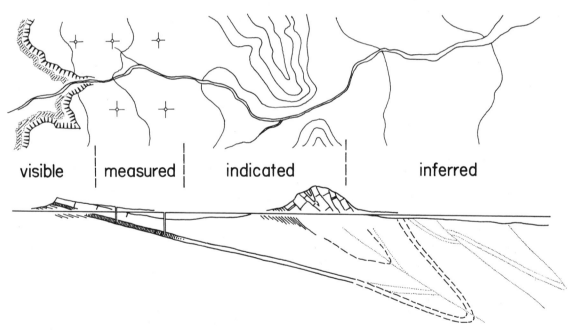

visible | measured | indicated | inferred

64 · EVALUATION OF MINERAL RESERVES. Four ways by which mineral reserves may be estimated (see the text). Outcrops in the visible section and drillings in the measured section establish the quantity and quality of reserves beyond doubt. In the part marked *indicated*, geologists are able to establish tonnage and grade within reasonable limits on the basis of the conditions found in the first two sections. In the *inferred* section, however, surface indications and others permit different interpretations of the geological character of the deposit, of which two possibilities are shown here (broken and dotted lines).

coal problem in general, and differs from one country to another. Little can be done about it from the producing side; the only solution lies with consumers, who may reduce their requirements through technical improvements or metallurgical manipulations.

THE MINING INDUSTRY

The coal mining industry has to provide coal to satisfy the variety of demands mentioned above. From the moment the decision has been taken to open up a new mine until the time when production enters into full swing, there is a lapse of several years. In European deep-shaft mining, it takes about 8 to 12 years, counting all installations. Thereafter the mine must be operated for several decades before the initial and current investments are all written off; the time period in this case largely depends upon the price of coal and legal regulations. Though these are purely economical questions, the economic geographer should be well aware that the coal mining industry, like other industries, is a long-term enterprise. Thus, among other things, a correct assessment of the reserves for each coal basin seems essential.

An evaluation of coal reserves is always based upon a careful geological analysis. The coal seam is clearly visible at an outcrop, but its underground continuation can only be inferred. An appraisal is needed of its horizontal extent as well as its probable thickness and qualitative aspects. The geologist will suggest places where his conclusions might be tested by taking drillings; if they are relatively close spaced, they may offer sufficient test of predictions regarding the seam within the tested area. If a seam has been firmly established in this manner and the amount of coal reserves calculated, we may call this figure "measured." An experienced geologist with sufficient geological indications to go by would not hesitate to step beyond the measured area in his estimations; the figures thus obtained are called "indicated." Finally, he may venture an opinion that, taking every known fact into account, the extent of the coal basin is perhaps even larger; the amount of coal reserves thus estimated are open to controversy among geologists. We may call them "inferred."

These are the terms used by the U.S. Bureau of Mines; the Institute of Mining and Metallurgy, London, differentiates between visible, probable, and possible; other countries and institutions employ still different classifications. Whatever the terminology may be, it always refers to reserves which are known to exist with a varying degree of certainty and quality. Here ends the work for the geologist, and the economist steps in. His work consists in evaluating the known deposits as to their exploitability. A common denominator for all the factors involved, such as depth of deposits, technical difficulties of mining, location of mine, etc., is as a rule the cost factor. Improved transportation facilities with a subsequent reduction in cost, changes in market prices for the product of the mine, and many other variables may alter the position of a deposit from exploitable to unexploitable or vice versa within a relatively short time.

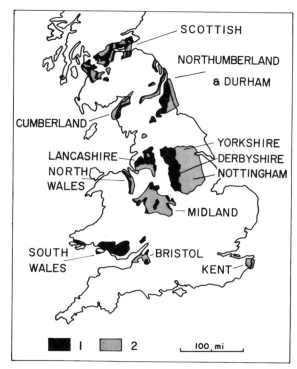

65 · COAL DEPOSITS OF GREAT BRITAIN. (1) Exposed coal fields; (2) concealed coal fields.

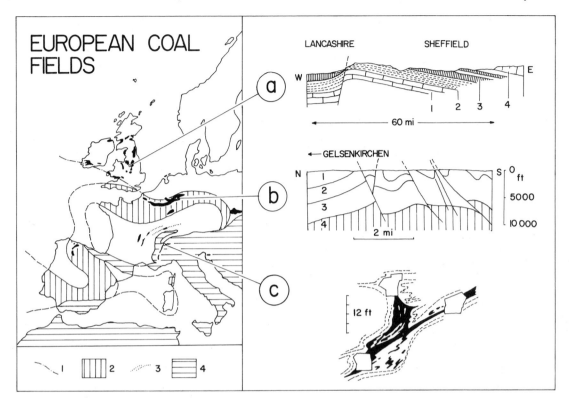

66 • TYPES OF COAL FIELDS in Europe. *Legend for the map:* (1) Branches of the late Paleozoic mountain chain. (2) The late Paleozoic mountain chain. (3) Structural lines of the late Paleozoic time south of the major chain. (4) Tertiary mountain chains of the Alpine type. Coal fields are shown in black. Diagrams on the right show types of coal fields: (a) Foreland type in England with only slightly folded and faulted Paleozoic coal beds (3) in a Paleozoic series (1-4). (b) Type found within the major chain, where the coal measures (1, 2, 3) are strongly folded and faulted as in the Ruhr basin illustrated here. Overthrusts and nappe structures occur locally as in the Belgian coal fields. (c) Type where the Tertiary orogeny was superimposed upon the late Paleozoic folding, resulting in highly complicated structures of the Carboniferous. This is a detailed mine profile from Chandoline, Switzerland, where seams vary from less than an inch to several feet. Economic implications of such differences in geologic structure can easily be understood.

Statistical appraisal of world coal reserves is in general only concerned with the first phase, namely with geological assessment. Such figures are found in the reports of the various World Power Conferences. One of the early estimates made in 1913 accounted total reserves to be $7398 \cdot 10^{12}$ tons, of which 10 percent was actual or measured, and 90 percent possible plus probable; another estimate of 1948 gave the figure of $6266 \cdot 10^{12}$ tons, of which 11 and 89 percent were measured and probable respectively, excluding the reserves counted only as possible.

Significant is the shift in percentage figures among various continents and countries.

DISTRIBUTION OF TOTAL WORLD RESERVES OF COAL		
	1913	*1948*
North America	68%	49%
Europe	10	10
USSR	3	19
China	13	16

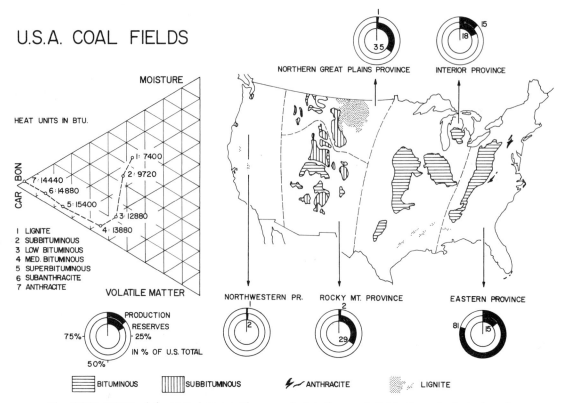

U.S.A. COAL FIELDS

67 · COAL FIELDS of the United States. The map depicts the areal distribution of principal coal deposits by types of coal and provinces. The share in each province of total reserves and production is shown by modified pie charts. The diagram on the left shows seven classes of coal ranging from lignite to anthracite; the classification is based upon the content of fixed carbons, volatile matter, and moisture. The use of such a trilinear chart greatly facilitates a comparison of a series of data in terms of three variable characteristics.

For most of us, such absolute totals are incommensurably large and do not convey very much as they are; they simply mean that there is no foreseeable danger that coal reserves will be exhausted, even if annual production, which has not yet reached $2 \cdot 10^{12}$ tons, should increase in the future. The shift in percentage figures reflects the amount of geological surveying that has been carried out in such countries as China and the USSR. But what strikes us most is the fact that 96 percent of all known coal reserves are located in the Northern Hemisphere. This is certainly of the utmost significance as long as coal remains a basic source of energy and raw material for industry and transport.

Coal seams date from different periods of the earth's history. Younger coals of Tertiary age occur in the form of lignite of low calorific value and fuel ratio (ratio of fixed carbon to volatiles). Bituminous coal is dispersed among Mesozoic sediments, but the greater mass is of late Paleozoic, i.e., Carboniferous, age. Calorific value and fuel ratio increase progressively with the age of the coal as a result of tectonic pressure. The carboniferous strata which contain the most important coal seams occur today in connection with an enormous mountain system of late Paleozoic age that encompasses the North Atlantic, reaching from southeastern United States through the Appalachians to Newfoundland and continuing into Europe from the south of the British Isles through northern France, Belgium, the Ruhr, and Silesia to southern Russia.

In relation to this mountain chain, bituminous (and sometimes anthracite) coal deposits are found in two positions. (A) Within the mountain chain proper, the coal seams are incorporated in the foldings and often metamorphosed to anthracites. The geology of the deposits is complex; folding, overthrusting, and faulting not only disrupt the continuity of seams, but bring them down to great depths with high temperatures, and necessitate mining operations on steeply inclined planes. (B) In the foreland to the north of the mountain chain the strata lie horizontally or are only slightly folded. Here mining usually proceeds from outcrops by way of slope mines which follow the dip of the seams, in contrast to shaft mines in case A. The two cases are represented in the United States by the anthracite mining area in Pennsylvania (A), and the Pittsburgh-Appalachian Plateau region (B). In Europe, type A is represented by the major coal zone of Ruhr-Belgium-northern France, while most mines in England belong to type B. It is important to distinguish between these two types; mining is not only more difficult but also much more costly in the mines of type A. Mechanized cutting is not always feasible, and more workers are occupied with bringing the coal to the main shaft and to the surface. Differences in production ratio (tonnage per worker and shift) reflect not only various stages of technical development but also diversity of working conditions. The following tabulation gives some idea about the differences among major producing countries in different years (in tons):

	1913	1930	1949
United States	3.8	5.1	6.0
United Kingdom	1.1	1.4	1.6
Germany—Ruhr	1.2	1.7	1.4

In countries where mining conditions are more adverse, the ratio drops further. In Japan, for example, the production per laborer per day is less than half a ton.

PROBLEMS OF THE COAL INDUSTRY

In an expanding world economy if one sector remains stagnant or even becomes retrogressive, like coal, it gives rise to some fundamental problems. The "coal problem" became apparent for the first time during the interwar years and has been the subject of numerous studies ever since. The problem is involved with multiple contributory factors. Some have already been mentioned —shifts in consumption, differentials in production cost, and so forth. Two additional factors have now to be taken up.

The first concerns long-range planning and investment. If the outlook of an industry shows uncertainty and little promise, it is usually first reflected in a slowdown in investment, which initiates a vicious circle. Outdated equipment and production methods lead to higher production costs; old mines are usually high-cost producers and badly in need of general overhauling. Economists have established the law of diminishing returns, which is particularly applicable to mining enterprises. Only by substantial capital investment in order to modernize production, as well as by closing down obsolete mines, can the industry be brought back to a competitive level. Self-financing is impossible in many cases; consequently, the government steps in to put the necessary financial means at the disposal of coal producers. This government interference stems in large measure from the fact that the private capital is not available for an urgently needed investment into coal mining. It is particularly true in Europe, where many mines are badly in need of modernization.

The second factor may be called the social factor in coal mining. In principle the problem is quite simple: around 1950, there were 350,000 laborers engaged in the coal mines of the United States, producing an aggregate of 500,000,000 tons, or about 1,500 tons per head; in the same year 100,000 laborers in oil and gas production accounted for—in coal equivalents—270,000,000 tons of natural gas plus 400,000,000 tons of petroleum, or 6,700 tons per head. Coal production in other countries shows considerably lower figures, while petroleum and gas production in many areas is much higher than in the United

States. In short, coal production is an extremely labor-intensive sector of our economy. It was even more so in the past; coal mining areas therefore coincide with large concentrations of population all over the world. Labor-saving devices can be applied only to a certain degree, and in some mining areas the opportunity is extremely limited. In this respect coal mining does not conform to that modern trend according to which we should be able to produce more with less physical human labor. Coal mining is also a strenuous and dangerous occupation, and even with considerable material temptations like high wages, insurance, good housing, etc., it is growing more and more difficult to recruit young miners. A large concentration of working population under such circumstances has everywhere led to trade unionism of a rather militant type.

An economist may summarize all this by stating that there will necessarily be a continual rise in production costs and that, since most of these factors are nonexistent in petroleum production, the competitive situation of coal wherever it may be replaced by other fuels will deteriorate. For the economic geographer, coal mining areas are actual or potential problem areas, particularly because of the large number of people involved.

COAL IN INTERNATIONAL TRADE

The coal problem is further affected by continuous and immoderate changes in the flow of coal in international trade. Despite the fact that coal deposits are distributed unevenly over the earth, international trade in coal comprises only about 5 percent or slightly more of the total production, as compared with about one-third for petroleum. Coal was found near the place where the Industrial Revolution had its beginning, and even today, mainly for historical reasons, industrial concentrations cluster at or around the centers of coal production.

Coal is not an easy item to transport; it is a bulk commodity and costly to load and unload; certain types entail heavy losses en route. Coal requires the traditional means of transportation, namely railroads or waterways. Railway lines bringing out coal from West Virginia to the Great Lakes or to Hampton Roads, or from Pennsylvania to the metropolitan zone of the Middle Atlantic Coast have by far the heaviest weight haul per distance in the whole of the United States. The same is true all over the world. Preference is given to cheap water transportation wherever possible, e.g., on the Ohio and the Rhine, since the specific value of coal as freight goods is relatively low.

Comparing the interwar years with the recent postwar period, the dominant change that occurred in international coal trade is probably that Europe lost her importance as the leading exporter and supplier of coal to deficit areas all over the world. Competition before these changes occurred was mainly intra-European: Great Britain, Germany, and Poland were the most interested suppliers, while Scandinavia, the Mediterranean, and some Central European countries constituted the major deficit areas. Well known is the case of Denmark, which bought coal from England and supplied the latter in return with breakfast necessities, such as eggs and bacon. Equally well known and more tragic is the case of Italy, for which the importing of coal was an absolute necessity; approximately 15 million tons, required annually by the highly developed Italian industries, could be supplied either by Great Britain or Germany. It is still fresh in the memory of Europe how this dependence brought Italy into two world wars on one or the other side. Outside of Europe, the major single market was Latin America, especially Argentina; between Argentina and Great Britain a similar bilateral trade of coal against meat products developed. All this drastically changed after the Second World War. By the late fifties European exports of coal to other continents, which before the war had ranged from 30 to 40 million tons, practically ceased. In fact, European countries imported an equal amount of coal from the United States and Canada; reasons for this are sometimes quite complicated, defying any simple explanation. For example, the Federal Republic of Germany (West Germany), by far the most important exporter, imported nearly as much coal as she herself exported; about half of the imports came from North America. Today, the great bulk of coal exports, about four-fifths of the world total, originates in North American and European countries. While European countries today trade mainly within Europe, North America directs at least three-fourths of her coal exports toward Europe. As for total quantities, all other flows are of minor order, i.e., below 10 million tons. The United States provided about two-thirds of the considerable Japanese requirements (3-4 million tons), and India supplied Pakistan with 1-1.5 million tons. Latin American countries had largely been resorting to liquid fuels; their imports thus totaled only between 2 and 2.5 million tons, most of which came, in striking contrast to the prewar situation, from the United States, but some also from Poland. A considerable volume of international trade in coal developed behind the Iron Curtain where Poland assumed the role of the major coal exporter, equaling in certain years the United States in quantities exported. The USSR itself imports a large amount of Polish coal, but toward the end of the fifties its own exports surpassed imports. East Germany and Czechoslovakia are the main net importers, both supplied by Poland and the

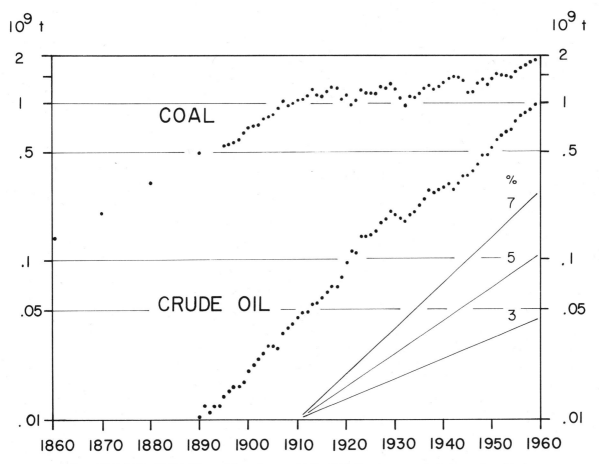

68 · COAL AND CRUDE OIL, world production, 1860–1960. The data are plotted on a logarithmic scale (world totals in billions of metric tons). In the lower right-hand corner, three curves indicating the annual increase rates of 3, 5, and 7 percent are shown as references. Oil production during the past seventy years has almost continuously maintained a uniform increase rate of 7 percent a year, while coal production has shown a great deal of fluctuations and its increase rate has been well below 3 percent for the past half-century.

USSR. South Africa and Australia offer only minor quantities to the world market; Australia contributes to the Far Eastern requirements in a small way, while South Africa serves the African market primarily, but also reaches out as far as Europe and the Far East.

Petroleum and Natural Gas

If a comparison is made between the petroleum and coal industries, we are immediately struck by one important difference. On the way from the place of origin to the ultimate consumer, oil (and to a certain extent gas as well) undergoes a number of processing operations in oil refineries which may completely alter its physical and chemical properties. Unlike coal, crude oil can be adapted to changing market demands; such bottlenecks as those in the coal industry, created by an unsatisfactory ratio of steam and coking coals, do not exist in this case.

Originally, oil refining was a very simple process which consisted of the removal of various admixtures from crude and the separation of light fractions from heavy ones by fractional distillation. At first the original qualities of crude oil, which vary from one oil field to another, were of vital importance. In the early days of the industry when the demand was primarily for kerosene to light lamps, crude oil with a high gasoline content was of little value; the situation was reversed later when the gasoline engine came into use and electric lights replaced the old kerosene lamps. Changes in the demand pattern forced the refining industry to add a third step in treating the crude, such as the cracking process by which the gasoline output could be raised almost regardless of the original quality of crude oil.

Our discussion will take up consumption, refining, and production in order of priority. The required quantitative and qualitative characteristics of oil products are the commanding factor in consumption; refining functions as an intermediate manipulator, and production has to see to it that the necessary quantities of crude are available. The oil industry is an excellent example to demonstrate how logical it is to reverse the usual sequence of production to consumption.

THE MARKET SITUATION

Not until the automobile industry and the invention of the diesel engine (R. Diesel, Germany, 1893-1895) created a larger market which had to be supplied exclusively with this new fuel, did production of oil really get under way. While the automobile may be considered an additional oil consumer, the diesel engine installed in locomotives and ships as well as in stationary apparatus represents a keen competitor of coal. We do not want to recount all the advantages of oil products; some of them are well-known from household use, where oil and gas have virtually driven out coal and anthracite in many countries.

We have repeatedly used the expression "oil products," which encompasses an ever-increasing number of products ranging from lubricating oil to diesel fuel and various grades of gasoline for automobiles and airplanes. All these products can be converted numerically into crude oil or coal equivalents, and total consumption can also be so expressed. Of a total of approximately $3700 \cdot 10^9$ tons coal equivalent of energy consumed in 1958, including solid and liquid fuels, natural gas, and hydroelectricity, 31 percent was derived from liquid fuels and 14 from natural gas, or a total of 45 percent. North America is by far the largest market (62 percent) followed by Western Europe (12 percent) and the USSR (11 percent). The latter was until recently shut off from the world market so that from the point of view of the world oil economy North America and Western Europe together represented the major outlets for oil products.

The market situation varies a great deal from one marketing area to another. The United States market demands mainly gasoline (almost 50 percent), while Western Europe needs more fuel oils, which make up more than 70 percent of the total consumption of oil products. The shift of the center of gravity to gasoline and to fuel oils, respectively, clearly exemplifies certain differences in the way of life between these two continents. In both, however, other market demands than those mentioned above cover the same wide range of oil products. In smaller markets, demands may be highly unbalanced; for example, in one country there may be no demand for aviation fuels or special lubricating oils; instead bunker oils and kerosene may make up the major portion of the consumption.

OIL REFINERIES

The quantity and quality of market demands will be decisive for the location of the oil-refining industry. A specific figure for the minimum quantity of oil required in the economical operation of a refinery cannot be given. It depends upon a number of factors, some of which are strictly of a local character. But one thing is certain: large refineries are operated more profitably than smaller ones. Therefore, a small market does not generally justify the erection of a refinery, and it is preferable to ship refined oil products in barrels, tins, etc. The universal trend at present is to build refineries close to actual or potential markets, since it is obviously more economical to transport crude oil in tankers as near to the market as possible, thus reducing costly freight charges for oil products conveyed as cargo or by truck or railroad. There are other reasons to support this development: a country which possesses its own refineries and imports crude is in fact cutting down its import requirements in money value; in this way it can profit by the processing, is in a better bargaining position in buying crude, and has an opportunity to build up a fuel reserve in the form of crude oil.

Within the United States, this trend has expressed itself in the erection of large refineries close to major population centers like Chicago and New York-New Jersey. They are supplied with crude oil by mass transport facilities—pipelines or tankers—and distribute hundreds of oil products by truck and railroad to retailers. A similar development has occurred in Europe more recently. Until the Second World War, only France and Italy imported crude in large quantities to process it within their national boundaries. The rest of Europe imported oil products, mainly gasoline and fuel oils, from the Americas. Consequently, the refineries were lo-

cated at the head of the shipping routes, i.e., either along the Gulf Coast of the United States or in Curaçao, the latter serving the Maracaibo fields of Venezuela. After the Second World War, oil refineries were given priority in the economic rehabilitation of Europe, and large sums were made available for their construction under the Marshall Plan. Today European refineries can meet the total demands and Europe has become an importer exclusively of crude, with all the advantages just mentioned.

An advantage of possessing refineries which has not yet been mentioned has come about with modern technical development in the refining industry. The major steps in processing crude oil, i.e., refining, fractional distillation, and cracking have already been referred to. Cracking is a process whereby complicated molecules of the hydrocarbon family are broken down into simpler ones which make up the light fractions; by this means the output of gasoline can be increased. Cracking takes place in so-called cracking towers at high temperatures or with catalysts at lower temperatures. Some chemically active olefins are separated out as by-products and become a basic material in the petrochemical industry. (Implications of this and further processing will be discussed under Petrochemical Industries.)

The great advantage the United States has over Western Europe in oil is the fact that the latter must import from overseas the raw materials for the refining industries. So far it has been technically and economically feasible only for the liquid fuels, but not for natural gas. Thus, while the United States is able to utilize both oil and gas as energy sources as well as raw materials for the petrochemical industry, Europe has to restrict herself for the time being to crude oil. Natural gas has many advantages over oil for a number of uses; hence Western Europe takes a great interest in obtaining an adequate supply of gas. There are two immediate possibilities: one is to import gas in liquefied form at low temperatures in tankers and the other is to build a gas pipeline from North African fields crossing the Mediterranean to a point in southern Spain. Another gas pipeline from Middle Eastern fields to Europe has been discussed but does not seem to be realizable soon.

Today, refining capacity is distributed over the earth in accordance with the market capacity. As the following figures show, this has been accomplished only recently. The refineries in Curaçao and Aruba as well as those in the Middle East have lost some of their relative importance. For the former, it should also be mentioned that Venezuela as a producer of crude oil successfully insisted on processing a major portion of it within her own territory. In earlier years, the Middle Eastern refineries had to serve a far-reaching market area with a relatively low consumption capacity, which stretched from South Africa through the Indian Ocean as far as the Pacific. Here it looked most logical to have the refining industry at the base, i.e., in Abadan (Iran). But with an increase in consumption, local refineries appeared everywhere within the marketing area, and exports of crude oil from the Persian Gulf gradually increased. New refineries in the Middle East are, as a rule, small and intended to satisfy only local demands. Percentage increases of the refining capacity in Europe and the USSR have been explained, and hence implicitly the relative decrease in the United States.

DISTRIBUTION OF REFINING CAPACITY IN PERCENT OF WORLD TOTAL		
REGION	*1950*	*1958*
United States (about half in Texas and California, and half in the Chicago and New York-New Jersey area)	59	42
Curaçao and Aruba	5	3
Europe (mainly France and United Kingdom)	8	15
Middle East	8	7
USSR	6	11

Oil Production and Oil Reserves

If we now turn to oil production, it will first come to our notice that, unlike coal fields, oil fields are scattered and generally far away from centers of processing and ultimate consumption.

Consequently, transportation is of much greater importance for oil than for coal. In round figures, world production of coal is $2000 \cdot 10^9$ and that of oil $1000 \cdot 10^9$ tons. While coal is hauled over relatively short distances, oil is usually carried a long way across the seas or continents. Large quantities and the specific character of oil and gas rendered it possible to develop a unique transportation system—pipelines and tankers—for these products, but they cannot be used for any other commodity. In some countries, as in the United States, the pipeline system is a common carrier, much like the railroads; but in other countries it is reserved for one or a group of users. A classical example of a highly complex pipeline network extending from coast to coast is to be found in the United States. In the USSR, too, pipelines have long been a major means of transportation. In Europe, however, they have appeared only recently; they were not needed as long as Europe was mainly importing oil products, for which the traditional carriers served the purpose. The refineries built soon after the Second World War were usually located at or near the tidewater. But newer ones exist now further inland; therefore it became necessary and economical to transport crude oil by pipelines.

We are now coming to that sector of the oil industry which is responsible for securing the necessary current production as well as providing the industry with ample measured reserves. In principle the situation does not differ from the coal industry, since, both are long-term enterprises. Construction of the oil transportation and refining systems is an undertaking of such tremendous magnitude that the future development of various markets as well as the potentials of production should be correctly assessed in order to avoid false investments. One of the major issues in modern times in this respect is related to the uncovering of the large Middle Eastern reserves in the late thirties and during the Second World War. A casual glance at the map and the relative location of production area and market seems to tell us that these fields should be the obvious production basis for Europe; the often heard statement that "Middle East oil is at Europe's doorstep" is, however, quite wrong.

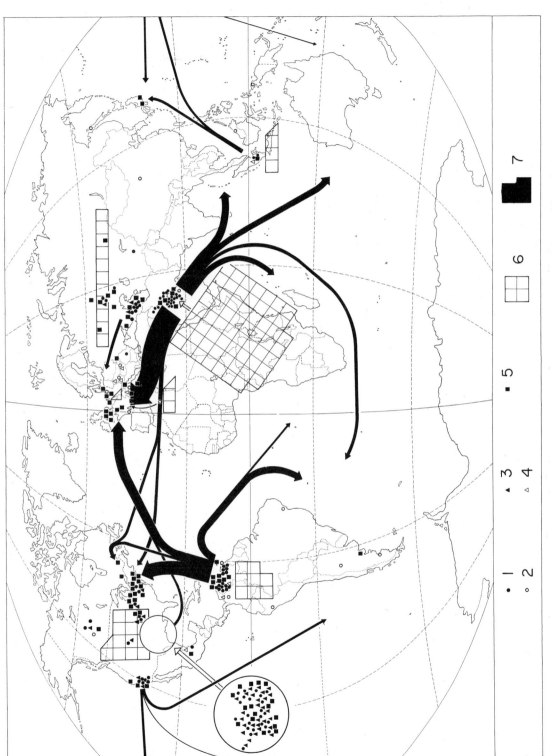

69 • PETROLEUM AND NATURAL GAS. (1) Each dot represents 1 percent of the world production of crude petroleum, or about 10 million tons. (2) Lesser producing centers with more than 1 million tons of production. (3) and (4) Production of natural gas. In potential energy, 1,000 cubic meters of natural gas is equivalent to 1 ton of crude petroleum. Each symbol represents an equal amount of energy contained in one dot worth of crude petroleum. (5) One percent of total output of crude petroleum. (6) Oil reserves, each square representing 1 percent of world total as known around 1960. (7) Movements of crude petroleum. Widths of the flowbands in the legend represent 500 and 1,000 million barrels, respectively.

Distances cannot be measured solely in miles. Since the new discoveries were located along the southern coast of the Persian Gulf, there were three possible ways to bring the oil to Europe: one, by pipeline across the Arabian desert to the Mediterranean and hence by tanker to Europe; another, all the way by tanker through the Suez Canal, where considerable duties are charged for the passage; and still another, around the Cape of Good Hope. From the economic point of view, these routes are longer than those from the Gulf of Mexico or from the Caribbean. A strong influence toward basing Europe on Middle East oil was also exerted by the fact that the balance between available reserves and greatly increased consumption within the Western Hemisphere was such that continued large exports of oil to Europe were looked upon by America with disfavor. There still remained the problem of how fast the East, where more than half of the world's population is living, would become industrialized and subsequently how it would develop as an oil market within the next decades. This huge area, which also comprises the whole of the Pacific, has only negligible known oil reserves. In the years after the Second World War, the oil industry was always in the foreground whenever a major decision was taken to reorganize the whole structure of production, refining, and marketing. Without entering into details, which are beyond the scope of our present discussion, the new structure that gradually emerged consisted more or less of the intra-Western Hemisphere unit and the Middle East-Europe unit. The Middle East also supplied crude within the traditional realm from South Africa to the Far East, supplementing their local production wherever necessary.

Large flows of oil from the areas of production to those of consumption, therefore, occurred mainly outside of the USSR and her associate countries; with a few exceptions, the world oil

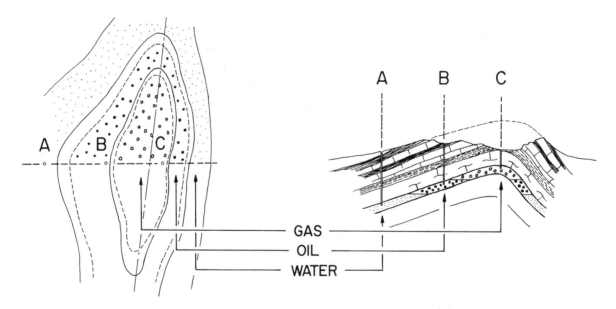

70 · OIL STRUCTURE. Oil deposits of the most common type are found in anticlinal structures as illustrated here. The cross section on the right shows how oil and gas are entrapped in a certain formation (stippled, sandstone) which is capped by an impervious layer, and how gravity separates oil, gas, and water. A, B, and C are three drillings. The map on the left indicates the form of the oil structure: the surface of the oil-bearing formation is represented by solid contour lines. Light broken lines delimit the occurrence of gas, oil, and water. The location of the cross section is marked by the heavy broken line along with the position of the drillings.

industry was also a classical example of capitalistic and private enterprise. It should be observed that the USSR has of late not merely expanded her production to an amazing degree to meet the entire domestic requirements, but has furthermore entered into the world market at different places of the earth. In the production statistics of crude oil, the USSR is currently moving from the third place (after Venezuela) to the second, surpassed only by the United States, and is able to make substantial contributions in the European and other markets at competitive prices. This development is coincident with an overall saturation of the market and a subsequent lowering of oil prices; it is a process from which consumers benefit, but has an adverse effect upon countries which receive their major income from oil revenues.

If we view the ratio of known oil reserves to production in the light of these facts, it is apparent that the former has always been increasing in the past in proportion to the growing production. Whenever there was overproduction, exploration slowed down, and vice versa. At the moment, known oil reserves are sufficient to last for more than a quarter of a century at the current rate of exploitation. Certainly, oil is a non-renewable resource; not only is the ratio of reserves to production much smaller than for coal, but oil consumption is likely to increase rapidly in the future. Some day an end will come to this continuous expansion of known reserves keeping pace with expanding future demands. That day has not yet arrived, as new discoveries in the immediate past have proved. But this reprieve only holds when the world is taken as a whole. The situation is different for the major consumer and producer, the United States, where reserves have not increased proportionally; it has more and more to rely on imports from Latin America and the Middle East.

Oil exploration is a longer and more complicated task than assessing coal reserves. Surface shows seldom exist to indicate the presence of hidden sources of oil or gas. Long and tedious geological, geophysical, and paleontological investigations lead to conclusions which finally justify the drilling of test wells. Once oil has been found, perhaps at different horizons, more drilling is required to ascertain the extent and the conditions of the field for future production. Gradually we arrive at figures comparable to the "measured reserves" for coal. Through much experience, oil geologists have been able to establish certain general rules regarding the probable locations where oil may be found or where it is thought futile to search for it. It is, therefore, not surprising that continuous geological research and oil prospecting give an ever-changing pattern of known reserves. In the older, geologically well-known areas, there are still some limited possibilities of increase in the figures for reserves, and above all, for current production. But unexpected discoveries come from faraway areas, as in the Middle Eastern countries in the past decades, or more recently in the Sahara and the continental shelf regions.

Even within a few years the statistical situation may alter considerably, as illustrated by the following table. Proved oil reserves ($95 \cdot 10^{12}$ barrels in 1951 and $260 \cdot 10^{12}$ barrels in 1958) were distributed among different continents and major producing areas as below:

PROVED OIL RESERVES		
AREA	*1951*	*1958*
North America	29%	14%
United States	28	13
Latin America (mostly Venezuela)	13	8
USSR	6	5
Europe	1	1
Asia	52	70
Middle East	49	62
Africa	—	1

The principal function of this sector of the oil industry is to furnish adequate supplies of crude oil. On the whole, exploration is always ahead of production, and reserve-production relationships of particular areas differ widely. The most notable discrepancies exist in the Western Hemisphere and in the Middle East, as the summarizing table clearly shows.

Finally, another significant difference between coal and oil industries should be mentioned. Since its early beginnings, the oil industry has been organized as large-scale enterprise. The names of the leading oil companies are well-known, but we do not intend to start a discussion of their history here. With a very few exceptions, they are traditionally private companies and hence outstanding examples of capitalistic economy. Even though the history of the oil industry is full of bitter fights between different companies, modern developments show equally clearly that they safeguard their position as a group with basically common interests against any outside interference. For the past few decades, as well as at present, the greatest danger for the oil companies has been the mounting tendency to nationalize oil reserves and oil production in countries where the companies are regarded as foreign, and consequently as outside exploiters of national resources. There is an essential difference in legal matters that exists between the United States, on one side, and the Middle East, for example, on the other. In the United States, the right to exploit oil rests with the title to the land; it is familiar to us that landed property increases its value rapidly once oil has been found near by, and that the land-owners may become rich almost overnight. Under these circumstances, oil companies can get hold of the industry only by controlling the transportation system, the refineries, or the marketing organization. In the Middle East, and in most other areas, on the other hand, the right to explore and to exploit is in no way bound to the title to the land, but is granted in the form of concessions. Such concessions gave the oil companies exclusive rights. The conditions under which they are granted have continually changed. Until the Second World War, flat compensations and royalties on the oil produced were the rule. Later on, the countries granting the concessions were given a share in the net profits arising from production, running as high as 50 percent, and in certain cases even 75 percent. Finally, a participation in the overall profits was demanded. Mexico was the first country to nationalize the oil industry in 1938. The venture was successful because she found outlets for her crude in markets (e.g., Germany and Italy) which were not under the control of big oil companies; later her own domestic market expanded so rapidly that it soon became large enough to absorb all her crude. However, the case of Iran demonstrates the almost unsurmountable difficulties with which the nationalization is confronted in less-developed countries. In possession of rich oil fields and the greatest refinery in the Middle East, Iran was unable to find means to transport her oil and an access to the market. She finally had to conclude a new agreement with an international group. The current tendency definitely does not point toward nationalization, but is to bargain and to obtain the most favorable conditions. The Middle Eastern countries together with Venezuela have joined forces to that effect in recent years. In this connection, we should observe that the location of refineries near the consuming end instead of in the area of production, weakens the bargaining position of countries which have merely oil reserves. As the Suez Crisis in 1956 demonstrated, it also makes it possible for the consumers to shift the source of supply readily from one continent to another one.

Much of what has been outlined so far applies to crude oil only. For natural gas there still exists an obstacle barring economical transportation. The natural gas deposits of the Middle East, the Sahara, the Caribbean—in short, of all the distant producers and particularly of producers separated from potential markets by sea —have not yet been ranked among the "exploitable." To liquefy gas and to transport it at low temperatures by tanker proved technically feasible, but up to now, it has been done only on an experimental scale.

The various sectors of the oil and natural gas industry also constitute problem areas from the point of view of an economic geographer. Unlike coal, however, problems derive from the dynamic nature of the industry which reveals itself in almost every aspect we have touched upon.

Other Sources of Energy

Coal, oil, and natural gas are nonrenewable sources of energy. Continuous exploitation will in time lead to exhaustion of these resources. There are enough known reserves of coal to last for several thousand years at the current rate of consumption, but oil and gas will be rather short-lived. Unremitting geological research coupled with improved techniques of mining and utilization might somewhat prolong the period during which these resources are still available in sufficient quantities. Yet ever-increasing energy consumption has already opened a search for new sources. Most of them have been known for a long time as potential sources, but the ways to transform them economically into usable energy have yet to be found. Some of the additional sources which may play an important part in the future are also nonrenewable like coal and oil, but others are classified as renewable and inexhaustible within certain broad limits.

Probably the most important nonrenewable source of energy in this group is fuelwood, which has already been discussed in relation to the general energy balance. We should not think solely of domestic users: in some countries fuelwood takes the place of coal to an amazing degree. Iron and steel plants with a total capacity of half a million tons are using charcoal, produced in the company's own forests, instead of coal or coke, as in Minas Gerais, Brazil. Plants of similar size in the Ural Mountains are also operated with charcoal. Railroads in Finland use wood as fuel. In a way, fuelwood is a borderline case between nonrenewable and renewable sources, because the time required for natural replenishment of the wood is so short that, for instance, the above-mentioned steel plant in Minas Gerais owns forests large enough to maintain an adequate supply of wood for the industry. Fast-growing species—eucalyptus in this case—are indispensable in such an economy.

Definitely nonrenewable is atomic energy. The source materials are used in much the same way as coal, i.e., by first producing heat which in turn may be converted into mechanical and hence into electric energy. As for atomic energy, once its production becomes cheap enough to allow competition with the traditional energy sources, it will be of special interest to the student of economic geography, for transportation costs of the source material are negligible. Atomic power plants could therefore be placed as close to the market as is desired, and losses involved in the transportation of electric power would be minimized. At the moment the great problem seems to be the disposal of the waste products so as to avoid harm to living beings. Statistics on the availability of the source material are scarce and incomplete, but according to the figures published by the United States Bureau of Mines enough reserves are known to exist to satisfy demands for a long time to come.

In a stimulating article which appeared 1948 in the *Proceedings of the American Petroleum Institute,* E. Ayres discussed the major sources of energy. He estimated the total energy on the earth available from renewable or continuous sources to be approximately $13,000 \cdot 10^{12}$ kw hr, only a fraction of which is utilized for the time being (about 1/10,000). Solar radiation, waterfalls, and the earth's heat are the most important sources, the first accounting for more than 96 percent. Other well-known sources are the wind, the tides, and the heat energy of water, which can be recovered by the use of the heat pump.

The difficulty with solar energy is that it is not constantly available and that in many parts of the world sunshine is never dependable. It is particularly awkward for all those who need energy at a certain time, as for cooking, radio, lights, etc.; other needs are more flexible—for example, the need to operate water pumps for irrigation or to heat boilers. Technically, utilization of solar energy has been possible for a long time. It has been found in India that during the period of maximum insolation, solar energy available from a 1-acre space is equivalent to 4 tons of coal. But as yet solar engines are operated with extremely low efficiency (only a few percent) and energy thus derived is expensive. Another disadvantage for general use is that the mirrors with which the heat of sunrays is collected and concentrated are apt to be easily damaged.

Water power has played a much more conspicuous role. In the past flowing water was chiefly used to drive water wheels and turbines; today its transformation into electricity in hydroelectric power plants is of the greatest importance; it will be discussed separately in the next chapter. Theoretically available water power can be calculated by determining the arithmetic mean of the volume of flow for every point along a water course and by multiplying this figure with the altitude above sea level. Available water

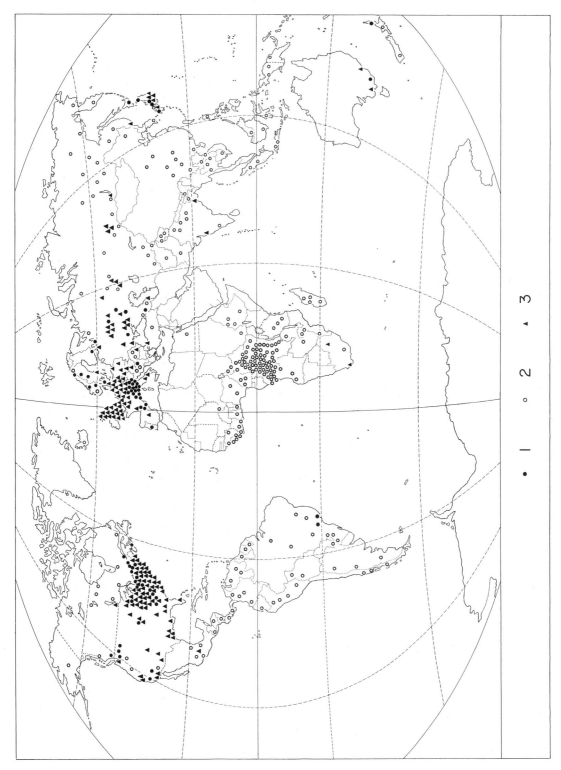

71 · WATER POWER AND ELECTRICITY. Legend: (1) water power, installed capacity; (2) water power, not yet used but usable; (3) thermal power, installed capacity. Each symbol represents a capacity of 2 million kilowatts.

power was thus calculated on the global scale by the 1950 World Power Conference. However, only a small portion of it is actually usable for water-power development. The United States Geological Survey estimated that only about 10 percent or 500 million kw were to be classified as usable. Still more interesting is its distribution: 40 percent is in Africa, 23 in the Americas, 13 in Asia, 3 in Europe, and more than 5 percent in the USSR. They show that most of water power is available far away from the centers of industrialization and has not yet been developed.

Unless transformed into some secondary form of energy, water power cannot be transported. Consequently, users will have to settle in the immediate vicinity of the water course. In the early days of European industry, when water power was the traditional form of energy used, this obstacle was partly overcome with mechanical transmission by steel wire.

The efficiency rate is high in the case of water power; two-thirds or more of its total energy can be made available in modern plants. If a rough comparison between known coal and oil reserves and usable water power is made, using the efficiency coefficients that have been discussed in an earlier chapter, we will find that oil and water power are about equal while coal is much more important. The values are $n \cdot 10^{12}$ kw hr against $n \cdot 10^{15}$ kw hr; n is about 2 to 3.

The economic geographer should particularly observe the relationships between available water power on the one hand and the precipitation regime and land forms on the other hand. Areas of former glaciation are characterized by a great number of small water-power sites, because after the last deglaciation (about 10,000 to 20,000 years ago) the reestablished drainage system was no longer able to find the former one which had already been graded, and there has not been time enough so far for streams to degrade the numerous falls and cataracts in their present courses. In the tropics, on the other hand, the rate of erosion is greatly reduced, and falls of structural origin have been worn down over a much longer period than in mid-latitudes. For example, the block-fault systems which shape the African continent generally date back to the late Mesozoic

age. They give rise to the waterfalls and cataracts of the major African rivers shortly before the rivers reach the sea. Owing to their equatorial location they carry a large volume of water throughout the year. In subtropical latitudes strong seasonality in the rainfall regime reduces the amount of water power available and so does the cold period in higher latitudes, with precipitation in a solid form. Water power and solar energy will make up excellent subjects of study on the relationships between the supply of energy and the environmental conditions.

The same can be said for wind power. Wind power is unreliable, and an important factor from the standpoint of engineering is its rapid shift in force. It can be profitably used wherever availability at a given time is not essential, as in the old-fashioned flour mill; there the grain was milled when the wind blew. Wind power could also be utilized for the production of electricity in combination with thermal plants. Recently this has been tried in Denmark and met with success. Power units there are small, about 30 to 70 kw, while in England where similar trials are carried out the capacity may rise to 100 kw. This source was considered so important by the Organization for European Economic Cooperation (OEEC) that a special Wind Power Working Party has been engaged with these problems since 1950.

In the near future, more important than wind power may be the power of the tides. Tides present no problems of irregularity or unreliability. In fact, it is amazing that tidal-power plants have not yet been started. Since tidal power would in practically all instances have to be transformed into electricity, preferred sites would be where there is a considerable difference between the high and low tides and a coastal topography that facilitates the construction of dams. Such a combination is found on both sides of the Atlantic, from Maine to the Maritime Provinces, and in western France. In both areas projects have already been worked out, and their realization may not be a very long way off. In colonial days, small tidal plants were in operation in New England as well as in Europe for flour milling; there the characteristic production curve oscillating with the tide between zero and a maximum value did not matter much, as in the case of the traditional wind-driven flour mill.

ELECTRICITY, A SECONDARY FORM OF ENERGY

Secondary Energy

The sources of energy mentioned above may all be used to produce a supply of power in the form of electricity, if the market requires energy in that specific form, or as in the case of water power, when their primary uses are greatly limited. Electricity has many advantages over other forms of energy which make it particularly suitable for certain consumers. It can, for example, be distributed in small quantities and is thus ideal for use in households, craft shops, and small industrial plants; for the same reasons it is widely used in densely populated rural areas. In transportation, electricity simplifies the maintenance of engines, and electric motors support and respond better to temporary peak loads. More and more railroads are therefore electrified even in countries where coal is available in abundance. Electricity is clean; nowadays we would not consider steam-driven street cars. For certain purposes, among them electric lighting and electrometallurgical processes, electricity is indispensable and irreplaceable by other forms of energy.

Yet electricity also has serious disadvantages; one of them is that a special transportation system is needed all the way down to the last user, which is costly and very often vulnerable. Another weakness is that electricity can be stored only in very limited quantities in batteries and accumulators. This is perhaps the most serious disadvantage; it means that electricity must be consumed at the same rate as it is produced, or rather vice versa. Other methods of storing electricity have been tried out without much success, such as to heat up rock masses inside of a mountain with surplus energy and to recuperate the heat energy later when it is needed. This of course is a very wasteful undertaking. More widespread is the use of surplus energy to pump up water into artificial lakes at higher altitudes,

from which it is recovered by hydroelectric power plants when regular production falls short of demand. Finally, and of great importance in economic geography, is the fact that electric power transmission by wire entails considerable losses. These generally limit the economically feasible distance between place of production and place of consumption to about 300-500 miles. All the foregoing remarks emphasize the unique nature of electricity as a specific form of energy, which is demanded in ever larger quantities. Atomic energy, coal, natural gas, oil, water power, wind power, etc., may be transformed into electricity. However, electricity is not—and this fact justifies its separate treatment—a source of energy in itself.

Comparatively speaking, only a fraction of the total energy is consumed in the form of electricity. The aggregate production or consumption of electric energy, which is rapidly increasing, is about $2 \cdot 10^{12}$ kw hr a year. Approximately one-third comes from the conversion of water power, and the rest from other sources. For the latter the usual way is first to convert the primary forms of energy into heat and thence into mechanical and finally into electrical energy. Thus we speak of thermal plants in antithesis to hydro plants; each group has its own characteristics and its own advantages as well as disadvantages.

The Structure of the Power Industry

Thermal power plants can be located near the place of consumption. Such location reduces the cost for transmission and distribution and involves only negligible transmission losses. A preferred location is near the waterfront where the bulky primary materials such as coal and oil can be brought in by cheap water transportation. Thermal plants are often found adjacent to unloading sites, especially of coal (oil can be shipped for some distance by pumping at lower cost). Another preferred location is in the vicinity of coal mines to avoid a long-distance hauling of the solid fuel by rail. This is particularly true if coal mines are not too far away from large population centers or if the coal is of low quality. An outstanding example of this is the brown coal mining districts in Germany. Thermal plants have the great advantage that the production of electric energy can be adjusted to variable demand.

For hydroelectricity the regulation of production is achieved by storing water in reservoirs. This necessitates heavy capital investments for the construction of large artificial lakes. Generally, two types of hydroelectric power plants can be distinguished: those capable of storing large quantities of water in reservoirs, and others which utilize the water power available from the flowing stream.

The supply of electricity within an economic region or a country usually presents complex problems. They arise basically from the constantly fluctuating curve of demand for power. A certain amount of basic load is taken by transportation; railroads show a fairly even curve, but streetcars and trolleys have pronounced peaks during the rush hours and corresponding lows at night. More pronounced are the fluctuations of the domestic demand. Cooking hours send the curve up, as do evening and radio or television hours. Electrometallurgical plants have probably the smoothest curve, especially those working on a twenty-four-hour basis. The power industry must be able to supply at all times the exact amount of electricity required. This means that the installed capacity of the power plants should be equal to the maximum consumption. Thus a large part of the power installations must lie idle most of the time. Since thermal plants operated with coal need four to five hours before they are ready to deliver the electric current, it is clear that an excellent solution can be found through combining the two types in such a way

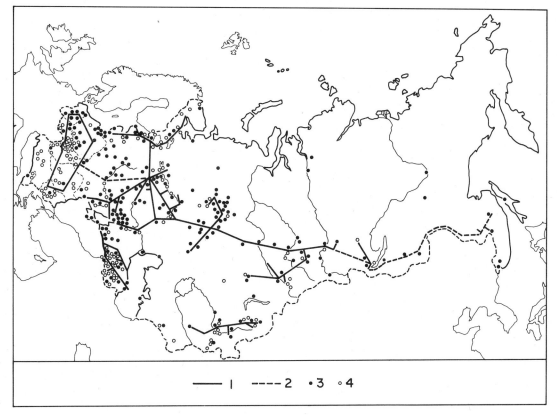

Krüger, 1960; *Oxford Regional Economic Atlas*, USSR and Eastern Europe, 1956; and Kish, 1960

72 · A CONTINENTAL POWER GRID: USSR and Eastern Europe. *Legend:* (1) high-tension power lines, existing; (2) the same, projected; (3) thermal power plants; (4) hydroelectric power plants.

that thermal plants supply the base load and hydro plants the additional peak load. Thermal plants using oil have in this respect the same advantages and may play the same role as hydro plants. The combination of different types of power plants makes necessary a general grid system with multiple interconnections and exchange or switch points. This power structure is very common; a typical example is to be found in England.

A different solution has been found in Switzerland, a mountainous country where electricity is practically the synonym of hydroelectricity. Here, water power of different kinds has been made available in sufficient quantities to meet various needs of electricity consumers. The base load is carried by hydro plants in the lowland without reservoirs, and the peak load—especially in winter when the lowland rivers have a diminished flow—is supplied by plants in the mountains. The latter take relatively small quantities of water, usually from artificial lakes, but have the advantage of a considerable head. Here again all the important power plants are interconnected with a grid system which permits the exchange of current during normal peak loads or for emergency. In short, we will find in every country a different solution, based on the availability of primary sources and on the nature of the market.

Which solution to adopt is finally decided in consideration of relative production costs. It is generally, but wrongly, believed that hydroelectric power is cheaper than thermal power. The truth is that there exists cheap as well as expensive power in each category; consequently it has to be determined first which one is actually more advantageous. Hydro plants are usually low in operational expenses, but represent an enormous capital investment. For thermal plants it is just the opposite. Hydro power becomes more costly as the available water-power reserves near exhaustion; in a country like Switzerland, where nearly 100 percent of electricity is generated from water, thermal electricity, the source materials of which have to be imported over long distances, is able to compete with hydroelectricity today.

In general, electricity is consumed not far from the place where it is produced. It plays a minor role in international trade, for only a fraction of the total production crosses international boundaries. The obstacle of long-distance transmission can now be overcome by new super-high-voltage transmission lines and by sending electricity somewhat in the same fashion as aligned billiard balls hit one another in succession from the place of original impetus.

This is of particular importance for Europe. There are two zones where hydroelectricity is predominantly produced—the Scandinavian countries and the southern mountain chains extending from Spain to Yugoslavia. Between them lies a large zone where thermal plants dominate; Great Britain, Belgium, Holland, northern Germany, and Denmark are almost exclusively dependent on thermal power. There exist plans for an integrated European power system which involves, for instance, an international exchange of the summertime surplus of hydroelectricity in Alpine countries for thermoelectricity in winter. In most of Europe power consumption follows an undulating curve with a high in winter and a low in summer; the production curve of hydro power is just the reverse, owing to a maximum precipitation in summer and solid precipitation in winter. For thermal plants adaptation to market demands is easier, but as has been mentioned, a considerable portion of the installations is not utilized to full capacity for a greater part of the time. The result is the relatively high price of electricity that has to be paid by the consumers. While coal and oil are sold at prices which are variable only according to their quality and quantity, but otherwise much the same for any customer, the price for electricity varies in general according to the class of consumers. Those who require a constant amount are favored with lower prices, since their demand makes up the base load of the plants. Those using electricity during peak hours (and the foremost such users are households) pay a price many times higher for what is seemingly the same commodity.

Power Capacity and Power Production

When we analyze the situation in an individual plant or in a country, we should make a primary distinction between the installed capac-

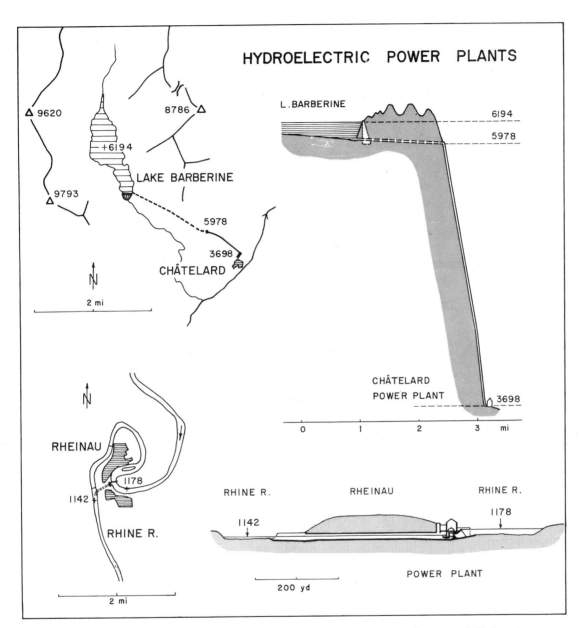

73 · TYPES OF HYDROELECTRIC POWER PLANTS: the two plants, Barberine and Rheinau in Switzerland, as described in the text.

ity measured in kilowatts (kw) or horsepower (1 hp = 0.764 kw), and the production of electric energy measured in kw hr (or hp hr). The first gives us an idea of the size of the installa-

tions, but the second is more significant in characterizing the functions of the plant. A typical river hydro plant in the Swiss lowland (Rheinau) has, for example, an installed capacity of 40,000 kw (at the generator), but the actual production is 118 million kw hr in summer and 97 million kw hr in winter, or a total of 215 million kw hr during the whole year. Barberine, a plant in the high mountains with an artificial lake of 50 million cubic meters content, has the following corresponding figures: 46,000 kw, 12.5 million kw hr + 85.5 million kw hr = 98.0 million kw hr. The ratio of the actual production to the theoretical maximum is 61 percent and 24 percent in the first and the second case, respectively. For Switzerland as a whole the ratio is only 39 percent. In the United States, where only 19 percent of the installed capacity is of hydro, the ratio runs as high as 52 percent. In the United Kingdom the hydro power capacity shares only 3 percent of the total, the ratio being 39 percent as in Switzerland. These figures are set down merely to illustrate the general problems that have been presented above.

In the global energy balance, hydroelectricity does not play an important role. Even if all the available water power (excluding tidal power) were harnessed, very little change would come about in the overall picture. In the preceding section on water power, mention has been made of the total available and usable water power. Theoretically the 500 million kw would give a total of 4380 billion kw hr, or if we use a coefficient of 40 percent for efficiency on the basis of our discussions, probably somewhere around 2000 billion kw hr; this is equivalent to 250 million tons of bituminous coal, according to ERW.

The picture is quite different if we study the situation by particular areas. Africa has 40 percent of the usable water power, as mentioned above, equivalent to 100 million tons of coal; it is a considerable amount compared with the current energy consumption of 45 million tons of coal equivalent only, most of which is actually derived from solid fuels. It is particularly the crescent area paralleling the coast from West Africa all the way to the equator that might prove to be of great interest in the future. In the years preceding the movements toward independence in that part of the world, a tremendous hydro-power development plan had been put into blueprint by the colonial powers, mainly for metallurgical industries. It remains to be seen how much of these projects will materialize under the changed conditions. Another area which should be watched carefully is the Himalayas, where some of the largest potentials in Asia are found. In all these cases the regional importance of hydro power is extremely great, although in the world-wide view it must not be overrated.

To conclude, it should be stressed that electricity is only one, though the most important, of the secondary forms of energy. Manufactured gas is another form; from a certain point of view coke, as well as various oil products, can also be considered as such, but this is a matter of definition.

THE MAJOR INDUSTRIES

9

CONSUMER GOODS

From the economist's point of view, one of the most logical divisions of manufacturing is into consumer-goods and capital-goods industries. The former manufactures things that are actually consumed, such as foodstuffs and clothes, or things used in the way that furniture or cigarettes are used. Capital goods, on the other hand, comprise such machines and other equipment as are used in manufacturing other goods; hence, they are sometimes called production goods.

The consumption of consumer goods often corresponds roughly to the number of inhabitants. Such is the case with almost all kinds of foodstuffs. The daily intake of food per capita, expressed in calories, is somewhere between 2000 and 3000, and only in certain areas does it deviate considerably. The market for clothing is more elastic and may be influenced by external factors to increase consumption. For foodstuffs, changes in consumption must rather be followed as a long-term trend, either in quantity or in nutritional quality. Whether the quantity of consumer goods that can be absorbed by the market is relatively elastic or not, one thing is certain: the controlling factor is the population at large. For example, hundreds of thousands of housewives do their daily shopping to satisfy the needs of hundreds of thousands of families; they demand our full interest, if we make a study of

the economic geography of consumer goods of a certain kind. It is quite different with capital goods. There the customers are relatively few. They invest their capital in order to produce other goods.

Apparently, the two divisions shade into each other. For example, to buy a car was, and in many ways still is, a capital investment; in this case cars are not to be considered consumer goods. Today in many parts of the world, however, they are regarded as consumer goods as much as furniture is.

Our selection of industries under this heading includes manufacturing of forest products in addition to such traditional consumer goods industries as manufacturing of foodstuffs and clothing. Other typical consumer-goods industries are not taken up here simply for lack of space, though they may be of great importance, like tobacco manufacturing or breweries. Consumer-goods industries are usually found to be the first-comers in most countries during the early stage of their industrialization.

Food and Feed

In a primitive society most processing takes place within individual households; some of it has to do with making harvested products suitable for storage, but a larger part is concerned with simple preparations of the daily meal. In a complex economy like ours, the way from the producer to the ultimate consumer is much longer and much processing is involved along the route, usually at the most advantageous location from the economic and technical standpoint. To an ever-increasing degree even some penultimate preparations like peeling potatoes and precooking certain foodstuffs are carried out as large-scale enterprises before the food reaches the consumer. Therefore, the food industries generally expand more rapidly than the corresponding agricultural production. An important cause is to be found in the fast-growing nonagricultural population and urban centers.

In most countries the food industry is a very important sector of industrialization. In general, the plants are smaller than those of other industries, and the number of people employed is high in relation to the value added by processing. It has been estimated that the group "food, drink, and tobacco manufactures" accounts for 20 to 30 percent of the gross value of the national industrial output in most industrialized countries, and for 30 to 40 percent in predominantly agricultural areas. Perhaps even more significant is the fact that in many countries food industries are the first manufacturing enterprises to appear. This has been particularly true for overseas territories, where the necessary installations for processing export products marked the beginnings of secondary occupations.

The degree of economic development manifests itself especially in products which may be consumed without processing. Most fruits and vegetables are such, and they form a distinct class. In a simple economy they are usually sold in a produce market daily or every other day directly by the producer, who perhaps lives within a trade area of a few miles radius from the ultimate consumer. In a more advanced economy, what is required is not only huge quantity but also constant supply of fresh farm products regardless of the season. This demand leads to express delivery systems over larger areas by railroad and trucking, even by airplanes, and also to a characteristic way of selling and buying wholesale, usually on the spot and at rapidly varying prices, which is similar to the marketing of fish. Here processing means that the produce is to be made less perishable, whether by drying,

canning, or deep-freezing. To make the resulting higher prices more attractive, food is generally prepared for cooking, an important consideration in a modern household.

Almost all the processing industries are located close to the place of production. In order to maintain a supply large enough for economical operations, farmers within each area are induced to specialize their production and to deliver the produce under a contract which guarantees volume and price. Production for distant markets, therefore, results in specialized producing areas with mutually coordinated processing units. An important exception to this is commercial banana production, where practically no processing takes place. Production of most other fruits and vegetables shows to some degree the development which has just been outlined.

Preparing foodstuffs for storage is but one phase of processing. Preparing them for transportation, grading them for the market, and rendering them ready for consumption are also to be included in processing. Though all this may be carried out at or near the place of production, as was mentioned above, some processing industries show a strong tendency to concentrate near the place of consumption. Still others are rather indifferent in respect of location. Finally, the size of operational units is an important factor; it can lead to either spatial concentration or dispersal of industry. It is with these remarks in mind that we will examine some of the more important industries in this group.

An outstanding example of a processing plant located close to the place of production is a sugar *central*. Sugar cane requires, especially if the cane fields are burned over before harvesting, immediate processing; sugar cane is seldom transported over a long distance, though some export trade takes place among the Caribbean islands. Sugar beets withstand transport far better and are often shipped over a considerable distance from the farmer to the mill. The radius of an area within which a cane sugar *central* draws the raw material is therefore much smaller than that of a beet sugar mill. Since both are large-scale operations, the difference is reflected in a much higher density of sugar cane cultivation than that of sugar beets; beets are usually grown as

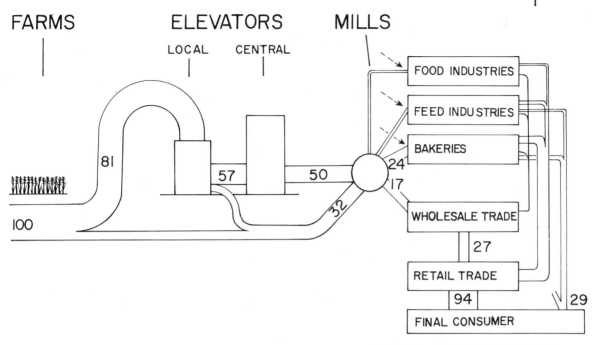

FARMS   ELEVATORS   MILLS

LOCAL   CENTRAL

FOOD INDUSTRIES

FEED INDUSTRIES

BAKERIES

81

57   50   24

17

100   32

WHOLESALE TRADE

27

RETAIL TRADE

94   29

FINAL CONSUMER

Simplified after *Atlas of the World's Agricultural Resources*

74 · THE FLOW OF GRAIN PRODUCTS. A typical case of the processing of agricultural products. The total grain production is represented by 100; all the other figures are the percentages of the total at various stages of processing. Note that the final sum becomes 123, for other materials are added through processing, mainly in the food and feed industries as well as in the bakeries.

part of a crop rotation, while sugar-cane growing represents a typical monoculture.

Once the cane has been processed into raw sugar, the product gains keeping qualities and its transportation and marketing become easier. The sugar refining industry does not have to be in juxtaposition to sugar mills; in fact, refineries can occupy any intermediate location between the *central* and the market. In the United States, sugar refineries until recently were largely supplied with raw sugar by Cuban *centrals*. The reason for this spatial distribution is not technical or geographical, but a tariff policy favoring the import of semifinished products.

Other industries in this group prefer a location close to the market. A typical example is the flour mill. Unmilled wheat is an almost ideal commodity for storage and transport; if stored in a dry and well-ventilated place, it can keep for years without showing any deterioration. Loading and unloading can be manipulated

pneumatically, and no sacking is necessary. All these qualities disappear as soon as wheat is milled into flour. Furthermore, milling produces many different kinds of flour from an identical variety of wheat with diverse baking and nutritional qualities. It is therefore advantageous and even necessary to move the milling industry toward the market and near to the centers of population. European countries where large quantities of wheat are stored for emergencies have developed their own milling industry, even when their domestic production is far short of covering requirements and imports are made from distant countries.

A similar situation used to prevail in the meat industry. Slaughterhouses were located as close to the place of consumption as possible. Cattle were moved over long distances and slaughter and processing were done near the consuming end. Later on, improved techniques in canning, cold storage, and deep-freezing freed the industry from this locational restriction. The size of the operational unit increased and the industry was concentrated in large packing plants. Since livestock were usually shipped by special block trains, large processing plants at rail centers were in an advantageous situation. This is well exemplified by the meat-packing industry in the Chicago area. Examples in other countries indicate that the converging point of railroads and overseas shipping lines is a favored location for the development of the industry, as in the La Plata area (Argentina, Uruguay). Large-scale operations had many important advantages, for example, the most economical utilization of by-products (blood, bones, etc.). An increasing use of trucks for the shipment of live cattle began to modify in the United States the former locational factors of the railroad age and have gradually led to a certain degree of decentralization of the industry with a shift in preference for shorter-distance shipment.

Particularly noteworthy are the locational requirements of plants for the extraction and processing of vegetable fats and oils (peanuts, coconuts, oil palm, etc.); in some cases this industry is found near the place of production, but in other cases close to the market. In view of the bottleneck in oils and fats that generally exists in the industrialized countries of middle latitudes, these vegetable products of largely tropical origin assume great importance in world commerce. On the whole it may be said that the United States would rather import the finished products, whereas European countries prefer to import oil-bearing raw materials and do the processing in their own domains. The reason for this difference is as follows. A very important by-product of the extracting industries is the residues that yield feed cakes; much tighter supplies of animal feed in Europe necessitate a thorough utilization of raw materials, but the United States imports vegetable oil for human consumption only. Another difference, one of less significance in the present context, lies in the fact that the United States imports more coconut oil than any other kind, while palm oil and, above all, peanut oil are preferred in Europe.

In general, the size of the operating unit tends to increase. The result is often important struc-tural changes in marketing final products. Typical are two basic supply lines, bread and meat. Small-scale bakeries and butchers are now partially or wholly replaced by large-scale bread and meat factories as processing units and by general chain stores, cooperatives, etc., as distributing and retailing organizations. Similarly, the collection, processing, and distribution of milk have changed, though at different rates in different countries.

In following these processing operations step by step, we will undoubtedly encounter statistical difficulties, because the unit of measurement may change from one step to the next and frequently something is added or dropped out. With the help of conversion factors, various goods can be made comparable. A simple example is rice milling: rice as it is harvested is generally called paddy; later it passes through the successive stages of husked, milled, and polished rice, at each of which some substance is removed as a waste or a by-product. The conversion (by weight) is quite simple in this case. Taking paddy as 100, processing reduces its weight roughly in the following order: husked rice = 90, milled rice = 65, and polished rice = slightly less than 65. The difficulty arises from the fact that rice statistics often fail to specify the stage of milling. Rice is thus a good illustration of the way a product may undergo continuous decrease in total weight through processing. In the next chapter we will come across a case in which the weight remains practically unchanged, i.e., the manufacture of textiles from spinning to finishing. Rice milling gives rise to by-products, while the textile industry does not know them. By-products play an important part in an appraisal of an industrial process. What is considered waste in the early stage of an industry will be fully utilized in the course of time to bring additional profits. The by-products have often turned out to be more interesting economically than the original main product. Wood processing (dealt with below), like rice milling, entails considerable losses, but unlike it in no way at a fixed rate. For wood, losses may be much reduced through intelligent handling. Further, valuable by-products are obtained from waste materials of sawmills, etc. Finally, there are products for which a considerable amount of material is added through processing; printing paper, for example, may have as much as 30 percent of its original weight added in the form of fillers, mostly mineral.

The industries in this group are of very diverse character. Taken together, they hold an important place in the national economy. In the United States their importance is surpassed only by the production of machinery, transportation equipment, primary metals, etc.; certainly they outrank the next group in our discussion, viz., the textile industry (excluding apparel and related products). In countries whose exports consist mainly of agricultural products that have to be processed before shipping, this group assumes the leading role in industrial activities.

Clothing

If all the industries concerned with the different phases of the manufacture of clothing (textile mills, apparel, and related products, according to the classification used in the United States statistics) are taken together, their total magnitude becomes truly impressive. In number of employees and workers, this combined group occupies the first place among all the industrial groups in the United States. However, it is surpassed by food industries in the number of establishments, and by metals, machinery, and transportation equipment in values added. Throughout the following discussion these characteristics will prove to be of major consequence.

The textile industry is the sector of industrial activity in which the new production techniques were first applied in the eighteenth century. Revolutionary inventions were made in England, born of a generally high level of rational, scientific thinking. In the early days of industrialization the selection of a particular site for a new industry was to a large degree influenced by natural factors. An abundant supply of clear water and—particularly for cotton textile mills —a humid maritime climate were often determining site factors. Small water-power sites also played an important role in the early development of the textile industry, in Europe as well as in New England. The first-mentioned loca-

tional factor, human inventiveness, soon lost its decisive meaning because textile machinery was exported, clandestinely or otherwise, and developed further in other countries. The second group of factors, natural site, lost its significance after the industry outgrew the local energy sources and operations were carried out in an artificial climate inside the factory. Thus, the textile industry was able to take roots in other parts of the world, first in the middle latitudes and later in any regions, regardless of climatic conditions.

In view of the outstanding importance of the textile industry in economic history, and above all, of the leading position occupied by the textile products in the earlier European export trade, this dispersal throughout the world should be considered a major change in the structure of world economy. There are two main reasons why the textile industry is usually among the first to develop in the course of industrialization: (1) since food and clothing are prime necessities, home production of these essential goods will improve the trade balance of a nation; (2) textile industries provide work for more people than most other industries do. However, since the ratio of man-hours to values added is relatively high, the textile industry is more sensitive to the wage level than other industries.

The misery of the textile workers in the infancy of the industry is well-known. A combination of mining and textile industries was quite frequent, as in the Appalachian valleys or in the Ruhr, where women and children found an additional income in the textile mills while men worked in the mines. The dispersal of the textile industry was favored by the rising wage level in the older industrial areas and countries; the industry emigrated to territories of lower wages. The tendency to follow the gradient of wages is more pronounced in the cotton industry than in the wool or silk industry, and within the cotton industry it varies from one section to the other. Despite a considerable wage differential in its favor, a newly established textile industry cannot in all cases compete with the traditional exporters; but in view of the importance of the industry within the national economy, it is generally allowed to grow behind a substantial protection of tariffs and other economic manipulations.

The first massive competition in the world market in modern times came from the side of Japan, but even Japan is no exception to the general trend and feels the influence of steadily rising wages at home. Just as European textile exports declined earlier, Japanese textile exports are now rapidly falling off. This general statement requires immediate specifications. Not only did the exports of textiles decline, but also in the remaining portion a change is observed, a shift toward specialties—high-quality fabrics and man-made fibers for one thing, and garments and finished goods for another. The older textile areas have the advantage in this respect on their side, but with regard to unspecialized mills the industries developed in new areas were favored by their lower wages. The rapid development of new textile capacities in newly industrialized countries affects primarily the older production areas in Europe, the United States, and also to a large degree Japan. Adjustments are difficult and made mainly by structural changes and by rationalizing production; rationalizing includes reduction of man-hours by improving production methods, elimination of outmoded and uneconomical units, developing new fabrics, etc.

Cotton is by far the most important raw material for the world's textile industry, and therefore some aspects of the location factors of the cotton textile industry will now be summarized. The complete process of the industry may be divided roughly into the following steps: (*a*) the harvested cotton is separated from the seeds by ginning; (*b*) the lints are spun into yarn; (*c*) the yarn is woven into textiles (in the strict sense of "woven fabrics"); (*d*) by further processes, of which bleaching and dyeing are the most important, finished cloth is made; (*e*) finally, the clothing industry and other industries make use of these fabrics for various ends.

The cotton textile industry with its vertical structure shows features that will be even more outstanding if compared with the iron and steel industry delineated in Chapter 10. (1) In the flow of the material through a textile mill, practically everything entering into the manufacturing process emerges at the end as something usable. Only a small fraction drops out in the beginning as unspinnable waste. Further, the end products are actually consumed and not returned in some way or other into the process. The consumption of raw cotton by the textile industry is consequently equal to the consumption of finished goods. (2) As a result of this one-way flow of materials it is very characteristic of the textile industry that its different sections are relatively independent of one another, and each can select the most economical location. Freight rates are a factor that might work against this possible spatial disintegration of the textile industry; they are generally higher for manufactured goods and therefore induce the industry to shift toward the consuming end. (3) Textile manufacture requires only a low capital investment in comparison with the heavy industries. This enables the textile industry to adjust its location to changing cost factors. The distribution pattern of this industry is thus fluid, changing from one period to another. The textile industry does not form industrial centers of gravity of the same permanence as industries with a high inertia. As a result of the high number of workers, this fluidity creates special problems of a social and political order.

As for the location factors affecting particular sections of the cotton textile industry, cotton gins are necessarily within or near the cotton-growing areas, since the seeds constitute about two-thirds of the weight of the harvested cotton; in fact gins are found widely dispersed over the whole cotton area and in every respect unrelated to succeeding steps in processing. The clothing industry and the fashion industry in particular are equally rigid in their location, needing to be close to the market. Rome and Paris in Europe, New York and Los Angeles in the United States, may serve as outstanding examples of this. Spinning, weaving, and finishing take intermediate positions, but their inclination to follow wage differentials decreases from spinning to finishing. Spinning mills respond quickly to changes and are usually the first to seek a new location in areas of lower wages. Finishing remains nearer to the market for a number of reasons. Finishing mills need to maintain close connections with the clothing and chemical industries, and wages are less important in the cost structure than for other sections.

In the early stages of mechanized production the mutual independence of the component sectors was significant. If we do not count the cotton gin, which was invented in 1793, the new production techniques saw their first general application in the field of spinning. It brought about a concentration of the yarn production and of yarn workers in steadily growing mill towns, while weaving was still carried on by hand as a cottage industry.

In northeastern Switzerland such changes also took place, following the typical sequence. In 1787 the Zürich canton had 170,000 inhabitants and was one of the most highly industrialized regions of Europe, with 24 percent of its population actively engaged in the making of textiles. At that time all work was done by hand. More than four-fifths of the textile workers were occupied with spinning. The first spinning machines were introduced from England in 1800 and the years immediately following. Even as late as 1840, when spinning had already been mechanized completely, there were only two weaving mills, with a total of 60 to 80 workers, and 17,000 hand looms in addition. In that interval the share of the spinning industry had dropped from four-fifths to one-third of the total textile workers, the rest being mostly weavers. The number of workers had been rising steadily during that period because of a mounting production of yarn and the subsequent expansion of demand for textiles in general. The introduction of mechanized weaving drastically reduced the number of weavers, and hence the ratio of textile workers to the total population. In contrast to eighteenth-century Zürich and its 24 percent of textile workers, in the United States today all manufacturing industries together employ about one-tenth of the total population! This also illustrates the revolutionary changes that occurred in textile regions in the nineteenth century as a result of mechanized production; political and social repercussions during the period were cushioned by the rapid expansion of industry in general that served as a shock absorber.

In England the cotton textile industry developed within the traditional framework of the wool industry around the Pennine Chains. After 1500 the guild system was replaced by the domestic system, by which the centrally located merchants and entrepreneurs gradually improved their position, whereas the spinners and weavers were impoverished. The eighteenth century witnessed the basic inventions which increased productivity, forcing the industry to utilize new sources of raw materials. In 1736 the sale of fabrics containing cotton was permitted for the first time by the Manchester Act, and in 1774 the manufacturing of pure cotton fabrics was authorized by act of Parliament. Toward the end of the eighteenth century the domestic system had been completely replaced by the factory system, many decades earlier than in other European countries. England then commanded a unique position in the world and was by far the most productive economic area. In the following century stiff competition came from other European countries; the textile industry in America grew rapidly behind rigid tariff walls, and Japan, Egypt, India, and Latin American countries also emerged later as competitors. Despite all this, England was able to hold a leading position in world textile exports until the First World War. In 1910 cotton yarns and woven fabrics made up one-quarter of her exports. By the middle of the century the proportion had dropped to but a few percent, though outdated spinning and weaving mills had been rapidly and systematically closed down to be replaced by modern machinery.

Well known is the development in the United States, where the first textile mill was built in New England at Pawtucket, Rhode Island, in 1793. Many waterfalls characteristic of postglacial drainage, combined with a suitable climate—particularly, high humidity to guarantee a smooth production process—were important site factors. Stronger influence was exerted by human factors—enterprising men with capital, labor recruited from the surrounding farm areas and later through immigration, and last but not least, an economic policy which protected the high-cost industry of the young United States against the old low-cost producers in Europe. In this way the New England textile industry grew

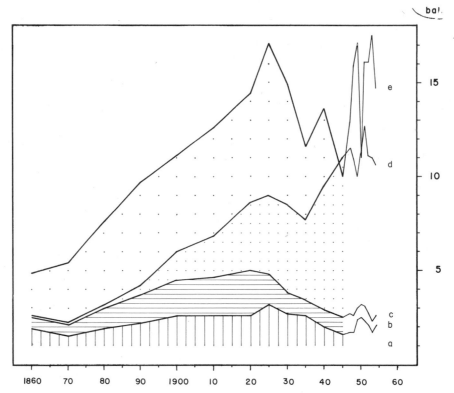

75 · COTTON IN THE UNITED STATES, 1860–1954. *Band a-e: total production of cotton in the United States. Band a-b: cotton exported from the United States. Band b-c: raw cotton consumed in the New England states. Band c-d: raw cotton consumed in the southern states. Band d-e: others, including stocks. Data were plotted at ten-year intervals between 1860 and 1920, at five-year intervals between 1920 and 1945, and at one-year intervals after 1945. The vertical scale is in million bales, each bale representing 500 pounds.*

together with the rapidly expanding national market. Until about 1870 its spinning mills had been using about three-quarters of all the raw cotton consumed in the whole of the United States. From that time onward their share steadily declined to less than 10 percent after the Second World War. The absolute amount of raw cotton consumed by New England mills, however, continued to increase until 1920. After the First World War it also began to diminish, reaching the amounts of a century before in the 1950's. These relative and absolute changes that took place in the New England textile industry were first felt in the spinning sector. New England had achieved a high wage level through industrialization and urbanization. Spinning mills were the first to seek a new location in low-wage areas, which they found in the Piedmont Region

of the Appalachians, formerly a cotton-producing area but at that time already largely abandoned by cotton farming. Here, as in other cases, the spinning industry was by no means attracted by the nearness of the cotton producing area, the cotton belt of the Southern States. As was pointed out above, no advantage accrues to the spinning industry from being located near the cotton farming area. On the contrary, freight charges being higher for manufactured goods than for the raw material, a location near the source of the latter has decided disadvantages; but they may be compensated for if there is abundant cheap labor available. Incidentally, the Piedmont Region gained the great advantage of being equipped with up-to-date installations, like most of the textile areas in newly industrialized countries. This is all the more important as wage

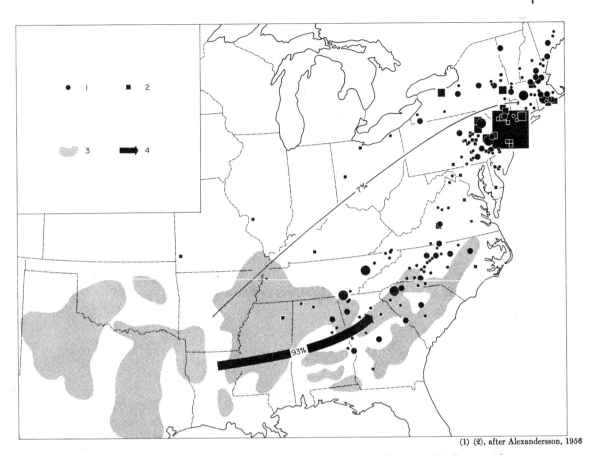

(1) (2), after Alexandersson, 1956

76 • TEXTILES: an example of a nonintegrated industry. (1) Textile towns. (2) Towns with apparel industry dominant. Note that the distribution of (1) and (2) do not represent the distribution of these industries, but of the towns where the textile and apparel industries play a dominant role. The size of the symbols is proportional to the importance of the industry, expressed in terms of number of workers. (3) Principal cotton producing areas in the southern states. (4) Major movements of raw cotton, of which 93 percent is consumed by the industry located in the cotton-growing states and 7 percent in New England (1960).

differentials tend to decrease with increasing industrial development. Certain initial advantages will gradually disappear, as they did in the South of the United States or in Japan. Spinning was the first to seek the way to cheap labor, followed by weaving, but to a lesser degree; finishing remained rather static. The originally highly concentrated textile industry of the United States thus became more dispersed.

Two major conclusions are to be drawn from the foregoing discussion. (1) Historical experience demonstrates that there is constant change in every sector of the industry. The present situation and problems are not essentially different from those of a hundred years ago; only the stage and the players have changed. (2) The cotton textile industry manifests certain features of its own. This will become clearer as we proceed and take up other industries by comparison. Though the manufactures of wool and silk differ in many respects from cotton, they will be omitted in this text simply because we are under pressure to concentrate our attention on the more salient examples.

Wood as a Raw Material

The forests of the world, as described in Chapter 3, constitute a major source of raw materials. In many parts of the earth they are still considered inexhaustible, and there the expression "timber mining" indicates the kind of exploitation carried on. In other countries, strict forest laws based on the principle of sustained yields have led to a method of utilization called "timber cropping." This is an excellent expression, since trees are cultivated under this system with the same care and according to the same general principles as apply to any other crops. Scientific forestry was one of the significant improvements in land utilization, in Europe practiced for many centuries. Yields have constantly improved, and the kinds of trees grown have been selected in quick response to changing demands. In the United States the psychological approach to the forest problem was entirely different. There the land had to be cleared of primary growth not many generations ago, and the supply of timber seemed inexhaustible. Under these circumstances it was only natural that replanting did not make much sense; consequently, the secondary forests that took over were of rather poor quality. Timber mining may have paid for the time being, but in the long run it proved to be an extremely destructive form of land use.

The yields of the forests of the world are generally underestimated. The total quantity of all the fellings in weight is more than five times that of all the wheat grown, or more than three times as much as all the iron ore mined. Much of it is used for nonindustrial purposes; but more than half of all the fellings are ultimately directed into one of the channels which are classified as industrial. Because the big forests are peripheral to the main industrial regions, forest products also play an important role in international trade. The two main trade routes lead from northern into central Europe, and from Canada into the United States. Exports from the USSR are fluctuating. Those from tropical countries to higher latitudes are quantitatively small, but they furnish some important high-quality woods used in furniture, in ply-

wood products, and for other special purposes.

At the present time the tropical forest occupies an insignificant position in the wood industries of the world, for the following reasons. (1) The tropical forest is by nature highly mixed, composed of trees of very different qualities; this makes logging operations costly and demands selective treatment in processing. (2) The haul between the source area and the market is usually long, which adds to expenses; having a low specific value, wood is sensitive to freight charges. (3) Industries, particularly the pulp and related industries, are at the moment interested in coniferous softwoods and not in hardwoods of the tropical forests. It is quite possible that the relative importance of the tropical forest will increase in the future. The wood industry may be forced to develop new techniques and processes in order to utilize tropical hardwoods, and consumers will ultimately have to bear the added expenses of shipment, etc.

In contrast to the textile industry, the vertical structure of the wood-using industries is highly varied. The felled trees enter into different channels to be used in a variety of ways. A great bulk consists of saw logs and veneer logs, which are processed to sawnwood, sleepers, and plywood. About one-fifth of what is industrially used is pulpwood. It is manufactured into wood pulp and later into pulp products—newsprint, fiberboard, etc. The third group, which historically played an outstanding role in the utilization of forest products but has fallen in recent years to 1 or 2 percent, is made up of pit props used in mines.

These are global figures. The situation in particular countries or continents is quite different. The ratio of industrial wood to total fellings drops to about 10 percent in Latin America and Africa, where most of the fellings are used for nonindustrial purposes, primarily as fuel. On the other hand, the ratio becomes higher than 80 percent in North America and lies above the world average in the USSR and in Europe.

Trends in international trade reflect changes in the location of the wood industries. Generally, trade in roundwood, as compared with the trade in processed wood, such as sawnwood or pulp, is decreasing, which means that the wood in-

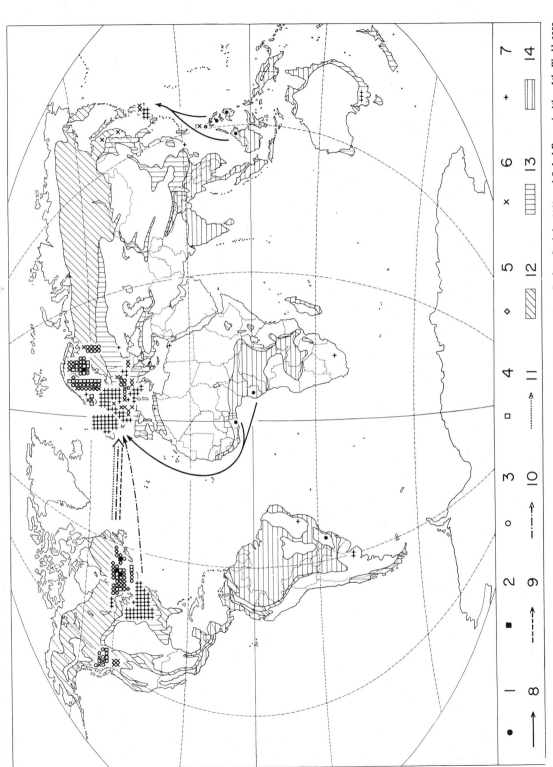

77 · FOREST PRODUCTS—TRADE. Each symbol from (1) to (7) represents 1 million cubic meters of roundwood equivalent: (1) exports of sawlogs and veneer logs; (2) exports, pulpwood; (3) exports, sawn wood; (4) exports, wood pulp; (5) exports, newsprint; (6) exports, other products; (7) imports, undifferentiated. Principal intercontinental trade relations are indicated by arrows. Each arrow represents the volume of trade that exceeds 1 million cubic meters of roundwood equivalent; (8) trade in saw logs and veneer logs; (9) trade in saw wood; (10) trade in wood pulp; (11) trade in newsprint. Types of forests distinguished here are: (12) coniferous forests; (13) temperate mixed forests; and (14) tropical hardwood forests.

FAO Yearbook of Forest Products Statistics, 1961; and Oxford Economic Atlas of the World, 1955

1	2	3	4	5	6	7
•	■	○	◇	12	×	+
8	9	10	□		13	14

dustry tends to move toward the raw material base. This is true both for the lumber industry and for the pulp industry. Unprocessed wood is a commodity with a relatively low specific value and is consequently sensitive to freight charges. The losses through waste are also important in the sawmills, i.e., in the first stages of processing. We should also consider the interest which wood-producing countries must have in utilizing the forest resources for their own industrialization and in processing the raw material as far as possible within their own boundaries.

The location factors of the lumber industry are easily understood and need no further comment. Wood is by far the most important raw material for the pulp industry. The ideal source of wood pulp is trees of coniferous species. Wood is disintegrated into pulp either mechanically or chemically. One ton of mechanically processed wood pulp corresponds roughly to 2.5 cubic meters of roundwood, in contrast to 5.0 cubic meters for chemically produced wood pulp. Pulp in turn is used for a vast variety of purposes— newsprint, printing and writing paper, paper board, fiber board, etc.—as well as for the manufacture of synthetic fibers of the cellulose type to be discussed later. The pulp plants were the first ones to be established at the raw-material base. Later came mills using pulp for further processing, especially for making newsprint. This trend resulted in a decrease of raw materials and semiprocessed goods in international trade, but such items as newsprint increased considerably.

A salient feature in world wood statistics is the outstanding importance of the United States and of North America as a whole. There the per capita consumption of all the products mentioned above far exceeds that in Europe or the USSR. A visitor coming from Europe to the United States is startled by the enormous quantity of paper products consumed daily, from the well-stuffed Sunday paper to cardboard boxes that are burned instead of being nicely folded and used again. Sawmills also impress our visitor, because all the cuttings are treated as waste and burned on the spot. He could think of a host of ways in which sawdust and other waste products are made use of in Europe, where wood has been a scarce commodity for centuries and good husbandry expresses itself not only in the careful management of the forests but also in the thorough utilization of their products. In the eyes of a foreigner, the high per capita consumption of forest products in the United States does not necessarily reflect a higher standard of living, but rather a habit, which dates back to the times when the whole continent with all its natural resources was still at men's free disposal. It is a habit which will have to be changed sooner or later and adjusted to the rate of natural rejuvenation of the forests.

THE MAKING OF IRON AND STEEL

Iron and steel had been made for many centuries, but it was not until the Industrial Revolution that the demand for them increased beyond all expectations. The whole technical development of the past two hundred years has been based largely upon this sector of industrial economy. The iron and steel industry is also called "heavy industry" for obvious reasons, or "basic industry." Iron and steel are basic because they go into the making of many consumer goods, but above all they are the dominant metals used in the manufacture of capital goods, mostly machinery and transportation equipment, upon which modern economy so largely rests. In the United States the primary metals industry, fabricated metal products, machinery (electrical and other), and transportation equipment together comprise more than one-third of all the industrial employees and almost two-fifths of the total value added by manufacturing. Of course, other raw materials are included in that total, but iron and steel are by far the most important. For the economic geographer the iron and steel industry is basic for other reasons than these. We will see that this industry requires an areal integration of various steps in production which in turn leads to highly concentrated large industrial agglomerations. Once such centers have been established, the industry shows a high degree of inertia and remains in the location that was first selected. The inertia of the iron and steel industry leads to severe problems, because the optimum location is likely to change in the course of time; older steel centers are rarely capable of an optimum utilization of resources and of production-consumption relationships.

It can be truly said that this industry has been the basic industry of the nineteenth and at least of the first half of the twentieth century. It will therefore be discussed in more detail than other industry groups.

Locational Factors

THE LESSONS OF HISTORICAL STUDY

A historical approach to the problems of the iron and steel industry reveals to us the two primary features: (1) the influence of an expanding and, with respect to the kind of products, changing market upon production methods and (2) the instability of the so-called optimum location. Through historical studies we gain an appreciation of the importance of dynamics in economic geography and avoid the danger of assuming the present situation to be something fixed forever. This is particularly important in view of the part that iron and steel industry performs today in the large-scale planning of many countries.

The year 1556 witnessed the appearance of a book by Georgius Agricola in Basel, Switzerland, called *"De Re Metallica"* [On Metallurgy] which became a leading authority on iron metallurgy for a long time. The situation described by Agricola marks an important turning point of the iron industry, prompted by an increasing demand from what we would call today the armaments industry. Before, iron had been made in a hollow furnace about 8 feet high and 2 feet in diameter; the furnace was charged with iron ore and charcoal, and only a small quantity of iron (not more than 20 pounds or so) was obtained at a time. This iron was malleable and could be worked into nails, horseshoes, and swords. Artillery, which came into existence shortly before Agricola's date, demanded large quantities of cannon balls made of iron. In order to cope with increasing demands the obvious thing was to build larger furnaces. They were made higher, air was blown in to stimulate the smelting and reduction process, and soon a shaft

furnace was able to produce 1,000 to 2,000 tons of iron per year. Less iron remained in the slag, which attests a great improvement in the metallurgical process. But the iron was high in carbon content and for this reason no longer malleable unless it was subjected to a second smelting in which part of the carbon was burned away or oxidized. For such foundry products as the cannon ball or the cover for an oven—another major product of the industry in those days—the high-carbon iron proved excellent because it was very fluid in the molten state. These blast furnaces consumed much more charcoal than the earlier simple furnaces—about 1½ times as much. More and more iron was produced in areas where there still remained large forest reserves, and the ore was carried over amazingly long distances to the furnaces. It was chiefly in the forested mountainous parts of Central Europe and in peripheral areas that iron furnaces and charcoal kilns were found. Thus the Alps and the Jura Mountains, the mountain chains in central Germany, as well as in Sweden and Russia, became major producing areas. In England, where the importation of iron was prohibited in 1597, the forests were soon depleted. Consequently, in the middle of the eighteenth century on the eve of the approaching Industrial Revolution, England was again importing about nine-tenths of her iron requirements.

After lengthy experiments Abraham Derby succeeded for the first time in using coke instead of charcoal. This not only freed England from dependence on iron imports; perhaps more important, it freed the iron industry in general from dependence on forests. The invention of the steam engine by James Watt in 1770 ushered in the possibility of building blast furnaces and iron works at a distance from water power, a strong locational factor in the past. By the early nineteenth century the use of coke had become universal in England, but in continental Europe charcoal was only gradually being displaced by the new method.

Coke, which was much harder and denser than charcoal, and the introduction of the hot blast in 1820 made the construction of larger and more efficient furnaces possible. At the end of the eighteenth century a blast furnace already had a capacity of 6 tons or more per day, and this was gradually raised to several hundred tons. (Modern furnaces turn out between 1,000 and 2,000 tons of iron each day!) The iron so produced was much like iron from the charcoal blast furnace. It was high in carbon and excellent for making foundry products, but it had to be reworked if malleable materials were required. At first the market was mainly asking for foundry iron, but demand shifted more and more toward the other kind. We will henceforth use the terms "iron" and "steel" to distinguish between these two types.

The technology of the blast-furnace process has remained essentially unchanged since the early eighteenth century, though improvements were added in more than one respect, achieving considerable economy in the production of iron. On the other hand the making of steel, which was demanded in increasing quantities and varying qualities, underwent major changes. Finally an increased output itself exerted an important influence upon iron and steel production. Some of these improvements and new techniques will be discussed in the next section as far as they are relevant to the study of economic geography.

THE VERTICAL STRUCTURE OF THE INDUSTRY

All the iron used in industry is ultimately derived from iron ores. A number of factors determine whether a rock containing iron should be classified as an iron ore. The most important is the iron content, which varies from 30 percent or so in low-grade ores to as high as 60 or 70 percent in rich deposits. Iron is usually found in ores in the form of iron oxides, but there are other compounds which are economically significant, like FeS_2 or pyrites. Of particular importance is the amount of "impurities" present, such as silica and lime, or small quantities of sulfur and phosphorus, since they may require special metallurgical treatment. Many iron ores can be used in the blast furnace without further treatment except screening. But the practice of enrichment or beneficiation in order to raise the iron content of the ore by various means is applied more and more in order to save fuel in the furnace. Ores may be hydraulically or magnetically enriched. Fine or soft ores are also

sintered into pieces of uniform size. Finally, different ores are mixed to obtain just the composition desired for the blast furnace and to assure the best subsequent results. It is usual for plants for the enrichment of iron ores to be located at the mines or at the first point of transshipment. Treated ores have a higher specific value and can withstand the rough handling of loading, unloading, and transportation better than untreated soft ores; the latter may lose as much as a fourth of the original weight in a long distance shipment. Treated ores also simplify blast-furnace operations from a technical point of view. Untreated ores are being more and more displaced by iron ore that has been enriched and sintered.

The next step in processing ores is the blast furnace. Its function is to reduce the iron oxides to iron and to separate iron from slag through smelting. The double function of reduction and smelting is achieved by coke. Some ores present difficulties in the separation of the slag, particularly so-called acid ores. Acid ores have a high silica content and demand an admixture of limestone or dolomite as flux. Thus iron ore, coke, and sometimes limestone usually make up the charge. Slag and iron are regularly drained off in a molten state from the bottom of the furnace, and gases escape through the top. The availability of large quantities of water for cooling is an additional important requirement for blast-furnace operation.

The amount of coke needed for producing one ton of iron is of the greatest interest to the economic geographer. Around 1800 it was about 2.5 tons of coke, or 4.0 tons of coal. Improvements in the making of coke and in furnace operations reduced this gradually to about 1.0 ton of coke in the thirties, and further to 0.7-0.8 ton in recent years. Despite this reduction in volume, the cost of the coke needed is hardly less, since the increase in coke prices has minimized the economic effect of these changes. However, increased efficiency in production, together with rising coke prices, has changed the locational factors of the blast furnace considerably. In the infancy of the industry the optimum location was obviously near the coal basin. As far as blast furnaces are concerned, however, this no longer

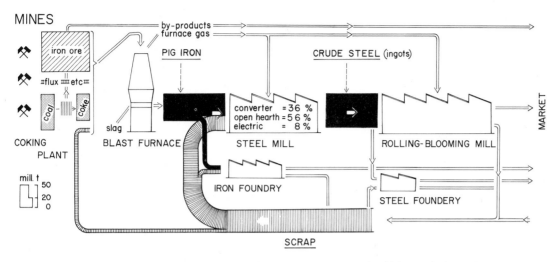

MINES

by-products
furnace gas

iron ore

PIG IRON

CRUDE STEEL (ingots)

flux etc

coal | Coke

slag

converter = 36 %
open hearth = 5 6 %
electric = 8 %

MARKET

COKING
PLANT

BLAST FURNACE

STEEL MILL

ROLLING-BLOOMING MILL

mill. t
50
20
0

IRON FOUNDRY

STEEL FOUNDERY

SCRAP

78 · THE FLOW OF MATERIALS in heavy industry. The diagram should be studied in conjunction with the text on the structure of heavy industry, which is basically the same everywhere in the world though materials that move from one section to another may vary in quantity according to local conditions. The case illustrated here represents something of an intermediate type, based on the average figures on coal, coke, iron ore, pig iron, crude steel, and scrap for Western Europe in the mid-fifties. Flow channels for by-products and furnace gas as well as outlets for finished products are shown without any quantitative indications. The percentage shares of the three steel-making processes are also for Western Europe. The share of converter steel is relatively high, owing to the special nature of European ores.

holds true. Coke has remained the major bottleneck in raw material supply in most countries; to reduce coke consumption, there is a tendency to shift toward higher-grade ores or enriched ores and to feed the furnace in part with iron scrap.

Another factor of great interest is the significance of blast furnace operations in relation to the whole of heavy industry. Since the early days of the iron industry, the blast furnace has been the most important sector whenever the market expanded considerably, since iron was there obtained in a usable form for the first time. In a more highly developed economy, and particularly in a saturated market condition, the importance of the blast furnace sector is greatly reduced. Much iron returns to the mill after a certain lapse of time as scrap or old metal to be reworked. Under these conditions the blast furnace acts as a sort of regulator; it becomes most important in times of increased demand, as in the war years, but falls back in other periods.

For these reasons coal or coke as a locational factor of heavy industry, as pointed out before, is no longer as significant as one might suspect at first.

The iron obtained from the blast furnace is called pig iron, for the red-hot iron bars, neatly arranged in rows, really look like little pigs. Pig iron contains 2.5-4.5 per cent carbon, melts at between 2300 and 2700° F, and then becomes very fluid. It can be directly used to make foundry products, but being brittle in a solid state, it cannot be hammered but must first be converted to steel. Essentially, steel making consists in bringing down the carbon content to 0.05-1.5 percent, depending upon the quality of steel (low- or high-carbon steel) and removing certain impurities which impair quality. Other materials may be added to give steel special properties for specific uses. (This will be discussed later in connection with alloys.) While the making of steel was becoming increasingly important, the market for foundry products remained rather limited. Today they make up about 10 percent of the pig iron produced; the rest is sent to the steelworks.

Two processes dominate modern steel making, —the converter process and the open-hearth process. The converter process, invented by Bessemer in 1856, can be simply described as follows: molten pig iron is poured into big, pear-shaped converters, into which hot air or oxygen is blown from the bottom. This produces a spectacular firework display lasting about twenty minutes during which all the carbon is burned out; later the right proportions of carbon and other materials are added to obtain the desired quality of steel. The conversion of iron into steel in this way is a process which does not require additional energy.

A modified form is the Thomas process. In this the converter is lined with a basic coating, e.g., limestone, capable of absorbing phosphorus in pig iron. A large part of sedimentary ores and others are high in phosphorus. Before the invention of the Thomas process (1879) high-phosphorus pig iron could not be used for the making of steel, since the presence of phosphorus proved to have a harmful effect. In both forms of the converter process primarily pig iron is used as the charge.

The other process can best be described as cooking pig iron slowly in a molten state. Gradually the carbon content is reduced and steel is made. The current name for this process is "open hearth" or Siemens-Martin. In the open-hearth furnace iron scrap makes up a large percentage of the charge. Martin steel is of a higher quality than converter steel, and market demands of highly industrialized countries are shifting from converter to open-hearth or Martin steel. This shift gives rise to a problem of increasing dependence of the steelworks upon a large supply of scrap, which is discussed below.

A third way of making steel is with the electric furnace. Only small amounts of special-quality steels are so made. Another process, which has recently assumed much importance, is the LD process named after the Austrian steelworks Linz and Donawitz at which it was first developed and has been in use since 1952. In the United States, commercial production of steel

by this process started in 1954. On the basis of current development plans, it is forecast that this process will probably account for one-third of world steel-making capacity in 1965. LD converters are especially designed for operations with manufactured oxygen. Installation and operation are more economical than for the open-hearth process. Scrap, which composes one-half or more of the charge in the open-hearth furnace and thus becomes a bottleneck in the making of Martin steel, is reduced in the LD process to about one-third of the charge. Finally, the new process is more versatile in meeting the specifications of various customers.

Steel leaves the steelworks in huge blocks called ingots. The capacity as well as the actual output of a heavy industrial establishment is customarily measured at this stage of the manufacturing process, i.e., in terms of ingot capacity or ingot production of crude steel. Ingots are sent either to the rolling mill, where they are pressed through rolling profiles in a red-white-hot state to be shaped into steel plates, rails, etc., or to the blooming mill, where they are hammered into the semifinished product. A small fraction also goes to the steel foundry.

There are two main reasons why all these units of the iron and steel industry tend to be physically integrated into one large compound plant. (1) A great deal of energy waste is eliminated if the material proceeds immediately from one stage to the next without cooling off. (2) Integrated plants reduce transportation of pig iron and crude steel in the one direction and scrap in the other, which results in considerable savings.

Scrap comes from two sources, ultimate consumers and the steel mills themselves. Scrap from consumers is called market scrap or, according to further specification, process or capital scrap. It is purchased in the market and shipped back to the steel mills. The mills turn out so-called circulation or home scrap. A relatively large portion of the material going through the steelworks does not reach the stage of marketable semifinished or finished goods; about 25 to 30 percent returns to various stations—blast furnace, the open-hearth furnace, etc.—as circulation scrap. In a modern heavy industry the amount of scrap used is considerable. Nearly half of the ingot output is eventually returned as circulation, process, or capital scrap to enter the process again, mostly by way of the steelworks. The balance is lost in the market, but replaced by pig iron from the blast furnaces.

In this dynamic industrial complex the steel plant occupies the central position. Practically all the materials have to pass through it, with the exception of small quantities of foundry iron. The blast furnaces serve only as a sort of regulating appendix, by which losses of a permanent nature or increased demands are taken care of.

Shortly after the Second World War, the optimum size of an integrated steel plant was calculated to be at least a million tons of ingot capacity. Ten years later this figure was increased to 2 or 3 million tons. Approximately the following quantities of raw materials are required to operate an integrated plant of that size. (a) The blast furnaces use 3.5 million tons of iron ore containing 50 percent iron, to produce 1.7 million tons of pig iron; and they use 2 million tons of coal, which yields 1.5 million tons of coke. Coke plants are usually included in an integrated plant. In addition, scrap and a million tons or less of limestone are needed, according to the quality of the ore. (b) In the foundries 200,000 tons of pig iron is used, to which 100,000 tons of scrap is added. (c) Besides 1.5 million tons of pig iron, 1.2 million tons of scrap goes into steel, but owing to losses incurred during the processing the final output measured in ingots will be about 2.5 million tons. (d) How much of this emerges from the blooming and rolling mills as finished products depends on the line of production. Altogether about 8 million tons of raw materials must be assembled in order to produce 2.5 million tons of crude steel. (Such average figures are subject to large regional variations, as we will see later.) There are plants which specialize in the production of pig iron, others in which the converter process is predominant, and still others in which the blast furnace does not exist at all.

The figures cited above are for the European steel industry. According to them, about 1.7 million tons of iron in ore and 1.3 million tons in the form of scrap are required for the alimentation of the industry. Note that iron ore mines and scrap producers are approximately equal in importance as sources of the basic raw material of heavy industry, a fact which is very frequently overlooked in economic geographies. The ratio of scrap to iron ore or pig iron varies, however, a great deal from region to region, as will be learned later in this chapter.

Unlike the textile industry the iron and steel industry is integrated. As integration leads to a high inertia with respect to the location that has been selected originally, heavy industry establishes permanent centers of industrialization. However, the so-called optimum location is constantly redefined with technological and structural changes, which means that older centers will in time find themselves producing under adverse conditions and that expansion is apt to take place in another location. Examples are widespread in Europe and in the United States and will be discussed in the regional sections of this chapter, together with the means for protecting the existing centers by economic devices such as the basing-point system of pricing.

Another notable difference between heavy industry and the textile industry lies in the role played by iron scrap. The textile industry does not know the problems of secondary material reentering the production process, which have become so important in the iron and steel industry. The introduction of secondary material into the production process implies that the quantities handled increase from one step to the next. If we take the amount of iron contained in the ore mined as 100, the indices for the world total of pig iron and crude steel are 107 and 148, respectively (in the late 1950's). For the United States the corresponding figures are 145 and 214, which clearly reflects the importance of the blast furnace as a regulator—in the negative sense—in a period of recession. On the other hand, a country like India, with indices of 57 and 49, appears as an exporter of iron ore and pig iron as well as a relatively undeveloped market for steel. West Germany has indices of 405 and 550, which points to her heavy reliance upon imported ores and a shifting of the center of gravity toward steel. The USSR, which exports large quantities of iron ore to Eastern

Europe, has a structure of heavy industry similar to that of the United States or of Western Europe, the indices being 77 and 107.

In summary, it can be said that the iron industry, which had been for many centuries in the vicinity of charcoal and water power sources, moved toward the source of coking coal during the nineteenth century. Incidentally the formerly dispersed industry became highly concentrated. Changes in technology and other matters freed it from its direct dependence on the coal basin, but the older established centers remained important as a result of the inertia of the industry. New centers are being drawn in the direction of the scrap market, generally large population centers. Another tendency is the shift toward tidewater as soon as imports from overseas become significant. Freight charges have been a major cost factor throughout because of the enormous bulk of raw materials fed into the blast furnaces and the steel mills.

Steel Centers of the World

In the foregoing pages a few principles concerning the structure of the steel industry have been discussed. They are now applied in reviewing the more important steel centers of the world. While the questions relating to coke have already been dealt with in the chapter on energy resources, the following discussion will include the iron ore deposits and the scrap situation in

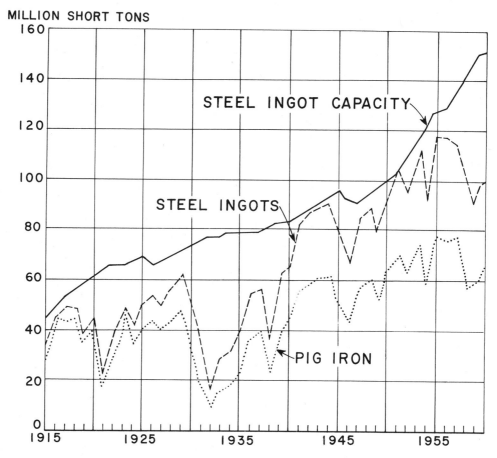

79 · DEVELOPMENT OF HEAVY INDUSTRY in the United States, 1915–1960. Ratios of pig iron to steel ingots and steel ingots to steel ingot capacity are of particular interest.

different countries. Each region is treated in the light of the peculiar problems to be encountered there.

THE UNITED STATES

There are different ways to measure the size of the steel industry. The most common check point is the crude-steel production in ingots; another is the production capacity measured with the same unit. Whichever method is em-

ployed, the United States turns up as the most powerful steel producer, leading the other nations by a wide margin, with a capacity of 150 million tons and an output of 100 million. However, the difference between her and the second ranking nation, the USSR, is becoming smaller every year. Furthermore, in the USSR all installations are used to maximum capacity.

The United States is important for more than the quantitative reasons. The country is in pos-

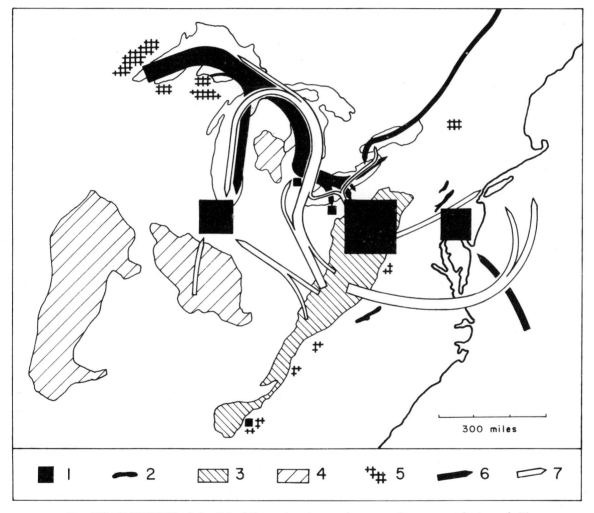

80 · HEAVY INDUSTRY of the United States: locations and sources of raw materials. *Legend:* (1) principal centers of heavy industry; (2) anthracite deposits; (3) bituminous coal deposits with a high percentage of coking coal and coal for chemical industries; (4) bituminous coal deposits— mainly steam coal; (5) iron ore deposits; (6) movements of iron ore; (7) movements of coal.

session of complete documentation and detailed statistics on the iron and steel industry to facilitate scientific research; the country has also remained an undivided whole during the period of industrialization, quite unlike the puzzling mosaic of economic and political units in Europe. Consequently a number of factors which exert grave influence upon the industry in other parts of the world can be eliminated from our considerations. It would, however, be wrong to assume that under such circumstances heavy industry would be found today in all cases at the economical optimum location. The first disturbing influence might be called the historical factor. The settlement of the American Continent, in its later phases, took place at about the time that the first steel mills were coming into being. The iron and steel centers that were established behind the rapidly westward-moving frontier in the already settled parts profited by the inertia of heavy industry simply by being there first. Secondly, the ideal of an economically homogeneous territorial unit is only partially fulfilled by the United States, as is familiar to every student of economic history. Various economic policies favoring regional division of the national territory were actively pursued, particularly in the last century, and are still influential today. They were carried out on the administrative level, for example, through tariffs, and in a free capitalistic economy, being most forceful where private economic interests can exercise their influence by means of pricing policies, freight rates, etc.

It was an especially fortunate coincidence that the Northeastern United States possessed all the essential raw materials for iron smelting and steel making in a relatively densely settled area and close to the major markets. The charcoal-operated furnaces of colonial days were soon abandoned, and heavy industry established itself firmly on the basis of coking coal. The optimum location at that time was the Pittsburgh area, followed by the Middle Atlantic metallurgical zone. An expansion of production and markets, however, soon necessitated additional sources of iron ore, which became scarce within the favored region. Large iron-ore deposits were discovered in the Lake Superior district, and these have since become the most important source of

iron ore for the steel industry of the United States. Lake Superior ores are high-grade, containing 50 percent or more of iron. The transportation system by which they are shipped to the blast furnaces resembles the one from North Sweden to continental European steel centers, except that the latter carries only a fraction of the total ore requirements while the former is responsible for practically the entire supply. Another point to be considered in drawing such a comparison is the fact that the heavy industry of North America has an inland location on the western side of the Appalachian Mountains. Later developments induced by the erection of steel plants at points of transshipment along the south shore of Lake Erie and at market centers, such as the Chicago area, were only to stress this characteristic. The tripolar structure of this steel industry, based upon the iron ore deposits of the Lake Superior district, the coal measures of western Pennsylvania, and the big inland industrial centers, constitutes a unique feature among the iron and steel industries of the world; it is quite distinct from the examples of Western Europe, or from those in Communist countries, where the distribution of heavy industry is planned and more even. We will not enter into the discussion of more economic problems, such as basing-point system, freight differentials on railways, etc., which attempted to maintain this concentration of production facilities rather than to allow their gradual dispersal. The case of Birmingham, Alabama, where coking coal and iron ore (though of lower grade, containing only 36 percent iron, much resembling European iron ores) are found within a few miles of each other, is illustrative; lacking its proper market and being at a disadvantage for reasons of an economic order—as mentioned above—Birmingham remained for many decades a producer rather of pig iron than of steel, and functionally tributary to the Northeast. For similar economic reasons the westward movement of heavy industry was greatly retarded. At the end of the Second World War the four northeastern districts— Pittsburgh, Cleveland, Chicago, and the East —combined still had 90 percent of the total steel capacity, the Pittsburgh district alone accounting for 42 percent. Perhaps more significant is the fact that 70 percent of the new investments in the period 1940-1945, just when elsewhere the decentralization of heavy industry was sought for strategic and economic reasons, still fell within this area, and 31 percent within the Pittsburgh district alone.

Inertia and concentration in connection with the tripolar structure and inland location may be considered most characteristic of the spatial structure of United States steel production. It was made possible by the tremendous vertical integration of a few big concerns. Of these the United States Steel Corporation is by far the largest, controlling nearly one-half the production of ores and steel as well as the intermediate transportation systems. If the ten largest steel companies are taken together, their aggregate production runs between 80 and 90 percent of the total United States production.

The ratio of iron ore : pig iron : crude steel produced is 1 : 1.5 : 2.1, reflecting the highly developed status of the industry as a whole, as described in the preceding section.

The most significant change in more recent times is caused by the need to replace the Lake Superior ores of present quality, which are no longer considered available in limitless quantities. According to the most generous estimates, they will not last much longer than a few decades. There are various alternative possibilities. One alternative is the low-grade ore called taconite. There are huge deposits of taconite from which the richer surface ores were originally derived by weathering processes in the Lake Superior district. Its iron content is only 27 percent, but it can be beneficiated and shipped to production centers by the current system of transportation. On the other hand, high-grade iron ores may be imported into the United States from outside sources. Owing to the inland location of the industry and an enormous volume of ores involved, this was only practicable by means of cheap water transportation all the way, i.e., by the construction of the Great Lakes-St. Lawrence Seaway, as long as the production centers remain where they are at present. A third possibility is to shift production toward the coast, as in Europe. Though all these possibilities have equally been considered, the last one

has been regarded as feasible only to a very limited degree. The completion of the Seaway in 1959 was hailed in the press mainly as opening the interior of the continent. It should not be overlooked, however, that the major function of the Seaway has so far been to serve heavy industry, as is indicated by the fact that ores make up by far the largest share of cargo. Whether to import high-grade ores or to beneficiate taconite is mainly a question of economics and of national economic policy. In this connection, steel companies in the United States have been actively engaged in developing iron-ore mines in Canada (Labrador), in Latin America (especially in Venezuela, Brazil, Chile), and in West Africa, and imports of iron ores are growing year by year. The supply of other raw materials, namely coke and scrap, is sufficient; furthermore, the United States is by far the largest exporter of scrap, which is primarily destined for consumption in Japanese steel mills.

While other countries find themselves hardly capable of coping with rising demands even with their steadily expanding production capacity, a large part of available installations are not used to capacity in the United States. Fluctuations in the domestic market and rising prices, favoring competition from overseas countries (Europe, Japan), constitute a major brake upon further expansion of the steel industry.

WESTERN EUROPE

Western Europe holds a unique position in the economic geography of iron and steel. This is the part of the world where the technology described above first evolved; consequently, we can expect to find here representatives of all types of heavy industry. The earliest centers of iron smelting practiced in the forested mountains and in peripheral areas have virtually ceased to exist; they persist only in a rudimentary or much changed form—e.g., as centers of metalworking industries. The transition from the charcoal furnace to the coke blast furnace marked the establishment of the nuclei of the future heavy-industry centers at or near the coal basin, as in England, Northern France, Belgium, and the Ruhr. All of them developed further in conformity with the growth of the market.

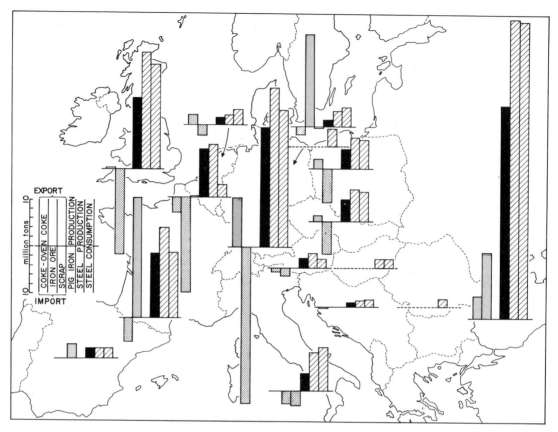

81 · HEAVY INDUSTRY IN EUROPE.

The later expansion of heavy industry followed definite trends. The changed ratio of coke to iron ore, coupled with an increase in coal prices, made it more economical to erect new plants near the source of iron ore. In England this shift took place within relatively short distances, since the iron ore deposits and coal measures there run roughly parallel to each other and diagonally across the island from northeast to southwest. More important changes occurred on the continent. The two largest ore deposits in Europe, in Lorraine (France) and Salzgitter (Germany), became the sites of integrated steel plants. In Lorraine this development started after 1870 and was made possible by the invention of the Thomas process which could utilize the high-phosphorus Lorraine ores. At that time Lorraine belonged to Germany, and so it was easy to bring the

Ruhr and Lorraine into one functional unit through the mutual exchange of coke and ores. Today the heavy industry of Lorraine relies almost exclusively on coal deposits in France and Belgium owing to their greater proximity and, until recently, to closer economic and political ties. The Salzgitter plant located at the second largest ore deposits of central Europe was started during the late thirties on an ambitious scale never to be completed; partially dismantled following the war and then reconstructed, it has remained a torso. Salzgitter is connected with the Ruhr basin by a canal over which ores and pig iron move in one direction and coal in the other. A few other examples of steelworks located over ore deposits are found in northern Spain (Bilbao at the ore base, Asturias near the coal) and in northern Sweden (Lulea).

Another more recent trend was brought about by the shifting center of gravity within the industry from pig iron to steel. Any large agglomeration of metal-working industries, where there is usually also a concentration of important railroad centers and other users of iron and steel, is a source of huge quantities of process or capital scrap and may thus develop into a new center of steel production. The most outstanding example of this development on a nationwide scale is Italy. Owing to large deficiencies in coal and iron ore, the ratio of ore : pig iron : crude steel production in Italy is 1 : 5 : 10; she is, therefore like Japan, a major market for all kinds of scrap.

The specific nature of iron ores in Europe and the fact that many important heavy-industry centers there have moved toward the iron-ore deposits are reflected in the unusually high percentage of converter steel produced in Europe, namely 37.2 percent, as against 52.3 percent of open-hearth steel; the rest is produced by electric and other methods (1955). The corresponding figures for North America are 2.7 and 88.8 percent, and for the USSR 4.4 and 88.0 percent. Europe is so poor in high-grade ores that she is compelled to rely on highly siliceous and phosphorous ores such as those of Lorraine, Salzgitter, and England. The only high-grade ore available in large quantities comes from northern Sweden (Kiruna district). The Lorraine ores contain about 32 percent of iron, Salzgitter 30, Northamptonshire 30, and Sydvaranger and Dunderland (Norway) 30-35, but the Kiruna ores yield 63 percent of iron on an average.

For the time being the problem for Europe has more to do with the quality of ores than their quantity, and imports of high-grade ores from overseas are assuming increasing importance. North and West Africa, Latin America, and recently Canada (Ungava) and Newfoundland are the major sources of iron ore imported into Europe. The annual iron ore imports into Western Europe, measured with respect to the iron content, now exceed 7 million tons, and it is estimated that they will increase to as much as 30 million tons in 1972 to 1975, or about one-fourth of the total requirements at that time.

This development is already indicated by the very latest trend in the localization of European steel plants at the ends of ocean routes, e.g., Ijmuiden, Dunkirk, Newport, Oxelösund.

In contrast to the United States, the situation in Europe is made more complex by the interference of the political factor. While the development of heavy industry was going on, Europe consisted of a large number of political and economic units, each having its own economic policy and tariff system. In addition, strategic considerations tended to draw industries away from the national boundaries, as in the case of Salzgitter, which at the time of its foundation was centrally located within Germany. The first tangible form of intra-European cooperation on a large scale was the European Coal and Steel Community, i.e., a common market for coal, iron ore, and scrap created in February 1953, which was followed by the establishment of a common market for steel in May of the same year. The existence of a common market should facilitate the most economical utilization of resources; its prerequisite is to abolish all discriminatory practices, restrictions, etc. The European Coal and Steel Community comprises Belgium-Luxemburg, France, Italy, the Netherlands, and West Germany. The total crude-steel capacity of Western Europe in 1960 was 111 million tons, of which the ECSC countries had a share of 66 percent. The most important outsider was the United Kingdom, whose capacity amounted to 23 percent of the total.

With respect to other raw materials we may again regard Europe as a whole. In the past scrap was supplied mainly from European sources, capital scrap constituting about one-half of the requirements. Overseas trade in scrap was meager, only about 10 percent coming from the United States. It is expected that despite an increase in steel production, scrap will continue to be supplied by European sources in sufficient quantities. Problems relating to coke have been treated in an earlier chapter. In Europe, too, heavy industry is the largest consumer of coke, the bulk of which is used in the making of pig iron.

An analysis of markets, even if in a rough

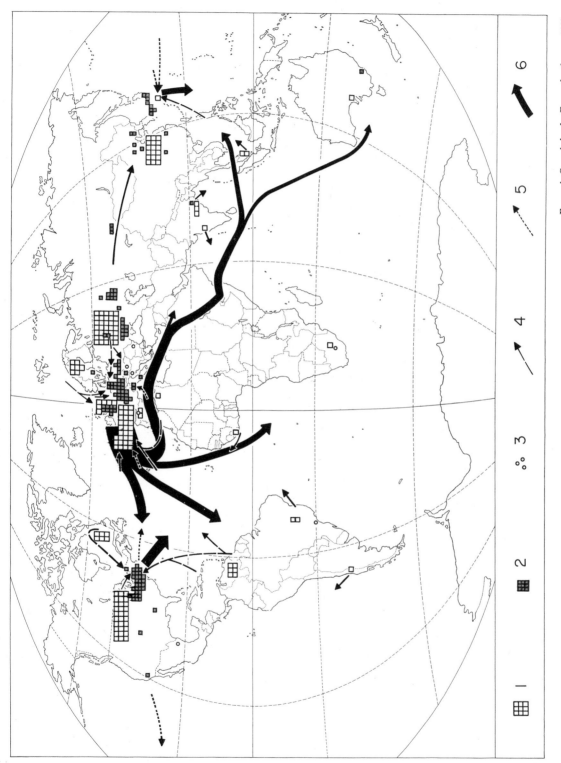

82 · IRON AND STEEL. *Legend:* (1) production of iron ore, one square = 3 million tons; (2) production of crude steel, one square = 3 million tons; (3) other important centers of steel production with less than 3 million tons; (4) major exports of iron ore, one bar = 3 million tons of ore; (5) major exports and imports of iron and steel scrap, one bar = 3 million tons; (6) international trade in steel products, width of the flow line in legend representing 2 million tons (intra-European trade excluded).

Economic Commission for Europe for the year 1960

approximation, forms a necessary part of the evaluation of European heavy industry. Taking rolled-steel products as an indicator, we can group the European countries into net exporters and net importers. If the total apparent consumption of iron and steel in any country is represented by the index 100, the indices of domestic production in the exporting countries are as follows (1957): Belgium-Luxemburg 345, Austria 176, France 133, West Germany 117, United Kingdom 117. All the others are net importers, Switzerland having the lowest index figure of 25. These data bring out the meshwork of intra-European trade in iron and steel products. Such an index figure for the whole of Western Europe has since 1913 fluctuated between 110 (1938) and 123 (1929), and was 116 in 1957. It implies that about 10-20 percent of the output of rolled steel products had always to be sold overseas. In the late fifties Europe exported approximately 10 million tons of semi-finished and finished steel to extra-European markets. These markets are found all over the world, but Latin America and the Far East are the most important ones, each absorbing about one quarter of the total exports. Africa, North America, and the Middle East import close to or somewhat more than a million tons each, while Eastern Europe, the USSR, and Oceania account for the remaining portion. The prominent exporting countries are Belgium-Luxemburg (28 percent), West Germany (23), France (20), and the United Kingdom (14). In absolute quantities European exports have shown a steady increase despite the great shocks caused by the two world wars, depressions, and growing industrialization all over the world. Industrialization in overseas territories and in underdeveloped countries actually stimulates exports, because of the increased demand for specialized products that cannot yet be obtained from the national producers. Of nearly 30 million tons of steel that entered world trade in 1957, Europe contributed two-thirds, half of it destined for intra-European exchange. This still leaves twice as much for extra-European markets as the total United States exports. Western Europe's exports to North America were larger by 50 percent than imports from North America. European steel

production must therefore be always evaluated in terms of domestic consumption as well as export possibilities. It is an amazing achievement, considering the adverse conditions with respect to the supply of raw materials (low-grade domestic ores and imported high-grade ores) and a high material standard of living, that Europe has been able not only to maintain but even to better her position in the world market.

U S S R, INCLUDING EASTERN EUROPE

Probably the most striking feature of the iron and steel industry in Russia is the stagnation of consumption prior to 1930 (5.1 million tons of crude steel equivalent in 1913 and 5.4 million tons in 1929) which has since been followed by an unprecedent increase (22.5 million tons in 1951, 49.3 million tons in 1957, and 75 million tons in 1960). Per capita consumption in 1960 surpassed that of Western Europe but was still far below that of North America. Such a rise in consumption was made possible by a corresponding increase in domestic production. The USSR has always imported only a fraction of her needs from outside. Before 1929, imported iron and steel products amounted to approximately 5 percent of the total consumed, later to drop to but 1-2 percent. Western Europe (primarily France and West Germany) and Eastern Europe (Czechoslovakia and Poland) supplied the bulk of the imports. Furthermore, since the mid-fifties, the USSR has been able to export annually more than 2 million tons of finished steel; half of this was destined for Eastern European countries, and one-third for Far Eastern markets, mainly China.

Behind such achievements are envisaged the realities of mines, metallurgical centers, and transportation systems, but also politically motivated planning and economic and social conditions without which an understanding of the economic geography of that sector seems inexplicable.

Recognizing the basic nature of the steel production, the various five-year plans of the USSR have given first priority to heavy industry and the production of capital goods. This contrasts with the industrialization of Europe and North America, where consumer goods (mainly textiles) were the first to take advantage of the new production techniques. In the USSR, as is well known, consumer-goods industries were barely able to satisfy even a greatly reduced demand for a long time. Such a differential treatment of the various industrial sectors is possible only in a strictly planned economy.

The influence of the political factor is also felt in the spatial distribution of the centers of heavy industry. Soviet planners recognize the principles of "economic regionalization," by which they understand the division of the country by objective and scientific methods into economic regions which in some respects are self-sustaining but also perform a specific function within the framework of a higher national or supernational order. The functional center of such an economic region is an industrial nucleus, equipped with heavy industry and a large industrial, i.e., proletarian population. The actual situation, however, does not reflect these principles in a pure form, because the steel industry extends its roots into pre-Communist days and the principles of economic regionalization have undergone considerable modifications during the period of the Communist regime.

Prior to 1917 the steel industry was found in three areas: (1) in and around the large population centers like Moscow, (2) in the Ural Mountains, based on local iron ores and charcoal, and (3) in the Ukrainian SSR and the south of Russia between the Dnieper and the Donets rivers on the basis of coking coal and iron ore. The Ukrainian region has always been the main production center. Excellent iron ores containing 55 percent iron come from very large deposits at Krivoi-Rog west of the Dnieper; the coking coal deposits are situated in the Donbas, the hilly area within the big bend of the Donets. The industry is located directly over the coal field and also along the Dnieper, especially in the case of electrometallurgical industries.

When the Communist regime got under way with the five-year plans, there evolved the idea of the great *combinats,* i.e., the combination of a coal base with an iron ore base to form a large functional unit. Krivoi-Rog with Donbas was an example of a *combinat* already in existence. Another example, which was developed in the thirties, consists of the coal fields at Kusbas around Kuznetsk in Siberia, and the iron ore deposits in the Southern Ural Mountains, with the metallurgical centers at Magnitogorsk, Chelyabinsk, and Sverdlovsk. The railroad connecting the two poles of this *combinat* has a length of 1400 miles and is one of the major lines with the heaviest traffic. The original bipolar structure of that *combinat* has, however, developed into a much more complex form; coal was later found about halfway between them at Karaganda, south of the railroad line, and iron ores are now brought from mines closer to the coal field to the eastern pole, i.e., the industrial zone that stretches from Stalinsk to Kemerovo and beyond.

The Soviet steel industry is based on domestic resources which are widely distributed and adequate for future expansion; it is scheduled to produce 117 million tons of crude steel in 1972 to 1975. Since the necessity of importing raw materials will be practically nil, there is no pressure for the steel industry to move toward the coast. On the contrary, a rigid application of the principle of "economic regionalization" should lead toward a more even distribution of the industry over the entire area of the country.

Moreover, steel works in the USSR are run to capacity in order to meet domestic demands, and the exportable surplus is and will probably remain small.

This system extends over a tremendous area, and connections within it are for the most part made by railroad. If we consider the facts that about 5 tons of raw materials must be hauled to the steel plant in order to produce 1 ton of finished steel and that freight charges make up as much as one-third of the total production costs, the disadvantages encountered by the Soviet steel industry may become clearer.

They become even more significant if our survey is extended to take in the Communist countries in Eastern Europe. Today these countries are virtually incorporated into the vast network of economic regionalization through an organization called COMECON. Their crude-steel output has greatly increased during the fifties, with Czechoslovakia and Poland as the leading producers. Most of the steel is made in the open-hearth furnace. The inclusion of the Eastern European countries in the Soviet economic sphere led to even longer hauls of the raw material by railroad. These countries possess large deposits of coal, but lack adequate reserves of iron ore. Consequently, there results a heavy flow of raw materials between the USSR and Eastern Europe, iron ore moving westward from the Ukraine, and coal and coke eastward, mainly from Poland. Semifinished and finished products manufactured within one designated economic region according to the plans of the COMECON are also shipped to the other regions. On the one hand, such economic regionalization reduces long hauls because each region has to be self-sustaining in most respects. On the other hand, the assignment of specific production processes to individual centers in combination with a more or less regular spacing of industrialization gives rise to an ever-increasing problem of inter-regional transportation.

CHINA (MAINLAND)

There are two reasons why the future development of mainland China should be of great interest to any student of economic geography. (1) The mere size of the country (third in the world in area, with 3.7 million square miles after USSR and Canada, and the first in population, with approximately 700 million people) suggests potentialities hardly to be found anywhere else in the world. (2) The strictly planned economy of the present Communist government has a striking influence upon the distribution of heavy industry centers; it is not possible to understand the present as well as the future distribution of such plants without due consideration of the political factor.

In pre-Communist days, Chinese steel production was almost exclusively concentrated in Manchuria. There, in close proximity to large coal and iron ore deposits and not far from the sea, the big Anshan plants came into being after 1917. Before the Second World War, Manchuria was providing roughly 90 percent of the pig iron and steel produced in China. The ratio of steel to pig iron in the whole of China gradually moved from 1 : 30 to 1 : 4 during the thirties, but even the latter figure for 1939 clearly indicates that China—and that means above all Manchuria—was primarily a producer of pig iron, for the most part exported to Japan. During the war years steel exports increased; in the more normal, prewar years, however, the Chinese steel market was basically supplied through imports from overseas. Following the Japanese occupation of Manchuria in 1931, this dichotomy of the Chinese steel industry became complete: Manchuria (Anshan) was working for the Japanese market, and China proper, which possessed only small steelworks in various scattered locations, had to rely upon imports.

The Anshan plant, which had suffered relatively little during the Second World War, was severely damaged in 1945 during the Russian occupation through the removal of installations; as late as 1947 this most important plant was estimated to be producing only about 15-20 percent of its prewar output. In 1949 the People's Republic of China was proclaimed. The principle of economic regionalization has already been discussed in the section on the USSR, and the basic importance of heavy industry in a Communist country and in Communist planning has been stressed. These principles are perhaps best exemplified in the development of the iron and steel industry in Communist China, where, with the exception of Anshan, there were hardly any existing centers to speak of which might have predetermined the pattern of industrialization. The importance of what is taking place in China today can hardly be exaggerated since it may set an example to be followed in countries which are yet to be industrialized.

The first huge task was to reconstruct the plants that had been damaged by war and occupation. Steel production was still down to 0.2 million tons in 1949, and even in the Five Year Plan of 1953-1957 70 percent of the heavy industry quota of investments had to be allotted for reconstruction and only 30 percent for new installations. In 1957, however, the production of pig iron and crude steel was already as high as 5.9 and 5.4 million tons respectively. From 1958 to 1959, as a result of an all-embracing campaign, hundreds of thousands—Communist sources mention the figure of one million—of small local furnaces all over the country started to produce pig iron, which pushed the figure up to 10 million tons and beyond. The low quality of the iron thus produced soon led to the abolishment of this system and to the construction of modern steel plants. Large-scale geological exploration uncovered new deposits of coal and iron ore. On this basis it was systematically planned that each of the seven economic regions of China, i.e., Manchuria, East China, North China, Southwest China, South China, Northwest China, and Central China, would be equipped with at least one fully integrated plant. The Chinese steel industry, which had thus far been concentrated in the coastal area—Anshan, Shihchingshan (Peiping), Tientsin, Shanghai, and Maanshan (west of Shanghai)—began to move inland: Huanghsih (on the Yangtse near Nanking) and Szechwan in the South, and Taiyuan and Paotou in the North are the major plants that have so far been established in the interior, and Kiuchuan on the Lanchow-Sinkiang railroad will be even farther west. The production ratio of pig iron to steel is approximately 1 to 1, suggesting the rather developed character of the home market. The ratio of steel could perhaps be even higher, but scrap, especially capital scrap, is extremely scarce, though circulation and processing scrap are available in increasing quantities.

It is estimated by United Nations sources that production will increase in parallel with consumption and that in the seventies China will be the largest producer and consumer as well in Asia outside the USSR with a total of approximately 50 million tons of steel. It is also estimated that such a development would bring China up to third place after the United States (147 million tons) and the USSR (117 million tons). Sometimes even a factual study has to gauge future possibilities with all their uncertain prospects, and China seems to be just such a case.

JAPAN

Industrialization in Japan started after the Meiji Revolution in 1868 with the opening of the country and the introduction of Western ideas and knowledge. Unlike the countries which have embarked on industrialization in the middle of the twentieth century, Japan looked to Europe and the United States for guidance. Industrial progress and demographic changes were always checked against the experiences of the older industrial countries. Industrialization commenced with production of textiles, concentrated around the traditional trade centers of Osaka and Kobe. In 1896 following the war with China the Japanese government decided to build up a heavy industry center in northern Kyushu; in 1901 the Yawata Steel Works started production there. This center, which is now astride the Straits of Shimonoseki, has remained the nucleus of the present-day steel industry.

The plants in northern Kyushu are located at tidewater not far from the coal mines. The lack of high-grade iron ores and scrap constitutes the most critical bottleneck in Japanese heavy industry. Before the Second World War iron ore and pig iron came mainly from Japanese-controlled territories in China-Manchukuo, with some additional imports from the Philippine Islands, Malaya, India, etc. As far as scrap was concerned, the bulk of it was purchased from the United States. The production ratio of ore (Fe content) : pig iron : steel is $1 : 7 : 11$, which is quite unique in the world. After the Second World War, ore and pig iron had to be imported from a greater distance. Domestic production of iron ore was enough to cover only about one-fifth of the requirements, and iron ore was the fourth in value on the list of imported items after petroleum, cotton, and wool. About half of it came from Malaya and India, and one-fifth from North America. On the other hand, ships, iron, and steel together account for one quarter of Japan's exports, destined for almost every corner of the world.

As far as the steel industry is concerned, production costs remain high because of high assembly costs and despite relatively low wages and modern equipment. The fact that Japan is a high-cost producer in this section of industry is frequently overlooked. Since she has to compete with European, American, and other producers in overseas export markets, this is of great importance. Competition will become even keener as wages rise and the material standard of living improves in Japan.

Little can be done to improve the domestic

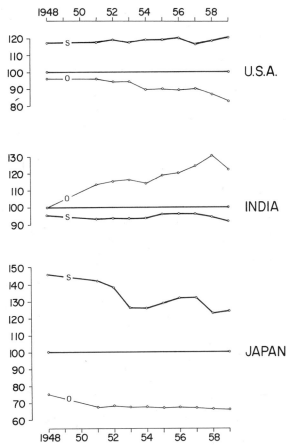

83 · RELATIVE TRENDS of iron ore, pig iron, and crude steel production, 1948–1959: U.S.A., India, and Japan. See the text for the significance of such relative trends. In all the three cases, the pig iron production of each year is expressed as 100, and the production of iron ore (O) —in terms of iron content—and crude steel (S) of the corresponding year as index numbers.

the steel industry away from its original site, Yawata, to other locations. This trend had been actively furthered by governmental measures taken during the interwar years to insure national security. After the war, new and modernized plants sprang up on the ruins of older ones.

Total production has made an amazing comeback, to a large degree with the American aid. In 1946 steel production (ingot) was only half a million tons. In 1955 it rose to 9.4 million tons, which was already higher than in any previous year, and in 1960 22 million tons were reached. The basic metal industries are now found in all major industrial areas of Japan. For number of people engaged, the most important area is the Tokyo and Yokohama (Kawasaki) industrial zone, followed by the Osaka-Kobe industrial zone. Northern (=Kita) Kyushu still boasts the biggest integrated steel mills in Asia. The district around Nagoya is much less important in this respect, though as an industrial zone it ranks next to Osaka-Kobe. Finally, mention should be made of heavy industry in Muroran (Hokkaido) at the coal basis of the North.

Japan is a fine example of how a country without adequate natural resources can develop a heavy industry of outstanding importance. Current production capacity far exceeds domestic consumption; hence Japan must by all means seek outlets in the overseas markets. For the reasons given above, exports of raw steel may be expected to decrease in importance, and more and more fabricated goods will take its place. Of these, capital goods required by underdeveloped countries in connection with their development plans will certainly play a significant role.

INDIA

Bharat, or the Indian Union, ranks third in Asia as a steel producer. The major center of iron and steel production is in the northeast of the Dekkan Peninsula, straddling over parts of the provinces of Bihar, Orissa, and West Bengal. The start of modern production was made by private investment, foreign as well as Indian. Since 1875 ironworks have been developed with British capital at Asansol in the Damodar Val-

supplies of raw materials. Iron ore deposits are scattered and insignificant. The more important mines are peripheral, located in northern Honshu (Kamaishi in Iwate Prefecture) and Hokkaido (Kutchan). Outside northern Kyushu, coal suitable for metallurgical purposes is found in Hokkaido (Yubari). For scrap, the industry relies heavily on large-scale imports.

Under such circumstances, the fact that all the major industrial agglomerations are at or very close to tidewater favors the spread of ley where coal was found; today they are known as the Indian Iron and Steel Corporation. In 1907 the Tata Iron and Steel Company was started further south near the iron ore base of Jamshedpur, involving only Indian capital. In the years between 1950 and 1960, the Indian government accepted offers from foreign countries to construct three new plants: two of them are close to the iron ore deposits in the southern part of the industrial district, namely, Bhilai (USSR) and Rourkela (West Germany), and the third is situated in the Damodar Valley near Durgapur (British). Finally a plant is planned at Bokaro in the upper Damodar Valley.

Thus, together with a smaller plant in Mysore, the aggregate steel capacity of India will reach approximately 11 million tons. Because of low assembly costs and low wages, India holds a favored position as an exporter of iron ore and pig iron, Japan being the most important customer. But the bulk of Indian steel production is channeled into the home market, which is rapidly expanding and at present still depends to a large degree upon imports. Even if per capita consumption of steel has increased nearly threefold within the last thirty years, it is still one of the lowest in the world—about one-fiftieth that of the United States.

Excellent iron ores are found in many locations throughout India. The most important deposits at the present time are those mentioned above. They are located in the Singhbhum and Mayurbhanj range about 100 miles west of Calcutta. Their quality is high (60 percent and more of Fe) and the quantity is considered practically inexhaustible (2 billion tons of measured and indicated reserves). The bottlenecks are presented by (a) coal, insufficient in quantity as well as in quality to guarantee the necessary supply of metallurgical coke in the future (Indian engineers are therefore much interested in any technical improvement concerning low-quality coal) and (b) scrap, which is now almost entirely derived from the works themselves. In connection with the latter, general industrialization, which is making rapid strides in the above-mentioned industrial district, gains additional importance.

AUSTRALIA

Richly endowed with all the necessary raw materials and provided with a fast-growing market for steel, Australia possesses all prerequisites for a large expansion of her iron and steel industry. However, heavy industry came relatively late to this continent. A small establishment in the town of Lithgow, about 80 miles inland from Sydney, operated an open-hearth steel furnace after 1900, until it was closed down in 1929; despite the proximity to coal and iron ore, the inland location proved to be uneconomical.

All the important raw material deposits as well as the major population centers of Australia are situated on or near the sea. The optimum location for heavy industry is thus along the tidewater. In 1915 careful investigations led BHP (Broken Hill Proprietary Company, Ltd.), the leading Australian concern, to start iron and steel production near Newcastle, some eighty miles north of Sydney, where large coking coal deposits are located in the lower part of the Hunter Valley. In the late twenties another center was established at Port Kembla in a similar location south of Sydney and, like Newcastle, on the coast. However, this new plant entered into full swing of production just at the time of the world economic depression, subsequently to become a subsidary of BHP in 1935.

BHP controls not only the iron and steel plants at Newcastle and Port Kembla, but also the nearby coal mines, the iron ore mines, and transportation by land and sea. Some ore is found in the hinterland of the steel plants, but the most important source is Iron Monarch Mountain in South Australia, not far from the head of Spencer Gulf.

In order to disperse heavy industry and out of other considerations as well, BHP erected a new plant in the vicinity of the iron-ore deposits at Whyalla, South Australia, just before the Second World War. Situated in an arid climate, the Whyalla plant presents special problems. One is the water supply; it was solved by the construction of a water pipe which brings water from the Murray River over a distance of 223 miles. Another is housing for the thousands of workers who had to be brought in from outside. Recently, another iron-ore mine has been opened up in Yampi Sound on the north coast of Western Australia.

According to reports, the real bottleneck in Australian heavy industry is created by labor questions in the coal mines. Australia is a low-cost producer thanks chiefly to low assembly costs, which are partially offset by high wages. It is expected that production will triple within the next ten years to reach about 9 million tons by 1972 with increasing exports to Asian countries.

REPUBLIC OF SOUTH AFRICA

Though South Africa is the most important producer of steel in the African continent, she ranks among such lesser producers as India, Hungary, and Spain, with only about 2 million tons of crude steel production.

The case of South Africa is unique and of special interest to the economic geographer, for the beginnings of the industry there were marked by the manufacture of steel only, based on scrap from the gold mines and railroads (period between 1910 and 1925). These steel furnaces were located on the Witwatersrand. Only in 1926 were sizable blast furnaces for the production of pig iron added, one at the coal basis in Newcastle (Natal) and the other at Vereeniging (Transvaal). In 1928 ISCOR (South African Iron and Steel Industrial Corporation) was founded as a government enterprise for the production of iron and steel.

The first integrated plant of ISCOR was built at Pretoria; it is strategically located at a railroad center with respect to the assembly of raw materials, i.e., iron ore from Thabazimbi (157 miles), coal from Whitbank (70 miles), and scrap from industries and railroads, as well as with respect to the market. In 1952 ISCOR erected another plant in Vanderbijlpark near Vereeniging, where the Union Steel Corporation already operated the largest steel foundry in South Africa and where other large-scale industrial establishments were located. While steel production has thus been concentrated in the Vereeniging-Pretoria area, smaller plants have been built in other parts of the republic. In near-by Rhodesia, steel is also made in limited quantities.

South Africa today possesses a fully developed heavy industry with a production ratio among iron, pig iron, and steel equal to 1 : 1.1 : 1.3. This means that all the iron ore is made into pig iron, and that all the pig iron except the amount used in the foundries is further processed into steel. South Africa, therefore, is a self-contained unit which neither exports nor imports essential raw materials—or processed goods, for that matter. The industry has an extremely fortunate location as regards the assembly of raw materials and the distribution of products within the home market. On the other hand, transportation to coastal cities and overseas markets is long and expensive. Existing development plans envisage an output of 6.5 million tons of steel for 1972-75. If this is compared with the probable gross consumption of 5 million tons, or per capita consumption of more than 300 kg, an exportable surplus of 1.5 million tons is to be expected. This equals about one-half of the estimated needs for the rest of Africa.

LATIN AMERICA

For many decades Latin American countries have constituted an important market for steel exporters, but recent developments have made it possible for an increasing percentage of the apparent consumption to be supplied with domestic production. The apparent consumption remained practically stationary from 1913 until the late thirties, averaging 2.5 to 3.0 million tons of steel per year for the whole of Latin America. In 1951 a consumption of 5.2 million tons was attained. However, if individual countries are considered, interesting changes are observed. Between 1913 and 1951, while the share of Argentina dropped from 38 to 28 percent, that of Brazil increased from 19 to 23 percent and that of Mexico likewise from 8 to 18 percent. These trends persisted throughout the fifties, but were overshadowed by the rapid development of Venezuela. In 1957 consumption amounted to 8.0 million tons which was shared among the major markets in the following percentages: Argentina 17, Brazil 23, Mexico 17, and Venezuela 19 percent.

In 1913 no domestic production existed in Latin America. As late as 1938, only 14 percent of the total consumption was covered by domestic production (Brazil and Mexico). In 1957, however, its share increased to 43 percent of the total consumption; the major consumers (with the exception of Venezuela) show much higher figures: Brazil 78, Mexico 67, Chile 78, Argentina 53 percent. It implied that in 1957 a deficit of about 5 million tons had to be covered by imports. Estimates for 1972-75 are the following: production of crude steel 18.7 million tons, consumption in crude steel equivalents 22.3 million tons, imports to be expected 3.6 million tons. All these figures reflect the rapid growth of the iron and steel industry in Latin American countries.

The leading producer, past as well as present, is Brazil. Her output of steel is well above the million-ton mark. Blast furnaces of small size have been operating for a long time in the interior of the state of Minas Gerais on the basis of local high-grade iron ores and charcoal. The most important plant in this area today is Belgo Mineiro's Monlevade with a production capacity of half a million tons of steel. It is unique because charcoal from planted eucalyptus forests is used for smelting and reducing instead of coke. In the forties the nationally owned Volta Redonda Steel Plant was built also in the State of Minas Gerais but nearer to the coast. This integrated plant has a much better location than Monlevade with respect to the markets, being situated only ninety miles from Rio de Janeiro on the way to São Paulo. Raw materials have to be hauled to the plant exclusively by rail, iron ore from the interior of Minas Gerais and coal from the coast. Coal is in part supplied from domestic sources in Southern Brazil, but high-grade coking coal has to be imported and mixed with national coal.

Mexico is another important steel producer of relatively long standing. She has a yearly output of about a million tons. The main center is located in the north of the country at Monterrey, equipped with a fully integrated plant producing pig iron and steel. A secondary center is near the capital city, specializing in steel.

Latin American countries currently undertaking the establishment of large-scale steelworks with a capacity of over a million tons are Venezuela, Argentina, and Chile, closely followed by Colombia.

Yet the importance of Latin America for the world iron and steel industry is not fully indicated by these remarks. In 1958 the Latin American iron mines produced about 18.0 million tons of ore (Fe content), most of which was not made into pig iron in domestic blast furnaces but exported to overseas consumers. Approximately 2 million tons came from each of Brazil and Chile, 1.5 million tons from Peru, and 10 million tons from Venezuela. North American and to a lesser degree European steel firms developed the mines and constructed the railroads and port facilities. In most cases these companies have since been nationalized in accordance with local law, but their interests still remain outside Latin America. In 1955 the United Nations published an estimate of world iron-ore resources, including only deposits which are "exploitable for usable material under existing economic and local conditions." According to its estimate, Brazil is credited with one-fifth of the world's total resources, some of which is of very high grade, and Latin America as a whole with about one-fourth. This compares with 15 percent in North America or Europe. It is to be expected that these figures will be revised in the future. Nevertheless, such enormous deposits will undoubtedly assume increasing importance in the export trade in coming years and bring about a shift toward tidewater location in European and possibly also in North American heavy industry.

THE PRODUCTION OF OTHER METALS

Out of all the mineral deposits other than iron, only a few examples of metallic minerals are picked out here for discussion. The nonmetallic minerals are excluded, though some of them, used as building materials, refractory materials, fertilizers, etc., are of very great economic importance. The reader is accordingly advised to refer to special publications for the nonmetallic minerals. Compared with iron, all the other metals are of secondary importance. Most of them depend directly or indirectly upon heavy industry in the broadest sense.

The Ores: Deposits,
Mining, and Treatment

The metallic elements generally occur in nature in the form of chemical compounds, such as oxides or sulfides. Usually these compounds form crystals, but some were precipitated in an amorphous state. The metal-bearing compounds are invariably found in combination with other materials which may or may not be of economic value. A rock is called an ore if the concentration of the desired elements is high enough to warrant exploitation.

Evaluation of an ore deposit follows the same general rules that were discussed in the section on coal. But a few points need to be made clear, and the example of molybdenum will bring them to light. Molybdenum is a metal which is used primarily in the making of special alloy steels. In most cases it occurs as MoS_2, the crystal molybdenite. This mineral is often found concentrated in quartz veins, in which it may constitute in many deposits 3 to 4 percent of the total weight of the rock. But the most important molybdenum deposits in the world (Climax, Colorado) contain molybdenite in a very different state; it is found diffused throughout a granite massif into which the vapor containing molybdenum had been injected. In such deposits the mineral content averages only 0.6 to 0.7 percent. We must therefore clearly distinguish between ore, mineral, and the metal: thus a lode ore deposit of, say, 5,000,000 tons containing 2 percent

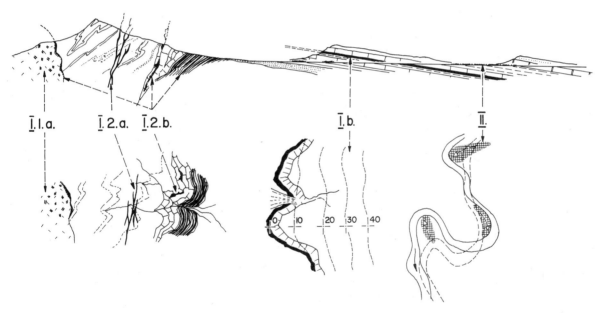

84 • TYPES OF MINERAL DEPOSITS. Refer to the classification of mineral deposits in the text. The profile shows how such deposits may appear in a geological cross section, which is further clarified by the geological maps below. (I.1.a) Ores occurring in a magmatic body, or syngenetic primary deposits. (I.2.a) Ores occurring in veins, or epigenetic primary deposits. (I.2.b) Replacement and contact deposits, epigenetic and primary—three subtypes indicated by arrows. Contact ores occur in the neighborhood of a magmatic body, while replacement takes place in a limestone series or in schist which has been infiltrated by metalliferous magmatic vapors. (I.b) Primary deposits of the sedimentary group. (II) Secondary deposits, often found along a stream course as placer deposits, as illustrated here.

MoS_2 yields 100,000 tons of molybdenite or 60,-000 tons of metallic molybdenum. Unfortunately it often happens that the data on reserves fail to differentiate clearly between these different possibilities. The statistics published by United Nations specify whether the given figures refer to the metal content, the mineral, a certain concentrate, or the ore. Attention should always be paid to the footnotes in the statistics.

A genetic classification of the more important mineral deposits shows the following types:

TYPES OF MINERAL DEPOSITS

I. PRIMARY DEPOSITS
   1. Syngenetic deposits
      a. Magmatic
      b. Sedimentary
   2. Epigenetic deposits
      a. Veins
      b. Replacement and contact
      c. Weathering
II. SECONDARY DEPOSITS (placers)

"Syngenetic" means that the metallic minerals originated at the same time as the rock formation in which they occur. "Epigenetic" deposits were formed sometime later. A common case of syngenetic deposits is of magmatic origin. Magma which came near to the surface of the earth became solidified through the process of cooling, and the various components crystallized as mineral compounds—quartz, feldspar, etc. When some of them have an economic value, the rock is classified as an ore.

In sedimentary syngenetic deposits, the valuable compounds were precipitated in the lake or the sea together with sand, clay, etc.; many iron and manganese deposits have been formed in this way. While such sedimentary deposits are stratified and interbedded among strata of no economic value, magmatic deposits usually occur as massifs.

Epigenetic deposits are also frequent. Emanating from a deep-seated magmatic body the mineralized vapor seeks an exit toward the earth's surface, following every possible line of least resistance, such as cleavage and fault planes. Continued cooling results in fractional crystal-

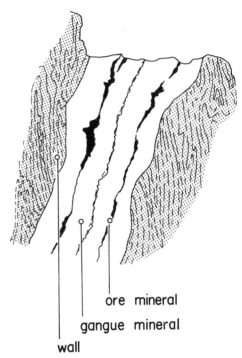

ore mineral

gangue mineral

wall

85 · A VEIN ORE DEPOSIT. The diagram illustrates a primary epigenetic deposit, i.e., a quartz (SiO_2) vein containing sphalerite (ZnS). The surrounding rocks are shown stippled.

lization of all the elements, contained usually in the form of a quartz vein (lode deposits). Mineralogists have established the typical sequences of crystallization and association of minerals in the succeeding zones of deposition. Veins are particularly valuable sources of some rare elements which are here concentrated by natural processes. There are other cases, like the above-mentioned molybdenum, in which vapors infiltrate entire rock bodies that may eventually be altered completely. This process is called "replacement"; the original rock constituents are replaced by new ones, and ores thereby formed are replacement ores (disseminated or compact). The contact zone of intrusive magmatic bodies with the neighboring rocks is another example of similar deposits.

Finally, a very important alteration occurs through the weathering of rocks. This may give rise to such a concentration of certain minerals that they can be classified as ores; some iron and manganese deposits are of this type. The outstanding example of this group are probably the bauxite deposits. Through residual weathering a complex mixture of hydrous oxides of aluminum becomes concentrated to such a degree that commercial extraction of aluminum from this residue is made possible.

In all the cases cited so far it may occur that metallic minerals are later removed by gradational processes from the place of primary formation and deposited at a secondary location where they accumulate in sufficient quantities to constitute ore deposits: hence the term "secondary deposits." Since the specific gravity of practically all the metallic minerals is much higher than that of the matrix rock material, natural separation takes place along the river courses, especially in meandering streams, as well as along the seashore. Other types of secondary deposits—moraines, talus slopes, etc.—are also possible.

Two excellent examples of primary and secondary deposits are offered by tin and gold. Primary deposits of tin are found as epigenetic quartz veins, frequently together with tungsten minerals, in the form of SnO_2 (cassiterite). In Bolivia tin comes from underground mines which follow the veins. In Southeast Asia cassiterite is found primarily in secondary deposits, in river-formed alluvial beds. While lode deposits contain up to 8 percent tin, placer deposits—the term for secondary deposits of this type—yield less than 1 percent. But since in a placer, cassiterite is found mixed with loose sands and clays, the separation of tin is easy and low in cost. Gold occurs in primary deposits like tin. The best-known example is probably the Mother Lode district in California; corresponding placer deposits are found in Tertiary, Pleistocene, and recent river deposits in the same area.

The type of deposits determines not only the mining methods but also to a very large degree the methods by which the ore is further treated. With respect to mining methods little can be added to what we already know from earlier discussions. Underground deposits are mined in shafts and slope mines in much the same way as coal. Open-pit mining is extensively employed for large deposits of types 1.a, 1.b, 2.b, and 2.c,

if the overburden can be stripped off. Modern techniques utilizing bulldozers and, for unconsolidated placer deposits, hydraulic methods have made many deposits accessible. As is well-known, hydraulic mining methods played an important role in California's gold production in early days. The gold-bearing sand and gravels were loosened by powerful jets of water and swept to the treating plants by the resulting flow; at the same time the water carried the waste material downstream. Consequently, reservoirs were gradually filled with the greatly increased load, canals for irrigation choked and overflowed, and a general deterioration of the hydrological situation ensued. As soon as the necessary laws were enacted, laws which made

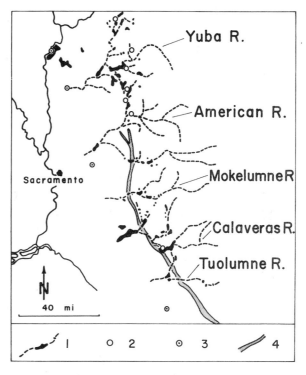

Jenkins, State of California Dept. of Nat. Res. *Bull.*, 141, 1948

86 · SECONDARY ORE DEPOSITS: gold in California. *Legend:* (1) Tertiary river courses, indicated by gravel deposits; (2) placer mines; (3) areas where dredges have been used; (4) Mother Lode which consists of vein deposits of gold quartz ore. It played a prominent role as primary deposits in the later development of gold mining in California.

the mining companies liable to pay for the damage caused, the hydraulic system was abandoned and the Californian gold mining industry concentrated on primary deposits that were worked by shaft mines.

The type of ore not only determines the technicalities of treatment, but frequently the location of the metallurgical operations as well. The most common forms of ore treatment are the following:

(a) Separation of the desired from the undesired minerals by hand, a practice followed only in countries where labor is very cheap and mostly with lode ores.

(b) Separation by different specific weights, e.g., gold and tin, by magnetic properties, or by affinities to certain substances. The last method is known as flotation. The finely crushed ore passes through a bubble bath in which ore minerals swim with the bubbles, coated with oil, up to the surface while other minerals collect at the bottom.

Methods a and b serve simply to obtain the concentrates of desired ore minerals. They are followed up by other steps to produce metals, namely:

(c) According to the chemical composition of the ore minerals, concentrates or crude ore are deoxidized (reduction process), roasted (sulfuric compounds), and smelted to separate metal from slag in much the same way as for iron.

(d) More and more ores are treated by electro-metallurgical or electrochemical methods which make possible the production of virtually pure metals. These methods also have the advantage of being easily adaptable to automation and cheap bulk handling, since the material is treated in liquid solution.

A comparison between tin and copper will reveal the importance of the ore type upon the economic geography of mines, metallurgical plants, and consumption. Tin ore from placer deposits is processed to tin concentrates on the same dredge that is mining the alluvial deposits; sand is thrown out as tailings, filling in the cavities excavated by the dredge. In underground lode deposits, e.g., in Bolivia, the mined products are usually separated by hand first and later crushed and processed to a concentrate containing 60 to 70 percent tin. These operations also take place in the immediate vicinity of the mines. Tin is obtained in the form of oxides (SnO_2); the ores are reduced and smelted much like iron with charcoal, coke, etc. Smelters may be established either near the mines or near the market, the major determinants being the availability of fuel and the economic policy of the country. The quantity of ores obtained from one underground mine is frequently too small for economic operation of a smelter. In such a case the products of the various mines are exported as concentrates which are already sufficiently high in value to make long-distance shipping profitable.

Copper ores are for the most part sulfides, though oxidized ores occur near the surface. If the copper content is very low—about 1 to 3 percent—copper ores have to undergo flotation first; otherwise they may be sent to the smelter directly. In the United States, where large-scale operations permit the use of lower-grade ores, the average copper content of ores to be concentrated is as low as 0.9 percent, and of ores which are directly smelted, about 3.5 percent. As much as nine-tenths of the copper ores mined in the United States are first concentrated. Smelting produces a copper which somewhat corresponds to pig iron and likewise has to be refined in a converter. The product of the smelter is called copper matte, and that of the converter blister copper. The latter will be electrolytically refined for uses in electrical engineering. Oxidized copper ores can also be treated by leaching and electrochemical precipitation of the copper, the method practiced in some districts of northern Chile. The low metallic content of the copper ores makes it necessary for the copper smelters to be located close to the mines. If fuel for smelting is not available there, it must be brought in to the mining area. In the form of matte or blister copper the metal can be profitably transported over long distances. Electrolytical copper is produced near the electric power plant, close to the source of water power or of other cheap primary energy such as natural gas or oil. While for copper the ratio of ore and smelter production (in relation to world totals) is practically identical in the different countries, it varies significantly for tin, where ore and smelter production are often areally separated.

The Occurrence of Ores and the Production Structure

Ores do not occur haphazard. On the contrary, the conditions under which ore deposits were formed determine their distribution with respect to time as well as to space. It is possible to identify well-defined metallogenetic provinces and distinguish characteristic combinations of valuable mineral compounds. We will limit ourselves here to a few examples, to demonstrate the principles.

Deposits of the type I.2.c (i.e., primary-epigenetic, resulting from weathering) are necessarily formed only within certain climatic zones; hence they occur within certain latitudinal belts. Bauxite, for example, which is nothing but a climatically controlled soil formation, is found in tropical and subtropical latitudes in either hemisphere. Older bauxite deposits follow a zonal arrangement which reflects an earlier climatic control, but these deposits are few and can be clearly separated from younger ones. Important deposits of bauxite in the Old World extend from southern France through many Mediterranean countries into equatorial Africa, mainly West Africa. In the New World the most important deposits are in the equatorial part of South America and the Caribbean as well as in southern United States. The major producing countries in Asia are India, Malaya, Indonesia, and tropical Australia. The structure of the production of aluminum from bauxite consists of three steps: (a) mining, mostly by the open-pit method, screening, crushing, and drying of the ore, which is made up of a colloidal mixture of hydrous oxides of aluminum and other admixtures, (b) transformation of the hydrous oxides into Al_2O_3 (alumina) by a process which requires a large amount of energy in the form of heat, and (c) reduction of alumina to aluminum by an electrometallurgical process. On an aver-

age 4 tons of dry bauxite will give 2 tons of alumina, or 1 ton of aluminum. All the processes mentioned under a generally take place at or near the bauxite mines. The location of b and c is governed primarily by the availability of low-cost energy in the required form. Were there two equal possibilities, the plant would move as close to the preceding step as possible in order to reduce unnecessary transport of waste material. Recent changes in the cost of energy (discussed in Chapter 8), are altering the traditional structure of the aluminum industry. In the United States large deposits of steam coal in the Interior Plains were used for the production of alumina from bauxite. This part of the industry was centered at St. Louis, and ores were brought in via New Orleans and the Mississippi; from there alumina was shipped to places of hydroelectric power production, such as Niagara Falls and vicinity, for the final transformation into aluminum. In Europe a similar south-to-north structure was observed—mines in the Mediterranean and Balkan countries, and aluminum refineries in the Alps and in Scandinavia.

Competition between coal and oil and between hydroelectricity and thermal electricity (especially based on oil and natural gas) has affected and changed this simple structure. Aluminum plants were erected on the Gulf Coast in the United States or in the Southwest of France near natural gas production, and alumina plants in Jamaica based on Caribbean sources of oil. Likewise the harnessing of West African rivers will eventually lead to the shift of plants toward the source of the ore in the Afro-European sector. Similar plans have been discussed for Latin American deposits, already with a view to possible utilization of nuclear energy.

Deposits of the types I.1.a, I.2.a, and I.2.b are characterized by their mineral associations as well as by their regional distribution. A few of the more common associations—some of which have been mentioned earlier—are Ag + Au, Ag + Pb, Pb + Zn, Pb + Zn + Cu, Cu + Au, Ni + Cu + Au, Fe + Mn, Sn + Wo. Each combination necessitates a special technique and installation for the separation of the various components. Each also gives rise to some economic problems, since the production of one metal en-

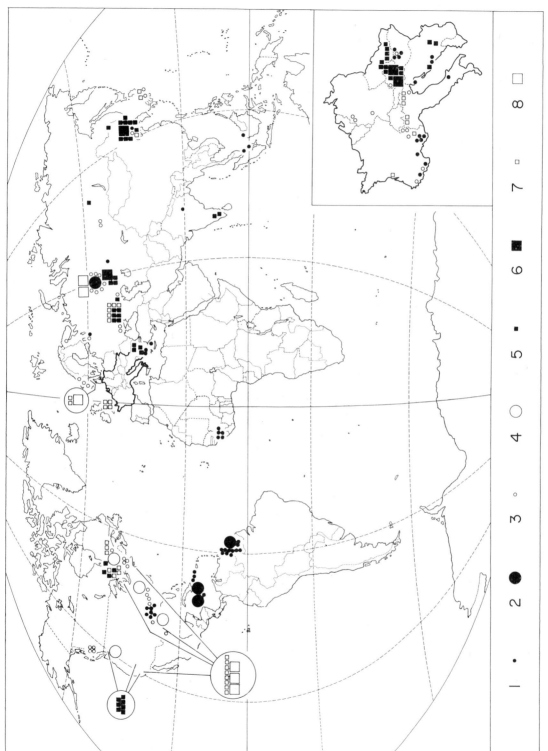

87 · ALUMINUM AND MAGNESIUM. *Legend:* (1) bauxite production, 1 percent of world total; (2) bauxite, 10 percent; (3) aluminum production, 1 percent of world total; (4) aluminum, 10 percent; (5) magnesite production, 1 percent of world total; (6) magnesite, 10 percent; (7) magnesium production, 1 percent of world total; (8) magnesium, 10 percent.

tails that of another metal. A typical example is the nickel-copper deposit of Sudbury, Ontario, which dominates world nickel production. We are not concerned with the geology of the deposits here; it will suffice to point out that the nickel-copper ratio varies from $1:0.6$ to $1:>1$, and that consequently increased demand for nickel inevitably brings about a considerable increase in copper production, gold being an additional by-product. In such instances it becomes very difficult to exercise control on the production of any one metal.

A special case is presented in many mining areas by so-called *stockworks*, each of which is impregnated with one or more ore minerals. Stockworks occur especially in lode deposits where a drop in temperature of a magma produced differential crystallization of minerals toward the earth's surface. Certain sequences of mineral compounds are found along a vein so regularly that some of the associations can be used, so to speak, as fossil thermometers. Hypothermal, mesothermal, and epithermal deposits are thereby distinguished. The extent of a given ore deposit is usually limited to one stockwork and as mining proceeds, the properties of the mine alter. An example may be given from the Butte district in Montana, one of the most famous copper mining areas in the world. There veins of different periods and different mineral composition traverse the rocks, producing a very complicated system of deposits; three major systems are recognized by the mining engineers. Mineralization changes from the central through the intermediate to the peripheral zone of each vein; the copper content decreases outward, while (for instance) that of silver increases. Furthermore, oxidation and subsequent weathering have removed copper and silver in places.

Some well-defined metallogenetic provinces in the North American continent are the copper province of the Rocky Mountains, the silver-gold deposits of the Basin and Range area, the quartz vein deposits of gold extending from California northward to British Columbia, young vein deposits of rare metals throughout the Rocky Mountains, especially in Colorado, and the large pre-Cambrian gold belt in the Canadian shield.

Similar metallogenetic provinces can be identified in the other continents.

The Availability of Ores

Ores are distributed unevenly over the earth, and many important raw materials are known to exist in only a few localities, often far removed from the places of consumption. In a number of cases—a few are mentioned below—this creates serious difficulties and bottlenecks in satisfying the demands of the market.

The first group of such highly important metals comprises those which are used to make alloy steel (ferroalloys). Molybdenum has already been mentioned; most of the world production comes from one mine in the United States (Climax, Colorado), and European consumers are largely dependent upon American exports. Vanadium shows a similar statistical situation. For tungsten, however, approximately half of world production comes from the Far East (mostly mainland China) and Southeast Asia. Almost half of the total cobalt production comes from the Congo, and Canada dominates the world production of nickel. All these metals are indispensable for any highly developed industrial country, for they are used to impart to steel certain desired properties—hardness, resistance to extremely high temperatures, etc.

A special case is presented by manganese. It is used in steel making to remove oxygen and sulfur; about 12 pounds of manganese are required for each ton of steel produced. Manganese is also used to give steel a certain hardness. This metal is almost completely absent from the main industrial centers of the Old and the New World. The United States produces only about 2 to 3 percent of the world total and is compelled to import practically all the manganese it requires. The USSR, on the other hand, can count on about half of world production, coming from large deposits in the Ukraine and the Caucasus. India is the major producer outside of Russia. Recently large mines have been developed by American concerns in the north of Brazil, and from there manganese is imported into the United States in increasing quantities. Manga-

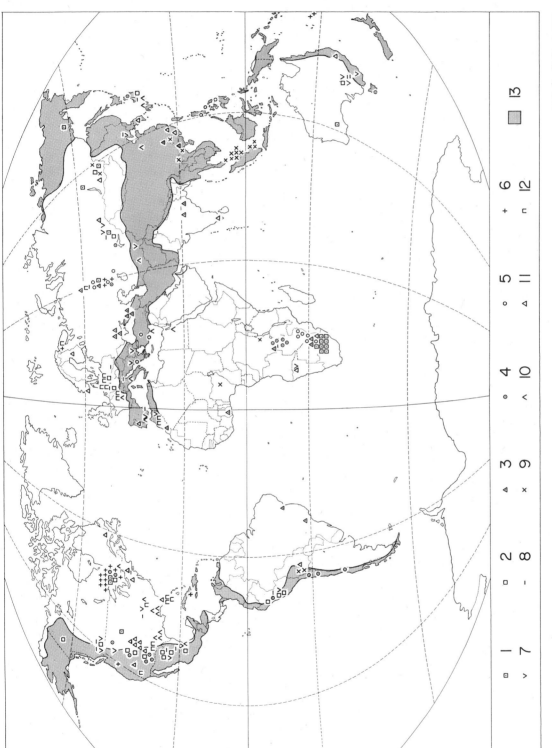

88 · VARIOUS MINERAL PRODUCTS. The production of various minerals in relation to the major structural units of the earth. Each symbol represents 5 percent (2.5–7.5 percent) of the world total production of the respective mineral in 1960. Legend: (1) gold; (2) silver; (3) manganese; (4) copper; (5) chromium, expressed by chromite; (6) nickel; (7) lead; (8) zinc; (9) tin; (10) sulfur, including sulfur obtained from pyrite; (11) tungsten, molybdenum, vanadium, and titanium; (12) potash and phosphates; (13) Tertiary mountain chains separating the northern and southern continental shields.

(18) after R. Staub, 1928

nese is to be considered an indispensable ingredient in steel making. The dependence of the United States on overseas supplies is a major bottleneck that can only be counteracted by the accumulation of large emergency reserves. Consequently, imports of manganese ores have been, in recent years, much larger than current consumption.

Another unique case is that of gold, which has been a major stabilizing factor in international monetary relations. Production is concentrated in a few countries. Most gold is produced in mines that were from the beginning specialized and destined for the production of gold, though quite a large percentage is obtained as a byproduct in other mining operations. Nearly half of world production comes from the famous Rand district and others in the Republic of South Africa. About a fourth—the exact amount is not disclosed—may be produced in the USSR, and some of this is used to maintain the balance of payments with countries outside the Soviet economic sphere. The existence of a sizable portion of the world gold reserves and of gold production under the control of the USSR must be considered a potential source of economic disturbances on a world-wide scale. Canada holds third place in the group of major gold producers with a share of 11 percent.

To assess the importance of each mining district is an interesting problem in economic geography. Two points should be observed. First, the absolute importance of the ores produced cannot be measured in units of weight for obvious reasons, even though the production figures are generally given in tons and pounds. In order to reach comparable figures, we must use their money value as a common denominator. The second point is the relative importance of the production, in other words the question of whether the mining district under consideration holds a dominant position in relation to world production or not.

Outside of the central industrial areas, characterized by their heavy industry, we find the following major regions of secondary mining resources and associated industries: the cordillera systems, the continental shields in Canada and Brazil, and the bauxite areas in the Guianas,

all in the Western Hemisphere; the West African coastal zone and the big mining belt extending from Congo and Katanga through Rhodesia into the Republic of South Africa; the Indian subcontinent; Southeast Asia and China, through the combination tin + tungsten. Some areas, like the bauxite areas, are mainly mining districts; others have developed considerable industrial annexes with concentrating plants, smelters, etc. These industrial zones are not basic like the heavy industrial centers, but are tributary to the latter. Their riches will undoubtedly play an important role in the development of the countries concerned, but will not help them to become economically independent, at least not more than they were before; the effect would rather be the contrary. They may, therefore, be called secondary industrial regions.

THE METALWORKING INDUSTRIES

A Few Basic Facts about This Group

A wide array of raw materials are used in the metalworking industries, and respective requirements differ from one sector to another—for example, the light metals in the aircraft industry, copper in electrical equipment, various steels in machinery in general. Yet if the industries of this group are taken together, a simple quantitative comparison confirms that iron and steel lead all the other metals by a wide margin. In addition to approximately 300 million tons of crude steel, more than 10 million tons of pig iron, used in iron foundries, is consumed by the metalworking industries each year. Iron and steel are followed by aluminum, copper, zinc, and lead, each with a total of between 2 and 3 million tons; other metals appear with even smaller quantities. Thus steel can truly be called the basic raw material of present-day metalworking industries.

In our earlier description of the production of steel and its role in world trade we did not touch upon the proportions consumed by consumer groups. These groups in their totality constitute the steel market. The pattern of steel consumption characterizes the technical as well as the general development of a country. The shares of the various consumer groups undergo continuous change as the economy of a country changes, and steel production must therefore quickly respond to the changing pattern of demand.

In the United States the steel market is highly diversified today; consequently, steel production has become highly specialized. Mining and permanent construction account for 28 percent of total steel consumption, metal products for 30 percent, and transport equipment for 26 percent. The single most important sector is the automobile industry, which absorbs 20 to 25 percent or more of the total, depending upon business conditions. This is about half of sheet steel production, and one-fourth of light sections. These figures underline the key position of the automobile industry in the United States.

In Europe machinery has a much larger share, while permanent construction, owing to the almost complete lack of oil wells and pipelines, is smaller; such products as tubes, which are prominent in the United States, are becoming unimportant. On the other hand, shipbuilding is more important in Europe.

The metal-working industry assumes great importance as a location factor of the steel industry as a producer of steel scrap (so-called process scrap). The amount of process scrap, however, is small in comparison with circulation or capital scrap. In 1955 the figures in the United States were 19 percent for process scrap and 35 for circulation scrap; in Europe 14 against 37. However, the 19 percent of the United States constitutes in absolute figures 14 million tons!

A large part of the capital goods will ultimately become obsolete. Installations will be dismantled, and ships will be wrecked. While the availability of circulation and process scrap can be fairly accurately estimated, since they are derived directly from manufacturing, the available amount of capital scrap is much more difficult to assess. The average lifetime of capital goods has been calculated to be on the order of 17 to 20 years in the United States and Western Europe, and somewhat higher (25 to 28 years) in the underdeveloped countries. Because capital scrap is the most important source of the scrap needed in the steelworks (53 percent in

North America, 42 percent in Western Europe), it is extremely important to know how much of the finished capital goods is absorbed by the home market and how much is exported. In the United States the metal-working industries that are the steel consumers produce mainly for the home market; only 10 percent of the steel availabilities is exported. In the United Kingdom, 34 percent is exported; in Western Germany the share is even 40 percent. These figures include exports of semifinished and finished steel as well as processed steel, the latter accounting for more than half of the total steel exports in volume. Japan exports 20 percent of her steel, of which two-thirds is so-called "indirect export" in the form of ships, capital, and consumer goods.

The foregoing discussion may bring to light the complex situation which confronts a student of this group of industries. Their main function is to provide capital goods for manufacturing and the transportation equipment necessary for shipping raw materials, products, and people. In the United States, production of machinery (including electrical machinery) and transportation equipment together accounts for more than one-fourth of the number of employees, production workers, and value added in all sectors of manufacturing. These figures are fairly representative of all the highly industrialized countries of the world.

Machinery

Only a few selected examples will be discussed here, either because they are of outstanding importance or because they serve to illustrate certain principles.

An important sector of manufacturing which requires a constant, large-scale replenishment of machinery is the textile industry. As is well known, in the early days of industrialization the British government prohibited the exportation of machinery or plans of machines. The question is still frequently debated whether it is advantageous or detrimental to export capital goods into countries which have been important export markets for consumer goods. While there is no doubt but that such exports curtail the export of textiles, for example, to underdeveloped countries, there are other sectors of the national economy which profit. The older industrialized countries are usually so far ahead in technical progress that they can switch their exports from consumer to capital goods and generally profit by the industrialization of the still underdeveloped countries.

The restrictive British policy with regard to the exportation of textile machinery has fostered the development of a textile-machine industry in the United States and Europe. Americans recall the story of Samuel Slater, who got the New England textile industry off to a start by reproducing from memory the designs of Arkwright's cotton machinery. Less well-known is the fact that the beginnings of many machine plants in Europe which became famous later were closely associated with the textile industry. Such a plant usually started as a small workshop for repairing the imported textile machines and went on to develop into a complete manufacturing establishment wherever inventiveness and enterprising capital were available. In this way the textile-machine industry is generally found near the market for textile products.

The textile industry also teaches the lesson that outmoded machinery should be replaced regularly. Wages make up a large portion of the production costs for textiles. Consequently, there is a constant challenge to manufacturers and their research departments to invent new machinery which is as nearly automatic as possible. This tendency is the basis for guaranteeing a continuing market for their products. The highly industrialized countries in Europe—the United Kingdom, France, Belgium, Germany, Switzerland, Italy—are very much advanced and specialized in the production of textile machinery, and so is the United States, especially New England and the Middle Atlantic States, where this sector of industry is concentrated. More recently Japan has become an important producer as well as an exporter of textile machinery.

Another important outlet for the machine industry is agriculture. Agriculture draws more heavily upon manual labor than the textile industry and has a high input of man-hours. Its mechanization has therefore been looked upon everywhere as a means for bringing agricultural production closer to the level of industrial production. Until the end of the First World War, mechanization of agriculture was under way mainly in the United States. The first tractors appeared in the early twenties in Europe and somewhat later in the USSR. It is not always to be attributed to backwardness or stubborn traditionalism that farmers do not take immediately to new production techniques. A number of conditions (see p. 57) had to change before European farmers began to employ tractors and other mechanical devices on a large scale. In Soviet Russia the technical and social conditions were more favorable for mechanization. It is therefore not surprising that as late as 1937 the United States and the USSR were by far the leading producers of tractors, with 75 percent and 14 percent of the total output, respectively. Since the end of the Second World War, mechanization has made rapid strides everywhere. The FAO publishes full statistics on the number of tractors used, because of their importance as an indicator of mechanization. In the decade from 1949 to 1959 the number of tractors used in agriculture doubled throughout the world, reaching a total of more than 10 million. About half of them are found in North America, mainly in the United States, but there the relative as well as the absolute increase was small. In the USSR the absolute increase in the number of tractors was even less, about 1 million. On the other hand the number tripled in Europe, to reach 3 million. Relative increases in other continents which have much smaller absolute numbers of tractors were as follow: South America, 250 percent; Asia, 330 percent; Africa, 200 percent; Oceania, 177 percent. Regional totals were 220 percent for the Near East and 450 percent for the Far East.

Again, the older industrial countries (the United Kingdom and continental Europe) together with the USSR and more recently Japan, increased their share of the production, stimulated by the growing demand in the domestic market as well as in the export market. The relative importance of the United States, on the other hand, was appreciably reduced. In contrast to the textile industry, the market for agricultural machinery is rapidly expanding.

In the old days of traditional craftsmanship,

there was a common saying that one has to have good tools in order to do a good job. The same still holds true; only, modern machine tools are highly complicated and often precision instruments of the first order. They are fully automatic and capable of producing parts accurate to a microscopic degree. The machine-tool industry is probably more dependent than the textile and agricultural machine industries upon highly developed engineering skills and experience. This is also a type of machine making in which smaller producers are in a more advantageous position than mammoth establishments, because standardized mass production is relatively less important. Thus countries like Sweden and Switzerland play a more important role in this sector of machine making than in others. Finally, the machine-tool industry exemplifies the precept that the manufacturing industry should always be in close connection with the market to be able to deliver exactly the type of machine required for a specific purpose. This industry is generally found within the area of high industrialization.

Transportation Equipment: Automobiles

The automobile industry well exemplifies certain principles of economic geography of modern manufacturing. First come the basic inventions, the fruit of long, costly, and frequently unsuccessful efforts, leading to the construction of early prototypes of the vehicle. In these infant stages, which fall at about the turn of the century for the automobile industry, Europe played an important role. This first stage is followed by production for the market. Here a correct analysis of the market, current as well as future, becomes essential for the successful planning of the industry. Until recently an automobile was not considered a necessity in Europe for the population at large; it was either a luxury item or a necessity to serve a specific purpose. In the United States the situation was entirely different, and the automobile soon became the generally accepted vehicle for individual transportation. It is a question whether this was due to the absence of adequate public transportation, the need to cover long distances, the lower prices of motor fuels, clever advertising of cheap cars, or social characteristics. The fact remains that the American automobile industry was producing for an entirely different market than its European counterpart, a market which was much larger, was less differentiated and exacting in the details of demand, and had a much more rapid turnover.

An automobile is a highly complicated piece of construction. Approximately ten thousand pieces are put together into the parts, and these in turn are assembled into the finished vehicle. Large-scale mass production cuts down the costs of manufacturing, but any change in a model produces a chain-reaction of other changes and increased expense. Standardized production also facilitates maintenance and repair of the products through the principle of interchangeability of parts. In the United States agreements on standardization were made among automobile manufacturers as early as 1912. This must be regarded as an essential factor in creating such a quick-growing market for automobiles.

The interwar years were marked by an enormous expansion of the United States' market and production. However we measure "motorization," there is no doubt that the United States was leading the rest of the world in every sector by a wide margin. What struck a European visiting the United States in those days was the symbiosis of man and automobile, the latter being practically a member of each family, and the far-reaching system of excellent highways that were built solely for automobiles. In Germany such highways were built in the 1930's, but their purpose was primarily military. Italy constructed a few *autostrade* in the North which people from other European countries visited and traveled on as a curiosity. France had her straight, poplar-lined *routes nationales*, which formed an excellent road network but were much too narrow for modern traffic, since they dated back to the last century. Britain's highways were inviting for leisurely drives around sharp curves in the country and through narrow medieval streets in the towns, but one always had the feeling that it would be much more pleasant to hike through the lovely countryside of Britain than to go by car. Such a description may seem exaggerated or unscientific, but it serves to emphasize the contrast between the prewar and postwar period on both sides of the Atlantic.

Following the Second World War, profound changes occurred in the automobile industry, which are duly reflected in the statistics. Such statistics are nearly complete and reliable since automobiles are required to have license plates in every country. During the ten-year period from 1948 to 1958, which may be considered as the first postwar decade, the number of automobiles in use doubled, reaching in the whole world a total of 86 million passenger cars and 22 million commercial vehicles. The United States remained the most motorized country, owning about 65 percent of the passenger cars and 51 percent of the commercial vehicles. However, the relative increase had been less than in the rest of the world, namely 170 and 145 percent respectively; Europe on the other hand experienced an increase of 350 and 190 percent, leading in the expanding world market for passenger cars. An increase in commercial vehicles was relatively more significant in Asia and Africa than in Europe. Corresponding figures for the Soviet bloc are not available, but it is well-known that commercial vehicles are much more important there than passenger cars. The United Kingdom, France, and West Germany are the European countries with the highest number of motor vehicles, but relative increases were much higher in some of the smaller countries where the number of cars increased four to five fold in those ten years.

The market situation for automobiles has therefore changed considerably since the Second World War. In addition to the more or less stable demand based on the replacement of old cars, in Europe and to a lesser degree in other continents there appeared a new, rapidly expanding market for passenger cars; the market for commercial vehicles grew everywhere in the world, but more in overseas countries than in the United States or in Europe.

Automobile production in the United States had developed in a direction which was not suited to demands of the European market. American passenger cars gradually became so big that they were hard to maneuver in the narrow streets that are still very common in Europe; they were not economical, and their fuel consumption was too high. What the European market wanted, above all, was a small, sturdy, economical car, with less emphasis upon external looks. The European automobile industry made a come-back by supplying exactly the type of car in demand. British manufacturers were perhaps the most conservative with respect to outside appearance, and the French the most revolutionary. German manufacturers specialized in sturdiness, and with the Volkswagen came a type that could be sold without essential changes during the whole period under review. Italians made speedy and elegant small and medium-size cars.

During the decade 1948 to 1958 world production of passenger cars increased from 4.6 to 8.6 million units, but that of commercial vehicles remained fairly stationary. In the United States, despite rapid fluctuations in productions, the average did not change very much; the American share of world production was about 50 percent in 1958 against 87 in 1948. On the other hand, European producers achieved a steady and sharp increase of their output without exception. Germany and the United Kingdom (each with more than a million units) were leading, and France was close third, followed by Italy with 370,000 units. At present the whole of Western Europe accounts for about two-fifths of the world output of passenger cars and shares the world market with American producers.

All these changes took place within a few years' time following the Second World War. European cars are sold primarily in the home market, but exports to all the continents are increasing, including the United States, where in fact small European cars found a good market. Such an expansion of the European automobile industry could only be achieved by applying to the manufacturing process the same principles that had proved so advantageous for the American producers. A European automobile factory is a replica of the most modern American factory, characterized by long assembly lines and other features of complex mass production. The attitude of Europeans toward automobiles has also changed. Like Americans, they have come to regard the car as a convenience for daily life that should be within the means of the majority of the public. The visible landscape also began to change slowly under the impact of automobiles: modern highways, garages, and super gasoline stations, motels, and drive-in offices (only drive-in movies are rare, because of the rainy and cool European climate) sprang up everywhere.

As for location, the principle discussed above applies. The automobile industry tends to concentrate within major industrial areas. This is the case in the United States, the United Kingdom, France, and Italy. In Germany it applies to all plants except the big Volkswagen plant at Wolfsburg. This plant is now close to the East-west boundary, but it was originally planned to be within the central industrial area of an undivided Germany, the nucleus of which would have been Salzgitter. It may be said that the automobile industry shows a higher degree of spatial as well as structural concentration than the machine industry. On the other hand, the manufacturing of different parts is usually dispersed; they must be assembled at the central plant, where only the heavier parts, such as the motor and body are manufactured as well as assembled.

Transportation Equipment: Shipbuilding

The shipbuilding industry not only makes a major contribution to world transportation but is also an important consumer of steel. In the United States only about 1 percent of the total amount of steel available has gone into shipbuilding in recent years; this contrasts with 6 percent in the United Kingdom, 5 in West Germany and in the USSR, and 13 in Japan. For West Germany and Japan, sales in international markets were more important than those in the domestic markets. The statistics above indicate the most important shipbuilding nations and their relative positions in the world trade of ships.

The postwar market for ships witnessed a moderate increase of total tonnage from 80 to 120 million gross registered tons (1948-1958). The most conspicuous increase occurred in the tonnage of tankers from 15 to 34 million gross

registered tons. These figures, however, conceal the realities of postwar shipbuilding activities, which were largely directed toward replacing obsolete and uneconomical units.

The greater part of world shipbuilding industry is located in Western Europe. In 1958 four-fifths of the total tonnage launched (9.3 million gross registered tons) came from Western European shipyards. The United Kingdom led during the period 1948-1958 with an annual average output of about 1.3 million tons, but West Germany took a long stride forward after 1950, even slightly surpassing the United Kingdom in 1958. An outstanding development was the swift rise of Japan as a shipbuilding nation. By the end of the fifties, Japan had become by far the most important producer, with more than 2 million gross registered tons. The role of the United States, the USSR, and the Eastern European countries is in comparison negligible.

CHEMICALS AND PETROCHEMICALS

The Chemical Industry in General

The development of chemical industry is an excellent indicator of the inventiveness and development of an industrial country. Probably no other industry matches chemical industry in its heavy dependence upon research laboratories. A stream of inventions pours forth new processes and new products to meet particular needs and specifications. Perhaps the most amazing thing about this industry is that the basic raw materials are usually such common substances as water, air, coal, limestone, petroleum, natural gas, sulfur, salt, and wood. These are transformed by intricate processing into exceedingly complex compounds with long chemical formulas that can be sold in minute quantities at very high prices. Thus, the chemical industry should by no means be regarded as a compact and unified industrial sector; on the contrary, it is so highly diversified that any generalization seems almost impossible.

The iron and steel industry was an example of a straight production line with several check points on the way (pig iron, ingots, etc.) where capacity and production could be accurately measured. The whole structure of the chemical industry defies such straightforwardness. Numerous roots extend from the main trunk, and the most complicated and interwoven relationships hold between different production lines. Summarizing statistics are all but lacking; only the statistics for individual products, such as sulfuric acid, are available. But compounds like sulfuric acid, hydrochloric acid, and nitric acid for which production data are easily obtainable belong to a first group of chemicals which are produced in bulk and further processed. We will call this group the industrial or heavy chemicals. The other group, called special or light chemicals,

is characterized by an almost complete lacuna of statistical data, with respect to both quantity and value.

The two groups also differ in locational characteristics. Industrial chemicals are usually produced near raw-material sources, along inland waterways, or along the seacoast, for transportation costs are paramount in importance. Specialized chemicals are most commonly found at or in the vicinity of large population centers which serve as commercial centers and at the same time attract high-quality research workers.

The distribution of chemical industry in the United States shows these characteristics very clearly. Leading port cities like New York, Phila-

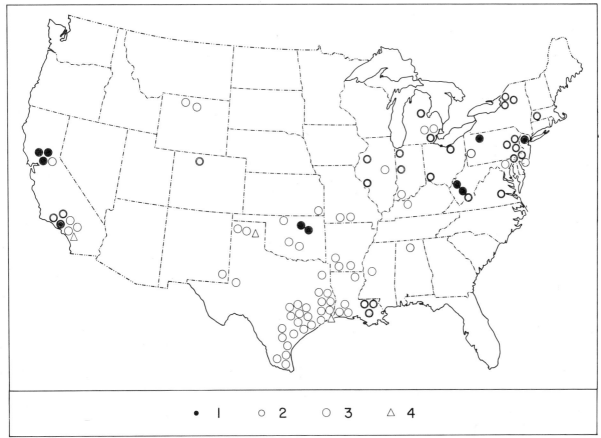

W. Isard and E. W. Schooler, U.S. Department of Commerce, 1955

89 · PETROCHEMICAL INDUSTRY: the youngest and the fastest growing of all the industries.
Legend: (1) location of petrochemical plants that existed in 1930; (2) location in 1940; (3) location in 1951; (4) plants proposed in 1951.

delphia, and Baltimore with their satellite cities represent major centers of the industry of both groups. The Appalachian Plateau is more of a raw-material-oriented section; here hydropower forms another inducement. The industry is widespread, but nodes occur here and there as in the Great Kanawha Valley. In the Northeast along the Great Lakes from Buffalo and Niagara Falls to Chicago, a very high concentration of chemical industry is found again. Other centers are large agglomerations such as St. Louis, Kansas City, San Francisco, Los Angeles. More recently rapid development of chemical industries has been observed along the Gulf Coast of Texas and Louisiana, based on local raw materials (sulfur, lime, and salt serving one section and petroleum and natural gas another) and cheap water transportation on the Intracoastal Canal. Besides the requirements mentioned above, other general points to be considered are cheap power and a good water supply, as well as the facilities for the disposal of waste products.

The chemical industry is one of the youngest industries, characterized by rapid expansion and constant quick changes in production techniques. This is particularly true of the production of specialized chemicals. Industrial chemicals are more static; some production processes are in fact between fifty and a hundred years old. For example, sulfuric acid, a most important heavy chemical in many industries, has been produced by essentially the same method since the latter half of the nineteenth century. The process of making caustic soda from salt and limestone, invented by the Solvay brothers in 1863, is still in use today. There are more such examples of basic materials that will not be mentioned here. Yet they are on the whole exceptions to the general rule that everything in the chemical industry is continuously changing. Almost every day new discoveries are made; some are for immediate use and some are for a potential future.

The unusual importance of research in the field of specialized chemicals greatly affects the economic geography of the chemical industry. One aspect is the extreme concentration of the industry in the hands of huge concerns and interest groups—for example, Imperial Chemical Industries (Great Britain) and IG-Farben (Ger-

many). They safeguard the results of their basic research, facilitate the exchange of information within the group, and develop the market for their myriad different products. Another aspect is that even a small country is capable of developing a chemical industry of importance, particularly at its light end, provided that the necessary facilities for continued research are available. If exports are measured in relation to the total exports of a country, Switzerland is the world's leading exporter of chemicals. While industrial chemicals are the leading export items in France, the United Kingdom, and West Germany, pharmaceuticals and dyes are at the top in Switzerland. In the United States also pharmaceuticals hold first place, followed by plastics and industrial chemicals.

The accompanying table summarizes the development of chemical industry (after German sources). The figures are indicative of only the overall development, since it has proved impossible to separate the various groups of chemical products.

CHEMICAL PRODUCTION IN LEADING COUNTRIES				
	1913	1927	1951	1957
World production in millions of dollars	2400	5400	39,600	63,200
United States	33.8%	41.7%	43.2%	41.0%
USSR	2.9	3.6	10.8	13.0
Western Germany	23.8	15.9	5.8	7.1
Great Britain	10.9	10.2	8.8	6.5
France	8.4	6.5	3.5	4.7
Japan	1.5	2.4	3.9	4.7
Total of these countries	81.3%	80.3%	76.0%	77.0%

As the utilization of atomic energy is in the forefront of modern development in energy production, so chemical industry is in the forefront of twentieth-century manufacturing. There have so far been published few works, general or special, on the economic geography of the chemical industries. The development is still too young, and the picture is highly complex and ever changing.

Man-Made Fibers

It was in the field of the textiles that the public at large felt the rising importance of chemical industry for the first time. Toward the end of the nineteenth century and early in the twentieth century, several new processes were developed for dissolving natural cellulose materials. The solution was then pressed through the tiny holes of spinnerets into a chemical bath which solidified it into a filament. Such artificial fibers are called cellulose-derivative fibers, or cellulose fibers for short, to distinguish them from the truly synthetic fibers which appeared much later.

The first commercially successful fiber of this type was made in 1884 by Chardonnet in Besançon, France. Cotton linters were treated with nitric and sulfuric acids to form nitrocellulose, which was then dissolved in ether and alcohol. The resulting artificial fiber had the disadvantage of being inflammable, and the solvents were responsible for the high production costs. Quite unlike natural fibers, this one had a shiny luster, a feature rather common in the early artificial fibers. The term *rayon,* used ever since to designate this goup of fibers, derives from the French word for ray and suggests their sheen.

The fiber produced by Chardonnet was a nitrocellulose rayon. There are at least four major groups of rayons, but the most important is the one produced by the viscose process, first used in 1905. Viscose is made from bleached sulfite wood pulp dissolved in caustic soda.

Like natural silk, rayon is produced in a continuous filament. While the silkworm presses his liquid through only two holes, an artificial spinneret may have up to forty holes. The solidified filaments are then taken together and spun into a rayon yarn. From here onward it follows the steps of weaving, dyeing, etc., described earlier for the textile industry.

Because of its likeness to silk and its low price, rayon first affected the silk market. Filament rayon was always cheaper than silk, but until about 1930 it was still more expensive than wool, raw cotton being the cheapest of all the raw materials. In the twenties the continuous filament yarn was gradually replaced by a sort of chopped-up rayon or *rayon staples,* which could be mixed with cotton or wool staples to be processed through the spinning and the weaving mills. From the very beginning viscose rayon staple commanded a lower price than that of raw wool, and now has almost reached the level of raw cotton. That rayons have not made inroads into the wool market, in the same way as they have practically destroyed the silk market, is explained by the fact that most artificial fibers do not yet possess certain distinctive qualities of natural wool. However, the impact of rayons is strongly felt in the cotton market.

The start of the rayon industry was made in countries which already possessed a highly developed textile industry but lacked a domestic supply of the necessary natural fibers. Rayons, especially those made by the viscose process and used as staples, seemed to offer a way out of that difficult situation. Consequently Germany, Italy, and Japan had become the principal producers and consumers of rayon staples before the Second World War, while the United States had already been leading in the field of filament yarn as a substitute for silk (artificial silk). The first three countries mentioned above were together responsible for about nine-tenths of the world supply of rayon staples in the years between the two world wars; their total share of artificial fibers, including filaments, was more than half of the world production.

The distinction between filament yarn and staples is, therefore, highly significant in surveying the textile industry of a country. During the Second World War, i.e., after 1940 and especially after 1944, a definite shift from staples to filaments was observed in world statistics as a result of bombardments in Germany, Italy, and Japan. The postwar years witnessed a quick recovery of the staples, which came to share nearly 60 percent of the total output of rayons in 1958. Japan, Germany, and Italy were again among the leading producers, and together with the United Kingdom their production of staples constituted a little more than half of the world total. The United States remained the chief producer of filament yarn (31 percent), at the same time greatly expanding staple production (13 percent). Noteworthy is Japan, who came to occupy an important position in the production of artificial fibers (the first place in staples with 18 per cent, and the third after the United States and the USSR in filament yarn with 9 percent). Finally a rapid growth in the USSR seems indicative of the industrialization of that country (filament yarn 9 percent, staples 6 percent).

Rayon is truly a man-made fiber, but it is not entirely synthetic, for the basic material from which it is made is cellulose in some form or other and of natural origin. For the noncellulosic fibers like Nylon, Perlon, and all their kind, the raw material from which we start is first broken down into unsaturated and chemically active molecules, from which entirely new materials are obtained by chemical synthesis. Important initial raw materials will be discussed in the following two sections, on the coal tar and the petrochemical industries. They are hydrocarbons; together with oxygen and nitrogen they form the basic compounds from which synthetic fibers are chemically constructed. To put it in an extremely simplified way, it may be said that air, water, and coal are the raw materials for synthetic fibers.

Synthetic fibers are newcomers, and their production is not yet equal to that of the rayons; the production ratio of rayons to synthetic fibers in the late fifties was roughly 5:1. The United States was by far the largest producer, having a share of 53 percent of the total world output, followed by Japan with 11 percent. Aggregate production of the European countries amounted to 29 percent, Germany, the United Kingdom, France, and Italy being the most important. The share of the USSR was 4 percent.

The industry's start may be assigned to the year 1937 when DuPont had the process for nylon patented. Other well-known names of synthetic fibers are Orlon and Vinyl in the United States, Terylene in England, and Vinylon in Japan. An entirely different line of chemical synthesis starts from vegetable and animal proteins (milk, soy beans, peanuts, etc.), reaching the end product called protein fibers. These fibers do not yet have the importance of synthetic resins.

In one respect synthetics have not yet altered the traditional pattern of industry. Once the fiber has been produced, whether in the form of filament yarn or staples, it goes through the regular process of spinning and weaving to the finishing stages. It means that the entire process of manufacturing synthetics involves the following steps: (1) preparation of industrial chemicals (e.g., in the case of nylon, amide salts from wood pulp); (2) production of specialized chemicals and hence filament yarns or staples; (3) the traditional steps in making textiles from spinning to finishing. While the first two steps require separate new establishments, those under head 3 may be accomplished in the long-established textile industry for natural fibers. This situation might alter in the future if synthetics should no longer be produced by way of yarns and staples, but directly manufactured into a fabric which will not deserve the name of a textile, but might better be called a garment-plastic. Such a process has already become important for certain purposes, especially where water-repellent fabrics are required.

The first man-made fibers were *ersatz* in the true sense of the word, fibers of generally lower quality than the natural fiber. For example, nitrocellulose rayons were inflammable, and most rayons have a luster which is not always pleasing to the eye. Once a product has been identified merely as an *ersatz*, the public takes a long time to be convinced that in many instances chemical research has succeeded in developing man-made fibers which are definitely superior to natural fibers in certain respects. Though these qualities can be objectively proved, yet in many parts of Europe synthetic fibers are still met with skepticism, much more so than in the United States. The basic fact which is often overlooked is that the market is now in a position to instruct the manufacturers as to the type of fiber demanded and that the chemist can elaborate a new process to meet exact specifications. This is something even the best of geneticists cannot do with cotton or with sheep. Once the process is worked out, materials of identical quality can be produced at any place and at any time; there is no restriction imposed by nature upon production, climatic or otherwise, nor any such problem as the deterioration of seeds. For these and many other reasons man-made fibers have practically wiped out the production of natural silk, are keen competitors of cotton, and gradually encroach upon the wool industry. The continuation of this process should be very carefully watched.

The Coal-Chemical Industries

Coal, which has so far been regarded only as a fuel and source of energy, is also one of the principal raw materials in an important sector of the chemical industry. In recent years petroleum and natural gas have made great inroads into the field of coal chemistry (see the section below on the petrochemical industry), but in all countries where coal is plentiful and relatively cheap, this industry still commands an important position.

The beginnings of the coal-chemical industry are closely associated with the production of gas and coke, especially gas. We already know the technological changes in the making of coke— that is, the replacement of the beehive ovens by modern by-product ovens, which was accompanied by a locational shift of the coking industries from the coal mines to the integrated steel factories. In some instances this was more of a structural than a geographical change, as in the Ruhr area; but elsewhere coke production sometimes wandered far away from coal mines as, for example, to the Calumet District south of Chicago.

In modern coke ovens, not only are the by-products recaptured, but the whole process can be regulated in such a way that certain desired by-products are obtained. While high-temperature coking processes give out so-called aromatics, low-temperature operations yield aliphatics in the tar fraction. Tar and gas are the basic raw materials for this section of the chemical industry.

The word "by-products" implies that tar and gas were originally thought to be undesirable and waste. Yet, but for the utilization of exactly these by-products, the ever-increasing price of coal might have financially wrecked the production of coke long ago. Here is a fine example of how the utilization of by-products can rescue an industry from a financial impasse. Since the bulk of the by-products are processed and used by the producers themselves, it is not easy to give statistical estimates and to ascertain the value of by-products. The following figures may help clarify the situation: at the end of the Second World War the coke ovens in the United States were fed with coal worth $450 million; they produced $450 million worth of coke and $900 million of by-products, of which 15 percent were sold in the market. Thus it may be said that the by-products pay all the operational expenses and make the profits as well.

The coal-chemical industry is relatively young. By-product ovens designed to recover gases and tars were first constructed in 1898 by Koppers in Germany, and a few years later were introduced into the United States. Germany was also well advanced in chemical research, and an increasing number of compounds were being produced from coal tar and coal gases. It is clearly demonstrated by Germany that an early start and continued research, backed by a strong organization for production and marketing, is of particular importance in the field of chemicals. Even before the First World War, Germany had practically monopolized the production of dyes, the core of the coal-tar industry at that time, accounting for 75 percent of the world output and 88 percent of world trade in dyes. After the war, the leading firms were incorporated in IG-Farben, which developed into the most powerful unit in chemical industry before the end of the Second World War, controlling nearly half of the total German output in chemicals. Similarly, Imperial Chemical Industries, Ltd., dominates the chemical field in England; in the United States companies mentioned above are of importance.

Very clear in this sector is the distinction between the two groups of chemicals, industrial and specialized. While the first group finds the most favorable location to be near the coke ovens, or at least along canals and waterways connecting coking and chemical plants, the second group may be found either in association with the first or totally separated. The Swiss chemical industry, centered in Basel at the head of the Rhine River navigation, offers a typical and important example. Based on imported industrial chemicals, the industry there concentrates on specialized products, mainly pharmaceuticals and dyes, which command a high price and give enough return to pay for extensive research laboratories.

Location factors therefore differ for different steps in processing. First a close locational association between by-product coke ovens and the coal-tar industry is observed. As long as the chemical plants handle the bulky industrial chemicals, long-distance hauls by rail are prohibitive; if water transportation is available, decentralization may take place. At the opposite end of the chemical industry, i.e., for the specialized products, other factors become more significant, such as historical roots, research facilities, and good living conditions. Generalization beyond this is obviously difficult.

The regulating factor for the coal-tar industry is the demand for (mostly metallurgical) coke, since tar is derived through the coking process. In an entirely different section of coal-chemical industry, coal is not first broken down into coke, gas, and tar, but is chemically treated in such a way that new compounds are brought forth. This field of coal-chemical industry, independent of any associate industries, came to blossom in coal-rich Germany and was primarily intended to relieve shortages of petroleum and natural gas. Chemically coal is very similar to petroleum; carbon and hydrogen are the major constituents, together with impurities; but the ratio of hydrogen to carbon is much lower in coal than in petroleum, and still lower than in natural gas. This ratio may be altered to approximate that of petroleum by a process called coal hydrogenation, originally developed by the German chemist Bergius and much improved during the interwar period. Germany was thereby able to produce liquid fuels she needed during the Second World War. The Fischer-Tropsch process achieved the same goal—namely, the production of gasoline from coal—by another method based on gasification and synthesis. These processes are theoretically and technically solved. Since their end products compete directly with petroleum products, the cost factor of petroleum vs. coal is the major determinant for their future. Unless there should be drastic changes either in the mining methods and consequently the production costs for coal or in the availability of petroleum and natural gas, the prospect is not very bright for the coal-chemical industry, particularly because a considerable portion of chemical production

earlier based on coal tar has been taken over by the petrochemical industry.

The Petrochemical Industries

Crude petroleum and natural gas are essentially a mixture of various hydrocarbons. Thus they can be used instead of coal as basic raw materials for the manufacturing of chemical products. Petrochemicals are pure chemical substances produced from petroleum or natural gas. The fact that coal prices have in the past risen faster than petroleum prices and are likely to continue higher has favored a rapid and constant development of the petrochemical industry, particularly in countries where oil and natural gas are cheaply available. Another advantage is that unlike coal they are easily handled in bulk and especially suited to modern production processes.

As in the early days of the coal-chemical industry, the petrochemical industries at first made use of cheap by-products from the oil refineries. In Chapter 8, the two basic processes of the oil-refining industry were mentioned, i.e., fractional distillation and cracking. Until 1936 cracking was done by the so-called thermic method; afterwards the catalytic method, which yielded more gasoline, came into general use. This change in technology has considerably affected location factors in the petrochemical industry. Thermic cracking yields a much higher percentage of olefines than the catalytic method. Olefines are unsaturated and therefore chemically very active molecules. They are the basic raw material for petrochemicals; their unsaturated nature is particularly desirable for the manufacture of synthetics. As long as thermic cracking was the prevalent method, the petrochemical industry, utilizing a by-product from the refinery, was locationally bound to the latter. With the introduction of the catalytic cracking process, however, the importance of the by-products lessened. The petrochemical industry came to depend directly on oil and natural gas, which are nowadays processed in special thermic cracking plants to give high olefine returns. Consequently the petrochemical industry became freer in the selection of its location. The fact that oil refineries and petrochemical industries are based on the same raw materials somewhat obscures this change in locational requirements.

For several reasons it is almost impossible to give an adequate treatment to the petrochemical industries. Theirs is the newest and most rapidly expanding field of modern industry. Prior to 1920 no pure chemicals were manufactured from petroleum. In the United States the start of the industry may be dated at the beginning of the Second World War, at least on a commercial scale. In 1955 more than a hundred plants were already producing as much as 13 million tons of chemicals. In Europe the petrochemical industry made a later start, around 1953, but has since been growing equally rapidly. The documentation in the form of statistics and other publications has already become quite voluminous, but comprehensive works in the field of economic geography are practically nil. Again, any generalization is made difficult by the heterogeneity of the industry. The synthesis of all the intermediate and final products presents a maze of ever-changing relationships, and so does the marketing. Thus the petrochemical industry cannot be dealt with in the same way as the iron and steel industry.

Nevertheless, a few facts relevant for the economic geographer already begin to stand out. In the years when refinery by-products were virtually the exclusive raw materials, the obvious location for the industry was near the refineries. After the raw-material base shifted from refinery by-products to crude oil and natural gas, the basic petrochemical industries became established either close to oil and gas fields or along or at the termini of shipping lines (pipelines as well as tankers). But their secondary branches may reach into areas where other raw materials— sulfur, salt, limestone, etc.—are available. Which of these locations is to be selected, other things being equal, depends first upon the transportation costs from the raw material sources to the industrial plants and hence to the markets. A study published by the United States Department of Commerce in 1955 gives a comparison between the Gulf Coast and the New York area in terms of this cost factor. To summarize the

results, it can be said that the various petrochemical products showed no general inclination either way. Some are better off at the Gulf Coast, for shipments made by water, while for products shipped by rail, the New York area is preferable. Like all other industries making use of automation, the petrochemical industries are also characterized by a high output per man-hour. The proportion of labor costs to the total is low, while capital investments, depreciation, plant maintenance, etc., are high. Large manufacturing units have a decided advantage over smaller ones.

The United States, where the petrochemical industries were first started, illustrates these facts clearly. The great development during the war years occurred primarily in the Gulf area from Louisiana to the Mexican border, and subsequently in the industrial Northeast in the vicinity of tidewaters, the Great Lakes, and the Ohio River, as well as in the Los Angeles area.

Products of the petrochemical industries cover an extremely wide range. Today they are found in increasing quantities in almost every sector of our economic life. Synthetic rubber, textiles, paints, solvents, detergents, pharmaceuticals, fertilizers, etc., are only a few of such products. Plastics are almost universal in their applicability and even encroach upon the markets for pipes and tubes and for steel for construction, appliances, and so forth. Synthetics are also infiltrating the market for certain agricultural products such as cream and ice cream. Just as for the coal-tar chemical industry, explosives are an important sector. In short, the petrochemical industry is becoming more and more indispensable for the development of any industrial nation.

For these reasons, the expansion of the petroleum refining industry following the Second World War was accompanied by a similar development in petrochemicals. As was pointed out in Chapter 8, Europe—France and Italy being the notable exceptions to the rule—was mainly importing processed products of the oil refineries before the Second World War. The immediate postwar period witnessed in practically all European countries a mushrooming of refineries large enough to produce all the petroleum products they needed. As a corollary to this development, the production of organic petrochemicals in Western Europe showed a spectacular increase of sixfold between 1953 and 1959; Great Britain and Germany were the leading producers, followed by France and Italy.

The special case of the United States somewhat obscures the general rule that a strong pull is exerted for refineries and therefore petrochemical industries to move away from the oil and gas bases toward the higher industrial centers. Discoveries of large oil reserves have recently been made primarily in industrially underdeveloped countries and sparsely populated parts of the world. Through their sister industry, the petrochemicals, the refining industries have become more and more affiliated and interrelated with the most complex sections of the industrial world. Plans have been worked out in Europe to transport natural gas by pipelines from the new fields in the Sahara and perhaps also from the Middle East to Central Europe. Other countries, like India and Japan, are building up their refining industry just as Europe did. Besides all the other advantages, such a development offers the guarantee to the countries concerned that they can have a share in the most modern industry of our century.

Part Three | THE SPATIAL ORGANIZATION OF ECONOMY
TERTIARY OCCUPATIONS

LEFT: This airphoto of the city of Sfax in Tunisia shows clearly the different patterns of the various sections: the modern rectangular street pattern of the harbour section, the typical arab pattern of the enclosed old town, and the suburban developments. (Courtesy, Institut Géographique National)

ABOVE RIGHT: Sydney (New South Wales, Australia) with her 2.2 million inhabitants, the busy harbour and the down-town district stands for the rapid development in the countries of the southern hemisphere. (Courtesy, Australian News and Information Bureau)

BELOW RIGHT: Wilmington and Long Beach Harbor (Los Angeles). (Fairchild Aerial Surveys)

10 | TERTIARY OCCUPATIONS

QUALITATIVE AND QUANTITATIVE APPROACH

The people engaged in tertiary occupations are responsible for the functioning of all activities that do not fall under primary production or processing. If the stress in the present text seems to rest upon economic activity, it is because we are concerned with economic geography. But there are important tertiary occupations which are more cultural or scientific in character than economic.

In most textbooks on economic geography little attention is directed toward tertiary occupations, and the subject matter is evenly divided between agriculture and industry. Of course, they do not negate the tertiary occupations as such, but these are left rather to the field of economics than to geography. Yet to judge by individual articles in the volumes of current geographical periodicals, there is a good deal of interest in this field among geographers. In general, geographers are chiefly concerned with individual case studies, i.e., with an idiographic approach, while economists tend to assume a nomothetic approach and deal with economic activity as such. Still, the boundary is fluid.

While it is easy enough to make qualitative statements about the tertiary occupations, statistical appraisal proves more difficult. We have already met with difficulties in assessing on the international level the percentages of the primary and secondary populations. The difficulty is still greater for tertiary occupations. There are two principal ways to obtain numerical results, (1) to calculate the difference between the total population and the sum of those engaged in the primary and the secondary occupations and (2) to use figures which refer directly to the tertiary occupations. Whichever way may be followed, the results must be viewed with caution. The following table gives estimates of the three occupational groups in percent of total population after Woytinski (*World Population and Production,* 1953) ; the figures in brackets represent the percentages of the agricultural population (after FAO) for the years 1945-59. Whatever the ac-

COUNTRY (YEAR)	PRIMARY, %		SECOND- ARY, %	TER- TIARY, %
United States (1940)	18.5	[13]	31.8	49.7
India (1931)	67.1	[70]	10.5	22.4
Japan (1947)	52.5	[41]	23.3	24.2
United Kingdom (1931)	6.0	[5]	46.1	47.9
Switzerland (1941)	20.8	[16]	43.5	35.7
Egypt (1937)	70.7	[64]	10.0	19.3

curacy of these figures may be, they show that the tertiary group surpasses the others in number in the industrialized and economically de-

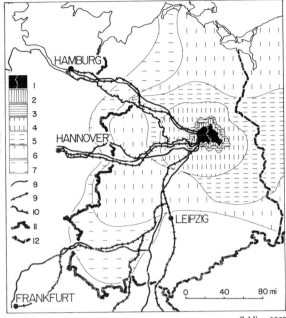

Schlier, 1959

90 · FUNCTIONAL ZONES OF BERLIN. The map shows how the functional organization of an area may by disrupted and altered completely in a very short time. *Legend:* (1) city of Berlin, today divided into West and East Berlin; (2) urbanized zone encircling (1); (3) commuters' zone; (4) zone of dominant urban influence; (5) Mark Brandenburg; (6) northeastern plain; (7) northeastern Germany; (8) Autobahnen connecting the Federal Republic of Germany with West Berlin; (9) railroads serving interzonal traffic; (10) waterways serving interzonal traffic; (11) boundary between West and East Germany; (12) other state boundaries, *de facto* status.

COUNTRY	PRI-MARY, %	SECOND-ARY,[a] %	TER-TIARY, %
United States	5	35	60
United Kingdom	4	45	51
West Germany	7	53	40
India	47	18	35
China (mainland)[b]	48	32	20
Japan	18	34	48
Congo	25	36	39

[a] Including mining, manufacturing and construction.
[b] Not including government services.

veloped countries and that even in the less developed countries it makes up about one-fifth of the total population.

Another possibility of quantitative evaluation is by way of the statistics on the gross domestic product which are regularly published by the United Nations for many countries. The coefficients of productivity for the various occupational groups vary so much that the resulting percentage figures differ necessarily from those in the foregoing table. The following table indicates the percentage shares of the gross domestic product by the three groups in 1958.

The outstanding importance of the tertiary group is again clearly brought out. A question is frequently posed: Does this group actually produce? For a farmer, a miner, or an industrial worker, his activity is unanimously accepted as productive. The question might be put, What difference is there between mining coal and bringing it to the surface on the one hand, and moving it from there to the final consumer on the other? In either case value is added and the gross national product increased. Similarly those working in offices, banks, administration, etc., as well as those engaged in commercial activities, contribute to the gross national product and consequently have to be considered producers in the broader sense of the word.

METHODS OF INVESTIGATION

Locational factors, as distinct from site factors and functional factors, assume increasing importance as we proceed from the primary to the secondary occupations. This trend continues farther as we move into the tertiary group. It entails a certain change in working methods. Interviews with informants, the use of statistical data, sociological studies, etc., become especially important. Environmentalistic theories are far less appropriate here than in agriculture. If we regard man as making his own decisions and acting upon his own free will, simple cause-and-effect relationships such as appear in the natural sciences are no longer applicable, but are replaced by what has been called possibilism.

As the functional approach gains in importance in this part of our study, there will be

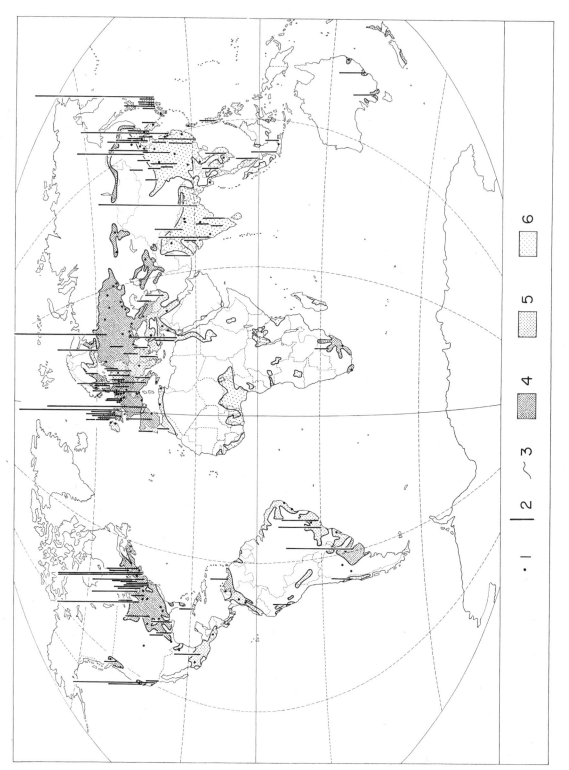

91 · URBANIZATION. *Legend:* (1) Cities with 500,000–1,000,000 people. (2) Cities with over 1 million people. The bar in the legend represents 2 million people. (3) Lines delimiting the areas with more than 25 people per square mile. (4), (5), and (6) indicate the degree of urbanization expressed in percent of population living in places of 20,000 or more inhabitants: (4) more than 29.1 percent; (5) 11.9–29.1 percent; (6) less than 11.9 percent. World average = 21.6 percent.

After Ginsburg, 1961

added another characteristic of functional structure. Formal and functional structures cannot be amalgamated in the final synthesis because they have different dimensions and qualities (see Chapter 6). Changes in the functional structure may also occur at a much faster tempo than changes in the formal structure. The difference derives from the simple fact that the formal structure is intimately bound to the tangible, while the functional structure consists of the immaterial for the most part.

It is not difficult to find examples which illustrate this difference. Some were mentioned earlier while discussing agriculture, and more will appear in Chapter 11 on urban settlements. Certainly any architect or city planner who is confronted with the task of building a new house or with the problems of urban planning is ambitious to achieve a complete harmony between form and function. With the passage of time,

however, functional aspects are likely to undergo much faster changes than the form. For example, the expansion of a city necessarily involves the inclusion of farm houses on its fringe. They retain the appearance of farm houses and may even be restored as such, but they house townsfolk. Form and function become discordant. It is to this aspect of geographical research, if anywhere, that the concept of harmony and disharmony can adequately be applied.

Theoretically this consideration also explains why study of the formal structure—in most cases, of its components—is one of the few ways in which the functional structure of former days may be reconstructed. Functional structures are ephemeral; once they become obsolete, they disappear, leaving no traces except in statistics and other documentary sources, as well as in those formal elements with which they were at one time in harmony.

11 | URBANIZATION

THE BIG CITY

Urban and Rural Population

Like a chain reaction, industrialization brought about a remarkable expansion of the tertiary occupations, and this in turn accelerated the growth of settlements that were neither agricultural nor industrial in character. Agricultural pursuits have rarely given rise to large agglomerations of population, though they are larger in some countries than in others. Where large landholdings and operating units are the characteristic features of rural areas, as in some parts of Spain or in densely settled parts of the East, the agricultural population lives in compact settlements having many thousands of inhabitants. In order to obtain a maximum of efficiency and to minimize the distance between the place of residence and the fields, farming settlements were on the whole kept small (villages and hamlets, scattered farmsteads).

The first marked change in the population distribution occurred with the appearance of factory towns; mining towns played a similar role. These developments are often considered the prime causative factors of a process called urbanization in modern times. This view, however, is of limited accuracy. An effect of continued industrial development was a steady increase in the number of those engaged in tertiary occupations. It is quite possible to disperse cer-tain industrial activities and to avoid dense agglomerations of industrial population; but the tertiary group is of necessity drawn together toward the central locations. This group is largely responsible for the recent growth of cities throughout the world. The Agricultural and Industrial Revolutions brought in their wake a striking change in the distribution and the living habits of the population. Urbanization is much more than a mere regrouping of the population or an expression of the increasing importance of the tertiary group, for an entirely new philosophy of life and reevaluation of many traditional concepts emerge.

Unfortunately the statistical basis for an evaluation of urban development is highly inadequate, at least for comparative studies on the international level. At the moment the ratio of so-called urban population to rural population will be taken as a measure of urban development.

According to the definitions of the United States Bureau of the Census, urban population comprises all persons living in (a) places of 2,500 inhabitants or more incorporated as cities, boroughs, and villages, (b) incorporated towns of 2,500 inhabitants or more except in New England, New York, and Wisconsin, where "towns" are simply minor civil divisions of counties, (c) the densely settled urban fringe, including both incorporated and unincorporated areas, around cities of 50,000 or more, and (d) unincorporated places of 2,500 inhabitants or more outside any urban fringe.

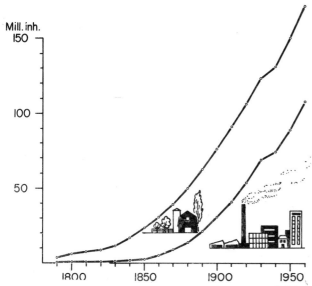

Mill. inh.

92 · POPULATION in urban and rural territory, U.S.A. The upper curve represents the total population. The urban and rural populations are separated by the lower curve as indicated by the pictorial symbols.

Thus even within one country, such a change in statistical definitions would make it difficult to compare results of different census reports unless they were given in both terms.

(3) The definition of urban and rural population differs from one country to another, rendering comparative studies very difficult. The scale value of 2,500 inhabitants, for example, is much too low for many parts of the world to separate two significantly different groups of settlements and hence population. Actually such a value should be based upon careful studies of the distributional pattern of settlements according to size within a country. Moreover, the term "urban" generally connotes the qualities of a large nonagricultural settlement.

In the USSR a settlement is called urban if it has a minimum of 12,000 inhabitants of which at least 85 percent must be classified as proletarian, i.e., as belonging to the working population according to Soviet definition. Within the Soviet Union, however, the critical number varies in accordance with regional differences.

Another extreme case is represented by Switzerland. There, no official definition of "urban" is extant, since every community is treated as equal in legal and administrative respects. The statistics simply give a tabulation of political communities which have, for example, more than 10,000 inhabitants, and it is customary to regard them as *Städte* and their population as urban.

How to Measure the Size of a City

Nobody suffers doubt about what to call an agglomeration of a hundred farmhouses or a huge urban metropolis like New York. The problem arises when one tries to differentiate settlements into different classes and to state the specific criteria of differentiation. This is again a problem that has been treated differently in different countries. Sometimes its solution was purely conventional—e.g., in Switzerland, as just mentioned—but in most countries there exists a certain legalized hierarchy of settlements in which each group possesses specific privileges and rights with respect to jurisdiction, administration, taxation, trading, etc. In the United

All other places are classified as rural. Naturally this definition entails a number of other things to be defined—for example, a "place." Such problems will, however, be disregarded for the moment, and attention called to three other points of major importance.

(1) The classification of a population as urban or rural does not refer to occupational status but only to the size of settlement units in which people live. Rural population is therefore in no way equivalent to farm population or the primary group. Many people are classified as rural but not engaged in farming; on the other hand one finds in certain areas not a small part of the urban population occupied with agriculture.

(2) The United States Bureau of the Census redefined the urban area in 1947; the result was a substantial change in the number of people thus classified. In 1950 the urban population was 96.5 million according to the new urban-rural definition, but only 88.9 million according to the old one. The new definition did not alter the value of 2,500 inhabitants as the lower limit, but was expanded to include closely built-up areas around the central cities previously excluded.

States two primary subdivisions of settlements are legally recognized: incorporated and unincorporated places. The 1950 census defined for the first time the so-called urbanized areas by virtue of the characteristic urban land use; the boundaries of an urbanized area are not legally fixed, but based upon on-the-spot observations, say, land-use mapping. On the other hand, the boundaries of a standard metropolitan area follow those of counties and comprise "the entire population in and around major cities, whose activities form an integrated social and economic system." The number of inhabitants for different subdivisions of settlements in the United States is shown in the following list (1950). Not only

SUBDIVISION	NUMBER	INHABITANTS
Unincorporated places with 1,000 or more inhabitants	1,430	3,565,496
Incorporated places	17,118	96,062,627
Urbanized areas	157	69,249,148
Standard metropolitan areas	168	84,500,680

are there large numerical differences among them but they also present different aspects of geographic reality and may therefore be used differently.

A world-wide survey of settlements would reveal a bewildering number of different systems, making it virtually impossible to arrive at comparable results. Instead of discussing this problem further, we shall now consider three methods by which the size of cities can be measured.

MEASUREMENT ACCORDING TO AREA

It has some emotional value for people who are apt to confuse greatness with bigness to express the size of cities in numerical terms. Precise quantitative expressions are also required in scientific investigations. To measure the size of a city in square miles is one way to achieve that goal. It presents no particular technical problem once such a settlement has been defined with respect to its boundaries.

Theoretically the problem of delimiting urban settlements in terms of surface area is easy in the case of incorporated places as well as in all the others where the total area within the given jurisdictional boundaries is defined to constitute a city, or whatever that particular urban agglomeration may be called. However, the municipal boundaries and the functional boundaries of a city seldom coincide. There are innumerable instances where large tracts of farm land are contained within the city limits or the built-up area extends far beyond the municipal boundaries. Notwithstanding these difficulties, the acceptance of such an administrative unit as a basis for urban studies has the advantage that it is quite clear and indisputable. Yet it may be disadvantageous for the geographer, since it does not necessarily correspond to the geographic reality of an urban agglomeration. He will certainly prefer to apply a definition according to urbanized area, or a similar one.

Among the various criteria for the determination of the size of a city, area has been taken up first because it is simply a matter of defining its boundaries.

MEASUREMENT ACCORDING TO NUMBER OF INHABITANTS

Population is generally considered the most appropriate and convenient means for measuring the size of a city. The ranking of cities by size is usually based upon population.

The basic problem remains unchanged, i.e., the problem of delimiting the statistical unit either with politico-administrative boundaries or according to urban land use. A number of other problems arise. People are generally counted at their actual or legal place of residence at the time of census taking. For farmers this is normally the place where they live and work, but for city folk it is increasingly the place where they sleep.

The problems of commuters are familiar to us all. They travel daily or regularly to and from places of work, and they are thus likely to travel from one administrative unit to another. In fact, the statistical evidence of a commuter hinges on whether at least one boundary of the census enumeration units is crossed. Commuting within any single unit, even though it may involve a long journey, does not appear in the statistical data.

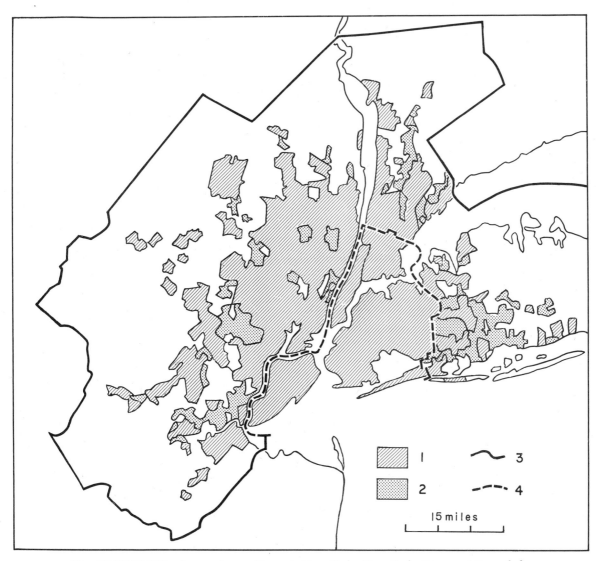

93 • DELIMITATION of an urban settlement: New York. New York City, consisting of five boroughs, lies within the dashed line (4), whereas the solid line (3) delineates the standard metropolitan area of New York, which extends beyond the area shown here including the whole of Long Island. The urbanized area of New York comprises the incorporated (1) and unincorporated (2) parts.

Place of residence and place of work must be in different enumeration districts and the person involved should travel regularly, daily or weekly, between the two.

The traveling distance of a daily commuter is best measured in travel time. Half an hour is the most usual distance; one hour is still acceptable, but more than one hour is rather unusual. Whether the commuting area of a city is large or small depends upon the efficiency of transportation facilities. Commuting is a curse of modern times inflicted upon millions of people who spend an hour or more each day just to reach places of work without accomplishing anything.

If we accept the principle that people are counted at the place of residence, it is not difficult to know accurately the population for a specific place. There remains the problem of grouping all the places into certain classes according to the number of residents. The usual procedure followed by statisticians is to select figures like 1,000 or 10,000, and so on. In order to gain more insight into the problem geographers usually proceed in a different manner. Population numbers of all settlements are first plotted on a frequency graph. On the basis of this frequency distribution, the numerical data are grouped into classes and scale intervals are determined. Experience has shown that the characteristic form of such a frequency curve varies from one region to another, reflecting the structure of the region. Whenever we are concerned with regional studies, the latter method is preferred, though the former may be more useful for comparative purposes on the international scale.

The number of inhabitants is certainly an essential characteristic by which the size of a city can be expressed. At any rate it is much more important and satisfactory than the surface area. Nevertheless, its significance is overrated even by students of geography. It is not so much the number of people who currently live in a certain place, but what they stand for and accomplish that really determines the size as well as the importance of a city.

MEASUREMENT ACCORDING TO FUNCTIONS

Urban settlements perform functions which are quite different from those of nonurban or agricultural settlements. The very nature of these functions accounts for the presence of large numbers of human beings living close together and hence for the development of urban agglomerations. In certain industries the mere size of the manufactural establishments requires a large working population residing within commuting distance. A modern blast furnace, for example, with its associated establishments requires about 10,000 inhabitants (workers and their families, etc.). Other industries of the heavy type tend to cluster around the iron and steel centers, while light industries may be able to avoid such crowded conditions and to select their locations elsewhere. For some light industries the maxim holds true that "industry settles where people want to live." Mining operations are like heavy industries, being bound to a place —the deposits. Coal-mining areas are characterized by high densities of population and urban agglomerations of a special type. Many tertiary activities cater to the people in such industrial agglomerations—retail businesses, marketing, communal service industries, etc. The size and number of their activities are proportional to the number of residents who are directly served by them.

In addition to such functions as have been mentioned above, cities perform other functions to an increasing degree. One large group may be called central functions or central services (to be discussed below). They tend to be drawn to specific points within the functional structure, or more specifically, they form characteristic groupings in urban centers or central places. Other functions group themselves of necessity at nodal points of the connecting lines of communication, i.e., railroad junctions, harbors, and so on. Some services have more freedom in the selection of their location. For instance, political and administrative centers are frequently established away from large urban centers; similarly, educational and research institutions tend to move toward small and quiet towns.

The importance of a city obviously depends not on the area it covers nor the number of its inhabitants, but above all on the dominant functions it performs. Geographic studies of cities have therefore placed particular emphasis on urban functions. An excellent example of this kind of work is *The Industrial Structure of American Cities* by G. Alexandersson (1956). The author first classifies urban functions into two major groups, manufacturing industries and service industries. The latter correspond closely to what have been called the tertiary occupations in the present text. The following list illustrates the variety of the service industries:

TRANSPORTATION AND COMMUNICATION INDUSTRIES—Railroads, trucking, warehousing, other transportation, telecommunications, utilities, and sanitary services.

TRADE INDUSTRIES—Wholesale trade, food stores, eating and drinking places, other retail trade.

OTHER SERVICE INDUSTRIES—Finance, insurance, real estate, business service, repair service, private households, hotels and lodging places, other personal services, entertainment, medical services, education, other professional and related services, public administration.

Alexandersson's study of the distributional patterns of the various industries has a weakness inherent in all studies based on occupational statistics, i.e., on the number of people gainfully employed in each occupation. The overall labor intensity is not the only criterion; the weight of a managerial staff member, for example, is in reality never identical with that of a mill worker. However, labor statistics are frequently the only source available and we have to content ourselves with this only possible solution. Typical service cities are, according to Alexandersson, Washington, D.C. (political and administrative), Urbana, Illinois (education), Daytona Beach and West Palm Beach, Florida (resort), Pocatello, Idaho (railroad), and so on.

A given hierarchical order exists only in a few of the services mentioned, e.g., in the realm of the politico-administrative functions. How the relative rank is established in other cases is a problem that requires further investigation; it will be taken up later in relation to the central functions. It is certain, however, that the number of people engaged is in no way a satisfactory criterion.

URBAN GEOGRAPHY

Urban geography has lately become a preferred field of studies among geographers. Reasons for this are the following: (a) urban settlements are the exponents of the most modern development in the economic geography of the world; (b) a city can be clearly delineated in terms of an urbanized area and subsequently studied like an organism, independent of its umland; (c) as cities figure prominently in the field of planning, it has become necessary to study them in all their complexity before problems of planning are solvable. Geographers have approached the study of cities in two ways, viz., the formal approach and the functional approach, whether or not actually so designated.

*Studies of the Formal Aspects
of Urban Settlements*

Formal studies of urban settlements are above all concerned with the ground plan and the projection of the buildings on a vertical plane. Studies of the vertical projection are few though they are theoretically of equal importance. Notable examples are the skylines of medieval European towns characterized by church steeples and fortifications, the typical Japanese town with a large expanse of one- and two-story houses, none of them allowed to go higher than the temple or shrine, or the characteristic downtown skyline of a modern American city. Parallel are studies of the frontage of individual buildings or whole street-fronts.

Studies of the ground plan are more numerous and also from many points of view more significant. Though there have been historical instances of a city once destroyed by war, fire, or other calamity and never being reconstructed, the rule is that a city cannot be extinguished without a complete disruption of the regional functional structure. If the latter remains, cities will be rebuilt at the former place and the preexisting pattern of streets is usually followed. Responsible for this are partly the property rights and also the fact that after complete destruction the only assets left usually lie underground. Excellent examples are found in European towns where the streets survived complete and sometimes repeated destruction of surface structures, to reappear through reconstruction. The central part of many towns is of Roman origin, characterized by a regular and rectangular pattern of streets in accordance with the Roman *castrum*.

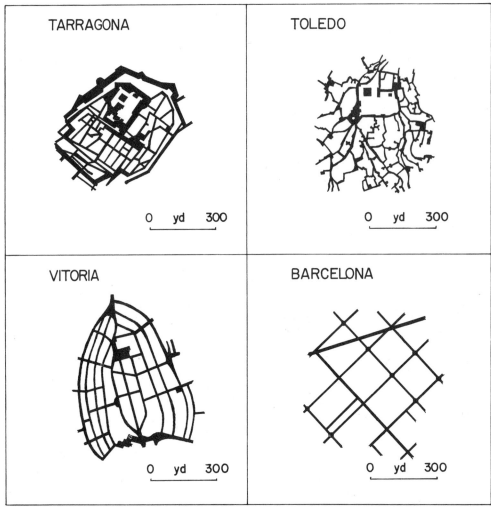

94 · STREET PATTERNS of Spanish cities. Spanish towns with their rich and varied past exhibit a variety of street patterns. Tarragona's old center lying within the city walls dates from pre-Roman days and is characterized by a regular rectangular pattern of Roman origin. The present cathedral occupies the site of the main Roman temple. The street pattern of Toledo, on the other hand, is typically Arabian. Toledo was invaded by the Moslems and remained an important Moslem center for more than 300 years until it came back under the power of Catholic kings in 1095. Vitoria is an example of a planned city of the twelfth century founded by the kings of Navarra at the outset of the *reconquista* of Spain. Barcelona has many faces; the section shown here is a part of the new development of the last century to the north of Plaza de Cataluna. The Great Diagonal—the popular name for the Avenida del Generalissimo Franco—is seen to cut across the systematic rectangular pattern.

It is surrounded by the medieval town, with its crooked streets, which is then followed by a more planned development of the nineteenth century. The latter usually terminates with a broad circular highway, the boulevards on the site of the former bulwarks, beyond which extend the twentieth-century additions. The vertical structure of urban settlements cannot be retraced

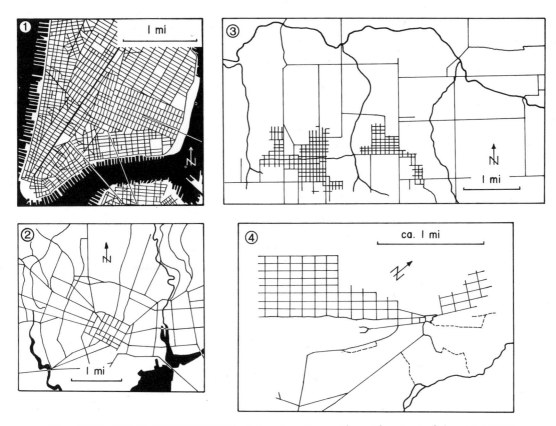

95 · RECTANGULAR STREET PATTERN of American towns. The grid pattern of American towns is of multiple origin. (1) Various grid patterns of lower New York represent different stages of the city's development, related to local considerations of the city planning. (2) New Haven, Connecticut, is an example of the original grid pattern of colonial settlements. Later expansion of the city took on the irregular road pattern of New England. (3) Webb City, Missouri, represents the characteristic checkerboard pattern in the public-land states oriented north-south and east-west. The layout of the growing settlements conformed to the formal pattern of the surrounding agricultural land. (4) The street pattern of present-day downtown Los Angeles dates back to Spanish colonial days.

beyond a rather recent period, but the ground plan enables us to follow it back to the earliest periods of history.

Studies of the ground plan bring also to light distinctive regional differences. For example, a typical Arab town is marked by few through streets and by numerous blind alleys running at sharp angles to one another. A rectangular pattern which resembles that of the Romans is characteristic of some oriental cities like Chiengmai in northern Thailand or Nara and Kyoto in Japan, pointing to the Chinese influence.

Geometric patterns lend themselves well to the typification of urban settlements. Rectangular patterns, for example, may have different origins, as is illustrated by North American towns. One of them is characteristic of the Spanish colonial town, where the spacing of streets was determined by legislation while their orientation was left to local conditions. Another dates back to the rectangular survey of agricultural land in the public-land states of the United States, where the urban streets were superimposed upon a rigidly oriented network. Still another is found

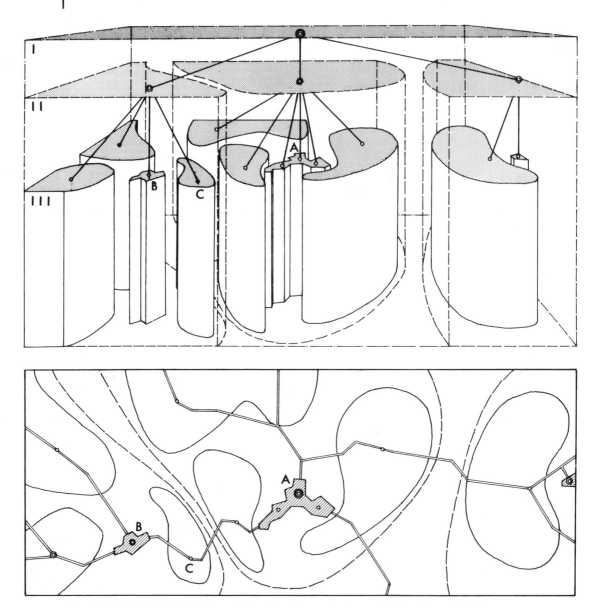

96 · FUNCTIONAL STRUCTURE and hierarchy of central places. The locality marked C stays on
the lowest platform, III; B performs additional functions on a higher platform, II; and A extends
its functions on all the three platforms, I, II, and III. These relationships are shown as a three-
dimensional model as well as in the form of a map. In the latter (below) the solid lines delimit the
functional areas on the lowest platform, and the broken lines those on the intermediate platform.
The whole area shown belongs to the functional area on the uppermost platform commanded
by the central place A.

in the rectangularly planned cities in the Eastern States, where neither the size nor the orientation of the mesh conforms to any prescribed rules and may change within the same city. It is through these relatively minor details that the "typical" American grid-pattern town can be differentiated into a number of different lines of development which merge at present into a seemingly identical formal structure. Such a development may be called a formal convergence.

These remarks should point up how wide open the field is for both idiographic and nomothetic research into formal structure.

Studies of the Functional Aspects of Urban Settlements

Only one particular group of function will be discussed here, namely, those which might be called the central services. Central services are characteristically located at central places where they form clusters of definite types. Each serves an area or, in other words, commands an area over which it performs its function. This area will be called the functional area. The theory of central places, services, and functional areas was first developed by a German geographer, W. Christaller. It has become the foremost sector in the study of functional structures and plays an important role in regional planning.

The study of urban functions begins with the listing of all the services to be considered and the mapping of their regional distribution. It will soon be noted that certain combinations of services occur repeatedly. Such distributional characteristics can be used for the classification of settlements based on central services. In hamlets, central services do not exist as a rule. In villages of Central Europe, the characteristic set of service establishments consists of various craftsmen, postoffice, country inns, collecting and distributing servcies, etc., as demanded by the needs of such an agricultural community. Market towns are in addition equipped with physicians, dentists, and veterinarians, notaries public, printing offices, banking facilities, and subsidaries of other larger business establishments found only in large urban centers. A still smaller group of settlements stands out through the

existence of cultural and scientific centers, headquarters of banking and insurance business and of commercial firms, as well as other services which together place them at the top of the hierarchical order of central places. The function or functions which perform the most extensive services are in fact the most characteristic of a central place, for whether a settlement is classified as a village or a market town or anything else depends upon them, regardless of the number of inhabitants or the size of the built-up area.

If the functional structure could be visualized as a three-dimensional model, various classes of central places and their functional areas would be represented by different platforms and by the

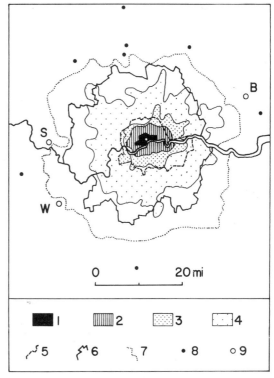

Walter, 1958

97 · FUNCTIONAL ZONES OF LONDON. *Legend:* (1) nucleus of urban agglomeration; (2) inner suburbs; (3) intermediate zone; (4) outer suburbs; (5) boundary of the London county; (6) outer limit of Greater London; (7) outer boundary of green belt; (8) new towns; (9) preexisting towns of Billericay, Woking, and Slought.

area occupied on each platform. Central places become fewer as we ascend to higher levels, but corresponding functional areas grow larger.

The selection of the central services which are to be used in the classification of central places should be based on a thorough study of the economic and social conditions of the region concerned. The location of the services may be ascertained by direct field observation or by the use of local directories, statistics, etc. The extent of a functional area is generally established through interviews or by field observation. Functional structures in different parts of the world are not basically dissimilar, though the set of services which are characteristic, the hierarchical order of central places and their designation, and the size of functional areas vary with local conditions. Thus the functional structure of central services constitutes a distinctive characteristic of a given area and lends itself well to comparative analyses.

To turn to the internal structure of an urban agglomeration, in addition to services of the highest order which characterize an urban center, there also necessarily exist in that same place all the services of the lower orders. The former are usually concentrated in the central business district while the latter are nucleated in neighborhood centers.

Studies of functional structures of the kind just described have become most important in urban planning. Local governments or planning agencies may direct many services so that they can be located most effectively. Without undue regimentation of the population, the planners can create nuclei which tend to grow and lead urban development in the desired direction. Outstanding examples of that kind of planning carried out in close cooperation with geographers are the settlements of the new polder areas of the former Zuider Zee in the Netherlands and the so-called new towns in England.

RECREATION

THE NEED for recreation and the possibility of fulfilling the desire for it are both immediate outcomes of industrialization and urbanization. In the preindustrial stage of economy, recreation is either nonexistent or takes a very simple form; it is marginal in relation to all other activities. Recreational studies have revealed that there is a very high correlation between "intention to travel" and "size of the place of residence" and that even in an industrialized country recreational trips originate primarily in the industrialized urban centers.

Comparisons between agriculture and industry may well point up the decided advantages enjoyed by those engaged in industry with regard to productivity and the application of modern production techniques. Yet not so long ago industry and urban life were equated with squalor and poverty, because the profits were unevenly distributed among those who contributed capital and labor. Radical changes occurred with a greater improvement in productivity, but social evolution contributed even more toward a greater participation of the working population in the net profit of the production process. Industrial workers, who used to work without any provision of social security and to earn comparatively less than agriculturists, achieved a status which has gradually reversed this situation. The problems of recreation are directly influenced by two factors—reduced working periods with early retirement

age, and highly increased purchasing power. Thus no form of recreation is any longer a monopoly of a small and well-to-do circle, but all forms today lie within reach of the people at large.

A hundred years ago the majority of the world's population was fully occupied with work; in fact, there prevailed an immense ethical valuation of work. Today in every highly industrialized and socially developed country, the best ways to spend leisure are sought out, in harmony with the trend toward higher income and less time for work. These problems are not immediately relevant to economic geography, but they point to the underlying causes of certain developments which are of an increasing importance in our field.

Recreation has a dual aspect: one is the daily recreational activities; the other is vacationing. Taken together they make up a considerable and increasing part of the national economic life in all the more developed countries.

The first group comprises a very wide range of activities, including amusements, sports, and other diversions and is generally organized as big-business enterprises. Recreational facilities of the same kind, e.g., theaters and cabarets, tend to cluster in certain districts of a city, and this fact attracts the interest of geographers. The entertainment business is characteristically a street-customer-oriented industry, like a department store. If the customer is not pleased with the goods offered in one place, he will go to another in order to find what he is looking for. Advertisements play an important role in luring the people on the street into these establishments, for most of the time they have not yet decided what they really want to see. Like other functional centers of a city, those of recreational activities are of much interest to the student of economic geography.

The other aspect of recreation, vacationing, is often synonymous with tourism. Why and where people travel is largely attributable to contemporary mass psychology, as well as to the power of advertising. Most people reason in a different way than that Boston lady who is said to have exclaimed, "Why should I travel? I am already here!" They all long to go elsewhere and do something else. Big-city life draws them more and more to camping and other forms of outdoor recreation, while countless vacationists from small towns are drawn toward the metropolis to spend their vacation there. There were times when vacationing meant mainly visits to religious sanctuaries (such as Santiago de Compostela in the pilgrimages of the Middle Ages) or architectural monuments and other places of cultural interest. As late as the eighteenth century the beauty of natural landscape was scarcely appreciated enough to attract tourists. Though the dawning interest in nature, waterfalls, glaciers, and mountain peaks gradually developed into tourism, such travel was at first a contemplative way of vacationing, that is, more in the way of looking at the landscape than entering into it.

Tourism has become a regular item of commerce, its sale dependent upon a large amount of advertising to attract the potential traveler to the desired spot. During the past thirty years or so traveling by individuals has been increasingly replaced by group and mass travels. The new mode not only cuts down overhead costs but also makes accessible to the mass many places that were reserved for a select few in former times.

This whole development is of interest to students of sociology, economics, and other such disciplines. What constitutes the specific interest of an economic geographer? It becomes first apparent when the phenomenon of tourism is viewed with respect to the formal structure of the landscape. In many regions the physiognomy has been completely altered through the mushrooming of hotels and other installations for the tourist industry, as is evidenced by such a term as "tourist landscape." Elsewhere the natural landscape has been zealously preserved and human influence excluded. The last hundred years have witnessed an increasing number of national parks and nature preserves in many parts of the world. In the United States alone there are today 187 national parks and monuments. These were visited by 80 million people in 1960, in contrast to 1.5 million in the early twenties. By the same year about one-tenth of the total land area of the country had been set aside for recreational and similar purposes, including the federal forests. In short, the impact of tourism upon the physiognomy of the landscape is significant, leading to two entirely different lines of development.

Equally important is the influence of tourism upon particular levels of the formal structure, as may be exemplified by characteristic changes in demographic composition. It is not surprising that this point has caught the attention of many geographers. In the late nineteenth and early twentieth century the mountainous areas in Switzerland, Austria, France, and Italy attracted a large number of tourists from the lowlands. The tourist industry became the chief livelihood in the mountain valleys. There agriculture, unable to compete with production elsewhere, had provided only a precarious living and consequently people had started to emigrate, sometimes abandoning a village altogether. Tourism truly marked a turning point in the whole way of life in such regions.

Another field of interest touches the role of tourism in the international functional structure, i.e., on the highest levels represented. The magnitude of its importance is staggering. The amount of money spent in recent years by American tourists abroad equaled about half the total of the major United States' foreign assistance (military grants and other aids), of which one-fourth was spent in Europe. In Mexico, which received a large share of American tourists, the income from the foreign tourists equaled the total export value of all commodities in foreign trade in 1960. These figures do not appear in the balance of trade but play a decisive role in a country's balance of payments. Even in Britain, a country often not considered to be a top-ranking vacation land, 1.7 million visitors brought in nearly 2.75 million pounds in 1960. The sums involved are on a par with the values of major import-export items, and tourism at mid-century should therefore interest the economic geographer in the same way as the movement of commodities from one country to another.

There is one peculiar aspect of the relationships established by international tourism. Traveling is not a necessity; it belongs to the category of nonessentials. And the destination of travel is of little consequence for the vacationer as long as he believes that he will find what he expects of a vacation. Thus, the flow pattern of tourists is not as rigid as that of essential commodities, but shifts a great deal in quantity and in direction. On the other hand, the tourist industry is capital and labor intensive and incapable of adapting itself to any other purpose. For obvious reasons the tourist industry is among the economic activities in which an especially large amount of money is spent on advertising.

The last characteristic aspect of this complex new development derives from early retirement age and prolonged life-expectancy, which account for a large increase in the number of retired people. This group, known in Europe for a long time, was formerly restricted to middle-class people who formed a distinct sociological group living on their ''rent'' and therefore called *les rentiers*. The sociological range of this group has since expanded and the number of those living in retirement increased manyfold. In the United States—and to a lesser degree in Europe —retirement often involves a change of residence; the preferred destination is somewhere in a sunny and warm climate. Florida and California, the Côte d'Azur, and the Mediterranean in general have become regions where large colonies of retired people are found, thus permanently and intensely modifying the settlement pattern as well as the demographic structure of the whole area.

The processes described in this chapter have only just seen their beginning, but their future importance is already envisaged. They are multifarious and complex, constituting a fruitful field for research in economic geography.

13 | WORLD TRADE

WORLD TRADE in economic geography is studied for the most part in close connection with functional structure. The geographer's prime objective is geographical analyses of commodity flow in terms of volume, value, and kind of goods. He also studies the physical facilities established to handle transportation in the broadest sense—both the centers from which operations are directed and the media of transportation. Such analyses will eventually lead to a differentiation of the world into major economic regions.

The particular aspects of the subject are frequently called *geography of transportation, geography of trade,* and so forth. They are treated here as subchapters of economic geography. In a treatise of the geography of transportation, the whole of geographic substance would have to be looked at from the point of view of transportation and all the facts would have to be arranged in a systematic order in accordance with such a view. Within the framework of economic geography, however, transportation represents only one facet of a highly complex structure, and the range of relevant facts is greatly narrowed.

TRADE AND TRANSPORTATION

The Flow of Goods: The Flow Charts

The foregoing chapters contained a large number of maps showing the flow of goods from the place of production to the place of consumption. Such maps are collectively called flow charts. They typify the geographic point of view, for geographers are used to visualizing such relationships in the form of maps or maplike diagrams which provide at a glance a clear characterization of the location and areal distribution. Economists may treat the same problem in an entirely different manner, either by means of tabulation or mathematical equations, or simply by descriptions. It is stressed again that in general the geographer turns his attention to the concrete situation of individual cases while the economist is more concerned with the problem of gaining an insight into the general laws that govern the trade relationships.

In order to compile a flow chart, adequate statistical data on the flow of goods, i.e., places of origin and destination, kind, volume, and route of movement, are required. Only in a very limited number of cases are all these facts established beyond doubt; consequently, flow charts must be viewed with caution.

This applies above all to flow charts which depict movements within the bounds of a single country, for statistical data are far from adequate in most cases, and little information is available beyond figures for loadings and unloadings at railroad and trucking stations. Such problems and an attempt to solve the difficulties involved are thoughtfully discussed by E. L. Ullman in his *American Commodity Flow* (1957).

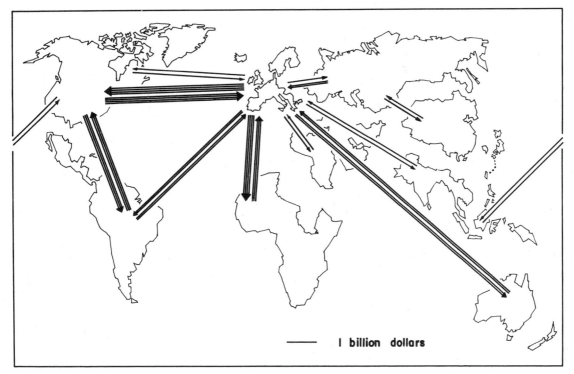

98 · WORLD EXPORTS. This map should be compared with Fig. 99. It is a much simplified presentation of essentially the same facts and consequently brings out certain features better. The world is divided into the following trade areas: North America, Latin America, Western Europe including the British Isles, Middle East, Africa, Far East, Australia and New Zealand, China, Eastern Europe, and the USSR. Only the interareal trade is shown.

The well-known maps of Great Lakes trade in iron ore, coal, grain, etc., exemplify undertakings for which flow charts can be constructed. These maps are analytical and deal with single products; their statistical basis was usually secured through painstaking analyses of particular industrial sectors. Maps of traffic flow on railroads, on highways, or any other means of communication appear at first to be a synthesis of such analytical maps; however, they generally do not portray the actual movement of goods, but simply the availability of transportation facilities.

The mapping of international trade is less difficult, since goods are checked at the border stations with respect to the kind, volume, value, origin, and destination, and uniform statistics are published for most countries of the world.

Unfortunately, the international statistics, such as the United Nations' *Yearbook of International Trade Statistics,* seldom arrange the material in such a way that flow charts for individual goods can be constructed in detail; consequently one has to have recourse to special publications of individual countries. Flow charts contained in this text represent both cases, namely, where it was possible to make detailed flow charts (e.g., coal) and where only the general direction of movement could be indicated (e.g., iron and steel).

A word of caution must be spoken concerning a large number of maps related to world seaborne trade. The legends of such maps should be read carefully; most of them show, not the actual flow of goods, but the density of shipping services. Moreover, only the scheduled liner services are considered as a rule, thereby eliminating the important group of tramp ships. Many maps also exclude tankers and limit themselves to dry bulk and general cargo. The world total of sea-borne shipments has increased from about 400 million metric tons before the Second World War to more than 1,000 million tons in 1960, of which tanker cargo constituted about 20 percent and 47 percent, respectively. Any map which does not include all classes of freighters and tankers must therefore be considered highly incomplete. Yet many maps published do not provide adequate information in this respect.

The Flow of Goods:
Statistical Check Points

Statistical check points make it possible to chart commodity movements in detail and between national boundaries. Some of the most important ones—inland stations and ports for loading and unloading, and national borders—have already been mentioned. For studies of international trade, the national trade statistics generally furnish satisfactory data on origins and destinations of international commodity flow. More difficult to obtain are data on the gateways and the routes of movements. Additional check points would be necessary to provide a more detailed and correct picture of flow of international trade.

Especially in large countries, as well as in countries with a long coastline or more than one coastline, the question of the gateway becomes paramount. The point of entrance or departure is often predetermined by the geographical location of the point of origin. For instance, it is correct to say that in all likelihood United States coal exports pass through ports on the Middle Atlantic coast even if there should be no data available to prove it. Sometimes the relationships are not so clear and additional information must be secured, as for Swedish iron ore exports from the northern fields; they leave either via the Swedish port of Lulea or via Narvik on the Atlantic. This and similar problems can generally be solved only with the help of special publications. Statistical data on port traffic are frequently lacking or insufficient, giving only totals

without specifications. Highly useful are the statistics published by the Institute for Shipping Research in Bremen (Germany) containing, among other items, international statistics on shipping, seaports, and sea-borne trade.

In 1957-1958 ports with more than 20 million tons of inbound and outbound cargo showed a very characteristic pattern of distribution. They were found on both sides of the Atlantic, New York (38.4 million tons), Philadelphia (23.8), Baltimore (29.1), Norfolk (29.9), and Newport News (24.6) on the North American coast and London (55.8), Rotterdam (73.8), Antwerp (35.8), and Hamburg (27.3) on the European coast. Marseilles (22.2) is the only world port located outside the area mentioned. Even if lesser ports with 10 to 20 million tons are included, the overall pattern of distribution does not change very much: Montreal and Portland on the American side of the Atlantic, and Liverpool, Belfast, Le Havre, and Amsterdam on the European side are added. Other ports in this class are New Orleans, Vancouver, Genoa, Tokyo, and Santos (Brazil).

Other convenient check points are inland navigation systems, i.e., canals, rivers, and lakes such as the Panama Canal, the Suez Canal, the St. Lawrence Seaway, the canals of the Great Lakes system, and the Rhine River. The relevant statistics can be used, for example, to indicate the routes of Australian wheat exports to Europe, whether by way of Suez, Panama, or the Cape. The use of these very important statistics in geographic studies is often precluded since they are not included in the regular statistical publications but have to be sought in national documents that are frequently difficult to obtain. Again the publications of the Institute for Shipping Research in Bremen are helpful in providing at least general information.

Of the two major canals of the world, the Panama Canal and the Suez Canal, the latter is far the more important, accounting for 17,842 transits totaling 154 million net registered tons compared with 9,187 transits and 45 million net registered tons for the Panama Canal (1958). The Suez Canal increased in importance as the Middle East became an outstanding producer of petroleum. Once forming a major link in intercontinental trade between Europe and India, the Far East, and Australia this 101-mile-long sea-level canal, which was opened as early as 1869 and admits ships up to 37 feet draft, performs a function very different from what it used to be. Today two-thirds of the traffic is made up of liquid bulk (tanker cargo). The tankers are loaded on their northbound voyage, but return empty on the southbound voyage.

For the Panama Canal as for the Suez Canal, the number of transits and the volume of cargo nearly doubled in the 1950's. There is a slight but significant difference between the two; the volume of cargo carried through the Panama Canal increased relatively less than the number of transits, pointing toward the dominance of large tankers at the Suez Canal. The percentage distribution of cargo carried over the principal ocean trade routes focused at the Panama Canal are as follows (1958) :

East coast of U.S. and	South America	26%
	Far East	15%
Europe and	West coast of U.S. and Canada	11%
	South America	11%
U.S. intercoastal		6%

Of the total cargo, 65 percent was moving from the Atlantic to the Pacific, while only one-third was northbound; the number of transits was about equal in the two directions.

Among the most important inland canals are those connecting the Great Lakes. Their function is mainly within the structure of North American heavy industry, and its ups and downs are reflected in the statistics of lake shipments. The St. Mary Falls Canal had 69.6 million short tons of cargo in 1959 but 115 million in 1955; corresponding figures for the Detroit River were 92.6 and 132. Though the Great Lakes are international waters and normal ocean freighters have had access to the lake ports through the St. Lawrence Seaway since 1959, a greater part of traffic on the Great Lakes is functionally considered inland transportation. Traffic on the Seaway has been less than was anticipated in the planning, and a large part of it consists of iron ore for United States consumers. This is not the place to discuss the problems involved, but we should not forget that not only the use of the canal and river systems but also access to Montreal is prohibited by ice for several months.

With the help of these and other check points, the economic geographer will be able to construct flow charts which indicate routes of commodity movement with a fair degree of accuracy.

Transportation Facilities: Economic and Technical Considerations

Generally speaking, the value of a commodity increases as it moves from one place to another; this resembles somewhat the increase in value through manufacturing (secondary production) and it expresses in terms of money one section of tertiary production. Therefore, price quotations for goods are not uniform along the way from the producing point to the consuming area. Here it suffices to mention two of the most important quotations. The first is *free on board* (f.o.b.), which implies that in addition to the initial costs of goods all the expenses for loading, export duties, etc., are borne by the exporter or seller. The importer or buyer, however, must be responsible for freight charges to the point of destination and the insurance during the transport, to mention the two most important items. The price upon arrival at the port of destination is therefore generally quoted as c.i.f., meaning *cost + insurance + freight*. We will return to this subject later when world trade in general is discussed, because export figures are usually based on f.o.b. prices and import figures on c.i.f. prices.

Insurance is a determining factor in the final cost structure; it plays an important role in the competition between different carriers, e.g., rail and sea transport, and especially in the competitive position of air transportation, for the higher freight rates of the latter may be offset by greatly reduced rates of insurance.

The ratio between initial production costs of a commodity on the one hand and freight and insurance rates on the other forms a good indicator of how sensitive a commodity price is to transportation costs. Low-value bulk goods, such as industrial raw materials, are generally shipped by the cheapest means, while goods with a high specific value are much less sensitive to freight rates. Water shipping is on the whole cheaper than overland transportation (rail or trucking), and air transport is the most costly as far as freight rates are concerned. But freight rates can be manipulated in various ways so that they do not necessarily represent the effective transportation costs. They are consequently used as one of the most efficient and important tools in planning and directing commodity movements and hence the total economy. The concept of the freight structure of an economic area derives from this manipulation. The freight structure may be constructed in favor of one specific means of transport, one specific route, traffic in one particular direction, or for one kind of goods. Examples to that effect are copious throughout the history of economic development as well as in the economic geography of any region.

Besides these economic factors, technical factors should also be taken into consideration. Bulk raw materials, such as ores or raw cotton, demand different media of transportation than manufactured goods, though both may be shipped by rail, truck, or ship. It becomes apparent if we think of electricity, for example, which is transmitted exclusively through its own transportation system, by wire; or of coal, which has not so far been susceptible of pipeline transportation but may be so soon; or of oil and gas, which are preferably shipped by pipeline. Natural gas poses a great problem for ocean transport, in part solved recently through liquefying it at low temperatures. It is thus not the cost factor alone that determines the media of transportation.

Transportation Facilities: Availabilities

The availability of transportation has been studied and mapped in many different ways, of which the following three are employed most frequently: (1) a regional division based on the dominant type of service available or on characteristic combinations of such services; (2) density of transportation nets, generally including a strip of land twenty to thirty miles wide on both sides of the line of transportation. Such maps are very effective for portraying the areas with or without adequate transport services and are thus found in many publications; (3) qualification of available services based on traffic density, carrying capacity, etc. A number of maps which were discussed earlier under Flow Charts may be included here.

All these generalized representations necessarily neglect a number of points, some of which may be of the utmost importance. In rail transportation, as in all the other services, the efficiency with which goods are loaded and unloaded is a decisive factor. Efficiency means not only achieving a maximum turnover in a minimum time at a minimum cost, but also keeping damages and losses to a minimum. For certain soft iron ores, for example, losses incurred during transporting operations may run as high as 25 percent.

No road is better than the weakest link of the system. Furthermore, viability is frequently hindered by seasonal climatic changes. In all the tropical countries, highways are classified primarily into dry-weather and all-weather roads. In middle latitudes the cold season replaces the rainy season of the tropics as obstructive to road traffic; mountain roads are blocked for months by deep snow and avalanche danger. In fact, before the coming of modern road transport, winter presented a less serious obstacle to mule and sled trains traveling over Alpine passes in Central Europe; today only a few are kept open, at great cost, to permit the passage of automobile traffic.

Ocean transportation is greatly affected by the size of the vessels, since port facilities must be made accordingly. Many shipping centers have lost their significance and moved elsewhere because modern vessels require ample depth of water. The decline of Macao and the rise of Hong Kong are one such example. The recent introduction of the supertanker in petroleum transportation has caused wide repercussions of a similar nature.

Likewise the size of aircraft and their speed largely determined the structure of air transportation. A number of first-class airfields have dropped out of international air traffic since the introduction of long-distance jet flights, and a new system of feeder lines and trunk lines has been instituted. Changes like these are motivated in the first place by the availability of a certain type of conveyance.

Trade Services

So far we have been concerned with the transportation of commodities, i.e., of tangible objects moved from one place to another. One exception was the tourist trade mentioned earlier. Incoming foreign tourists may be regarded as equivalent to the exports of goods, and outgoing native tourists as imports. However, there are still many other functional connections within the structure of international trade which ought to be included here. Equal in importance to tourist trade are capital exports and imports, whether they are in the form of investments, grants in aid, or transfer of earnings. Communications media, like telephone, telegraph, radio, mail, form another segment.

While all exchange mentioned so far may come under *flow of goods* in a broad sense, certain central services responsible for the functioning of the whole system, and the central places where these services are located, should also be considered within the functional structure of the highest international order. What may be included there is shown in the following paragraphs.

Headquarters of international business organizations are generally located at the turntables of world commerce. However, there are some notable exceptions; for instance, the prominence of Connecticut or Zürich (Switzerland) in the insurance business, or numerous financial centers of international importance. Banking and insurance are other fields in economic geography where few case studies have so far been made. Likewise studies of the locational factors of commodity exchanges (wheat, cotton, rubber, etc.) and stock exchanges, which are found close to production areas, at centers of commerce, or near the market, are almost completely lacking.

On the other hand a substantial geographical literature is available on the role of switching points like seaports, railroad centers, etc., and the reasons for their being. A special case is represented by the free ports or foreign-trade zones wherever foreign trade touches the national territory. Such free-trade zones were established to facilitate the re-export of goods. Though goods are unloaded and stored, they do not pass the customs and therefore do not enter the national territory from the customs' point of view. Free ports came into existence primarily where re-exports make up a substantial portion of the traffic. Outstanding examples are Penang, Singapore, and Hong Kong, all of which have played an important role in the entreport trade. A foreign-trade zone may be limited in extent, but sometimes extends over a large territory as in the above-mentioned cases, where it includes whole islands and the adjacent territory. Usually foreign-trade zones in U.S. ports have a very limited area, and so do those in European countries.

FOREIGN TRADE

Definition and Statistical Basis

Foreign or external trade refers to all the commodities that enter or leave the customs area of a country; in the event that they merely pass through a country, they generally do not appear in the statistics. Commodities which are not cleared for domestic consumption but are re-exported are included in figures referred to as "general trade," whereas they are excluded from "special trade." Definitions of statistical data should always be carefully consulted in using trade statistics. Explicit commentaries are given in the United Nations *Yearbook of International Trade Statistics*.

As already mentioned, the quoted price of an export commodity corresponds to its f.o.b. value and that of an import commodity to the c.i.f. value. A number of other special considerations explain the discrepancies which any student will observe between the values of corresponding export and import figures given by two different countries. For example, cargo may be rerouted on the way or may be still en route at the end of a fiscal year. In 1959 the total world exports calculated by the United Nations was 100,600 million dollars and the imports 105,100 million dollars (excluding the trade of Albania, Bulgaria, mainland China, Mongolian People's Republic, North Vietnam, Czechoslovakia, Rumania, and the USSR). The total world trade is defined as the sum of total exports and total imports.

A great deal of standardization effected by the United Nations Standard International Trade Classification (S.I.T.C.) facilitates international comparisons. It groups commodities into the following large commodity classes:

0 Food
1 Beverages and tobacco
2 Crude minerals, inedible, except fuels
3 Mineral fuels, lubricants, related materials
4 Animal and vegetable oils and fats
5 Chemicals
6 Manufactured goods classified by material
7 Machinery and transport equipment
8 Miscellaneous manufactured articles
9 Miscellaneous transactions and commodities

In order to construct flow charts the export figures are obviously more appropriate than the import figures.

Foreign trade is measured in terms of either volume or of value. Very instructive is a comparison of the development by index values. If 1953 is taken as index year, indices of development for the world in 1938 and 1959 are as follows:

	1938	1953	1959
EXPORTS:			
Food and raw materials	99	100	139
	*33	*100	* 86
Fuel	56	100	133
	*42	*100	*106
Manufactured goods	54	100	140
	*50	*100	*106
FOR COMPARISON:			
Population	82	100	109
Primary commodities production	77	100	116
Manufacturing, production	50	100	131

* = value index, all others volume index

These figures point to the discrepancy in price behavior among the different classes of commodities, especially between primary and secondary production; this was recognized above as one of the great problems that separate the industrialized and the less developed countries.

Balance of Trade and Balance of Payments

The statistical data mentioned so far refer to commodity movements, but not to movements of other kinds, like tourism. The balance of trade is the ratio between the total value of exports and that of imports. If the imports show a higher value than the exports, the balance of trade is called negative, and if vice versa, positive. The United States has a positive balance of trade while Western Europe has traditionally been negative. If a country had no other sources to compensate the negative trade balance, it would become poorer and poorer. Whether this is happening or not is indicated by the balance of payments, which includes the so-called invisible imports and exports. Important items of invisible imports and exports are income on investments, travel, transportation, miscellaneous services by the governments concerned as well as by private organizations. The striking example of Mexico, where the invisible exports have equaled the export of commodities in recent years, was cited above. In the United States they made up about one-third of the total "exports of goods and services" in 1960.

Colonial economy was generally characterized by the strong necessity of obtaining a positive balance of trade, since colonial territories had few opportunities to compensate the negative trade balance. Their balance of payments frequently tended to the negative side because of large payments of interest on foreign investments. The industrialized countries, on the other hand, benefited from an almost complete monopoly of secondary and tertiary production and the capital strength resulting from it.

Generally speaking, economic geographers pay undue attention to the balance of trade and overlook the significance of the balance of payments in evaluating the economy of a country. It is of course a borderline field between economics and economic geography; while the problem of establishing a correct balance of payments is within the realm of economics, an economic geographer should be fully aware of its importance.

Foreign Trade of the United States
and the World

Some of the considerations in the foregoing are applicable to two specific cases: (1) the changes that have occurred during the past hundred years in a country that rose from a quasi-colonial status to the highest degree of industrialization and (2) the situation in 1960. A number of statistical data are compiled from the original sources to bring out certain characteristics. The main sources are *Statistical Abstracts of the United States, Historical Statistics of the United States —Colonial Times to 1957,* and *Annual Reports of the International Monetary Fund.*

UNITED STATES

(1) The changing importance of the various commodity groups is indicative of the changing national economy. Exports of crude materials in any form and foodstuffs declined in importance as manufactured articles increased in volume and value, reflecting a shift in the occupational pattern from primary to secondary occupations. It is also evidenced in the corresponding development in the import trade—increase of crude materials and decrease of manufactures. The commodity groups distinguished here are (A) crude materials; (B) crude foodstuffs; (C) manufactured foodstuffs; (D) semimanufactures; and (E) finished manufactures.

CHANGING IMPORTANCE OF COMMODITY GROUPS IN FOREIGN TRADE

Export-Import, Percentage of Total

YEARS	A	B	C	D	E
1860	69-11	4-13	13-17	4-10	10-49
1900	25-33	16-12	23-16	12-16	24-23
1921-1925	28-37	10-11	14-13	12-18	36-21
1956-1960	13-22	7-14	6-11	15-22	59-31

(2) A further shift toward the tertiary occupations is clearly reflected in the balance of payments. At first it was virtually determined by the commodity trade in crude and manufactured goods; in later years it became much influenced by so-called invisible items—returns from financing, services, etc. On the debit side, American tourists abroad began to constitute an important item, as has been pointed out above. The heading E, "others," as a debit for 1960 was in large measure made up of military expenditures abroad.

BALANCE OF PAYMENTS ON GOODS AND SERVICES

(A) merchandise, (B) transportation,
(C) travel, (D) investments, (E) others
in percent of total

EXPORTS

YEAR	TOTAL IN BILLIONS OF DOLLARS	A	B	C	D	E
1860	0.4	91	8	—	—	—
1900	1.7	96	1	—	—	—
1929	7.0	76	6	2	16	—
1960	29.1	66	6	3	11	14

IMPORTS

YEAR	TOTAL IN BILLIONS OF DOLLARS	A	B	C	D	E
1860	0.4	86	4	4	6	—
1900	1.2	76	3	8	10	—
1929	5.9	76	9	8	6	1
1960	23.3	63	8	7	4	18

(3) Both the balance of trade and the balance of payments in the last century were frequently negative; since the turn of the century, however, both ratios have been on the positive side in most years (except during the 1930's following the depression). While the balance on goods and services has remained positive ever since, the total balance of payments has shown a deficit since 1958 owing to other factors not to be dis-

cussed here. Economic geographers who are concerned with the different stages of economic development from an underdeveloped to a highly industrialized state will find ample food for thought in the example of the United States.

(4) The changes that occurred within the United States are necessarily reflected in the country's trade relationships with other parts of the world. The following table is self-explanatory.

DIRECTION OF FOREIGN TRADE
Export-Import, in Percent of Total

YEAR	CANADA	LATIN AMERICA	EUROPE	ASIA	OTHERS
1860	7-7	14-23	74-61	3-8	2-1
1900	7-5	9-20	74-52	5-17	5-6
1929	18-11	19-25	45-30	12-29	6-5
1956	22-23	22-32	27-23	14-16	15-6

(5) Changes in the national economy and external trade relations had an effect upon the relative importance of the various customs districts, or in other words, the gateways of external trade. A close comparison of the following figures with those above will bring out significant changes.

RELATIVE IMPORTANCE OF THE CUSTOMS DISTRICTS
Export-Import, Percent of Total

YEAR	AT-LANTIC COAST	GULF COAST	MEX-ICAN BORDER	PA-CIFIC COAST	NORTH-ERN BORDER
1860	48-87	46-5	0-0	2-2	4-6
1900	69-82	17-3	2-1	5-7	7-7
1929	46-67	22-7	2-1	11-12	19-13
1954	44-58	19-11	4-1	11-9	22-21

THE WORLD

Mercantilism, which saw its heyday between the sixteenth and the eighteenth centuries, contended that world trade was above all an exchange of manufactured goods for raw materials. Consequently, the spread of industrialization to nonindustrial countries was considered to have an adverse effect upon international trade. Actually, trade between industrialized countries is very important, since the highly diversified economy of an industrialized country stimulates the exchange of such items as can be obtained only from another industrialized country. Not only is the volume of trade larger among industrialized countries, but the rate of its increase is also considerably higher in recent years than elsewhere.

For the purpose of analyzing the statistical data, all the countries are conveniently assembled into three groups: (A) industrialized countries —United States, Belgium-Luxemburg, Federal Republic of Germany, France, Italy, Netherlands, Denmark, Norway, Sweden, Austria, Switzerland, United Kingdom, and Japan; (B) the Soviet bloc, including mainland China (recently the countries of this group have been called "countries with centrally planned economies"); and (C) all the others. Only the export values (f.o.b.) expressed in billions of dollars will be considered. The situation may be summarized roughly as follows: about one-half of world exports are shared equally between groups A and C; one-third is within group A, while the

TOTAL TRADE, 1960
(WORLD EXPORTS, F.O.B.)
112.0 BILLION DOLLARS[a]

Trade within group A	37.3	(33%)
Exports from A to C	32.1	(54%)
Exports from C to A	28.7	
Exports from A to B	2.3	(4%)
Exports from B to A	2.0	

[a] Exclusive of trade of group B.

trade of B with either A or C is negligible. The remaining 9 percent is mainly the trade between different countries in group C. The trade within group A increased by 20 percent from 1959 to 1960, while the trade between group A and group C countries grew only by 8.5 percent. The United States contributed more than 60 percent of the exports from Groups A to C, but imported only one-third of the exports from Groups C to A.

What becomes clear from the preceding para-

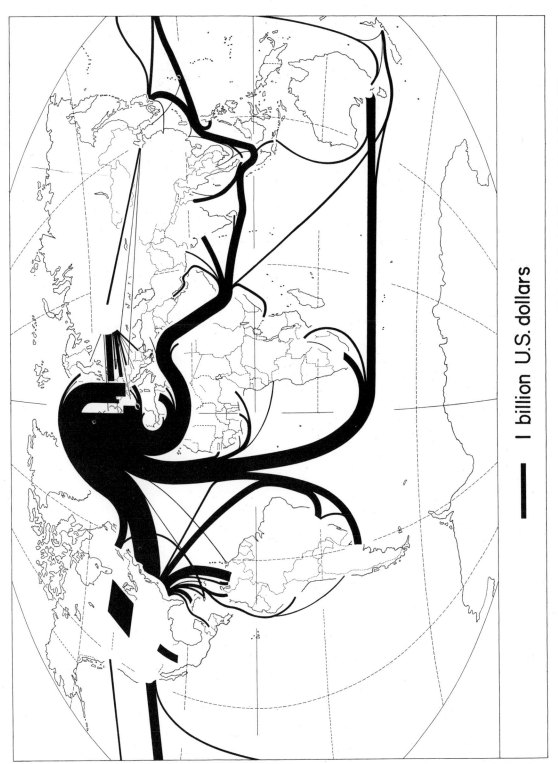

— 1 billion U.S. dollars

Statistical source: *United Nations Yearbook of International Trade Statistics, 1958*

99 · WORLD TRADE. Any foreign trade between two countries which exceeded 100 million dollars in one direction is included here, with the exception of intra-European trade in both western and eastern Europe. All the exceptions, restrictions, etc., mentioned in the source material are also applicable to the present map. Even though a systematic error arising from the exclusion of all the trade relationships of less than 100 million dollars was unavoidable, the map portrays correctly the major traffic flow of the world.

graph is the unique position of Western Europe in world trade. At different places in the present volume, it has been brought home that Western Europe as a whole constitutes the major deficit area for all sorts of crude materials—above all, foodstuffs. As much as one-half of all world imports and exports flow in and out of European countries; however, somewhat more than 50 percent of them represent the trade between European countries themselves. It brings us to a crucial point, namely, that foreign trade is defined to be the trade between customs zones of different countries. Foreign-trade statistics could fluctuate from one year to another without any appreciable change in the overall flow of goods if the statistical units were changed. Theoretically, foreign trade would be nil if all the countries of the world were united in one big customs area as long as one does not choose a new definition for foreign trade. On the other hand, if there were a larger number of nations and hence customs units than at present, the volume of foreign trade would also be larger, without any material change in the actual exchange of goods. If the trade within the European Economic Community and the Free Trade Area were excluded from the total world trade, the latter would be reduced by more than 10 percent; likewise if the intra-West-European trade were altogether excluded, the total world trade would be about one-fourth less.

As regards the trade between different countries of Group A, the exclusion of intra-European trade would alter the picture considerably. The trade within Group A would be reduced to a mere 12 percent of world exports and to only 8 or 9 percent between Western Europe and the United States.

Finally, it should not be lost sight of that the discussion on the foregoing pages is based exclusively on the value of exports, and not on the volume. The value of manufactured goods has remained strong, while the value of raw materials has been decidedly weak. In 1960, for example, the prices of cacao and copra underwent sharp declines while prices of jute and long-staple cotton showed upward trends. Let us repeat: on the whole the industrialized countries profited more from recent price changes than the primary exporting countries.

WORLD ECONOMIC REGIONS

The Problem of Regionalization

The task of dividing the earth's surface into economic regions presents the same problems as were discussed in Chapter 1 and in Chapter 6. Actually there is no such thing as a true system of regions which is to be uncovered through scientific research; on the contrary, any system of regional divisions is a product of our mental synthesis. It is therefore quite conceivable that different workers should arrive at different regional systems even if painstaking and scientifically correct procedures are employed.

Another consideration is that there are two entirely different avenues of approach to geographic analysis—the formal and the functional approaches. So far in the present chapter we have been concerned solely with functional aspects. The text will be concluded in the next section with a division of the world on a functional basis. This is quite natural, since functional aspects are necessarily brought forward in a discussion of world trade. Nevertheless, the problem of a regional division of the world on a formal basis will be considered briefly—even if only for antithesis and to stress the difference in outlook between the two approaches.

From the standpoint of economic geography, the primary division of the world is into ecumene and anecumene (or nonecumene). The anecumene should be further subdivided according to its potential uses. Since most of the physical factors find an integrated expression in the natural vegetation, it may best serve as a criterion for the first-order subdivision.

It is more difficult to find a sound principle for a similar subdivision of the ecumene. Some authors have suggested that the ratio of area in natural landscape to area in humanized landscape be used as an indicator. Most geographers however, have preferred to consider only the anthroposphere as the primary criterion. The first subdivision is based on the type of land use (urban, agricultural, etc.). Such regions are further differentiated on the basis of the degree of economic development. As an example we may refer the reader to the *World Occupance*

Types of Philbrick (1957), but there are many other studies as well.

An earlier statement that formal structure changes only slowly in comparison with functional structure becomes very important in this context. While functional structures may be changed overnight, any such changes have to take into account the existing concrete facts of the formal structure which alter only slowly. This is something one should never forget in considering the problems of development, nationalization, reconstruction, etc.

The Functional Structure of World Economy

REGIONAL VERSUS NATIONAL DIVISION

Before one seeks to study the functional structure of world economy and to plot it on maps, it is well to consider whether such a study should be based on individual national units or not. In general, political boundaries tend to be disregarded in geographic study, and certainly a formal regionalization will almost always do without them, except when the area of study is defined by such boundaries. Even then, the delineation of subregions is preferably based on nonpolitical (frequently called natural) boundary lines.

In economic geography the problem presents itself somewhat differently for two reasons. First, most statistical data are summed up by political, i.e., statistical units. One method of transferring such data on any desired areal unit is by way of dot maps; this has been mentioned in the beginning of our discussions. Still, it is a rather cumbersome and not always practicable way. The second reason is more significant. National units as realities play a decisive role in economic geography, and constitute one representative of functional areas themselves. In an evaluation of the various geospheric components, political (and implicitly, economic) boundaries assume an outstanding importance for the student of economic geography.

In plotting economic data, however, it seems advisable to consider only that part of the country which may be regarded as ecumene. This principle has been followed throughout the present volume, i.e., the boundary line between uninhabited and inhabited areas is considered to be represented by the isopleth of 1 inhabitant per square kilometer (about 2.5 per square mile).

THE GROUPING OF COUNTRIES

The conventional grouping, as by continents, gives way to one based on certain economic characteristics. A few possibilities are mentioned here.

A simple way is to divide the world into economic regions according to various trade agreements. In 1962 the following trade areas are recognized, among others: (*a*) Central American Free Trade Area, comprising El Salvador, Guatemala, Honduras, and Nicaragua; (*b*) Latin American Free Trade Association, comprising Argentina, Brazil, Chile, Mexico, Paraguay, Uruguay, Colombia, Peru, and Ecuador; (*c*) European Economic Community, comprising Belgium, France, Italy, Luxemburg, Netherlands, and the Federal Republic of Germany; (*d*) European Free Trade Association, comprising Austria, Denmark, Norway, Portugal, Switzerland, United Kingdom, and Sweden; (*e*) British Commonwealth; and (*f*) the Communist bloc.

Another division, used by the United Nations in the *Yearbook of International Trade Statistics*, is into developed and underdeveloped areas. The former include the United States, all the countries of Western Europe, Japan, Australia, New Zealand, and the Republic of South Africa. The Communist countries form a group by themselves (Albania, Bulgaria, China (mainland), Mongolian People's Republic, North Vietnam, Czechoslovakia, Eastern Germany, Hungary, North Korea, Poland, Rumania, and the USSR).

Still other significant divisions are based on the medium of currency, such as weak- and hard-currency countries, or the dollar and the pound-sterling areas.

A MAP OF WORLD ECONOMIC REGIONS

The map of world economic regions (Fig. 100) represents a simple and systematic attempt to depict the functional structure of world economy and should be studied in conjunction with the map of world trade. The statistical basis is pro-

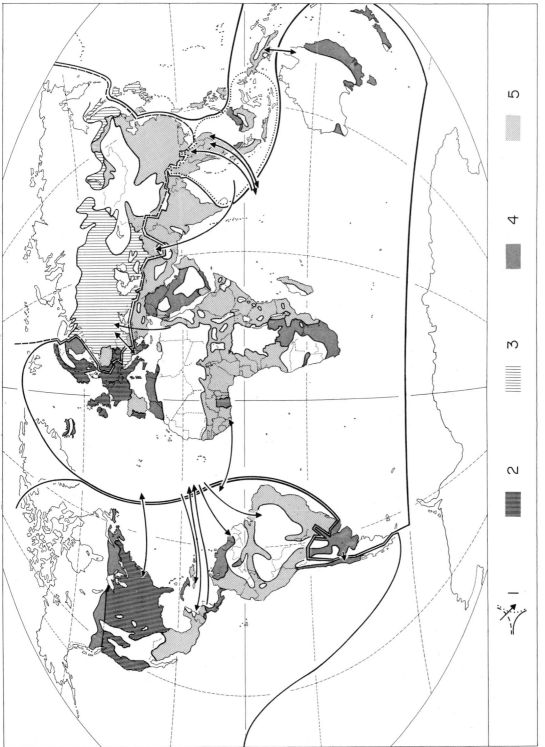

100 · WORLD ECONOMIC REGIONS. Legend: (1) Boundaries of major economic regions of the world, i.e., North American, Western European, Southeast Asian, and Communist Bloc regions. All the countries within each region are primarily oriented toward its center, named above, in their trade relations. Exceptions are indicated with arrows. (2) Countries exporting more secondary than primary products, i.e., industrialized countries where per capita foreign trade is above world average. (3) The same, below world average. (4) Countries exporting more primary than secondary products where per capita foreign trade is above world average. (5) The same, below world average. For a detailed explanation of the map, see the text.

1 2 3 4 5

vided by foreign-trade statistics. This is in many respects the most reliable source of information despite the fact that data from the Communist bloc do not conform to S.I.T.C. and that statistics on China were compiled entirely from secondary sources. To be sure, there may be other sources which are more significant in principle, but most of them are rather incomplete or less trustworthy than the foreign-trade statistics, which is an official register of all the items that pass through the customs.

The compilation of the map followed three steps. The first step was to establish the relative position of all the countries with respect to exports and imports. The flow of major imports and exports to and from each country was noted. The map provides at a glance the delineation of four major realms of interdependence oriented toward the North American center of gravity, Western Europe, Southeast Asia, and the Communist block. All the countries within each realm have common bonds insofar as the majority of

their exports and imports are directed toward the centers named above. There are notable exceptions, marked with arrows pointing in the direction where such anomalies occur. For example, one does not fail to note the inroads made upon the Western Hemisphere by the European realm, nor the still existing ties between the latter and the former French Indochina.

The second step consisted in determining from foreign-trade statistics the functions of each country according as its exports were made up mainly of manufactured goods or of crude materials. Unfortunately data relevant to tertiary production were not available for all countries; they would have helped to bring out still another important distinction.

The last step was to differentiate trade further in terms of the intensity with which a certain function is performed. Intensity was measured as per capita value of foreign trade; according as it is above or below the world average, the countries were divided into two groups.

BIBLIOGRAPHY AND READINGS

THE FOLLOWING LIST is not comprehensive but highly selective. The first part (Bibliography) includes the publications which one would usually find on the reserve shelf for constant reference during a course in economic geography. The second part (Readings) consists of a selection of articles taken from the leading periodicals in the English language that should be available in larger geography departments and libraries: *Annals of the Association of American Geographers (Ann. AAG), The Professional Geographer (Prof. Geogr.), Geographical Review (GR), Economic Geography (Econ. Geogr.), Geographical Journal (GJ), Geography (Geogr.), New Zealand Geographer (NZG), Geographical Bulletin (GB), (Malayan) Journal of Tropical Geography (Trop. Geogr.), Geographical Review of India (GRInd.), Indian Geographical Journal (Ind. GJ), Pakistan Geographical Review (Pak. GR)*. The selection is restricted to newer articles (since 1940) having a direct bearing upon what has been discussed in the text; consequently these readings are grouped in accordance with the main plan of the book.

The fact that certain fields have been neglected by geographers in the past is reflected in an uneven coverage of the subjects. There are, for example, relatively few studies dealing with agricultural commodities in world trade. It is therefore suggested that additional readings be selected from other sources, e.g., publications of the Food Research Institute, Stanford University. An invaluable source, though not everywhere available, is the series of Research Papers of the University of Chicago, Department of Geography, as well as other series published by individual departments and institutions. A few books are also mentioned in the text wherever reference is made to specific statements.

BIBLIOGRAPHY

ALEXANDERSSON, G.: *The Industrial Structure of American Cities*. Stockholm, 1956.

ALEXANDERSSON, G., and G. NORSTRÖM: *World Shipping: An Economic Geography of Ports and Seaborne Trade*. Stockholm, 1964.

AMIRAN, D. H. K., and A. P. SCHICK: *Geographical Conversion Tables*. International Geographical Union, Zürich, 1961.

BATEMAN, L. M.: *Economic Mineral Deposits*. New York, 1950.

DARBY, H. C. (ed.): *An Historical Geography of England Before A.D. 1800*. Cambridge, 1936.

DUNCAN, O. D., R. P. CUZZORT, and B. DUNCAN: *Statistical Geography—Problems in Analysing Areal Data*. Free Press, Glencoe, Ill., 1961.

EAST, W. G., and A. E. MOODIE (eds.): *The Changing World*. London, 1956.

GINSBURG, N. (editor): *Essays on Geography and Economic Development*. University of Chicago, Dept. of Geography Research Papers, No. 62, 1960.

GINSBURG, N.: *Atlas of Economic Development*. University of Chicago Press, Chicago, 1961.

GOUROU, P.: *The Tropical World*. London, 1955.

HARTSHORNE, R.: The Nature of Geography: A Critical Survey of Current Thought in the Light of the Past. *Ann. AAG*, 1939.

JAMES, P. E., and C. F. JONES: *American Geography —Inventory and Prospect*. Syracuse University Press, Syracuse, N.Y., 1954.

LÖSCH, A.: *The Economics of Location*. Yale University Press, New Haven, 1954.

McFARLANE, J., and C. F. W. R. GULLICK: *Economic Geography*, 5th ed. London, 1949.

Oxford Economic Atlas of the World. Oxford University Press, New York, 1955.

Oxford Regional Economic Atlases, Oxford University Press.

SMAILES, A. E.: *The Geography of Towns*. London, 1953.

STAMP, L. D.: *Land for Tomorrow: The Underdeveloped World*. Indiana University Press, Bloomington, 1952.

STAMP, L. D.: *Britain's Structure and Scenery*. London, 1955.

STAMP, L. D.: *Man and the Land*. London, 1955.

The Statesman's Yearbook (annual). Macmillan & Co., London.

THOMAS, W. L. (editor): *Man's Role in Changing the Face of the Earth*. University of Chicago Press, Chicago, 1956.

VAN ROYEN, W.: *Atlas of World Resources*: Vol. I, *The Agricultural Resources of the World* (1954); Vol. II, *The Mineral Resources of the World* (1952). Prentice-Hall, New York.

WAGNER, P. L., and M. W. MIKESELL: *Readings in Cultural Geography*. University of Chicago Press, Chicago, 1962.

WOYTINSKY, W. S., and E. S. WOYTINSKY: *World Population and Production—World Commerce and Governments* (2 vols.). Twentieth Century Fund, New York, 1955.

ZIMMERMANN, E. W.: *World Resources and Industries*. Harper, New York, 1951.

UNITED NATIONS: *Statistical Yearbook* (annual). *Demographic Yearbook* (annual). *Yearbook of International Trade Statistics* (annual). *Patterns of Industrial Growth 1938-1958* (1960). *World Energy Supplies 1955-1958* (1960).

————: *Humid Tropics Research Series* (UNESCO).

————: *Arid Zone Research Series* (UNESCO).

FAO (Food and Agricultural Organization of the United Nations): *Trade Yearbook* (annual). *Production Yearbook* (annual). *Yearbook of Fisheries Statistics* (annual). *Yearbook of Forest Products Statistics* (annual). *The State of Food and Agriculture* (annual). *Agricultural Commodities—Projections for 1970*, Special Supplement E/CN.13/48-CCP 62/5, 1962.

UNITED STATES: Department of Commerce: *Statistical Abstract of the United States* (annual). Department of Agriculture: *Yearbook of Agriculture and Agricultural Statistics* (annual). Department of the Interior: *Minerals Yearbook* (annual). *Historical Statistics of the United States—Colonial Times to 1957* (1960).

READINGS

CHAPTER 2

BENNETT, H. H.: Adjustment of Agriculture to Its Environment. *Ann. AAG* 33-4, 1943.

CRESSEY, G. B.: Changing the Map of the Soviet Union. *Econ. Geogr.* 29-3, 1953.

CURRY, L.: Climate and Economic Life: A New Approach, with Examples from the United States. *GR* 42-3, 1952.

DUCKHAM, A. N.: The Current Agricultural Revolution. *Geogr.* 44-2, 1959.

GINSBURG, N.: Natural Resources and Economic Development. *Ann. AAG* 47-3, 1957.

HEWES, L., and A. C. SCHMIEDING: Risk in the Central Great Plains: Geographical Patterns of Wheat Failure in Nebraska, 1931-1952. *GR* 46-3, 1956.

HUNTINGTON, E.: The Geography of Human Productivity. *Ann. AAG* 33-1, 1943.

JOHNSON, H. B.: Rational and Ecological Aspects of the Quarter Section: An Example from Minnesota. *GR* 47-3, 1957.

MENON, M. M.: Problems of Soil in Pakistan. *Ind. GJ* 35-1 & 2, 1960.

SMITH, J. R.: Grassland and Farmland as Factors in the Cyclical Development of Eurasian History. *Ann. AAG* 33-3, 1943.

TREWARTHA, G. T.: Types of Rural Settlements in Colonial America. *GR* 36-4, 1946.

VISHER, St. S.: Weather Influences on Crop Yields. *Econ. Geogr.* 16-4, 1940.

CHAPTER 3

ALBRECHT, W. A.: Soil Fertility and Biotic Geography. *GR* 47-1, 1957.

BARNES, J. A., and A. H. ROBINSON: A New Method for the Representation of Dispersed Rural Population. *GR* 30-1, 1940.

BENNETT, H. H.: Food Comes from Soil. *GR* 34-1, 1944.

BENNETT, M. K.: International Contrasts in Food Consumption. *GR* 31-3, 1941.

CARTER, G. F., and R. L. PENDLETON: The Humid Soil: Process and Time. *GR* 46-4, 1956.

CHATTERJEE, S. P.: Food Shortage. *GRInd.* 14-2, 1952.

CRESSEY, G. B.: Land for 2.4 Billion Neighbors. *Econ. Geogr.* 29-1, 1953.

ESPENSHADE, A: A Program for Japanese Fisheries. *GR* 39-1, 1949.

FIEDLER, R. H.: Fisheries of North America, With Special Reference to the United States. *GR* 30-2, 1940.

GAJDA, R. T.: The Canadian Ecumene—Inhabited and Uninhabited Areas. *GB*, 1960.

MACKAY, J. R.: Some Problems and Techniques in Isopleth Mapping. *Econ. Geogr.* 27-1, 1951.

MAY, J. M.: Medical Geography: Its Methods and Objectives. *GR* 40-1, 1950.

McCARTY, H. H.: A Functional Analysis of Population Distribution. *GR* 32-2, 1942.

ROBINSON, A. H., and R. A. BRYSON: A Method for Describing Quantitatively the Correspondence of Geographical Distributions. *Ann. AAG* 47-4, 1957.

STEWART, J. Q.: Empirical Mathematical Rules Concerning the Distribution and Equilibrium of Population. *GR* 37-3, 1947.

CHAPTER 4

AWAD, M.: The Assimilation of Nomads in Egypt. *GR* 44-2, 1954.

CLARKE, J. I.: Studies of Semi-Nomadism in North Africa. *Econ. Geogr.* 35-2, 1959.

CUMBERLAND, K. B.: High Country "Run." The Geography of Extensive Pastoralism in New Zealand. *Econ. Geogr.* 20-3, 1944.

CUMBERLAND, K. B.: The Agricultural Regions of New Zealand. *GJ* 112-1-3, 1949.

DICKINSON, R. E.: Rural Settlements in the German Lands. *Ann. AAG* 39-4, 1949.

DICKINSON, R. E.: Land Reform in Southern Italy. *Econ. Geogr.* 30-2, 1954.

DOBBY, E. H. G.: The North Kedah Plain—A Study in the Environment of Pioneering for Rice Cultivation. *Econ. Geogr.* 27-4, 1951.

DOBBY, E. H. G.: Some Aspects of the Human Ecology of South-East Asia. *GJ* 108-1-3, 1946.

DOERR, A. H.: An Operating Scheme for Humid Tropical Land Inventories. *Prof. Geogr.* 12-3, 1960.

ELAHI, M. K.: Agriculture in South East Asia. *Pak. GR* 14-2, 1959.

FARMER, B. H.: Problems of Land Use in the Dry Zone of Ceylon. *GJ* 120-1, 1954.

FOSBERG, F. R., B. J. GARNIER, and A. W. KÜCHLER: Delimitation of the Humid Tropics. *GR* 51-3, 1961.

GILLMAN, C.: White Colonization in East Africa, with Special Regard to Tanganyika Territory. *GR* 32-4, 1942.

GROTEWOLD, A.: Von Thünen in Retrospect. *Econ. Geogr.* 35-4, 1959.

HANCE, W. A.: The Gezira: An Example in Development. *GR* 44-2, 1954.

HIGBEE, E. C.: Of Man and the Amazon. *GR* 41-3, 1951.

MALIN, J. C.: Grassland, "Treeless," and "Subhumid": A Discussion of Some Problems of the Terminology of Geography. *GR* 37-2, 1947.

McNEE, R. R.: Rural Development in the Italian South: A Geographic Case Study. *Ann. AAG* 45-2, 1955.

MURDOCK, G. P.: Staple Subsistence Crops of Africa. *GR* 50-4, 1960.

MYERS, W. I.: Current Aspects of American Agriculture. *Econ. Geogr.* 19-4, 1943.

OOI, JIN-BEE: Rural Development in Tropical Areas, with special reference to Malaya. *Trop. Geogr.* 12, 1959.

PRUNTY, Jr., M.: Recent Quantitative Changes in the Cotton Regions of the Southeastern States. *Econ. Geogr.* 27-3, 1951.

PRUNTY, Jr., M.: The Renaissance of the Southern Plantation. *GR* 45-4, 1955.

SCOTT, P.: Transhumance in Tasmania. *NZG* 6-2, 1955.

STAMP, L. D.: Land Utilization in Britain 1937-1943. *GR* 33-4, 1943.

STAMP, L. D.: The Measurement of Land Resources. *GR* 48-1, 1958.

STERNBERG, H. O.: Agriculture and Industry in Brazil. *GJ* 121-4, 1955.

TREWARTHA, G. T.: Land Reform and Land Reclamation in Japan. *GR* 40-3, 1950.

VALKENBURG, S. VAN: The World Land Use Survey. *Econ. Geogr.* 26-1, 1950.

VALKENBURG, S. VAN: An Evaluation of the Standard of Land Use in Western Europe. *Econ. Geogr.* 36-4, 1960.

VISHER, ST. S.: Comparative Agricultural Potentials of the World's Regions. *Econ. Geogr.* 31-1, 1955.

ZINK, N. E.: A Dry-Farm Region in Utah. *Econ. Geogr.* 16-3, 1940.

ZOBLER, L.: A New Areal Measure of Food Production Efficiency. *GR* 51-4, 1961.

CHAPTER 5

ASCHMANN, H.: A Consumer Oriented Classification of the Products of Tropical Agriculture. *Econ. Geogr.* 28-2, 1952.

DEASY, G. F.: Geography of the United States Cottonseed Oil Industry. *Econ. Geogr.* 17-4, 1941.

DOBBY, E. H. G.: Padi Landscapes of Malaya. *Trop. Geogr.* 6, 1955 and 10, 1957.

DYER, D. R.: Sugar Regions of Cuba. *Econ. Geogr.* 32-2, 1956.

GARLAND, J. H.: Hemp; A Minor American Fiber Crop. *Econ. Geogr.* 22-2, 1946.

JONES, C. F., and P. C. MORRISON: Evolution of the Banana Industry of Costa Rica. *Econ. Geogr.* 28-1, 1952.

MATHER, E.: The Production and Marketing of Wyoming Beef Cattle. *Econ. Geogr.* 26-2, 1950.

MORRILL, R. L., and W. L. GARRISON: Projections of Interregional Patterns of Trade in Wheat and Flour. *Econ. Geogr.* 36-2, 1960.

MUNN, A. A.: Production and Utilization of the Soybean in the United States. *Econ. Geogr.* 26-3, 1950.

OOI, JIN-BEE: The Rubber Industry of the Federation of Malaya, *Trop. Geogr.* 15, 1961.

RUSSELL, J. A.: The Teas of Uji. *Econ. Geogr.* 16-2, 1940.

RUSSELL, J. A.: Fordlandia and Belterra, Rubber Plantations on the Tapajos River, Brazil. *Econ. Geogr.* 18-2, 1942.

SHAW, E. B.: Recent Changes in the Banana Production of Middle America. *Ann. AGG* 32-4, 1942.

SPENCER, J. E.: Abaca and the Philippines. *Econ. Geogr.* 27-2, 1951.

SUBRAMANIYAM, NALLAMMA: Tea Industry in Ceylon. *Ind. GJ* 29-4, 1954.

WAIBEL, L.: The Political Significance of Tropical Vegetable Fats for the Industrial Countries of Europe. *Ann. AAG* 33-2, 1943.

CHAPTER 6

ACKERMAN, E. A.: Geographic Training, Wartime Research and Immediate Professional Objectives. *Ann. AAG* 35-4, 1945.

ACKERMAN, E. A.: Regional Research—Emerging Concepts and Techniques in the Field of Geography. *Econ. Geogr.* 29-3, 1953.

BROEK, J. O. M.: Discourse on Economic Geography. *GR* 31-4, 1941.

CAROL, H.: Geography of the Future. *Prof. Geogr.* 13-1, 1961.

FINCH, V. C.: Training for Research in Economic Geography. *Ann. AAG* 34-4, 1944.

JAMES, P. E.: Toward a Further Understanding of the Regional Concept. *Ann. AAG* 42-3, 1952.

PLATT, R. S.: Determinism in Geography. *Ann. AAG* 38-2, 1948.

SAUER, C. O.: The Education of a Geographer. *Ann. AAG* 46-3, 1956.

SHABAD, TH.: The Soviet Concept of Economic Regionalization. *GR* 43-2, 1953.

SPATE, O. H. K.: Quantity and Quality in Geography. *Ann. AAG* 50-4, 1960.

THORNTHWAITE, C. W.: The Task Ahead. *Ann. AAG* 51-4, 1961.

CHAPTER 7

ALEXANDER, J. W.: Locations of Manufacturing: Methods of Measurement. *Ann. AAG* 48-1, 1958.

HARRIS, CH. D.: The Market as a Factor in the Localization of Industry in the United States. *Ann. AAG* 44-4, 1954.

LONSDALE, R. E., and J. H. THOMPSON: A Map of the USSR's Manufacturing. *Econ. Geogr.* 36-1, 1960.

MILLER, E. W.: Some Aspects of the Mineral Position of Eight Principal Industrial Nations. *Econ. Geogr.* 26-2, 1950.

RENNER, G. T.: Geography of Industrial Localization. *Econ. Geogr.* 23-3, 1947.

THOMPSON, J. H.: A New Method for Measuring Manufacturing. *Ann. AAG* 45-4, 1955.

CHAPTER 8

BALLERT, A. G.: The Coal Trade of the Great Lakes and the Port of Toledo. *GR* 38-2, 1948.

DALE, M. B.: The Location of Oil Refineries in Australia. *NZG* 15-2, 1959.

ESTALL, R. C.: The Problem of Power in the United Kingdom. *Econ. Geogr.* 34-1, 1958.

GUYOL, N. B.: Energy Consumption and Economic Development. In Ginsburg: *Essays on Geography.* University of Chicago, Dept. of Geography Research Papers, No. 62, 1960.

HARDING, G. E.: American Coal Production and Use. *Econ. Geogr.* 22-1, 1946.

HARRIS, CH. D.: The Ruhr Coal-Mining District. *GR* 36-2, 1946.

JONES, ST. B.: The Economic Geography of Atomic Energy: A Review Article. *Econ. Geogr.* 27-3, 1951.

MCNEE, R. B.: Centrifugal-Centripetal Forces in International Petroleum Company Regions. *Ann. AAG* 51-1, 1961.

MELAMID, A.: Geographical Distribution of Petroleum Refining Capacities: A Study of the European Refining Program. *Econ. Geogr.* 31-2, 1955.

MURPHY, R. E., and H. E. SPITTAL: Movements of the Center of Coal Mining in the Appalachian Plateaux. *GR* 35-4, 1945.

MUTTON, A. F. A.: Hydro-Electric Power in Western Europe. *GJ* 117-3, 1951.

PARSONS, J. J.: The Geography of Natural Gas in the United States. *Econ. Geogr.* 26-3, 1950.

STAMP, L. D.: Britain's Coal Crisis: Geographical Background and Some Recent Literature. *GR* 38-2, 1948.

STEVENS, JR., G. P.: Saudi Arabia's Petroleum Resources. *Econ. Geogr.* 25-3, 1949.

THIEL, E.: The Power Industry in the Soviet Union. *Econ. Geogr.* 27-2, 1951.

THOMAS, T. M.: Recent Trends and Developments in the British Coal Mining Industry. *Econ. Geogr.* 34-1, 1958.

VOSKUIL, W. H.: Bituminous Coal Movements in the United States. *GR* 32-1, 1942.

VOSKUIL, W. H.: Coal and Political Power in Europe. *Econ. Geogr.* 18-3, 1942.

CHAPTER 9

ABREU, S. F.: The Mineral Wealth of Brazil. *GR* 36-2, 1946.

ALEXANDERSSON, G.: Changes in the Location Pattern of the Anglo-American Steel Industry, 1948-1959. *Econ. Geogr.* 37-2, 1961.

BANERJEE, B.: A Study of Jute Cultivation in West Bengal. *Ind. GJ* 30-3, 1955.

BOAS, CH. W.: Locational Patterns of American Automobile Assembly Plants, 1895-1958. *Econ. Geogr.* 37-3, 1961.

BRIGHTMAN, G. F.: Cuyuna Iron Range. *Econ. Geogr.* 18-3, 1942.

COKER, J. A.: Steel and the Schuman Plan. *Econ. Geogr.* 28-4, 1952.

COLLIER, J. E.: The Aluminium Industry of the Western Hemisphere. *Econ. Geogr.* 20-4, 1944.

COLLIER, J. E.: The Aluminium Industry of Europe. *Econ. Geogr.* 22-2, 1946.

ERSELCUK, M.: The Iron and Steel Industry in Japan. *Econ. Geogr.* 23-2, 1947.

ERSELCUK, M.: The Iron and Steel Industry in China. *Econ. Geogr.* 32-4, 1956.

GRIESS, PH. R.: The Bolivian Tin Industry. *Econ. Geogr.* 27-3, 1951.

ISARD, W., and J. H. CUMBERLAND: New England as a Possible Location for an Integrated Iron and Steel Works. *Econ. Geogr.* 26-4, 1950.

KERR, D.: The Geography of the Canadian Iron and Steel Industry. *Econ. Geogr.* 35-2, 1959.

KESO, E. E., and H. SELF: The Magnesium Industry. *Econ. Geogr.* 25-4, 1949.

KIRK, W.: The Damodar Valley—"Valles Opima." *GR* 40-3, 1950.

KOHN, C. F., and R. E. SPECHT: The Mining of Taconite, Lake Superior Iron Mining District. *GR* 48-4, 1958.

KURIYAN, GEORGE: Industrial Development in India Since Independence. *Ind. GJ* 33-3&4, 1958.

LONG, R. G.: Volta Redonda: Symbol of Maturity in Brazilian Progress. *Econ. Geogr.* 24-2, 1948.

MARTIN, J. E.: Recent Trends in the Lorraine Iron and Steel Industry. *Geogr.* 43-3, 1958.

MILLER, E. W.: Changing Patterns in the Mineral Economy of the United States, 1939-1954. *Prof. Geogr.* 13-3, 1961.

MURPHEY, R.: China's Transport Problem and Communist Planning. *Econ. Geogr.* 32-1, 1956.

OOI, JIN-BEE: Mining Landscapes of Kinta. *Trop. Geogr.* 4, 1955.

PETTERSON, D. R.: The Witwatersrand—A Unique Gold Mining Community. *Econ. Geogr.* 27-3, 1951.

POUNDS, N. J. G.: Lorraine and the Ruhr. *Econ. Geogr.* 33-2, 1957.

POUNDS, N. J. G.: World Production and Use of Steel Scrap. *Econ. Geogr.* 35-3, 1959.

PRUNTY, JR., M.: Strategic Metallic Alloys and United States Dependence. *Econ. Geogr.* 17-4, 1941.

READ, T. T.: Economic-Geographic Aspects of China's Iron Industry. *GR* 33-1, 1943.

RODGERS, A.: The Manchurian Iron and Steel Industry and Its Resource Base. *GR* 38-1, 1948.

SCOTT, P.: The Iron and Steel Industry of South Africa. *Geogr.* 36-3, 1951.

SCOTT, P.: The Witwatersrand Gold Field. *GR* 41-4, 1951.

WHITE, C. L.: Water—A Neglected Factor in the Geographical Literature of Iron and Steel. *GR* 47-4, 1957.

WHITE, C. L., and R. H. CHILCOTE: Chile's New Iron and Steel Industry. *Econ. Geogr.* 37-3, 1951.

WILLS, N. R.: The Growth of the Australian Iron and Steel Industry. *GJ* 115-1-3, 1950.

ZIERER, C. M.: The Australian Iron and Steel Industry as a Functional Unit. *GR* 30-4, 1940.

CHAPTER 10

McNEE, R. B.: The Changing Relationships of Economics and Economic Geography. *Econ. Geogr.* 35-3, 1959.

VISHER, ST. S.: American Leaders, Where Produced and Used. *Econ. Geogr.* 24-2, 1948.

ZELINSKY, W.: A Method for Measuring Change in the Distribution of Manufacturing Activity: The United States, 1939-1947. *Econ. Geogr.* 34-2, 1958.

CHAPTER 11

ALEXANDER, J. W.: The Basic-Nonbasic Concept of Urban Economic Functions. *Econ. Geogr.* 30-3, 1954.

APPLEBAUM, W., and S. B. COHEN: The Dynamics of Store Trading Areas and Market Equilibrium. *Ann. AAG* 51-1, 1961.

BERRY, B. J. L., and W. L. GARRISON: Alternate Explanations of Urban Rank-Size Relationships. *Ann. AAG* 48-1, 1958.

BERRY, B. J. L., and W. L. GARRISON: The Functional Bases of the Central Place Hierarchy. *Econ. Geogr.* 34-2, 1958.

BRUSH, J. E.: The Hierarchy of Central Places in Southwestern Wisconsin. *GR* 43-3, 1953.

CAROL, H.: Hierarchy of Central Functions Within the City. *Ann. AAG* 50-4, 1960.

CRONE, G. R.: The Site and Growth of Paris. *GJ* 98-1, 1941.

DICKINSON, R. E.: The Morphology of the Medieval German Town. *GR* 35-1, 1945.

FUCHS, R. J.: Intraurban Variation of Residential Quality. *Econ. Geogr.* 36-4, 1960.

GIBBS, J. P.: Growth of Individual Metropolitan Areas: A Global View. *Ann. AAG* 51-4, 1961.

GOTTMANN, J.: Megalopolis or The Urbanization of the Northeastern Seaboard. *Econ. Geogr.* 33-3, 1957.

GREEN, H. L.: Hinterland Boundaries of New York City and Boston in Southern New England. *Econ. Geogr.* 31-4, 1955.

HARRIS, CH. D.: A Functional Classification of Cities in the United States. *GR* 33-1, 1943.

HUGHES, R. H.: Hong Kong: An Urban Study. *GJ* 117-1, 1951.

KLOVE, R. C.: The Definition of Standard Metropolitan Areas. *Econ. Geogr.* 28-2, 1952.

KLOVE, R. C.: Metropolitan Areas—A Review of Three Recent Publications. *Econ. Geogr.* 37-3, 1961.

LAMBERT, A. M.: Millionaire Cities, 1955. *Econ. Geogr.* 32-4, 1956.

MURPHY, R. E., and J. E. VANCE, JR.: Delimiting the CBD. *Econ. Geogr.* 30-3, 1954.

NELSON, H. J.: A Service Classification of American Cities. *Econ. Geogr.* 31-3, 1955.

SIDDALL, W. R.: Wholesale-Retail Trade Ratios as Indices of Urban Centrality. *Econ. Geogr.* 37-2, 1961.

SPELT, J.: Towns and Umlands: A Review Article. *Econ. Geogr.* 34-4, 1958.

STANISLAWSKI, D.: The Origin and Spread of the Grid-Pattern Town. *GR* 36-1, 1946.

STEWART, JR., CH. T.: The Size and Spacing of Cities. *GR* 48-2, 1958.

TREWARTHA, G. T.: The Unincorporated Hamlet: One Element in the American Settlement Fabric. *Ann. AAG* 33-1, 1943.

VANCE, J. E.: Labor-Shed, Employment Field, and Dynamic Analysis in Urban Geography. *Econ. Geogr.* 36-3, 1960.

WEHRWEIN, G. S.: The Rural-Urban Fringe. *Econ. Geogr.* 18-3, 1942.

CHAPTER 12

ALEXANDER, L. M.: The Impact of Tourism on the Economy of Cape Cod, Massachusetts. *Econ. Geogr.* 29-4, 1953.

CARLSON, A. S.: Ski Geography of New England. *Econ. Geogr.* 18-3, 1942.

DEASY, G. F.: The Tourist Industry in a "North Woods" County. *Econ. Geogr.* 25-4, 1949.

EISELEN, E.: The Tourist Industry of a Modern Highway: U.S. 16 in South Dakota. *Econ. Geogr.* 21-3, 1945.

GREELEY, R. B.: Part-Time Farming and Recreational Land Use in New England. *Econ. Geogr.* 18-2, 1942.

WOLFE, R. I.: Summer Cottagers in Ontario. *Econ. Geogr.* 27-1, 1951.

ZIERER, C. M.: Tourism and Recreation in the West. *GR* 42-3, 1952.

CHAPTER 13

ALEXANDER, J. W., S. E. BROWN, and R. E. DAHLBERG: Freight Rates: Selected Aspects of Uniform and Nodal Regions. *Econ. Geogr.* 34-1, 1958.

ALEXANDER, J. W.: International Trade: Selected Types of World Regions. *Econ. Geogr.* 36-2, 1960.

BALLERT, A. G.: Commerce of the Sault Canals. *Econ. Geogr.* 33-2, 1957.

CARTER, R. E.: A Comparative Analysis of the United States Ports and Their Traffic Characteristics. *Econ. Geogr.* 38-2, 1962.

CHEVRIER, L.: The St. Lawrence Seaway and Power Project. *GJ* 119-4, 1953.

FRYER, D. W.: World Income and Types of Economics: The Pattern of World Economic Development. *Econ. Geogr.* 34-4, 1958.

FULTON, M., and L. C. HOCH: Transportation Factors Affecting Locational Decisions. *Econ. Geogr.* 35-1, 1959.

GROTEWOLD, A.: Some Aspects of the Geography of International Trade. *Econ. Geogr.* 37-4, 1961.

KISH, G.: Soviet Air Transport. *GR* 48-3, 1958.

MANCHESTER, C. A.: How Poor Is Japan? (Abstract). *Ann. AAG* 48-3, 1958.

MAYER, H. M.: Great Lakes–Overseas: An Expanding Trade Route. *Econ. Geogr.* 30-2, 1954.

MOUNTJOY, A. B.: The Suez Canal at Mid-Century. *Econ. Geogr.* 34-2, 1958.

PATTON, D. J.: The Traffic Pattern on American Inland Waterways. *Econ. Geogr.* 32-1, 1956.

PATTON, D. J.: General Cargo Hinterlands of New York, Philadelphia, Baltimore, and New Orleans. *Ann. AAG* 48-4, 1958.

PEARCY, G. E., and L. M. ALEXANDER: Pattern of Air Service Availability in the Eastern Hemisphere. *Econ. Geogr.* 29-1, 1953.

PEARCY, G. E., and L. M. ALEXANDER: Pattern of Commercial Air Service Availability in the Western Hemisphere. *Econ. Geogr.* 27-4, 1951.

PHILBRICK, A. K.: Principles of Areal Functional Organization in Regional Human Geography. *Econ. Geogr.* 33-4, 1957.

SHIMKIN, D. B.: Economic Regionalization in the Soviet Union. *GR* 42-4, 1952.

TAAFFE, E. J.: Trends in Airline Passenger Traffic: A Geographic Case Study. *Ann. AAG* 49-4, 1959.

THOMAN, R. S.: Foreign Trade Zones in the United States. *GR* 42-4, 1952.

THOMAS, M. D.: Imports, Industrialization and the Economic Growth of Lesser Developed Countries. *Prof. Geogr.* 13-5, 1961.

ULLMAN, E. L.: The Railroad Pattern of the United States. *GR* 39-2, 1949.

WALLACE, W. H.: Railroad Traffic Densities and Patterns. *Ann. AAG* 48-4, 1958.

WEIGEND, G. G.: Some Elements in the Study of Port Geography. *GR* 48-2, 1958.

APPENDIX

TABLE I—AGRICULTURAL PRODUCTION
Sources: *Production Yearbook*, F.A.O. *Trade Yearbook*, F.A.O.

PRODUCTS	WORLD PRODUCTION, 1961		WORLD EXPORTS, 1961	
	Area in ha[a]	Quantity in t[b]	Quantity in t[b]	Value per $ t[b]
Wheat	200 300 000	243 700 000	40 541 000	$ 65.5
Wheat flour	—	—	4 541 000	85.2
Rye	29 120 000	37 200 000	1 831 000	54.2
Maize (corn)	108 900 000	224 200 000	13 768 000	49.9
Barley	62 800 000	93 000 000	7 331 000	48.2
Oats	43 600 000	60 400 000	1 364 000	48.5
Rice (paddy)	119 500 000	239 500 000	6 138 000	109.0[4]
Groundnuts	15 800 000	13 900 000	1 325 000[1]	175.0[1]
oil	—	—	273 000	346.0
Palm kernels	...	1 030 000	705 000	125.0
oil	—	1 170 000	586 000	210.0
Soybeans	21 700 000	27 300 000	4 158 000	94.5
oil	—	—	391 000	286.0
Potatoes	25 300 000	284 900 000	2 626 000	56.6
Cacao beans	—	1 085 000	1 024 000	478.0
Coffee	...	3 895 000	2 716 000	678.0
Tea	...	950 000[2]	580 000	1115.0
Sugar cane	...	413 600 000	20 385 000[11]	105.0[9]
Sugar beets	6 970 000	185 140 000		112.0[10]
Grapes (all purposes)	10 100 000	43 700 000	610 000	182.0
(for wine)	...	34 500 000	28 016 000[8]	192.0
Cotton (lint)	33 600 000	10 900 000	3 669 000	633.0
Cottonseed	33 600 000	20 500 000	344 000	78.2
Wool, greasy basis	—	2 527 000[2]	1 485 000	1092.0
clean basis	—	1 444 000[2]	1 020 000	1584.0
Livestock				
cattle	—	899 400 000[3]	3 920 000	129.0
pigs	—	520 700 000[3]	2 570 000	48.4
sheep	—	988 200 000[3]	—	—
Milk				
cow	—	310 000 000	—	—
goat	—	8 200 000	—	—
sheep	—	6 800 000	—	—
buffalo	—	15 700 000	—	—
total	—	340 700 000[2]	1 200 000[5]	308.0[6]
				317.0[7]

... = No information.　— = None or negligible or entry not applicable.　* Estimated.
[a] ha = hectares; 1 ha = 2.47 acres.
[b] t = metric tons; 1 t = 0.984 long ton = 1.102 short tons.
(1) shelled; (2) 1960; (3) numbers; (4) milled equivalent; (5) condensed and powdered; (6) condensed; (7) dried; (8) wine in hectoliters: 1 hl = 26.42 gal. U.S.; (9) sugar, raw; (10) sugar, refined; (11) sugar, raw basis.

TABLE II—MINERAL PRODUCTION

TABLE II—MINERAL PRODUCTION
Source: *Statistical Yearbook*, United Nations

PRODUCT	WORLD PRODUCTION, IN METRIC TONS,[a] 1961	NOTES
Coal	1 942 700 000	Anthracite and bituminous coal
Lignite	663 500 000	Lignite and brown coal
Crude petroleum	1 123 700 000	Excl. natural gasoline
Manganese ore	5 500 000	Mn content, high-grade ore containing 30% or more of manganese; excl. 1
Iron ore	230 300 000	Fe content, incl. manganiferous iron ores, excl. pyrites; excl. 1, 5
Copper ore	3 760 000	Cu content, incl. copper content of mixed ores; excl. 1, 2, 4, 5, 8
Lead ore	2 030 000	Pb content, incl. lead content of mixed ores; excl. 1, 5, 8
Zinc ore	2 810 000	Zn content, incl. zinc content of mixed ores; excl. 1, 2, 5, 7, 8
Tin concentrates	164 500	Sn content; excl. 2, 6, 8
Bauxite	25 090 000	Crude ore; excl. 1, 8
Chrome ore	1 320 000	Cr_2O_3 content; excl. 2, 3, 4, 6, 7, 8, Albania
Molybdenum ore	33 120	Mo content; excl. 1, 5, 7, 8, Spain, Yugoslavia
Vanadium ore	7 990	V content; excl. 8, Argentina, Congo (Leopoldville), Mexico, Morocco, Spain, Norway
Tungsten ore	20 400	WO_3 content; excl. 1, 5, 8
Nickel ore	300 000	Ni content; excl. 8, Albania, Bolivia, East Germany
Cobalt ore	17 000	Co content; excl. 8
Antimony ore	31 600	Sb content; excl. 1, 2, 4, 8
Mercury	7 030	Excl. 1, 2, 8
Gold	1 080	Fine gold content of ores mined; excl. 2, 7, 8
Silver	6 700	Content of ores mined; excl. 2, 7, 8
Diamonds	6.62	Gems and industrial diamonds, mine and alluvial production of uncut diamonds; excl. 8
Asbestos	1 640 000	Nonfabricated asbestos fibers and asbestos powder; excl. 1, 2, 8
Sulfur A	6 900 000	Recovered from pyrites; excl. 1, 8
B	7 600 000	Native sulfur; excl. 1, 8
Phosphate rock	35 600 000	Crude mineral with a variable phosphate content; excl. 1, 6, 8
Potash	8 930 000	K_2O content; excl. 1, 8
Magnesite	3 370 000	Crude magnesite ($MgCO_3$) mined; excl. 1, 2, 5, 8

[a] 1 metric ton = 0.984 long ton = 1.102 short tons.

1	China (mainland)	3	Bulgaria	5	North Korea	7	Rumania
2	Czechoslovakia	4	Hungary	6	North Vietnam	8	U.S.S.R.

TABLE III—STATISTICS FOR

Selection of the countries included in this table has been based upon the availability of statistical materials and the Nations *Statistical Yearbook* unless otherwise noted. Additional data can be found in the sources quoted.

COUNTRY	POPULATION[a]	ANNUAL INCREASE, % (1958-61)	TOTAL AREA SQ. MI. (KM.²)	CROPS	LAND USE[b] PASTURE	FOREST
AFGHANISTAN	13 000 000[8]	3.0[8–0]	250 000 (650 000)	14	5	2
ALGERIA	10 390 000[8]	1.9[8–0]	919 500 (2 382 000)	3	16	1
ARGENTINA	21 079 000	1.7	1 072 000 (2 777 000)	11	41	36
AUSTRALIA	10 508 000	2.2	2 975 000 (7 704 000)	4	56	5
AUSTRIA	7 081 000	0.3	32 370 (83 850)	21	28	36
BARBADOS	236 000	. . .	166 (431)	65	12	—
BELGIUM	9 184 000	0.5	11 780 (30 907)	32	25	20
BOLIVIA	3 500 000	1.4	424 200 (1 098 500)	3	10	43

. . . No information available.   — None or negligible or entry not applicable.   * Estimated.

0 = 1960   1 = 1961   6 = 1956   7 = 1957   8 = 1958   9 = 1959.

[a] Estimates of midyear population 1961 unless otherwise noted.

[b] Data from F.A.O. *Production Yearbook*. CROPS—arable land and land under tree crops; PASTURE—permanent meadows and pastures; FOREST—forested land.

[c] Products listed in Tables I and II for which the share of the country in question exceeds 2 percent of the world total as given in these tables.

COUNTRIES OF THE WORLD
general importance of the country. Statistical information is limited to a few basic data and comes from the United

CHIEF PRIMARY PRODUCTS[e]		ESTM. NAT'L INCOME	SOURCE[d]			EXPORTS, F.O.B. MILL. $ 1961	%[e]	IMPORTS, C.I.F. MILL. $ 1961	%[e]	COUNTRY
			A	M	T					
—		. . .	. . .	. . .	. . .	60[8]*	. . .	15[8]*	. . .	AFGHANISTAN
Grapes (all purposes)	5	10.3 bill.[8] new	21	22	57	368	93	1 024	11	ALGERIA
Antimony	2	francs								
Maize	2	686.0 bill.[0]	20	29	51	964	96	1 460	23	ARGENTINA
Wool, greasy	8	pesos								
Wool, clean[8]	8									
Sheep	5									
Cattle	5									
Grapes (all purposes)	4									
Sugar cane	2									
Tungsten	2									
Wheat	3	9.814 bill.[1]	. . .	. . .	. . .	2 324	86	2 093	25	AUSTRALIA
Oats	2	A.£								
Wool, greasy	29									
Wool, clean	29									
Sheep	16									
Sugar cane	2									
Copper	3									
Lead	14									
Zinc	10									
Tungsten	8									
Antimony	2									
Gold	3									
Magnesite	3									
Lignite	2	128.7 bill.[1]	11	55	34	1 202	26	1 485	39	AUSTRIA
Antimony	3	schillings								
Magnesite	53									
—		100.0 mill.[9] B.W.I. $	. . .	. . .	. . .	25	100	47	40	BARBADOS
—		472.9 bill.[1] francs	7	49	44	3 924 incl. Luxemburg	18 incl. Luxemburg	4 219 incl. Luxemburg	43 incl. Luxemburg	BELGIUM
Tin	13	. . .	. . .	. . .	. . .	56		73		BOLIVIA
Tungsten	8									
Antimony	21									

[d] Percentage distribution of industrial origin of gross domestic product: A—agricultural, forestry, fishing; M—mining, manufacturing, construction, electricity, gas, water; T—transport and communications, trade, all others.

[e] Percentage share of primary products according to Nos. 1, 2, 3, and 4 of the SITC code—namely, food, beverages and tobacco; crude materials, inedible, except fuels; mineral fuels, lubricants, related materials; animal and vegetable oils and fats. Data from the United Nations *Yearbook of International Trade Statistics.* For countries which are not using the SITC code the percentage share could in most cases not be calculated.

TABLE III—STATISTICS FOR

COUNTRY	POPULATION[a]	ANNUAL INCREASE, % (1958-61)	TOTAL AREA SQ. MI. (KM.²)	CROPS	LAND USE[b] PASTURE	FOREST
BRAZIL	73 088 000	3.6	3 286 000 (8 512 000)	2	13	61
BRITISH GUIANA	582 000	3.0	83 000 (215 000)	7	. . .	85
BULGARIA	7 943 000	0.9	42 780 (110 670)	42	9	33
BURMA	21 527 000	2.1	207 500 (678 000)	13	. . .	62
CAMBODIA	5 335 000	3.8	66 610 (172 500)	16	—	56
CAMEROONS	4 013 000[8]	1.0[8-0]	183 600 (475 500)	17*	17*	50*
CANADA	18 269 000	2.2	3 852 000 (9 977 000)	4	2	45
CEYLON	10 167 000	2.7	25 330 (65 610)	23	. . .	55
CHILE	7 827 000	2.4	286 400 (741 800)	8	1	22
CHINA (mainland)	646 530 000[7]	2.4[7-0]	3 692 000 (9 561 000)	11	18	1

COUNTRIES OF THE WORLD (Continued)

CHIEF PRIMARY PRODUCTS[c]		ESTM. NAT'L INCOME	SOURCE[d]			EXPORTS, F.O.B. MILL. $ 1961	%[e]	IMPORTS, C.I.F. MILL. $ 1961	%[e]	COUNTRY
			A	M	T[6]					
Rice	2*	1.879 bill.[0] cruzeiros	27	25	48	1 403	97	1 460	37	BRAZIL
Groundnuts	4*									
Cacao	16									
Coffee	46									
Cotton lint	4									
Cottonseed	4									
Cattle	8									
Pigs	9									
Sugar cane	14									
Maize	4*									
Manganese	8									
Iron	3									
Lead	5									
Phosphate rock	3									
Magnesite	2									
—		212.3 mill.[0] B.W.I. $	25	35	40	87	94	86	27	BRITISH GUIANA
Lignite	3	45.9 bill.[1] levas	. . .	. . .	. . .	661	28*	666	13*	BULGARIA
Lead	4									
Zinc	3									
Rice	3	5.18 bill.[1] kyats	43	3	54	220	98	216	21	BURMA
Groundnuts	3									
—		14.7 bill.[9] riels	41	12	47	63	100	97	18*	CAMBODIA
Cacao	6	. . .	. . .	. . .	. . .	98	. . .	96	. . .	CAMEROONS
Wheat	6	27.83 bill.[1] Can. $	6	39	55	5 811	54	5 694	28	CANADA
Barley	5									
Oats	12									
Cow's milk	3									
Crude petrol.	3									
Iron	4									
Copper	11									
Lead	10									
Zinc	13									
Nickel	70									
Cobalt	4									
Gold	13									
Silver	14									
Asbestos	65									
Tea	21	5.85 bill.[1] rupees	49	15	36	364	99	358	48	CEYLON
Copper	14	3.869 bill.[0] escudos	14	29	57	508	98*	585	30*	CHILE
Molybdenum	6									
Rice	36*	152 bill.[9] yuan	48	32	20	. . .	. . .	. . .	. . .	CHINA (mainland)
Soybeans	37*									

TABLE III—STATISTICS FOR

COUNTRY	POPULATION[a]	ANNUAL INCREASE, % (1958-61)	TOTAL AREA SQ. MI. (KM.²)	LAND USE[b]		
				CROPS	PASTURE	FOREST
CHINA (mainland *continued*)						
CHINA (TAIWAN)	10 971 000	3.7	13 885 (35 960)	24	2	49
COLOMBIA	14 443 000	2.2	439 500 (1 138 000)	4	12	61
CONGO (LEOPOLDVILLE)	14 464 000	2.4	905 600 (2 345 400)	21	1	43
COSTA RICA	1 225 000	4.4	19 575 (50 700)	6	14	...
CUBA	6 933 000	2.1	44 220 (114 500)	17	34	11
CYPRUS	577 000	1.1	3 572 (9 251)	47	10	18
CZECHOSLOVAKIA	13 776 000	0.7	49 370 (127 870)	43	15	35
DENMARK	4 617 000	0.7	16 620 (43 050)	64	9	11
DOMINICAN REP.	3 098 000	3.4	17 370 (48 730)	14	12	71
ECUADOR	4 455 000	3.2	104 500 (270 700)	4	8	62
EL SALVADOR	2 709 000	3.6	8 260 (21 390)	27	35	14
ETHIOPIA	21 600 000[s]	...	457 300 (1 184 300)	10	49	4
FINLAND	4 467 000	0.8	103 400 (337 000)	7	1	73

COUNTRIES OF THE WORLD (Continued)

CHIEF PRIMARY PRODUCTS[c]		ESTM. NAT'L INCOME	SOURCE[d]			EXPORTS, F.O.B. MILL. $ 1961	%[e]	IMPORTS, C.I.F. MILL. $ 1961	%[e]	COUNTRY
			A	M	T					
Tea	17*									CHINA (mainland *continued*)
Cattle	5*									
Sheep	6*									
Pigs	36*									
Sugar beets	2*									
Tin	15									
Sugar cane	2	53.53 bill.[6] N.T. $	34	26	40	196	. . .	322	30*	CHINA (TAIWAN)
Coffee	12*	21.82 bill.[0] pesos	34	26	40	434	98	557	17	COLOMBIA
Sugar cane	2									
Palm kernels	14*	48.185 bill.[9] francs	30	30	40	489[9]	96*	308[9]	44*	CONGO (LEOPOLDVILLE)
Palm oil	20*									
Manganese	2									
Copper	8									
Zinc	4									
Tin	4									
Cobalt	49									
Diamonds	55									
—		2.367 bill.[1] colones	37	15	48	84	95	107	14	COSTA RICA
Sugar cane	11	2.219 bill.[8] pesos	. . .	. . .	. . .	763[8]	95*	808[8]	27*	CUBA
Nickel	3*									
Sulfur	5	73.9 mill.[1] £	24	26	50	49	97	113	37	CYPRUS
Rye (incl. mixed grain)	2	. . .	14	74	12	2 046	. . .	2 024	. . .	CZECHOSLOVAKIA
Sugar beets	4									
Lignite	10									
Sulfur	2									
Barley	3	36.51 bill.[1] kroner	14	39	47	1 537	60	1 873	38	DENMARK
Cacao	3	659.8 mill.[9] pesos	. . .	. . .	. . .	143	98	69	19*	DOMINICAN REP.
Bauxite	3									
Cacao	4	12.59 bill.[1] sucres	37	23	40	127	98	101	17	ECUADOR
Coffee	2	1.102 bill.[1] colones	36	12	52	119	95	112	24	EL SALVADOR
Sheep	2	. . .	. . .	. . .	. . .	76	. . .	93	. . .	ETHIOPIA
Cattle	2									
Vanadium	7	12.782 bill.[1] new markkas	21	42	37	1 054	51	1 153	30	FINLAND
Sulfur (1960)	2									

TABLE III—STATISTICS FOR

COUNTRY	POPULATION[a]	ANNUAL INCREASE, % (1958-61)	TOTAL AREA SQ. MI. (KM.²)	CROPS	LAND USE[b] PASTURE	FOREST
FRANCE	45 960 000	1.0	213 800 (551 200)	39	24	21
EAST GERMANY	16 061 000	−0.4	41 660 (107 900)	48	12	28
FEDERAL REPUBLIC OF GERMANY (WEST GERMANY)	54 027 000	1.2	95 930 (248 450)	37	24	30
GHANA	6 943 000	. . .	91 840 (237 900)	22	—	64
GREECE	8 402 000	0.9	50 550 (130 900)	29	40	19
GUATEMALA	3 886 000	3.1	42 040 (108 890)	14	5	45
GUINEA	2 654 000[8]	. . .	94 925 (245 860)	Incl. with senegal		
HAITI	4 249 000	2.2	10 710 (27 750)	14	18	26

COUNTRIES OF THE WORLD (Continued)

CHIEF PRIMARY PRODUCTS[c]		ESTM. NAT'L INCOME	SOURCE[d]			EXPORTS, F.O.B. MILL. $ 1961	%[e]	IMPORTS, C.I.F. MILL. $ 1961	%[e]	COUNTRY
			A	M	T					
Wheat	5	233.2 bill.[1] new francs	9	46	45	7 210	25	6 678	35	FRANCE
Barley	6									
Oats	4									
Potatoes	5									
Cattle	2									
Cow's milk	7									
Sugar beets	10									
Grapes	22									
(all purposes)										
Iron	9									
Bauxite	9									
Tungsten	2									
Potash	22									
Potatoes	5	76.678 bill.[1] D.M.	12	75	13	2 042	. . .	2 019	. . .	EAST GERMANY
Sugar beets	4									
Lignite	36									
Potash	19									
Wheat	2	240.4 bill.[1] D.M.	6	57	37	12 687	11	10 941	55	FEDERAL REPUBLIC OF GERMANY (WEST GERMANY)
Barley	4									
Oats	4									
Potatoes	9									
Rye	10									
Pigs	3									
Cow's milk	6									
Sugar beets	7									
Grapes	2									
(all purposes)										
Coal	7									
Lignite	15									
Lead	2									
Zinc	3									
Silver	8									
Sulfur	3									
Potash	27									
Cacao	28	492 mill.[1] G. £	. . .	. . .	. . .	292	90	394	20	GHANA
Manganese	3									
Gold	2									
Diamonds	10									
Grapes	2	91.8 bill.[1] drachmas	30	27	43	223	90	714	28	GREECE
(all purposes)										
Bauxite	5									
Coffee	2*	586.0 mill.[1] quetzales	32	25	43	115	98*	134	24	GUATEMALA
Palm kernels	2	. . .	. . .	. . .	. . .	55	. . .	50	. . .	GUINEA
Bauxite										
—	7	. . .	. . .	. . .	. . .	32	. . .	35	. . .	HAITI

TABLE III—STATISTICS FOR

COUNTRY	POPULATION[a]	ANNUAL INCREASE, % (1958-61)	TOTAL AREA SQ. MI. (KM.²)	CROPS	LAND USE[b] PASTURE	FOREST
HONDURAS	1 893 000	3.0	42 290 (112 090)	9	18	43
HONG KONG	3 178 000	3.6	398 (1 031)	12	—	9
HUNGARY	10 028 000	0.5	35 920 (93 030)	62	15	14
ICELAND	179 000	2.0	39 850 (103 000)	—	22	1
INDIA	441 631 000	2.2	1 175 000 (3 042 800)	49	4	16
INDONESIA	95 655 000	2.3	575 900 (1 491 560)	12	...	61
IRAN	20 678 000	1.7	636 300 (1 648 000)	10	1	11
IRAQ	7 263 000	3.3	173 650 (448 750)	12	2	4
IRELAND	2 815 000	−0.4	27 175 (70 280)	20	48	2
ISRAEL	2 185 000	3.0	7 750 (20 700)	20	39	4
ITALY	49 455 000	0.5	116 300 (301 225)	54	17	20

COUNTRIES OF THE WORLD (Continued)

CHIEF PRIMARY PRODUCTS[c]		ESTM. NAT'L INCOME	SOURCE[d] A	M	T	EXPORTS, F.O.B. MILL. $ 1961	%[e]	IMPORTS, C.I.F. MILL. $ 1961	%[e]	COUNTRY
—		669.1 mill.[0] lempiras	44	16	40	73	98	72	22	HONDURAS
—		. . .	. . .	. . .	. . .	688	17	1 045	41	HONG KONG
Lignite	4	147.4 bill.[1] forints	23	68	9	1 029	. . .	1 026	. . .	HUNGARY
Bauxite	5									
—		6.811 bill.[1] krónur	. . .	. . .	. . .	71	99	75	31	ICELAND
Wheat	4	142.0 bill.[0] rupees	48	18	34	1 386	54	2 246	38	INDIA
Barley	3									
Rice	26									
Groundnuts	32									
Tea	34									
Cotton lint	9									
Cottonseed	9									
Sugar cane	21									
Coal	3									
Manganese	9									
Iron	3									
Magnesite	6									
Palm kernels	3	202.9 bill.[9] rupiah	56	15	29	784	99	794	30	INDONESIA
Rice	5									
Palm oil	12									
Tea	4									
Coffee	2									
Sugar cane	2									
Tin	11									
Sheep	3	. . .	. . .	. . .	. . .	300*[1-2] . . .		146*[1-2] . . .		IRAN
Crude petrol.	5									
Chrome	3									
Crude petrol.	4	303 mill.[6] dinars	. . .	. . .	. . .	662	98*	408	17*	IRAQ
—		572 mill.[1] £	25	30	45	505	69	732	38	IRELAND
—		4.087 bill.[1] I. £	12	32	56	239	38	577	36	ISRAEL
Wheat	3	17.151 bill.[1] lire	17	45	38	4 188	26	5 222	60	ITALY
Sugar beets	4									
Grapes (all purposes)	20									
Lead	2									
Zinc	5									
Mercury	27									
Asbestos	3									
Sulfur	10									

TABLE III—STATISTICS FOR

COUNTRY	POPULATION[a]	ANNUAL INCREASE, % (1958-61)	TOTAL AREA SQ. MI. (KM.²)	LAND USE[b] CROPS	PASTURE	FOREST
JAMAICA	1 631 000	1.6	4 727 (11 425)	20	22	25
JAPAN	94 050 000	0.9	142 730 (369 660)	16	...	67
JORDAN	1 690 000	2.0	37 300 (96 610)	9	8	5
KENYA	7 287 000	2.2	225 000 (582 650)	1	39	29
KOREA, REP. OF	25 375 000	2.9	38 030 (98 500)	21	—	39
KUWEIT	322 000	15.8	6 000 (15 540)	...	...	...
LAOS	1 850 000	2.7	91 430 (236 800)	4	4	60
LEBANON	1 569 000[8]	2.3[8-0]	4 000 (10 400)	28	...	9
LIBERIA	1 290 000[c]	...	43 000 (111 370)	20	3	51
LUXEMBURG	317 000	0.7	998 (2 590)	29	24	33
MADAGASCAR	5 577 000	2.8	230 000 (595 800)	2	63	20
MALAYA, FED. OF	7 137 000	3.2	50 710 (131 300)	17	—	72
MAURITIUS	656 000	2.8	720 (1 865)	48	21	19
MEXICO	36 091 000	3.1	761 600 (1 972 500)	10	34	20

COUNTRIES OF THE WORLD (Continued)

CHIEF PRIMARY PRODUCTS[c]		ESTM. NAT'L INCOME	SOURCE[d]			EXPORTS, F.O.B. MILL. $ 1961	%[e]	IMPORTS, C.I.F. MILL. $ 1961	%[e]	COUNTRY
			A	M	T					
Bauxite	26	217.1 mill.[1] £	13	34	53	178	95	211	34	JAMAICA
Barley	2	13.694 bill.[1] yen	15	43	42	4 236	11	5 810	79	JAPAN
Rice	7									
Tea	8									
Coal	3									
Copper	3									
Lead	2									
Zinc	6									
Tungsten	3									
Mercury	12									
Silver	6									
Sulfur	24									
—native	3									
—		93.8 mill.[0] dinars	4	16	70	15	96	117	43	JORDAN
—		224.8 mill.[1] £	39	15	46	116 incl. Uganda & Tan- ganyika	93	193	18 incl. Uganda & Tan- ganyika	KENYA
Tungsten	20	212.7 bill.[1] won	41	17	42	41	86	316	38	KOREA, REP. OF
Crude petrol.	7	. . .	. . .	. . .	. . .	23* excl. oil	. . .	280*	. . .	KUWEIT
—		. . .	. . .	. . .	. . .	1	. . .	17	. . .	LAOS
—		1.325 bill.[8] L. £	17	17	66	42	59	343	46	LEBANON
—		. . .	. . .	. . .	. . .	83	96	69	21	LIBERIA
—		18.2 bill.[1] francs	8	55	37	Included in Belgium				LUXEMBURG
—		. . .	. . .	. . .	. . .	78	. . .	103	. . .	MADAGASCAR
Palm kernels	2	4.535 bill.[0] Malay $	49	13	42	857	74	728	53	MALAYA, FED. OF
Palm oil	8									
Tin	35									
—		705 mill. rupees	27	27	46	62	100	68	41	MAURITIUS
Maize	2	126.0 bill.[1] pesos	. . .	. . .	. . .	826	75	1 139	5	MEXICO
Coffee	3									
Cotton lint	4									
Cottonseed	4									

TABLE III—STATISTICS FOR

COUNTRY	POPULATION[a]	ANNUAL INCREASE, % (1958-61)	TOTAL AREA SQ. MI. (KM.²)	CROPS	LAND USE[b] PASTURE	FOREST
MEXICO (*continued*)						
MOROCCO	11 925 000	2.8	171 300 (443 700)	16	22	13
NETHERLANDS	11 637 000	1.3	12 980 (33 610)	32	39	1
NEW ZEALAND	2 420 000	2.0	103 700 (268 700)	2	47	35
NICARAGUA	1 526 000	3.5	57 000 (148 000)	13	. . .	47
NIGERIA	35 752 000	1.9	356 700 (923 800)	16	. . .	34
NORWAY	3 611 000	0.8	125 100 (323 900)	3	1	23
PAKISTAN	94 547 000	2.1	365 500 (946 700)	25	. . .	3
PANAMA	1 109 000	2.7	28 750 (74 470)	6	7	71
PARAGUAY	1 812 000	2.4	157 000 (406 800)	1	2	51
PERU	10 365 000	2.0	496 200 (1 285 200)	1	10	56
PHILIPPINES	28 727 000	3.3	115 700 (299 700)	25	4	54
POLAND	29 965 000	1.4	120 400 (311 700)	53	14	25

COUNTRIES OF THE WORLD (Continued)

CHIEF PRIMARY PRODUCTS[c]		ESTM. NAT'L INCOME	SOURCE[d] A	M	T	EXPORTS, F.O.B. MILL. $ 1961	%[e]	IMPORTS, C.I.F. MILL. $ 1961	%[e]	COUNTRY
										MEXICO (*continued*)
Sugar cane	4									
Lead	9									
Zinc	10									
Antimony	11									
Mercury	9									
Silver	19									
Sulfur	16									
Manganese	5	716 bill.[1] francs	27	29	44	343	. . .	452	. . .	MOROCCO
Lead	4									
Cobalt	8									
Phosphate rock	22									
Sugar beets	2	36.22 bill.[1] guilders	10	42	48	4 307	47	5 112	42	NETHERLANDS
Cow's milk	2									
Wool, greasy	10	1.146 bill.[1] N.Z. £	22	32	46	793	97	901	21	NEW ZEALAND
Wool, clean	13									
Sheep	5									
—		. . .	. . .	. . .	. . .	61	97	74	21	NICARAGUA
Palm kernels	42*	942.9 mill. W.A. £	63	9	28	482	97	623	20	NIGERIA
Palm oil	31*									
Cacao	18									
Sulfur	5	26.253 bill.[1] kroner	12	38	50	931	37	1 616	28	NORWAY
Rice	7	24.069 bill.[1] P. rupees	56	15	29	400	95*	642	42	PAKISTAN
Tea	2									
Cotton lint	3									
Cottonseed	3									
Cattle	3									
Sugar cane	4									
—		407.3 mill.[1] balboas	24	18	58	30	99	124	26	PANAMA
—		25.947 bill.[1] guaranis	38	16	46	31	99*	35	30*	PARAGUAY
Sugar cane	2	42.225 mill.[o] soles	25	31	44	494	. . .	468	. . .	PERU
Copper	5									
Lead	7									
Zinc	6									
Antimony	2									
Silver	16									
Sugar cane	2	11.518 bill.[1] pesos	34	25	41	499	97	611	30	PHILIPPINES
Chrome	18									
Oats	5	415.8 bill.[1] zlotys	25	62	13	1 504	. . .	1 687	. . .	POLAND
Potatoes	13									
Rye	21									

TABLE III—STATISTICS FOR

COUNTRY	POPULATION[a]	ANNUAL INCREASE, % (1958-61)	TOTAL AREA SQ. MI. (KM.²)	LAND USE[b] CROPS	PASTURE	FOREST
POLAND (*continued*)						
PORTUGAL	9 196 000	0.8	35 340 (91 530)	47	. . .	28
RHODESIA AND NYASALAND, FED. OF	8 520 000	2.4	484 500 (1 254 900)	16	. . .	35
RUMANIA	18 567 000	0.9	91 700 (237 500)	44	18	27
SAUDI ARABIA	6 036 000[c]	. . .	620 000 (1 600 000)	—	6	—
SENEGAL	2 980 000	. . .	76 120 (197 160)	2*	5* (for terr. of former Fr. W. Af.)	24*
SIERRA LEONE	2 450 000	2.7	27 930 (72 330)	51	31	4
SINGAPORE	1 687 000	3.7	224 (581)	25	—	7
SOUTH AFRICA, REP. OF	16 236 000	2.6	472 350 (1 223 410)	9	71	1
SPAIN	30 559 000	1.0	194 900 (504 750)	41	2	12

COUNTRIES OF THE WORLD (Continued)

CHIEF PRIMARY PRODUCTS[c]		ESTM. NAT'L INCOME	SOURCE[d]			EXPORTS, F.O.B. MILL. $ 1961	%[e]	IMPORTS, C.I.F. MILL. $ 1961	%[e]	COUNTRY
			A	M	T					
Pigs	2									POLAND *(continued)*
Cow's milk	4									
Sugar beets	5									
Coal	5									
Zinc	5									
Sulfur (native)	3									
Grapes (all purposes)	4	64.2 bill.[1] escudos	26	41	33	326	45	656	40	PORTUGAL
Tungsten	9									
Sulfur	4									
Copper	15	473.6 mill.[1] £	20	37	43	579	33	434	20	RHODESIA AND NYASALAND, FED. OF
Chrome	19									
Cobalt	10									
Asbestos	10									
Maize	2	. . .	33	53	14	793	. . .	815	. . .	RUMANIA
Grapes (all purposes)	2									
Crude petrol.	6	. . .	. . .	. . .	. . .	. . .	. . .	270*[0-1]	. . .	SAUDI ARABIA
Groundnuts	6	. . .	. . .	. . .	. . .	124	. . .	155	. . .	SENEGAL
Palm kernels	6*	. . .	. . .	. . .	. . .	82	35	91	36	SIERRA LEONE
Diamonds	6*									
—		. . .	. . .	. . .	. . .	1 083	72	1 295	71	SINGAPORE
Maize	2	4.271 bill.[0] rands	11	38	51	1 333	66	1 406	19	SOUTH AFRICA, REP. OF
Groundnuts	2									
Wool, greasy	5									
Wool, clean	4									
Coal	2									
Manganese	10									
Chrome	30									
Vanadium	29									
Gold	66									
Diamonds	14									
Asbestos	11									
Antimony	34									
Sugar beets	2	495.8 bill.[0] pesetas	26	33	41	710	77	1 092	61	SPAIN
Grape (all purposes)	8									
Lead	4									
Zinc	3									
Tungsten	3									
Mercury	21[0]									

TABLE III—STATISTICS FOR

COUNTRY	POPULATION[a]	ANNUAL INCREASE, % (1958-61)	TOTAL AREA SQ. MI. (KM.²)	LAND USE[b]		
				CROPS	PASTURE	FOREST
SPAIN (*continued*)						
SUDAN	12 109 000	2.8	967 500 (2 505 800)	3	10	38
SURINAM	283 000	4.5	55 140 (142 820)	—	—	43
SWEDEN	7 520 000	0.5	137 950 (449 800)	9	2	55
SWITZERLAND	5 496 000	1.9	15 980 (41 288)	11	43	25
SYRIA	4 930 000	4.8	71 230 (184 480)	30	29	2
TANGANYIKA	9 399 000	1.8	455 500 (937 061)	9	37	35
THAILAND	27 181 000	3.0	198 500 (514 000)	19	...	28
TRINIDAD AND TOBAGO	859 000	2.9	1 980 (5 128)	35	1	46
TUNISIA	4 254 000	1.7	48 720 (125 180)	39	1	8
TURKEY	28 602 000	2.9	301 400 (780 600)	33	38	14
UGANDA	6 845 000	2.5	92 530 (239 640)	14	...	8
UNITED ARAB REP. (EGYPT)	26 593 000	2.5	400 000 (1 000 000)	3	—	—
UNITED KINGDOM	52 925 000	0.7	94 220 (244 030)	30	53	7

COUNTRIES OF THE WORLD (Continued)

CHIEF PRIMARY PRODUCTS[c]		ESTM. NAT'L INCOME	SOURCE[d] A	M	T	EXPORTS, F.O.B. MILL. $ 1961	%[e]	IMPORTS, C.I.F. MILL. $ 1961	%[e]	COUNTRY
Sulfur	14									Spain (*continued*)
Potash	4									
—		349.5 mill.[6] S. £	57	12	31	179	100	238	28	Sudan
Bauxite	14	...	...	...	...	41	94	54	27	Surinam
Iron	6	62.084 bill.[1] kronor	...	...	...	2 743	37	2 927	35	Sweden
Lead	3									
Zinc	3									
Sulfur	3									
—		34.740 bill.[1] francs	8*	47*	45*	2 041	8	2 707	35	Switzerland
—		2.357 bill.[1] S. £	32[9]	18[9]	50[9]	110	81	199	38	Syria
Diamonds	2	186.9 mill.[1] £	57	18	25	138	Incl. in Kenya	111	Incl. in Kenya	Tanganyika
Rice	3	50.026 bill.[1] bahts	38	19	43	477	98	485	21	Thailand
Tin	8									
—		740.5 mill.[1] B.W.I. $	13	52	35	346	96	336	52	Trinidad and Tobago
Phosphate rock	6	279 mill.[1] dinars	...	...	...	110	...	211	...	Tunisia
Wheat	4	46.434 bill.[1] liras	41	23	36	347	94	509	23	Turkey
Barley	4									
Sheep	3									
Sugar beets	2									
Grapes (all purposes)	6									
Chrome	16									
Antimony	4									
Coffee	3	156.2 mill.[1] £	62	11	27	1.6	Incl. in Kenya	74	Incl. in Kenya	Uganda
Cotton lint	4	1.188 bill.[8] E. £	33[6]	17[6]	50[6]	485	87	678	44	United Arab Rep. (Egypt)
Cottonseed	4									
Barley	5	21.552 bill.[1] £	4	48	48	10 308	13	11 864	66	United Kingdom
Oats	4									
Potatoes	2									
Wool, greasy	2									
Wool, clean	2									
Sheep	3									
Cow's milk	4									

TABLE III—STATISTICS FOR

COUNTRY	POPULATION[a]	ANNUAL INCREASE, % (1958-61)	TOTAL AREA SQ. MI. (KM.²)	CROPS	LAND USE[b] PASTURE	FOREST
UNITED KINGDOM (*continued*)						
UNITED STATES	183 742 006	1.7	3 615 210 (9 363 390)	25	33	34
URUGUAY	2 758 000[8]	1.3[8-0]	72 170 (186 925)	14	65	2

COUNTRIES OF THE WORLD (Continued)

CHIEF PRIMARY PRODUCTS[c]		ESTM. NAT'L INCOME	SOURCE[d] A	M	T	EXPORTS, F.O.B. MILL. $ 1961	%[e]	IMPORTS, C.I.F. MILL. $ 1961	%[e]	COUNTRY
										UNITED KINGDOM (*continued*)
Sugar beets	4									
Coal	10									
Wheat	15	424.5 bill.[1] $	4	37	59	20 755	35	14 702	54	UNITED STATES
Barley	11									
Oats	26									
Potatoes	4									
Rye	2									
Maize	49									
Soybeans	55									
Groundnuts	6									
Cotton lint	28									
Cottonseed	26									
Wool, greasy	10									
Wool, clean	4									
Sheep	3									
Cattle	11									
Pigs	11									
Cow's milk	18									
Sugar beets	8									
Grapes (all purposes)	6									
Sugar cane	4									
Coal	19									
Crude petrol.	32									
Iron	7									
Copper	28									
Lead	12									
Zinc	15									
Bauxite	6									
Molybdenum	91									
Vanadium	61									
Tungsten	23									
Nickel	4									
Cobalt	8[9]									
Mercury	16									
Gold	5									
Silver	16									
Asbestos	3									
Sulfur	6									
Sulfur (native)	73									
Phosphate	53									
Potash	28									
Magnesite	16									
Wool, greasy	3	. . .	. . .	. . .	. . .	175	. . .	208	. . .	URUGUAY
Wool, clean	3									

TABLE III—STATISTICS FOR

COUNTRY	POPULATION[a]	ANNUAL INCREASE, % (1958-61)	TOTAL AREA SQ. MI. (KM.²)	LAND USE[b] CROPS	PASTURE	FOREST
U.S.S.R.	218 000 000	1.8[9-1]	8 648 500 (22 402 200)	10	18	40
Venezuela	7 590 000	3.3	352 100 (912 050)	3	20	21
North Vietnam	16 690 000	2.1	61 400 (159 000)	8	...	57
Vietnam, Rep. of	14 520 000	3.9	65 950 (170 800)	16	17	31
Yugoslavia	18 607 000	1.1	98 770 (255 800)	33	26	35

COUNTRIES OF THE WORLD (Continued)

CHIEF PRIMARY PRODUCTS[c]		ESTM. NAT'L INCOME	SOURCE[d]			EXPORTS, F.O.B. MILL. $ 1961	%[e]	IMPORTS, C.I.F. MILL. $ 1961	%[e]	COUNTRY
			A	M	T					
Wheat	26	157 bill.[1]	...	...	...	5 998	48	5 832	34	U.S.S.R.
Barley	18	new								
Oats	20	rubles								
Potatoes	30									
Rye	44									
Maize	8									
Tea	4									
Cotton lint	14*									
Cottonseed	14*									
Wool, greasy	14*									
Wool, clean	15*									
Sheep	14									
Cattle	8									
Pigs	10									
Cow's milk	20									
Coal	19									
Lignite	20									
Crude petrol.	15									
Manganese	49									
Iron	30									
Crude petrol.	14	19.668 bill.[1]	6	51	43	2 413	99*	1 051	21	Venezuela
Iron	4	bolivares								
—		...	...	...	...	...	...	...	...	North Vietnam
Rice	2	...	...	...	...	71	...	255	...	Vietnam, Rep. of
Lignite	3	3.124 bill.[1]	27	50	23	569	50	910	30	Yugoslavia
Lead	5	dinars								
Zinc	2									
Bauxite	5									
Antimony	12									
Mercury	8									
Magnesite	8									

INDEX

Entries in the following index refer to regions, countries, and products. For other topics the reader should consult with the table of contents and the bibliography. Page numbers in *italics* refer to illustrations.